Studies in Multilevel Planning . . . I

Researches in Decentralisation

STUDIES IN MULTILEVEL PLANNING

General Editor : Shri B.N. Yugandhar

Forthcoming Volumes
By Amitava Mukherjee

Foundations of Decentralisation
Methodology and Database for Decentralised Planning
Techniques of Decentralised Planning
A Perspective Plan for Hill District
Manual on Decentralised Planning

STUDIES IN MULTILEVEL PLANNING : I

RESEARCHES IN DECENTRALISATION

With Special Reference to District Planning in India

AMITAVA MUKHERJEE
Advisor
District Planning Unit
Lal Bahadur Shastri
National Academy of Administration
Government of India
Mussoorie

General Editor : B.N. Yugandhar

HERITAGE PUBLISHERS New Delhi
INDIA 1990

IBSN 81–7026–157–0 (set)
81–7026–158–9

Published by B.R. Chawla, Heritage Publishers,
4C, Ansari Road, New Delhi 110002.
Laser Typeset at Compofast, 7/33, Ansari Road, New Delhi and
Printed by Solar Printer, B-64, Sector X, NOIDA

FOREWORD

The District Planning Unit at the LBS National Academy of Administration was established in 1989 for developing faculty in decentralised multi-level planning primarily for the training of the IAS officers who come on training here. Planning Commission, Government of India, in *The Report of the Study Group on Training for District Planning (New Delhi: 1989)* has envisioned that the LBS National Academy of Administration, Mussoorie, will have to be developed into the principal training centre in multi-level planning for I.A.S. officers. We are working towards that goal.

It was realised early that good research must precede good training and, therefore, it was felt expedient that research in decentralised multi-level planning ought to be an integral part of the District Planning Unit at the Academy. Samuel Johnson's famous quote:

> "Knowledge is of two kinds : either you know something yourself or you know where to find information about it"

reminded us that an appropriate starting point for research in decentralised multi-level planning would be to document what all has been written about decentralised multi-level planning both at home and abroad, with special reference to India. As an answer to this, it was decided that the first output of the District Planning Unit of the Academy, in the realm of its research function, ought to be a documentation on decentralised multi-level planning. It is here: I have great pleasure in presenting it to you, our readers.

As would be apparent from the pages to follow, there would be several volumes to be published in succession, ultimately culminating into the Manual on Decentralised Planning. The general tenor of the series makes it apparent that these volumes will be addressed to planners, administrators, trainers and academicians. We would feel our efforts amply validated if this series helps, even modestly, those working with, and interested in, decentralised multi-level planning.

I thank the Government of India, the Ministry of Personnel and Training, New Delhi and the Planning Commission, New Delhi for providing the necessary resources for the project and for their continued support in our future activities.

I wish to place on record my appreciation for the members of the Core Group for District Planning who are collectively guiding the affairs of the District Planning Unit.

Lal Bahadur Shastri
National Academy of Administration,
Government of India
Mussoorie.

B.N. Yugandhar

To

The Teeming Millions Of Our Countrymen

Whose Lives Have Not Been

Touched By The Fruits Of Planning

But Who Deserve Them Most

Contents

THE PRELUDE

This is an exercise in exploration. The concept of, and issues revolving around, decentralised planning has been with us for nearly half a century. Like many other concepts and techniques in developmental economics, the fate of decentralised planning have fluctuated between distress and fortune, but fortune has been the rarer phenomenon and distress the more dominant one. Economists, planners and our political masters, by underpinning their faith in planned economic development as the grand panacea of all economic evils, made a system of decentralised planning for the country with a federal structure, almost inevitable. However, its formulation, execution and implementation was not a picture, during those initial years, that inspired confidence: lack of "farsightedness" and paucity of "broadmindedness" of the managers of our planned economic development marred the whole canvass several times over.

Of late, however, there has been a resurgence of faith in decentralised planning because it is believed that the effects of our planned economic development, centralised for the greater part, have left untouched the lives of an overwhelming majority of our people. This renewed faith in decentralised planning as being the most efficacious instrument for eradication of poverty in this country, springs from the two fundamental tenets of the economic and political thinking of the day: one, decentralization of planning per se should be an article of faith. That makes the genesis of democratic functioning: "doing things wherein people matter". Two, small groups of people may have little problems when judged against the vast national scenario, but which are of immense importance to the small man. These small problems may not be intimately viewed at higher levels of planning and administration. Thus, participation of the people at large for whom planning is undertaken, to reflect collective wisdom and to incorporate the will of the masses in planning is important.

The faith reposed in decentralised planning now, as an instrument for economic development, and agrarian change, can be redeemed well only if we know why hopes were belied and expectations frustrated. Research in decentralised planning is, therefore, justified by the need to see where we went wrong, how we went wrong and what should we do (or what we should not do) so as not repeat our past mistakes in future. This is important because failure of planning at improving the conditions of poor people is not a painless process. Impatience is writ large on the faces of the masses for whom planning in directed: impatience with the slow process of development, impatience with the failure of the planning process itself, impatience with the deprivation and privation which they undergo.

The researches on decentralised planning undertaken by us is against this background. The scheme of research in decentralised planning that we have taken up should be viewed as an effort in the continuum to help planners, economists and administrators, present and future, at the lower levels of planning, particularly at the district and sub-district level, to prepare, implement and monitor, a better plan for the respective territorial tiers under their charge. It was felt, therefore, that the first thing to do is to have one long hard look at the wide landscape we have left behind us over the last forty years or so, and figure out what has been written and what all has been spoken about decentralised planning in India relevant in its present incarnation, by people who have trudged this weary path before us.

An increasing number of people are seemingly concerned with decentralisation and decentralised planning, but the researcher involved, finds it not an easy task to obtain information about approaches to the problem and about comparative temporal experiences with decentralised planning under diverse circumstances. It is generally agreed upon that dissemination of existing body of knowledge is inadequate on the subject. An aim of the bibliography is, therefore, to fill this gap by attempting at providing a guide, on a modest scale, to the literature, on decentralised planning, development and related areas to those who are most interested in these processes and even to the layman having interest in the fascinating complexities involved.

The fundamental problem in compiling a bibliography of this sort, is first presented by the conceptual tangle of defining decentralisation and decentralised planning. Decentralisation as accepted in this research scheme is that the function of planning for the entire country is delegated to several territorial tiers in the country. The national economy as a whole is conceptually divided into several regions and for each region, a plan is prepared, by a functionary, authorised to prepare a plan for accelerated economic development. In effect, there are several territorial tiers (conceptually) in the country and there are several plans operating, one for each tier of territory. The content, character and scope of planning for different territorial tiers can vary, but the existence of several tiers, with a system of planning for each tier is an abject reality. Decentralised planning, therefore, is taken as synonymous with multi-level planning, and this is perfectly consistent with the concepts of space, region and regionalisation.

The country as a whole can be conceived of as the "macro" region; several States collectively can be conceived of as "macro-meso" region; each state can be conceived of as a "meso" region; each district can be conceived of as a "micro" region and each community development block can be conceived on as "super- micro" region. This delineation of regions has a corresponding planning scheme and mechanism: there is: the National Plan for the "macro" region; the "Regional" plans for "macro-meso" regions; the State Plans for "meso" regions; the District Plans for "micro" regions and the Block Plans for "super-micro" regions. In current literature, however, the words "Regional Plans" include plans encompassing more than one State, or more than one district or more than one block at the sub-district level or even one area at the sub-District or sub-block level. In this bibliography we shall retain the current usage unless repugnant to the context or otherwise specified.

Judged in that perspective, decentralised planning, in the Indian context at least, encompasses planning of various hues and colours. Planning for each territorial tier is conceived of as a sub-system of a larger and total system of "regional planning". Therefore, while selecting contributions to decentralised planning, we have included in this bibliography, contributions to regional planning and regional plans, district plans, block plans, even on people's participation in planning, and plans of every description having relevance to planning at sub-national level except State Planning because that deserves a separate treatment altogether. The choices, however, have neither been indiscriminate nor arbitrary; the choices have not been guided by either vintage or contemporaneousness of the relative contributions. Selections have been made with the view to "maximise utility": utility in understanding the fitfalls of decentralised planning; and in envisioning the future scenario. Therefore, it is possible that some important contributions have not been included. We would like to guard ourselves against being possibly misunderstood: we have no pretension to claim that all that was intended to be included or should have been included has been included, because, for one, limits of space forces selectivity upon us and two, perhaps because we did not obtain access to all of them, despite our best efforts and clear intentions. These are, therefore, the obvious limitations which sobers the justification, need and usefulness of this bibliography.

Since the audience to whom we are addressing this research and for whom this research is being primarily prosecuted, would be the future planners and administrators of the country, who would man positions, where they will have direct interface with the stark realities of ground conditions, and who would be required to lead planning teams,under (in certain cases) disagreeable conditions, it was thought that the role of the administrator in decentralised planning ought to be reflected in the right perspective in this bibliography. This has been attempted in a small measure. More importantly, as has been accepted with virtual unanimity, decentralised planning and decentralised administration are necessary conditions for the success of a planning super-structure built around the foundations of a decentralised multi-level planning frame. This is the justification for including a separate section on decentralised administration, decentralised planning and development.

It is also essential that the future planners and administrators, with whom we shall be primarily concerned, would have a full grasp of project planning, project evaluation and project monitoring. Because, after all planning at the micro and super-micro level will essentially involve project planning and there is no escape from the fact that unless the future administrators and future planners are capable of, and are appropriately equipped to, evaluate monitor and scrutinize projects successfully, planning at lower levels in the territorial hierarchy will suffer from a serious handicap. A select bibliography on the more important contributions to project planning, evaluation and monitoring has been included, which would provide access to techniques and methods essential in project planning and appraisal.

This bibliography has been divided into thirteen parts:

Chapter I, contains a short recital on evolution of decentralised planning in India through the plan documents during the plan period up to the end of 1989. A short bibliography is appended to this recital on evolution of decentralised planning in India to make it a complete whole. This short bibliography, however, should not be taken as exhaustive because a staggering amount of matter has been written on these issues and the select bibliography should rather be deemed as supplementary to the general bibliography that has been provided at the end, to we shall come later.

Chapter II, deals with Regional Planning in India.

Chapter III, contains a recital on the rationale of decentralised planning, both in theoretical terms and in terms of their operationalisation in various countries of the world where decentralised planning has been in operation: with success in some and with failure in others. This recital on the rationale of decentralised planning is followed by a select bibliography on the various issued touched upon.

Chapter IV, deals with the concepts of space, spatial organisation; regions and regionalisation, which have bearing on the system of decentralised planning, supported by a select bibliography. The justification for inclusion of this discussion on spaces and spatial organisation and regions and regionalisation is that much of decentralised planning will revolved around, and be concerned with, these aspects in real life situations. A clear grasp of these would avoid many confusion in understanding the mechanics of a decentralised planning setup later.

Chapter V, will contain a narrative on the theories of development and decentralised planning, with a select bibliography of works cited in the narration. These theories provide the required ground work and insights into the thoughts and ideas of those who had the vision of decentralised planning, gave it a concrete shape and struggled very hard too, to operationalise it. The knowledge of the theoretical underpinning of development planning and of decentralised planning is essential for framing a dynamised decentralised plan which will keep pace with the movements of the basic parameters that determine the course of development, with the flux of time, in a highly stochastic world.

Chapter VI, briefly summarises the various strategies relevant for decentralised planning, with particular reference to micro-planning or district planning. These strategies are important because they tell us where we went wrong in our continuing effort to stabilise a system of decentralised planning; they tell us about what fails; they tell us all about the numerous crevices and they tell us the leeways to make for, for the success of the task to which we have addressed ourselves to. It is very important, therefore, to look at these strategies from a close proximity and take all the good that are embedded in them, so as to enable us to frame appropriate strategies for planning for a region, realistically and optimally.

Chapter VII, contains a short discussion on approaches to decentralised planning with special reference to micro planning or district planning, and a select bibliography. The wide spectrum of approaches applied for decentralised planned development in developed and developing countries is awesome and each had its limitation and strengths. A search into these approaches can be of great assistance in arriving at an approach to decentralised planning that would be most appropriate for a region (be at a state or a district or a block level), which will eschew the inappropriate components of the previous approaches and reduce the constraints and limitations to which a decentralised plan (or for that matter any plan) is subject to.

Appendix 'A' will have the bibliography on decentralisation administration, decentralised planning and development and Appendix 'B' will be a short bibliography on project planning, project appraisal and project monitoring, both of which we have already discussed earlier.

We will have a general bibliography which contains thoughts and ideas on decentralised planning, regional planning, area planning, block planning and project planning. This general bibliography is provided as a support, as a supplement, and as a reservoir to the relatively shorter bibliographies that have been included on specific areas in the earlier chapters.

In Appendix 'C' references of some regional plans and feasibility reports in underdeveloped countries (CRDR, Justus-Liebig-University: Regional Plans of Developing Countries, June 1980 and others) are provided to give an idea of the scope and diversity of regional planning. Since some of these regional plans are by individuals, some by Government agencies and some by private agencies, the authors have not been mentioned. And to distinguish the regional plans, the system followed in Appendix 'C' is different from the general scheme.

Appendix 'D' documents some of the more important Government of India Reports and of a few State Governments which have immediate relevance to the issues at hand

The preparation of this work reminded me of a few lines I had read many many years ago. Hark these words:

> "The more I study economics, the smaller appears the knowledge I have of it....And now at the end of half a century, I am conscious of more ignorance of it than I was at the begining".

My tinkering with the mass of literature on the subjects under review, have brought before me in flesh and blood the eternal truth contained in these lines of one of the greatest economists of all times.

No work that is fundamentally exploratory can flourish in a vacuum. This book is no exception to this general rule. I have drawn upon various sources, too numerous to be enumerated here but particular mention must be made of the materials provided to me by the Commonwealth Secretariat, London (for Appendix-A); Food and Agriculture Organization of the United Nations, Rome; The Institute of Social Studies, The Hague (for Chapter III-VII); Asian Institute of Technology, Bangkok; United Nations Research Institute for Social Development, Geneva; The International Labour Organization, Geneva; Centre for Regional Development Research, Justus-Leibig University, Giessen; Settlement Study Centre, Rehovot, Israel and the Regional Research Institute, West Virginia University, West Virginia, U.S.A..

In the conduct of this project I have had the support and assistance of a multitude of people both in India and abroad. They all deserve my best thanks but the list is too long to be paraded here. Nonetheless I thank each one of them very sincerely and look forward towards their continued support in future.

My special thanks are due to Shri B.N.Yugandhar, Director, L.B.S.National Academy of Administration, whose "passion" for research was germane to the creation of the District Planning Unit at the National Academy, and whose constant provocation and vigilance have been contributory factors in keeping this project move on. I thank Shri Lalit Mathur, Joint Director for his abiding interest and for the courtesies shown to me. I thank Shri Rajiv Takroo and Shri P.K. Deb, Deputy Directors, on the Core Group for District Planning Unit of the Academy for the support provided to me. Professor C.S. Prasad, Project-Coordinator for the District Planning Unit, deserves my thanks for the interest taken in running this Unit. I am grateful to Dr.D.M. Nanjundappa, Vice-Chancellor, Bangalore University for his encouragement. Shri R.K.Dar, Secretary, Textiles, Government of India as Principal Secretary, Hill Development, Government of Uttar Pradesh, had helped us in more than one way. To him we are grateful. To Dr. K.V. Sundaram, Consultant and Project Manager, Food and Agriculture Organisation of the United Nations at Kathmandu, I express my gratitute for his wise counsel.

My staff in District Planning Unit, particularly Shri Dharampal Singh, L.D.C., have provided me excellent support during all these months. My thanks to all of them.

The errors, both of omission and commission, that remain are solely mine.

Amitava Mukherjee

District Planning Unit,
LBS National Academy of Administration,
Government of India,
Charleville,
Mussoorie.
26th January, 1990.

CHAPTER I

INDIA'S PLANS AND DECENTRALISATION: AN EVOLUTIONARY PROCESS

The vision of a multilevel planning mechanism has been with us long before we embarked on the avenue of planned economic development in this country. Vishveswaraya (1942) conceived of a four-tier planning system in what was then Mysore State and thoughts of regional planning had dawned on our economists quite early (Balkrishna 1948) in our adventure to seek faster economic regeneration. The thoughts of a planned economy had always been served by a concern for people at every state of society and therefore, the thoughts of planned economic development have been conditioned by the need for a multi-level decentralized planning mechanism.

Today the multilevel decentralized planning framework has turned out to be a logical and natural consequence, of which the federal structure of our politico-administrative machinery as enjoined in the Constitution of India is a distinct antecedent. The division of powers and functions enshrined in Article 246 read with the Seventh Schedule of the Constitution of India, makes multi-level planning a near necessity, at least for administrative expediency, even if warranting economic conditions are non-existent. Under the present constitutional arrangements, all pastures where the State can intercede, can be classified into three neat clusters: Central, State and Concurrent. The Central Government is required to evolve National Plans and to chart out a cohesive policy to implement the national plans. The State Governments are required to confine their excursions in planning within the State list, but subjects like social and economic activities are to be within the domain of both National Plans and State Plans.

Even otherwise, socio-economic realities of India, marked by a multi-ethnic, multi-lingual and multi-cultural society, provided ample validation for a multi-level planning framework. Much of the social heterogeneity is space-specific, which is germane to much of space specific cultural, social and economic structures and patterns. Thus, spatially defined boundary points of socio-economic structures require space-oriented action, space-oriented planning and space-oriented approach, because that alone would be capable of reflecting the collective wisdom and "constructive" will of the masses, to meet demands of rising aspirations of the people relevant to each territorial tier. This explains largely the bias that had developed quite early in our planned developmental effort for a decentralized multilevel planning mechanism.

Our early economic thinkers were quick in perceiving the natural national ethos and in the early years of our planned economic development itself they recognised the need of breaking up the entire gamut of planning exercise into National, State, District and Local Community levels (First Five Year Plan 1951, p, 145). They did not, however, elaborate upon the modus operandi of operationalising, at ground conditions, the conceptual frame of decentralized multi-level planning and they left unexplained the disaggregation and co-ordination of the activities. Experimentation with community development programmes started with 'Pilot Project' on rural development of Mahela Block in Etawah District, whose findings resulted in the establishment of the Community Development Blocks (Misra & Sundaram 1980), and an infrastructure for co-ordination of developmental and administrative functions of the administrative machinery was established. The multi-dimensional task of developing a cluster of villages was assigned to the Community Development Blocks, which was tantamount to translating into reality the conceptual frame of micro-level planning in a modified form.

The planners in the country during the mid-fifties got two new elements injected into the planning process: One, the thought of Village Plans and the concept of District Development Councils; two, the idea of popular participation in planning through the process of democratic decentralisation, with clear emphasis on the district as the hub around which the structure of democratic planning would revolve. This marked the begining of a long process of carrying the plans at the sub-national levels, to the threshold of the common man as instruments for ameliorating his distress and privation, dominated by the grand idea of local community participation and self-help to mobilise local resources, effort,initiative and leadership (Government of India, 1956, p.58) for economic development at sub-national levels in areas such as community development, social welfare, primary education, primary health, agricultural production, rural development and Village Panchayats.

Several States concurrently sought the establishment of the District Development Councils, but these were not success stories because, for one, they did not fit into a decentralised planning frame, and for the other, they were not integrated fully with the fabric of economic struggle for accelerated development. The ennobling vision of the village level plans being drawn up according to the felt needs of the people, were reduced to mere charters of demands as no mechanism was provided to pitch those demands against the available resources. Their aggregation and assimilation to generate the district plans and eventually the State plans could not materialise.

Towards the closing years of the decade of fifties Balwant Rai Mehta Committee (Govt. of India 1957) reviewed the working of community development blocks and plan projects, and handed down the Report that mounted a plea of decentralisation of administration and democratisation of power, having a three-tier integrated organic structure with the Panchayats at the base, overseen by Panchayat Samities or Kshetra Samities and the Zilla Parishad at the apex in the district, to be collectively christened the Panchayati Raj Institutions. These recommendations were accepted by the Government, and different States enacted legislation for creation of these institutions with appropriate modifications, for making due allowance for regional variations.

During the early sixties the Panchayati Raj Institutions gave a good account of themselves, but with the flux of time, hopes were belied, with possible exceptions being experiences in Maharashtra, Gujarat, West Bengal and Karnataka, because they were either superseded or they only remained operating in truncated form. These supercessions had the fall out of erosion of the powers and activities of the Panchayati Raj Institutions in many of the States.

Regional planning made its debut with the "Pilot Regional Survey of the Mysore State" during 1956-58 and the "Diagnostic Survey of Damodar Valley Region" in 1957 for an audit of the resources and devising strategies for regional development (ICSSR,1972).

The hybernating concept of decentralised planning re-emerged during the Third Five Year Plan, with the basic concept that the respective States would formulate their plans for: (a) agriculture, minor irrigation, soil conservation, social forestry, animal husbandry, poultry and dairing; (b) cooperatives; (c) village industries; (d) elementary education; (e) rural water supply, minimum rural needs, link roads etc. and (f) works for fullest utilisation of human resources in rural areas, on the basis of district plans and block level plans (Government of India 1961, p.334). The ingredient for block level planning was enjoined to include all socio-economic activity of the villages under each Community Development Block, that required planning to be initiated locally and where coordination was necessary with the departmental plans, which were implemented within the bounds of the block area. But the plans could not be actually pressed into operation, because the planning machinery necessary to execute the task at the block level was conspicuous by its absence.

The problem of regional development and planning once again received a clear emphasis during the Third Five Year Plan, but a national policy, with clear contours, appertaining to spatial dimension of planning, was yet to emerge, and the success of regional approach to development remained more at the conceptual stage than at the operational state.

The issues of planning machinery at the various territorial tiers came under the scrutiny of the Administrative Reforms Commission (1967), whose Final Report spelled out that the entire gamut of district planning should be related to those areas where local variations in the pattern and process of development were likely to yield quick results in terms of growth; and that a clear picture should be provided to the district authorities about the resources that would be available with them for development purposes, leaving the district authorities to decide their financial outlay for different sectors.

The Fourth Five Year Plan (Government of India, 1969a) brought into sharp focuss the critical importance of regional, district and local planning, with the added requirement that the district plans should be more detailed and greater attention was necessary for development of infrastructual facilities. The concept of integrated area approach was brought to the fore, to locate appropriate socio-economic functions at appropriate places through people's participation and to decentralise developmental efforts, by relating State plans to physical features, resources and institutional machinery in each area.

The Planning Commission issued guidelines to the States on the formulation of district plans (Government of India 1969b), elaborating the concept of district planning and detailing the methodologies for drawing up a district plan, with clear indications that there shall be annual plans, medium term plans and a perspective plan. Researches on methodology of district planning at few key centres began in right earnest, though moderate in their content (Misra 1970). The Government had a close look at the planning machinery at the State and district level, and they were revamped in several States, with the Centre sharing half of the expenditure booked on this account by the States.

Based on the Planning Commission's guidelines several states prepared district plans but their incorporation in the annual plans did not fructify, with the exceptions of Gujarat, Karnataka and Maharashtra, each of whom had adopted their own variation of district planning with difference in criteria for devolution of plan funds to districts and monitoring of plan implementation. The period covered by the Fourth Five Year Plan was, however, significant on two counts: One, the "Lead Bank" scheme was pressed into operation with the designated Nationalised Bank being named lead bank for each district, who would prepare "District Credit Plans", (R.B.I. 1975) to be dovetailed with district development plans for channeling resources to areas of high priority in the district context. Two, a shadow of area planning could be seen to be introduced in the garb of area specific and beneficiary oriented programmes like the CADA, DDA SFDA, and MFAL, (Roy 1982) implementable through special agencies created for the purpose at the district or area level, without inter-programme inter-dependence. The success of these attempts, however, was limited, in part because the total district plans of the districts were not prepared by internalising these attempts, and in part, because these special programmes were not derieved from an overall district plan, which was non-existent in many cases.

The Fifth Five Year Plan outlined for the period 1974-79, (Government of India , 1974) was terminated in April 1978 to introduce the rolling plan scheme formated by the "new look" Government of India that was installed at the Centre in 1977. The development strategies of the Fourth Five Year Plan were carried into the Fifth Five Year Plan as well. The development strategy followed in the Fifth Five Year Plan had reflections of the "Growth Centre" and "Central Place Strategies", advocated in this country by the pioneering works of Lalit K.Sen (1971, 72, 73), Fisher (1979) and by the growth foci concept expounded by (Misra 1974). Need specific programmes like the 20-point economic programme of the Prime Minister (in 1975) and target specific programmes for harnessing science and technology for growth of rural areas were launched.

In 1977, the Government of India arrived at the consensus that anti-poverty programmes and development efforts directed at backward areas could be successful only when the truely poor were identified and plans formulated for ameliorating their conditions, which was not possible by planning at the district level. Hence they identified the block as the appropriate level where planning should commence. A Working Group on Block level planning was set up, which handed down its Report in 1978 (Government of India 1978) noting that the remoteness of planning agencies at the District level from the actual scene of action, distorted matching of financial allocations with location specific needs. Block was identified, therefore, as the appropriate planning unit, and it was thought of as the correct planning approach because that would make sub-national planning responsive to felt needs of the poor, and which would provide a link in the hierarchy between "cluster of villages" and the district, and then on to the regions, state and national levels. The recommendations of the Working Group on Block level planning was accepted and guidelines were issued by the Planning Commission, and Block level planning commenced.

Since the Panchayati Raj Institutions had fallen into disrepute, the Government of India in 1977 appointed a Committee headed by Sri Asoka Mehta to go into the working of these units. The Committee on Panchayati Raj Institutions in 1978 submitted its report (Government of India 1978b) arguing that developmental efforts ought to be fine-tuned to the stark needs of the poor and marked by a high degree of co-ordination, which was not achievable at the State level; the districts should be equipped with professionally qualified people and placed under the Zilla Parishad to be supervised by the Chief Executive Officer, and the Panchayati Raj Institutions should be made to evolve into machineries capable of planning the most appropriate schemes, which were most appropriate for areas of their immediate concern.

The Sixth Five Year Plan (Government of India, 1980) while highlighting the relevance of block level planning for poverty alleviation, over-emphasized the need to provide gainful employment to the poorest of the people, whereby reducing the block level planning exercise to a "one point planning" for employment generation without mirroring the integrated area development approach which was at its base. The Government of India, extended, however, the integrated rural development programme to all blocks (in 1982) and merged SFDA programmes with it, for comprehensive development. (Sisodia, 1983).

The Sixth Five Year Plan retained the concept of district planning in terms of "backlog-cum-problem oriented planning concept" and in terms "resource-cum-need based planning approach" as per guidelines issued by the State Level Planning Organisation. The district planning process was made a function of five factors: resource analysis; sectoral plan formulation; provision of communication services; formulation of spatial plans and planning for special target groups such as women, Scheduled Castes, Scheduled Tribes and Backward Classes (Government of Uttar Pradesh 1983, pp. 100-102).

The Economic Advisory Council of the Prime Minister with Prof. Sukhomoy Chakravarty as the Chairman, however, felt (in 1983) that the exercise of planning at the district level was of limited efficacy, because the district was too small a unit for planning some of the infrastructural facilities (E.A.C., 1984). The Council, therefore, favoured a cluster of four districts, on an average, as a territorial tier for decentralised planning, termed as Divisional Development Authority with a Policy Planning Council and Programme Executive Council and with funds earmarked for the Divisional Development Authority. The Economic Advisory Council was, therefore, advocating a regional planning set up with an additional planning tier (without a territorial tier being co-terminus with it) at the sub-state level but above the district level. These recommendations were, however, neither incorporated nor operationalised in the events to follow.

If anything, the Planning Commission thought that a re-look at district planning was overdue and the working Group on District Planning, with Prof. C.H. Hanumantha Rao as Chairman was set up. In its Report (Government of India 1984) the Working Group made detailed recommendations on district planning and hoped that the Report was sufficiently provocative to stimulate States to adopt a "stages approach" to district planning. The Working Group favoured viewing the district planning exercise as a sub-system in a multi-level planning framework with the entirety of planning activities of this sub-system invested in a single district planning body, capable of determining the priorities and allocation of funds amongst competing development sectors. (Govt. of India, 1984, p. 23).

In the meanwhile district planning made considerable progress in several other states notably in Andhra Pradesh, Uttar Pradesh, West Bengal and Rajasthan. Assam started by presenting another model of decentralized planning by resorting to Sub-Divisional Planning, more in line with the conceptualisation of the Prime Minister's Economic Advisory Council recommendation of 1983 but as a sub-district planning machinery rather than as a super-district level one. West Bengal resorted to the involvement of the Panchayats in perceiving the felt need of the masses, by incorporating the Panchayat Plans into the District Plans (Government of West Bengal 1985).

The Seventh Plan document (Government of India 1985a) was a re-affirmation of faith in decentralised planning with emphasis on district Planning. Though not much headway could be achieved during the period, the importance of planning at the district level for a realistic plan formulation was realised in greater measure.

In 1985 the Government of India appointed a committee to review the existing administrative arrangement for rural development under the chairmanship of Sri G.V.K. Rao, a seasoned bureaucrat. The report of the Committee (Government of India 1985b) reiterated the need for qualitative change in the district plans prepared, emphasising the critical importance of properly prepared district plan. The very important contribution of the Committee was the introduction of the concept of a district budget, for the Committee was of the opinion that in the absence of suitable modification in arrangements for preparation of district budgets, decentralised planning at the district level could not get off the ground (Government of India, 1985b, p. 33).

The Commission appointed by the Government of India under the Chairmanship of Justice Sarkaria to go into the existing arrangements for seperation of powers, functions and responsibilities between the States and the Government, dealt at length with issues relevant to decentralised multi-level planning set up in this country. The Commission reiterated the bearing that participation of people's representative has on planning and administrative machinery at the local level. An important recommendation of the Commission was the creation of a body like Finance Commission at the State level for devolution or transfer of resources to the districts, on an objective basis (Government of India, 1988).

During April, 30th and May 3rd, 1988, the "Workshop of Collectors and District Magistrates on Responsive Administration" held at Jaipur and addressed by the then

Prime Minister, in its Report (Government of India 1988a) dealt with the outlines and methodology of district planning. The focus of the Workshop was that the real worth of the district plan lay in its ability to reflect the aspirations of the people. The Workshop endorsed the recommendation of the Sarkaria Commission, to the extent that a clearly laid down system for devolution of resources from the States to the districts ought to exist, taking into account the levels of development in various districts and according to established criteria.

It was impressed upon the Government of India, that information gap and lack of appropriately trained manpower at the district level caused a serious impediment for the success of the district plans. The Government of India, therefore, constituted two Committees: One, the Committee of the Study Group of Information Gap (Government of India 1988b) and two, Study Group on Training for District Planning (Government of India 1988c), to examine the two aspects of the problem.

The report of the Study Group on Training for District Planning (Government of India 1989a) brought forth the staggering figure that over six lakh forty thousand people, who man the district planning machinery at various levels, need training for proper preparation, monitoring and implementation of district plans, without taking account of the personnel who ought to be ideally trained at 5143 blocks and 5,57,00 village (excluding uninhabited villages) in the country. Hopefully steps are being taken to implement the recommendation of the study group.

The Report of the Committee of the Study Group on Information Gap (Government of India 1989b) felt that for good planning, data at the sub-district level was inadequate and therefore, suggested detailed data collection, in optimum quantum, eliminating amassing of data that could hardly be put to use. The Report has indicated separately three sets of data requirement:-

(a) Data requirement at village level for the micro-level planning (Annexure IV).

(b) Data requirement at Block level for planning at block level (Annexure V).

(c) Data requirement for district level planning (Annexure VI)

Incidentally it may be mentioned in passing that to explore and exploit the vast opportunities offered by information technology, for accelerating and improving the planning process, the Government of India had set up the National Informatics Centre (NIC) as the nodal organisation for computer-based MIS. The NIC has set up a Satellite Based Computer Communication Net-work (NICNET) covering all districts, State Capitals and the Centre, facilitating the development of District Information System at the district level (DISNIC). And then under the programme on Computerisation of Rural Information System Project (CRISP) each of the DRDAs has been provided with mini-computers for developing data bases for different rural development programmes, to facilitate monitoring the schemes, and for processing and building village level information collected through report formats, for planning purposes. Natural Resource Data Management Systems has also been set up on Pilot Scale at nine places in varying geo-environments.

The Eighth Five Year Plan which was scheduled to commence in 1990, is likely be delayed for at least one plan-year. Given the current economic ideas and inclination of the Government of India, (Datta Choudhary, 13th December 1989) and given the composition of the Planning Commission, (The Economic Times News Service, 26th December 1989) indications are clear that decentralisation would be the basis of the next Five Year Plan. Experts are of the view that for rejuvenating the economy, subsidies to the agricultural sector have to be cut, if not totally eliminated, which is best possible when a truly decentralised planning machinery, is combined with the political will of a leader whose credentials as a leader of the farmers is undisputed. It is safe to "predict" that decentralised multi-level planning is at a critical crossroad and the turn that it would take in the next few months will have far reaching consequences for the country.

Select Bibliography

India's Plans and Decentralisation: The Evolutionary Process

Balkrishna, R.:
Regional Planning in India
(Bangalore: Bangalore Printing and Publishing Co.) 1948.

Datta Chaudhari, Mrinal:
"New Government Committed to Decentralisation",
Economic Times, Dec. 13th, 1989.

Economic Advisory Council:
First Report of Decentralisation of Development and Implementation in the State,
4th October 1983, text published in Economic Times, New Delhi, 14th January, 1984.

Economic Times News Service:
"Planning Commission, Enter the Anti Poverty Crusaders",
Economic Times, 26th December, 1989, pp. 1 and 4.

Fischer, Benjamin H.:
"Growth Centre Planning in India",
in Misra R.P. and Sundaram K.V. (eds.):
Rural Area Development and Approaches
(Delhi: Sterling Publishers) 1979.

I.C.S.S.R.:
Survey of Research in India
(Bombay: Popular Prakashan) 1972.

Gandhi, Rajiv:
Responsive Administration,
Speeches at the Workshops of District Magistrates and Collectors on Responsive Administration in 1988 (New Delhi: Government of India) no date mentioned.

Government of India:
First Five Year Plan
(New Delhi: Planning Commission) 1951.

Government of India:
Second Five Year Plan
(New Delhi: Planning Commission) 1956.

Government of India:
Report of the Committee on Plan Projects
(New Delhi: Planning Commission) 1957.

Government of India:
Third Five Year Plan
(New Delhi: Planning Commission) 1961.

Government of India:
Final Report of the Study Team on the Machinery of Planning (New Delhi: Administrative Reforms Commission) 1967.

Government of India:
Fourth Five Year Plan,
(New Delhi: Planning Commission) 1969a.

Government of India:
Guidelines for the Formulation of District Plans
(New Delhi: Planning Commission) September 1969b.

Government of India:
Fifth Five Year Plan
(New Delhi: Planning Commission) 1974.

Government of India:
Report of the Working Group on Block Level Planning
(New Delhi: Planning Commission) 1978a. (M.L. Dantwala Group Report.)

Government of India:
Report of the Committee on Panchayati Raj Institutions
(New Delhi: Department of Rural Development, Ministry of Agriculture and Irrigation) 1978b. (Asoka Mehta Committee Report).

Government of India:
Sixth Five Year Plan
(New Delhi: Government of India) 1980.

Government of India:
Report of the Working Group on District Planning
(New Delhi: Planning Commission) 1984. (C.H. Hanumantha Rao Committee Report.)

Government of India:
Seventh Five Year Plan
(New Delhi: Government of India) 1985a.

Government of India:
Report of the Committee to Review the Existing Administrative Arrangements for Rural Development
(New Delhi: Ministry of Rural Development) 1985b. (G.V.K. Rao Committee Report)

Government of India:
Towards Improved Local Level Planning for Rural Development: Lessons From Experience
(New Delhi: Planning Commission, Multi-Level Planning Section) 1986.

Government of India:
The Report of the Commission on Centre State Relations, Part I & II,
(New Delhi: Government of India) 1988.

Government of India:
Report of the Workshop of Collectors/District Magistrates on Responsive Administration, 30th April to 3rd May 1988, Jaipur Group III, on Contents and Methodology of District Planning
(New Delhi: Government of India, Ministry of Personnel, Public Grievances and Pensions) 1988a.

Government of India:
Office Memorandum No. PC (p) 27/Study Group/ 88-MLP,
(New Delhi: Multi-level Planning Division, Planning Commission) 9th Sep. 1988b.

Government of India:
Office Memorandum No. : PC (p) 27/Study Group/88-MLP,
(New Delhi: Multi-Level Planning Division, Planning Commission) 9th September 1989 and Office Memorandum of even number dated 26th September 1989c.

Government of India:
Report of the Study Group on Training for District Planning,
(New Delhi: Planning Commission) June 1989a.

Government of India:
Report of the Committee of the Study Group on Information Gap,
(New Delhi: Planning Commission) July 1989b.

Government of Uttar Pradesh:
Decentralised Planning, Draft Annual Plan, Vol. I (Review),
(Lucknow: State Planning Department, Government of Uttar Pradesh) December 1983, pp. 100-102.

Government of West Bengal:
Village Based District Planning Process: An Outline of Methodology,
(Midnapore: District Planning Committee) September 1985.

Misra, R.P. and Sundaram, K.V. :
Multi-Level Planning and Integrated Rural Development in India,
(New Delhi: Heritage Publications) 1979.

Misra, R.P.; Parkasa Rao, V.L.S., and Sundaram, K.V.:
Regional Development Planning In India: A New Strategy,
(New Delhi: Vikas Publishing House) 1974.

Reserve Bank of India:
Report of Currency and Finance
(Bombay: Reserve Bank of India) 1975.

Roy, B.:
"Integrated Rural Development",
The Hindustan Times, 3rd January 1982, pp. 10 and 13.

Sen, Lalit K.:
"The Growth Centre and Its Application to Development Planning",
Administrative Staff College of India Journal of Management, Hyderabad 1971.

Sen Lalit, K.:
"Rural Growth Centres and Unemployment",
Kurukshetra, 1972.

Sen, Lalit K.:
Readings in Micro-Level Planning and Rural Growth Centres,
(Hyderabad: National Institute of Community Development) 1973.

Sisodia, H.G.S. :
"Graft Hits Plan for Rural Poor",
The Hindustan Times, October, 11th, 1983, p. 18.

Vishveswaraya, M.:
District Development Scheme-Economic Progress by Forced Marches,
(Bangalore: Bangalore Press) 1942.

CHAPTER II

REGIONAL PLANNING IN INDIA

In a multi-level planning set up, and a multi-level territorial hierarchy, where even planning at the national level could be conceived of as regional planning at the macro level, (Patnaik 1981, and Adisesiah 1989 even consider an agglomeration of several countries as a macro region) it is of interest to know the growth and development of regional planning in this country, where regional planning is taken to mean sub-national planning other than State Plans. The survey of literature on the subject has received a very competent treatment in the hands of Sharma (1989) but with obviously, greater emphasis on planning for social facilities and with good deal of academic flavour. We propose to follow the same scheme with some modification and extend it in terms of operational components of regional planning.

Conceptual work and work on Growth Centre and Central Places have received considerable attention in the literature on regional planning in India. The analysis of spatial dimensions of regional planning is very important. The contribution of Misra & Shivalingaih (1970), Misra (1970), Misra, (1971) and Sen (1971, 72) in the realm of growth pole and growth centre are pioneering contributions that had generated a whole range of applied research on growth centre and growth pole theories. Bhadouria (1976) makes interesting reading on the subject under immediate review. Even today there is a good deal of support for these theories as instruments of development amongst people who matter. Misra & Sundaram (1974, 1978) considerably extended the growth pole concept to the "Growth Foci", which is of major consequence for multi-level planning and have added a new dimension to planning for regional development. Though not much conceptual work has been done on central place concept comparable to the path breaking contributions by the distinguished band of German Scholars like Von Thunen (1926), Walter Christaller (1933) and August Losch (1944), there has been a mass of attempts at regional planning with "central places" and service centre as the focuss of attention. Mayfield (1967), Singh, O.P. (1974), Singh J. (1976), Singh O.P. (1978), Singh, J. (1979) and Sharma, A.N. (1980) are notable writings in this regard. Bhadouria (1971) made an assessment of the application of Loschian model to development Regions. Desai (1985) has examined the spatial aspect of settlement patterns on the basis of a case study. The contribution of Srivastava and Rai (1969) and the conceptual work of, amongst others, Pathak (1972) and Patnaik (1981) are worth mentioning, though the last named is in reality a sweeping overview of the entire gamut of regional development itself.

Rural Development in India has received considerable attention by scholars and practitioners even outside the government, where rural development is conceived of as not merely increases in productivity and employment in agriculture, but a comprehensive transformation of the total rural landscape. Mayer et al. (1958), Lal (1963), Das and Sankar (1972), Khatu (1975, Arunchalam et. al. (1977), Sarma and Mehrotra (1977); Sharma and Shastri (1984), and Rayudu (1989) are well written treatise, but the work done by Khatu (1975) and Sharma and Shastri (1984) are specially noticeable because the former deal with rural planning and the latter is a competent treatment of agro-politan approach to rural development. Thaha, A. and Thaha, M. (1979) also deserve a special mention because they were perhaps amongst the first to develop a manual on integrated rural development. The contribution of Misra and Sundaram (1980) in presenting an "integrated picture" of multi-level planning and integrated rural development cannot escape the attention of serious students of multi-level planning. Sivaiah et. al. (1985) deals with the field level implementation of rural development projects. The contribution by Maithani et al. (1986) could also be read with profit as an exercise in pure application. Aziz (1987 and 1989) are very relevant in this regard. Desai's seven volume work (1988) is the most exhaustive work on the entire sweep of rural development in India.

There has been a large number of attempts at developing Plans for area development, of every description: backward area development plan; tribal area development plan; integrated area development plan; drought prone area development plan; desert area development plan and command area plan. Prasad (1972), Pathak (1973), Sen et. al. (1975) and Sharma (1980) are important contributions. The contribution of Sen et al. (1976) and Bose (1978) on comprehensive area development; of Mathur and Misra (1974), and Routray (1984) on backward area development; of Khan and Ramesh (1977) on tribal area development, and of Sharma B.D.(1989) on tribal development are notable contributions. Sen and Das (1986) made a very useful study of Tungabhadra Command Area with regard to its problem of water utilization. Desai (1985) also made an intensive study of the Narmada Command Area but strictly speaking it does not contain a plan per se for development of the area.

It needs to be underscored that the concept of integrated area development planning was introduced for the first time (in the formal sense) in India by the Institute of Regional Development Planning, Wardha (1965), while the concept of integrated area plan through growth centres was introduced, by the Government of Madhya Pradesh (1974) in the wave of the "growth centre approach" emanating from the "Hyderabad-Mysore nexus" of Sen and Misra. The area development study by Centre for Development Studies and Activities, Pune, on Etawah some time in the mid seventies (no date mentioned) is an excellent work done, and could guide future research on the subject despite its vintage.

Area level planning has received considerable attention of economists, academicians and planners and the amount of literature that has grown around it, is staggering. Thaha (1974) is one of the more earlier attempts. Sen and Thaha, A. (1977) is an excellent specimen of Hill Area Planning, to be followed in many subsequent plans. Subramaniam (1987) is a more recent account of area level planning in one sense. And then there exists the considrable volume of literature, documented by Sharma (1989), namely, ISI (1962); Sen et al. (1971); Misra (1972); Bhat et al. (1976); Roy and Patil (1977); Singh H.P. (1978); UNAPDI (1980); Ram Chandran (1980); and Sharma A.N. (1980). The work by Kumara (1983) on Kanpur City is very interesting and deserves a serious reading. Verma (1985) and Nadkarni (1986) are studies of Bombay Metropolitan Area and drought prone areas of three Southern States respectively. UNAPDI (1980) is considered by several experts as among the first work on the nature and implications of local level planning and development with people's participation. Sharma (1989) rightly points out that several of the studies in area level planning were grounded on approaches to micro-level planning.

The contribution made in this regard by the Association of Voluntary Agencies for Rural Development (AVARD) New Delhi has been significant and should be dealt with separately. AVARD (1975) is a much quoted integrated rural development plan for Imphal East Meitie Villages. AVARD's (1976) integrated rural development plan for Kumarikata Panchayat, Assam, is one of the few attempts made at area planning in a state where decentralised planning has been operationalised even up to the sub-divisional level (Baisya and Mali (1989). AVARD (1976, 1985a, 1985b, 1986a, 1986b, 1986c, 1986d, 1986e and 1987) are some of the area level plans prepared by AVARD for various segments of the country. AVARD (1978) is a very interesting study of fringe areas of a sprawling megapolis like Calcutta. The contribution made by AVARD in area planning, where the area is conceived of as a cluster of villages, has been notable. Table I provides a list of 36 such area plans prepared by AVARD and it would have been worthwhile examining each separately but the number is too numerous and hence they are not discussed here individually. The block plan for Dharampur Block, in Valsad District Gujarat, by I.I.M. Ahmedabad has been discussed widely (Vyas et. al. 1979). Gupta (1980) has many thoughts that are still relevant to us today. The other institution worth mentioning in this regard is the National Institute for Rural Development, Hyderabad. Starting with the lead given by Sen and others the Institute has rendered notable service in the realm of area planning, the last being pilot project on District Planning in Nasik, Munger, Sitapur, Shimla and Tirunelvelli (NIRD. 1989).

It is too well known to be laboured here that regionalisation is an integral part of decentralised planning and methods of regionalisation ought to and does vary according as the purpose for which regionalisation is sought to be made varied. Sen Gupta (1961a, 1961b) and Sadasyuk (1961) did pioneering work on regionalisation in India during the Census Operation of 1961. Mukherjee (1962) and Sharma (1973) discuss Agricultural regionalisation; Tewari (1962) talk of industrial regionalisation; Kumar and Popov (1962) are concerned with economic regionalisation; Bhat & Prakash Rao (1964) and Nath (1965) discuss resources regions; Choudhury and Singh (1975) are concerned with physiognomic regions; Sandhu (1977) contributed her mite to the regionalisation in terms of backward and developed regions; and Dashrath (1979) and Yadav (1980) were concerned with locating the area of influence of the cities. The contribution of Patnaik (1981) in summarising various stands of thoughts of regionalisation could be of some relevance.

The issue of determining the appropriate unit for planning has long since agitated great minds. Vivekananda and Rao (1980) concerned themselves with what could be the proper regional unit for planning. Prof. Dantwala Committee (1978), even before Vivekananda and Rao, thought that the block was the appropriate unit for planning. The Economic Advisory Council of the Prime Minister (1984) under the Chairmanship of Prof. Sukhamoy Chakravarty, thought of the Divisional Development Authority consisting of several districts to be the appropriate region for planning. Hanumantha Rao Committee (1984) thought the district as the appropriate delineation of region for the lowest tier of planning in a decentralised planning set up. It must be mentioned to the credit of Pal, that in Pal (1963, 1973, 1974) he made path breaking studies by introducing quantitative techniques in regionalisation in India.

Regional Development and Planning have had their share of scholarly outpouring as well. The studies by A. Mitra (1965); Bahadur and S. Singh (1984) on identifying the levels of development; by A. Sen (1976), S. Prakash (1977), Hemlata Rao (1980), Sundaram (1982), Sudarshan (1982) and Mukherjee & Kishore (1982) on regional inequality and disparities; by T.B. Lahiri (1972), and M.L. Patel (1975) on balanced regional development, are some of the important contributions.

The literature on the problems of regional planning for social facilities has been brought out in abundance, of which Wanmali (1970), and Elhance (1983) are good examples. On the issues relating to the problems of individual facilities, services and amenities, of the numerous studies conducted, the significant examples are M.L. Makhija (1978) and S.D. Shinde (1978) on health facilities; D.N Singh (1970), and M.M.L. Srivastava (1976) on traffic and transport; by the I.I.M.C. (1979) on communication policies; V.K. Srivastava and H.O. Srivastava (1979), R.C. Sharma and A. Kumar (1981), and Tripathi and R. Chand (1983) on market facilities; by L.K. Sen and G.K. Misra (1974) on rural electrification; S. Lal (1977) on farm services; by S. Kant and K.N. Dubey (1984) on administrative units; by R.C. Tyagi et. al. (1982) on spatial organisation of film theatres; and C.B. Singh (1981) on tourist and Bihar tourism industry.

Select Bibliography

"Regional" Planning in India

Adisesiah, M.C.:
Regional Economic Arrangement (New Delhi: India International Centre & Lancer International) 1989.

Akhtar, R.:
The Geography of Health - An Essay and a Bibliography, (New Delhi: Marwah Publications) 1981.

Arunachalam, K. and Natrajan, M. (eds.):
Integrated Rural Development, (Madurai: Kodal Publishers) 1977.

Association of Voluntary Agencies for Rural Development (AVARD):
Integrated Rural Development Plan for Imphal East Meitie Villages, Manipur Central District, September 1975.

Avard:
Integrated Rural Development Plan for Kumarikata Panchayat, Kamrup District, Assam, June 1976.

Avard:
Integrated Rural Development Plan for Tribal Region -3, Banpur, Puri, Orissa July 1976.

Avard:
Integrated Rural Development Plan for Mayapur Panchayat, Hoogly District, West Bengal, November 1985.

Avard:
Integrated Rural Development Plan for Maturia - II Panchayat, Howrah District, West Bengal, November 1985.

Avard:
Integrated Rural Development Plan for Gaganpur Panchayat, Munger District, Bihar, January 1986.

Avard :
Integrated Rural Development Plan for Bara Sota Panchayat, Birbhum District, West Bengal February 1986.

Avard:
Integrated Rural Development Plan for Asanbani Panchayat, Singhbhum District, Bihar, November 1986c.

Avard:
Integrated Rural Development Plan for Bhadwar Panchayat, Dumaria District, Bihar, November 1986d.

Avard:
Integrated Rural Development Plan for Amthapur Panchayat, Cuttack District, Orissa, January 1987

Avard:
Fringe Areas of Calcutta -Development of Three Rural Situations, 1978.

Aziz, A.:
Studies in Block Planning, (New Delhi: Concept Publishing Co.) 1983.

Aziz, Abdul:
Formulation of IRDP: The Plan Integration Issue (1989), Manuscript, Bangalore.

Aziz, Abdul:
Approaches to Micro-Area Development Planning, (1989), Manuscript, Bangalore.

Bahadur, S. and Ahmad, A.:
"Levels of Development of Higher Education in India", Indian Geographical Studies, Research Bulletin No. 20, March, 1983.

Bhat, L.S.; Pal, M.N. et. al. :
"Problems of Regionalisation for Development of National Economy",
Sankhya, Series B, Vol. 25, 1963.

Bhat, L.S. and Prakash Rao, V.L.S.:
"A Regional Framework for Resource Development",
Bombay Geographical Magazine, Vol. 10, No. 1, 1964.

Bhat, L.S., et. al.:
Micro Level Planning :A Case Study of Karnal Area, Haryana, India,
(New Delhi: K.B. Publications) 1976.

Bhadouria, B.P.S.:
"August Losch's Model of Spatial General Equilibrium and Its Applicability to Development Regions",
Indian Economic Journal, Vol. XIX, No. 2, 1971.

Bhadouria, B.P.S.:
Disparities and Development Policies,
(New Delhi: Anmol Publications) 1986.

Bose, A.N.:
West Bengal: Possibilities - A Report on the Working of West Bengal Comprehensive Area Development Corporation, 1974-78, A Draft for Discussion,
(Calcutta: Comprehensive Area Development Corporation) Aug. 1978.

Centre for Development Studies And Activities:
Integrated Area Development Etawah
(Pune: Centre for Development Studies and Activities) no date mentioned.

Christaller, W. (1933):
Central Places in Southern Germany,
Translated By C.W. Baskin from German, (Englewood Cliffs: Prentice Hall) 1966.

Das, B.N. and Sarkar, A.K.:
"Rural Area Development, Karnal Area: A Case Study",
Indian Journal of Regional Science, Vol. IV, No. 2, 1972.

Desai, Anjana P. :
Spatial Aspect of Settlement Pattern: A Study of Narmada Command Area
(New Delhi: Concept Publishing Company) 1985.

Desai, Vasant:
Rural Development
(Bombay: Himalaya Publishing House) 1988, Vol, I to VII, 1988, particularly Volume IV Experiments in Rural Development.

Elhance, A.:
"Location of Social Facilities: An Analytical Foundation",
in A Geographical Approach to Settlement Planning for Integrated Area Development, (New Delhi: Ford Foundation) 1973.

Gopalaswamy, R:
"Regional Dimensions of Plan Development - Possible Approaches",
in Government of U.P.: Regional Dimensions of India's Economic Development (Lucknow: State Planning Commission) 1983.

Govt. of India:
South India Macro-Regional Survey (Mimeo),
(New Delhi: Indian Statistical Institute) 1962

Govt. of India:
Malkangiri Development Plan,
(New Delhi:Town and Country Planning Organisation) 1973.

Govt. of India:
Report of the Working Group on Block Level Planning (Dantwala Committee),
(New Delhi: Planning Commission) Nov. 5, 1977.

Govt. of India:
Decentralised Planning, Draft Annual Plan Vol.I (Review), 1984-85,
(Lucknow: Govt. of U.P., Planning Deptt.) Dec. 1983.

Gupta, Ranjit:
Prelude to Block Level Planning in Gujarat
(Ahmedabad: Indian Institute of Management) 1978.

Hermansen, T..
"Spatial Organisation and Economic Development",
Development Studies No. 1, University of Mysore, (Mysore: Institute of Development Studies) 1971.

Institute of Regional Development Planning:
Wardha District Plan
(Wardha: Institute of Regional Development Planning) 1965, mimeographed.

Hilhorst, J.G.M.:
Regional Development Policies
(The Hague: Institute of Social Studies) 1985.

Losch, A. (1940):
The Economics of Location,
translated from German by W.F. Stopler, (Connecticut, New Haven: Yale University Press) 1954.

Makhija, M.L.:
Locational Study of Educational Institutions in Udaipur Plateau,
Unpublished Ph.D. dissertation (Udaipur: Udaipur University) 1978.

Mathur, O.P. and Misra, R.P.:
Planning for the Backward Areas: Some Contributions, Development Studies, No.9,
(Mysore: Institute of Development Studies) 1974.

Mayer, A. and et al.:
Pilot Project, India, the Story of Rural Development at Etawah, Uttar Pradesh, India
(Berkeley: University of California Press) 1958.

Minocha, A.C.:
"Planning for Social Services in a Backward Region",
Indian Journal of Regional Science, Vol. VI, No. 2, 1974, pp. 181-198.

I.I.M.C.:
Rural Development and Communication Policies,
Proceeding of Seminar held at Hyderabad from Feb. 21st to 24th, 1979 by the Indian Institute of Mass Communication (IIMC).

Kant, S. and Dubey, K.N.:
"Spatial Structure of Administrative Units and the Development Process (A Case Study of Uttar Pradesh)",
The National Geographical Journal of India, Vol, 30, Part 1, 1984.

Khan, W. and Ramesh, K.S.:
Integrated Area Development Plan for West District, Manipur,
(Hyderabad: National Institute of Community Development), 1977.

Khatu, K.K.:
"Rural Planning System",
The National Geographical Journal of India, Vol. XXI, Pts. 3 & 4, 1975, pp. 213-219.

Kumara, V.K.:
Kanpur City-A Study in Environmental Pollution,
(Varanasi: Tara Book Agency) 1983.

Lahiri, T.B.:
Balanced Regional Development,
(Calcutta: Oxford & I.B.H. Publishing Co.) 1972.

Lal, R.:
Community Development-Principles, Practices and Problems,
(Calcutta: Bookland Pvt. Ltd.) 1963.

Maithani, B.P.; Nagaseshanna, A.; George, Jacob and Ramana, D.V.:
Planning for Integrated Rural Development
(Hyderabad: National Institute of Rural Development) April 1986.

Misra,B.:
"Growth Pole and Growth Centre Strategy in Metropolitan Regional Development",
Indian Journal of Regional Science, Vol. III, No. 1, 1971.

Misra, R.P.:
Regional Planning-Concepts, Techniques, Policies and Case Studies,
(Prasaranga, Mysore: University of Mysore) 1969.

Misra, R.P. & Shivalingaih, M..
"Growth Pole Strategy for Development in India",
Journal of the Insititute of Economic Geography, Vol. 1, 1970.

Misra, R.P.:
Growth Poles and Growth Centres in Urban and Regional Planning in India and Training Programme for Regional Development in Developing Countries: An Experiment in India, Development Studies No. 2, Institute of Development Studies
(Mysore: University of Mysore) 1971.

Misra, R.P. and Sundaram, K.V.:
"Growth Foci as Instruments of Modernization in India",
in Kuklinski, A. (ed.): Regional Policies in Nigeria, India and Brazil (Paris: Mouton) 1978.

Mitra, A.:
"Levels of Regional Development in India",
Census of India, 1961, Vol. I, Part I-A (i) and (ii), New Delhi, 1965.

Mukherjee, A.B.:
Agricultural Regions and Geographic Planning for Indian Agriculture,
National Geographer, Vol. 5, Dec. 1962.

Mukherjee, M.S. and Kishore, N.:
"Concept and Measurement of Poverty: A Development Index",
in Govt. of Uttar Pradesh: Regional Dimensions of India's Economic Development, (Lucknow: State Planning Commission) 1983.

Nadkarni, M.V.:
Socio-Economic Conditions of Drought Prone Areas: A Benchmark Study of Drought Districts in Andhra Pradesh, Karnataka and Tamilnadu
(New Delhi: Concept Publishing Co.) 1986.

Nath, V.:
Resource Development Regions and Divisions of India
(New Delhi: Planning Commission) 1965.

National Institute of Rural Development:
Pilot Project on District Planning Executive Summary
(Hyderabad: National Institute of Rural Development) 1989.

Pal, M.N.:
An Introduction to Regional Planning,
(Calcutta: Indian Statistical Institute, Regional Survey Unit) 1963.

Pal, M.N.:
"A Method of Regional Analysis of Economic Development with Special Reference to South India",
Journal of Regional Science Vol. 5, 1963.

Pal, M.N.:
"Operation Research Techniques in Indian National and Regional Planning",

Opsearch, Council for Scientific and Industrial Research, New Delhi, Vol. 2, Nos. 1 and 2, 1965.

Pal, M.N.:
"Quantitative Techniques in Regional Planning",
Indian Journal of Regional Science, Vol. III, No. 1, 1971.

Pal, M.N.:
"Regional Studies and Research for Constant and Optimal Plan Formulation: The Need for Right Kind of Orientation",
Indian Journal of Regional Science, Vol. V, No. 1, 1973.

Pal, M.N.:
"Regional Information, Regional Statistics and Regional Planning in India",
in Kulkinski, A. (ed.):
Regional Information and Regional Planning
(The Hague: Mouton & Co.) 1974.

Prakasa Rao, V.L.S. and Bhat, L.S.:
"A Regional Framework for Resource Development",
Bombay Geographical Magazine, Vol. 1, 1964.

Prakash, S.:
"Regional Inequalities and Economic Development With Special Reference to Infrastructural Facilities in India",
Indian Journal of Regional Science, Vol. 9, No. 2, 1977.

Prasad, H.::
"Integrated Area Development and Its Appraisal in Dehra Dun",
Indian Journal of Regional Science, Vol. IV, No. 2, 1972, pp. 186-192.

Patankar, P.:
"Planning for Micro Regions and the Plan of Infrastructure in Wardha",
(Mimeo), Wardha, 1968.
Dilemma of Balanced Regional Development in India,
(Bhopal: Progress Publishers) 1975.

Pathak, C.R.:
"Development: Search for a Conceptual Frame"
Indian Journal of Regional Science, Vol, IV, No. 2, 1972.

Pathak, C.R.:
"Integrated Area Development",
Geographical Review of India, Vol. XXXV, No. 3, Sept. 1973.

Pathak, C.R. and Kundu, A.:
"Regionalisation and Regional Planning-An Axiomatic Approach",
Indian Journal of Regional Science, Vol. V, No. 2, 1973.

Patnaik, S.C.:
Economics of Regional Development and Planning in Third World Countries,
(New Delhi: Associated Publishing House), 1981.

Ramchandran, H.:
Village Clusters and Rural Development,
(New Delhi: Concept Publishig Co.) 1980.

Rao, V.K.R.V.:
Planning Unit Areas for Integrated Rural Development-An Exercise,
(New Delhi: Ashish Publishing House) 1980.

Rayudu, C.S.:
Management of Rural Development
(New Delhi: Discovery Publications) 1989.

Routray, J.K.:
"Approaches to Backward District Planning: Case Study of Boudh-Khondhmal District in Orissa",
Indian Journal of Regional Science, Vol. XVI, No. 1, 1984.

Sen, A.C. et al. (eds.):
Comprehensive Area Development- Proceedings and

Papers of a Workshop, District Mirzapur, U.P., Feb. 17-22, 1975,
(Association of Voluntary Agencies for Rural Development: New Delhi) 1976.

Sen, D. and Das, P.K.:
Water Utilization at Farm Level: A Study of Tungabhadra Command Area
(Hyderabad: National Institute of Rural Development) November 1986.

Sen, L.K. (ed.):
Readings on Micro Level Planning and Rural Growth Centres,
(Hyderabad: National Institute of Community Development), 1972.

Sen, L.K. et al.:
Planning Rural Growth Centres for Integrated Area Development: A Study in Miryalguda Taluka,
(Hyderabad: National Institute of Community Development) 1971.

Sen, Lalit K.; and Thaha, A.L.:
Regional Planning for a Hill Area - Case Study of Pauri Garhwal, U.P.
(Hyderabad: National Institute of Community Development) 1977.

Sen, L.K. and Misra, G.K.:
Regional Planning for Rural Electrification: A Study in Suryapet Taluk Nalgonda District, Andhra Pradesh,
(Hyderabad: National Institute of Community Development) 1974.

Sen, L.K., et al.:
Growth Centres in Raichur: An Integrated Area Development Plan for a District in Karnataka,
(Hyderabad: National Institute of Community Development) 1975.

Sengupta, P.:
"The Principles and Techniques of Regional Planning",
The Geographer, Vol. XIV, 1967.

Shah, M.:
Rural Development Planning and Reforms,
(New Delhi: Abhinav Publications) 1977.

Sharma, A.N.:
Spatial Approach for District Planning - A Case Study of Karnal District,
(New Delhi: Concept Publishing House) 1980.

Sharma, B.D.:
Web of Poverty
(Shillong: North Eastern Hill Univesity and New Delhi: Prachi Publishers) 1989.

Sharma, P.N. and Shastri, C.:
Social Planning: Concepts and Techniques,
(Lucknow: Print House India) 1984.

Sharma, P.S.:
Agricultural Regionalisation of India,
(Delhi: New Heights Publishers) 1973.

Sharma, R.C.:
Regional Planning for Social Development
(New Delhi: Criterion) 1989.

Sharma, S.K. and Malhotra, S.L.:
Integrated Rural Development (Approach, Strategy and Perspectives)
(New Delhi: Abhinav Publications) 1977.

Shinde, S.D.:
"The Distribution of Population and Medical Facilities in Maharashtra",
Maharashtra Medical Journal, Vol. 25, No. 4, 1978.

Shiviah, M.; Balakrishna, S.; Narayana, Rao; Subramanyam, K. Siva; and Ranghacharyulu, S.V.:
Field Level Implementation of Rural Development Projects
(Hyderabad: National Institute of Rural Development) 1985.

Singh, C.B.:
Tourist and Tourism Industries in U.P.,
An unpublished Ph.D. Thesis in Geography (Gorakhpur: University of Gorakhpur) 1981.

Singh, D.N.:
"Regionalisation of Transport in North Bihar",
Uttar Bharat Bhoogol Patrika, Vol. 6, No. 1, June, 1970.

Singh, H.P.:
"Development Pole Theory: Review and Appraisal - A Case Study of Bundelkhand",
National Geographer, Vol. XIII, No. 2, Dec. 1978.

Singh, J.:
"Nodal Accessibility and Central Place Hierarchy - A Case Study in Gorakhpur Region (U.P.)",
National Geographer, Vol. XI, No. 2, 1976.

Singh, J.:
Central Places and Spatial Organisation in a Backward Economy: Gorakhpur Region- A Study in Integrated Regional Development,
(Gorakhpur: Uttar Bharat Bhoogol Parishad) 1979.

Singh, K.:
"A Scheme of Regionalisation for Bundelkhand",
The Geographical Obsever, Vol. 11, March, 1975.

Singh, O.P.:
"Central Places, Identification and Types",
Uttar Bharat Bhoogol Patrika, Vol. 10, Nos. 3 & 4, Sept. Dec., 1974

Singh, O.P.:
"Hierarchy of Towns as Service Centres in Varanasi Region",
Uttar Bharat Bhoogol Patrika, Vol. XIV, No. 1, June 1978.

Singh, R.N. and Kumar, A.:
"Classical Theories of Spatial Organisation: Scope and Limitations",
National Geographer, Vol. XVII, No. 2, Dec. 1982.

Singh, R.R.:
Studies in Regional Planning and Rural Development,
(Patna: Associated Book Agency), 1982.

Singh, S.:
"Measuring the Levels of Development-A Taxonomic Approach",
Indian Journal of Regional Science, Vol. XVI, No. 1, 1984.

Singh, T.:
"Resource Development and Regional Planning",
Geographical Review of India", Vol. XXVIII, No. 1, March 1966.

Srivastava, M.M.L.:
"Commuters Traffic Flow in Metropolitan Delhi",
The National Geographical Journal of India, Vol.XXII, Parts 3 and 4, 1976, p. 139.

Srivastava, V.K. and Rai, J.P.:
"Hierarchy of Market Centres: A Methodological Approach",
Uttar Bharat Bhoogol Patrika, Vol. 14, No. 2, Dec. 1979, pp. 97-104.

Srivastava, V.K. and Srivastava, H.O.:
"Distributional Pattern and Classification of Market Centres in the Sarupar Plan",
The Deccan Geographer, Vol. XVII, No. 1, Jan-June 1979.

Srivastava, V.K. and Viswanath:
"Demarcation of Market Area Region: A Methodological Approach",

Uttar Bharat Bhoogol Patrika, Vol. XI, No. 1, 1975.

Subramanian, S.:
Poverty Unemployment and Perspective of Development
(Allahabad: Chugh Publications) 1987.

Sudarshan, P:
"A Note on Inter-Temporal Differentials in Andhra Pradesh's Development",
in Govt. of U.P.: Regional Dimensions of India Economic Development (Lucknow: State Planning Commission) 1983.

Sundaram, K.V.:
"Measurement and Analysis of Development at the Regional and Local Levels",
in Govt. of U.P.: Regional Dimensions of India's Economic Development (Lucknow: State Planning Commission) 1983.

Somayajulu, V.V. and Mohan Raj, S.:
"Passenger Traffic Demand in Hyderabad-Secunderabad",
Indian Journal of Regional Science, Vol. XV, No. 1, 1983.

Thaha, M.:
Regional Approach to Development of Chotanagpur,
Unpublished doctoral dissertation, (Ranchi: Department of Geography, Ranchi University) 1974.

Thaha, Abdul L. and Thaha, Mumtaz:
A Manual on Integrated Rural Development
(Quilon: Faizy, A.A.) October 1979.

Tripathi, V.B. and Chand, R.:
"Micro Level Locational Planning for Market Facilities: A Case Study of Bulandshahar District",
The Geographer, Vol. XXX, No. 2, July 1983, pp. 63-75.

UNAPDI:
Local Level Planning and Rural Development- Alternative Strategies,
(New Delhi: Concept Publishing Co.) May 1980.

Varma, H.S.:
Bombay, New-Bombay and Metropolitan Region
(New Delhi: Concept Publishing Co.) 1985.

Vivekanand, M. and Rao, V.K.R.V. (eds.):
Planning Unit Areas for Integrated Rural Development-An Exercise,
(New Delhi: Ashish Publishing House) July 1980.

Von Thunen, H.J. (1926):
Von Thunen's Isolate State, Translated by C.M. Wartenburgh,
(London: Oxford University Press) First Published in German, 1966.

Wanmali, S.:
Regional Planning for Social Facilities: An Examination of Central Place Concepts and their Application- A Case Study of Eastern Maharashtra,
(Hyderabad: National Institute of Community Development) 1970.

Wanmali, S.:
"Clustering of Services as a Function of Population Distance in Settlement System",
Journal of Behavioural Sciences and Community Development, Vol. VI, No. 1, Hyderabad.

Table-I

PLANS PREPARED FOR CLUSTER OF VILLAGES BY ASSOCIATION OF VOLUNTARY AGENCIES FOR RURAL DEVELOPMENT, (AVARD) NEW-DELHI:

(As on 31st January 1985)

No.	Name of the Plan	Block	District	State
1.	2	3	4	5
1.	Rural Reconstruction Programme in Selected Areas	Musahri Block	Muzaffarpur	Bihar
2	Project Proposal forSelected Panchayats	Bochaha	Muzaffarpur Block	Bihar
3.	Rural Rcconstruction Programme in Selected Areas of Jamiui Block	Jamui Block	Munger	Bihar
4.	Project Proposal for for selected Panchayats in Khaira Block	Khaira Block	Munger	Bihar
5.	Detailed Work Plan Nagapalli Check Dam	Bolgarh	Puri	Orissa
6.	Development of Goatry in Bolgarh	Bolgarh	Puri	Orissa
7.	Proposal for Development of a Hill Recess		Almora	Uttar Pradesh
8.	Development of a Cluster of Villages in Banpur Block	Banpur Block	Puri	Orissa
9.	Integrated Rural Development in Chantongia Block	Changtongia Block		Nagaland
10.	Work Plans for selected schemes Naujil Block	Naujhil Block	Mathura	Uttar Pradesh
11	Work Plan forselected Schemes Adhura Block	Adhaura Block	Rohtas	Bihar
12	Work Plan for Selected Schemes	Dhamdham a Block	Kamrup	Assam
13.	Sericulture Development in Khaira Block	Khaira Block	Munger	Bihar

14.	Development of Sarifuddinpur Panchayat Block	Bochaha	Muzaffarpur	Bihar
15.	Development of Dumarkola Panchayat	Khaira Block	Munger	Bihar
16.	Rehabilitation of Bhoodan Families Ramdohar Panchayat	Dumaria Block	Gaya	Bihar
17.	Sarabannapalem Tribal Region-A Development		Visakha patnam	Andhra Pradesh
18.	Family DevelopmentProgramme, G.Udaigiri	G.Udaigiri Block		Orissa
19.	Need Based Plan for Bankura Champatagara	Mouza Masthol		West Bengal
20.	Continuing Schemes for the Development of a Hill Recess		Almora	Uttar Pradesh
21.	A Woman Development Programme in Oinem Thingal Panchayat.	Imphal West II	Central	Manipur
22	Selected Anti-Poverty Alleviation Schemes	Jamui	Munger,	Bihar
23.	Longathabal Panchayat		Central	Manipur
24.	Selected Poverty Alleviation Schemes	Musahri	Muzaffarpur	Bihar
25.	Development of Sangaiprou Mamang Panchayat,	Imphal West II Block	Central	Manipur
26.	Techno-Economics Survey -A Cluster of Drought Prone Village	Khanapur	Sangli	Maharashtra
27.	Development of Nauhatta Block-with Women in Focus-A Project Proposal	Nauhatta Block	Rohtas	Bihar
28.	Project Takhel GramPanchayat,		Central	Manipur
29.	Socio-Economic Development, Women in Chingnungkok Panchayat,	Nongem East Block	Imphal	Manipur

Table- II

INTEGRATED RURAL DEVELOPMENT BLOCK PLANS PREPARED BY ASSOCIATION OF VOLUNTARY AGENCIES FOR RURAL DEVELOPMENT (AVARD) NEW DELHI

No.	Name of Block	District	State	Month and Year
1	2	3	4	5
1.	Chintalapudy Block	West Godavari	Andhra Pradesh	January 1980
2.	Boath Block	Adilabad	Andhra Pradesh	December 1980
3.	Mudhol Block	Adilabad	Andhra Pradesh	June 1981
4	Angarka	Kamrup	Assam	September 1976
5	Dhamdhama	Kamrup	Assam	July 1977
6.	Adhaura Block	Rohtas	Bihar	June1976
7.	Barhara Kothi Block	Purnea	Bihar	February 1981
8.	Bhawanipur Block	Purnea	Bihar	January 1982
9.	Dhmdaha Block	Purnea	Bihar	November 1981
10.	Banmankhi Block	Purnea	Bihar	June 1982
11.	Rupauli Block	Purnea	Bihar	August 1982
12.	Bochana Block	Muzaffarpu r	Bihar	August 1984
13.	Khaira Block	Munger	Bihar	June 1982
14.	Dumaira Block	Gaya	Bihar	March 1971
15.	Musahri Block	Muzaffarpu r	Bihar	October 1971
16.	Nauhatta Block	Rohtas	Bihar	April 1983
17.	Karkala Block	South Kanara	Karnataka	June 1983
18.	Hiriyir Block	Chitradurga	Karnataka	March 1982
19.	Malakalmuru Block	Chitradurga	Karnataka	March 1982
20.	K.R.Pet Block	Mandya	Karnataka	April 1982
21.	Sagar Block	Shimoga	Karnataka	April 1982

22	Vellanad	Trivandrum	Kerala	March 1980
23	Imphal West	Central	Manipur	May 1983
24	Jiribam	Central	Manipur	September 1983
25	Khuladabad	Aurangabad	Maharashtra	February 1983
26	Joura	Morena	M.P.	April 1976
27	Kohima	Kohima	Nagaland	May 1975
28	Changtongia	Mokokchun g	Nagaland	May 19s75
29.	Krushna Prasad Block	Puri	Orissa	January 1982
30.	Koksara Block	Kalahandi	Orissa	September 1982
31.	Parlakhemundi Block	Ganjam	Orissa	February 1982
32.	G.Udaigiri Block	Phulabani	Orissa	February 1982
33.	Banpur Block	Puri	Orissa	February 1982
34.	Shannarpatty	Madurai	Tamilnadu	December 1983
35.	Naujhil Block	Mathura	Uttar Pradesh	May 1977
36.	Bahadurpur Block	Allahabad	Uttar Pradesh	
37.	Harahua Block	Varanasi	Uttar Pradesh	September 1979
38.	Kurebhar Block	Sultanpur	Uttar Pradesh	March 1980
39..	Masodha Block	Faizabad	Uttar Pradesh	August 19980
40.	Sohawal Block	Faizabad	Uttar Pradesh	May 1980
41.	Kudraha Block	Basti	Uttar Pradesh	June 1980
42.	Lakshmanpur	Pratapgarh	Uttar Pradesh	June 1980
43.	Dobhi Block	Jaunpur	Uttar Pradesh	February 1980
44.	Lar Block	Deoria	Uttar Pradesh	August 1979
45.	Bhathat Block	Gorakhpur	Uttar Pradesh	February 1980
46.	Paniara Block	Gorakhpur	Uttar Pradesh	January 1980
47.	Nawangagar Block	Ballia	Uttar Pradesh	January 1980
48.	Murli Chapra Block	Ballia	Uttar Pradesh	April 1980
49.	Ranipur Block	Azamgarh	Uttar Pradesh	December 1979
50.	Razapur Block	Ghaziabad	Uttar Pradesh	May 1974

51.	**Shadholi Quadim Block**	Seharanpur	Uttar Pradesh	April 1984
52.	**Bolpur Block**	Birbhum	West Bengal	August 1976
53.	**Dhaniakhali P.S.**	Hooghly	West Bengal	August 1976
54.	**Amta P.S.**	Howrah	West Bengal	August 1976
55.	**Bewaria P.S.**	Howrah	West Bengal	August 1976.

CHAPTER III

THE RATIONALE FOR DECENTRALISED PLANNING, REGIONAL PLANNING AND RURAL DEVELOPMENT

The position taken in this study is that multi-level planning and regional planning at several teritorial tiers, are virtually co-terminus, and therefore, any attempt at defining or delineating multi-level planning, must of necessity involve references to regional planning. It is, however, at once recognised that regional planning appertaining to a land mass or space that does not correspond to any teritorial boundary, such as the regional plan for Agro-Climatic Zones (1989); or the Damodar Valley Corporation to tackle concurrently the problems of generating hydro-electricity and control flood that cut across more than one State, could also be resorted to, in which event it would be "macro-meso" regional planning.

Friedman and Alonso (1964) held that "regional planning is made synonymous with regional development policy at the national level (balanced integration) with a process of decision making and design in elaboration of investment project at the regional level and with economic development programmes for sub-national areas. There is, in addition, an intimation that regional planning has something to do with metropolitan development resource management , and agricultural and community improvement". This definition, however, does not contribute much to making the concept and meaning of regional planning clear. "Regional Planning is basically spatial development planning" (Misra et. al. 1974). From this they go on to define "planning for socio-economic development at several territorial levels instead of a single national level ...... as multi-level planning" (Misra 1974).

Multi-level Planning, clearly, has a wide connotation, conveying different things to different people, and admits of different interpretations. One possible interpretation of multi-level planning could be that multi-level planning refers to the process of planning for various territoral tiers treated as regions for planning like the nation, the States or Provinces, Districts or Sub-District Levels (like Community Development Blocks in India or Up-Zilla Parishads in Bangladesh). An alternative interpretation could be that multi-level planning refers to the process of planning as applied to classification of the country according to the state of population density that is, as rural, semi-urban, urban and metropolitan. In either of these interpretations, a bias towards institutional setting and towards a decentralised approach is clearly common, which explains, at least in part, why multi-level planning and decentralised planning are taken as synonymous terms. In our usage throughout these studies, multi-level planning and decentralised planning would be taken as synonymous concept and will be used inter-changeably unless otherwise specified or is repugnant to the context.

It is also possible to attribute a third interpretation to multi-level planning, viz., that seperate development strategies have been selected and policies adopted for each regional or territorial hierarchy of the country, as principal instruments to attain regional developmental goals. We elect to accept the position that multi-level planning has been adopted as a strategic choice for development in different territoral settings, warranting resource mobilisation of every sector at the regional level, in support of objectives and for attainment of the targets, derived from a wide spectrum of development goals, set up by the different functionaries. In underdeveloped countries like India, where the locale of the vast majority of the people are in the rural areas, rural problems and rural development assume paramount importance. Underdeveloped countries, with regions which suffer rural problems but which are endowed with rural development potential, should attempt at rural development planning and at arranging the necessary co-ordination of inter-sectoral developmental activity between the sectors. It is obvious thus that such a conceptualisation enjoins that several tiers of planning, policy making and strategy formulation, including that of micro-regions like districts, sub-distric or even blocks in India have to be concurrently considered. (The concept of regionalisation of the economy is discussed in detail in Mukherjee Amitava: *Foundations and Theories of Decentralised Planning*, New Delhi: Heritage, forthcoming). The need for both inter-level and multi-sectoral orientation to multi-level plan ning can hardly be overemphasized.

In underdeveloped countries like India, the choice of a balanced intra-regional development, (such as between sectors, groups, areas and communities) and inter-regional development (such as those between the macro-regions, meso-regions and micro-regions) should be attempted with a bias towards rural areas where the incidence of poverty and deprivation is most pronounced and co-exists with substantive development potential. As a counter-balance to the urban biased-industry-dependent strategies adopted in the initial years of the fifties in the underdeveloped countries, including in India during and from the Second Five Year Plan onwards, which has created imbalances in terms of income and wealth, (we are not joining issue to the continuing debate started by Hirschman on Balanced vs Unbalanced Growth) a rural bias now for improving the quality of life of people living in the rural areas through agriculture and allied activities, has helped comprehensively in shifting the focus of attention to the hitherto neglected and weaker sections in society. A summary of the debate regarding choice of a balanced and an unbalanced growth strategy is found in Bejamin Higgins (1966).

A competent summary of the debate regarding a choice in favour of rural development strategy vis-a-vis industrial-urban development strategy in multi-level planning framework, is in Harriss (1982), particularly the papers by Johnston and Kilby, Michael Lipton, and Byres. The arguments set forth by Friedman and Doughlass (1978), Friedman and Weaver (1979), H.W. Richardson (1980), Hilhorst (1981) and Stohr and Taylor (1981) are relevant to follow the development of the debate. It may be mentioned that Harriss (1982) leads the debate from the general "a-spatial perspective", while the "spatial perspective", has been brought forth in sharp focus by Stohr and Taylor (1981), taking a more fundamental position of emphasising the need to re-examine the foundations of rural poverty and of growth imbalances, bearing in mind, at once, the varied potentials for survival and growth embedded in the regions, that we call "national terriory" of a poor country. The brilliant work by Sen (1981) where he brings forth ideas of deprivation and entitlement helps in having a close glimpse of the foundations of poverty. The excellent articles by Hansen (1981) and by Stohr and Taylor (1981) are of particular interest because of the justification that they attempt to provide for the extension of "planning from below" to spatial planning, and because they provide the picture of contrast to the brilliant analysis of Friedman and Douglass (1978) of the industrialisation paradigm "from above" and of its failure on the basis of Asian experience. These arguments are further extended in Friedman and Weaver (1979) and "agropolitan district approach", as an attractive alternative is very well argued. Hilhorst (1981) assesses the entire gamut of the debate and presents the complicating perspective that the normative dimension regarding devolution of powers and authorities to regional or local authorities seemingly lack political feasibility. Mukherjee (1989) in response to Chandra (1989) maintains that political will makes or mars the success of local level (district) planning. Sundaram (1989) makes devolution of powers to lower tiers of planning one of the principles of Multi-Level Planning.

Spatial Imbalances

It needs to be emphasized at this stage that whether one talks about national, sub-national or local planning, the spatial specifications emerge very sharply. The frequent reference in current literature to the need for a redressing of inter-regional and intra-regional disparities, is a mere reflection on some sort of spatial variation which will necessitate specific and detailed attention before an appropriate programme of action can be realistically chalked out.

The pivotal importance of space in regional planning, and the way how space is employed, can be best understood by having a closer examination of physical planning and by examining how space is viewed as the resource base that constitutes the immediate environment of the community for whom planning is sought to be prosecuted and how the choice of a site for alternative uses in the realm of planning for its optimum utilization is made. Naturally, the identification and development of homogenous spatial units is a pre-requisite to physical planning and the development of spatial units where each unit shares characteris tics, that make the unit particularly appropriate for certain purposes (like residential, commercial, industrial, business, agricultural and recreational) for physical planning is critically important.

The spatial logic entails three distinct dimensions(F.A.O., Institute of Social Studies Advisory Service: The Theory and Practice of Regional Rural Development and Planning, The Hague: ISSAS, 1986 mentions two specifically but talks about three.) One, a stretch of land on account of a combination of particular attributes has the quality of being suitable for specific purposes. Two, the location of the site in the universe of other sites is very important; Three, the relationship of the predominant activity of the area to other activities and the relative position of the place vis-a-vis other places becomes in creasingly important. The relevance of these dimensions to developmental strategies can hardly be over emphasized, because these dimensions unleash forces which amongst themselves determine, at least in part, the pace and location of development, which exhibit patterns that are not always spatially balanced. The seminal work on these issues is contained in Losch (1938, 1954); Perroux (1950, 1955); North (1955, 1956); Myrdal (1957); Hirschman (1958); Boudeville (1961, 1974), Davin (1964); Clark (1968) and Friedman (1969). It may be mentioned that Myrdal and Hirschman are in favour of unbalanced growth, just as Davin and Clark advocate favouring the choice of certain regions which can be developed first as, what we call "lead region". Myrdal, Hirschman, Davin and Clark are adherents to the idea that acceleration of the tempo of socio-economic development may be achieved in some areas or "region", even if required at the expense of other, in the adventure of spatial economic development and in a process of politico-social inter-regional and intra-regional differentiation.

It has to be recognised that the cohesiveness achieved in viewing the implicit social and spatial interface of development process, after a better understanding of the process of domination and ensuing centre-periphery relationship, has been brought into sharp focus by the seminal works of Friedman. It may be emphasized also that the theories underlying the distribution of people and activities have been impinged upon by the explanations regarding the optimal location of the firm resulting from transport cost minimization. Weber (1928), Hoover (1948), Isard (1950), Alonso (1964) and Richardson (1969) have been pioneers in this field. Mathur and Hashim (1969), Kundu and Raza (1982) and Kundu, Misra, and Meher (1986) are important contributions in the Indian context appertaining to location. Rushton, Sara and Ghosh (1981) have given a quantitative texture to the arguments for equilibrium location of public services in the context of regional development. A large number of firms and individuals trying to achieve optimality in location (determined by aggregate transport cost emanating from the need for socio-economic inter- action) generates a spatial structure, which imparts spatial imbalance the character of differential distribution of locational opportunities for firms as perceived by individual producers and not the character of a macro-induced process of economic transformation.

Orientation and Characteristics

If development of the rural areas is to overcome short term improvisations and sectoral narrowness, it is essential that the planning machinery at the various tiers be manned by people having professional expertise in inter-level and inter-sectoral synthesis. Well trained professional planners are required at every planning region, namely, at macro planning level (national level), at macro-meso-planning level (an area covering more than one State but below the national level), at meso-planning level (State or Provincial Level) at micro-planning level (District level) and at super-micro level (Block level). The paucity of trained manpower to man the planning machinery has been recognised more than once in several under-developed countries, notably in India (Government of India 1989). Boulding and Porter (1979), Hilhorst (1971) and Ackoff (1975), significantly enough, tend to agree that the sum of the parts is less than the whole, without facing the logical consequences of the operational requirement for "Wholeness Specialists".

One possible solution to solve the paucity of professional planners at different tiers of planning could be to transfer professionally equipped planning personnel from national or other levels of planning, to lower tiers of planning in a decentralised set up, but this unfortunately will not be enough because the peculiar conditions of planning at each level in the multi-level super-structure and peculiar problems of each territorial tier, require special understanding and capability to handle the specific planning task, which would not be available in a multi- disciplinary team whose members share a specific outlook as the result of training and experience at a given level in the planning hierarchy. Thus where development of the under-developed countries will have to be in terms of a greater bias for rural development, planning has to be decentralised. van Ray (1981), and Gant (1979) note that the division and the dispersion of the workload of the regional institutions will circumvent the problem of congregation and bring in the services and facilities that improve the quality of life with different characteristics. Training for decentralised planning ought, therefore, be a part of an overall scheme for initiating a new decentralised planning structure or for revamping an existing one (Tongyingsire 1980). Small wonder then that Mathur (1982) raises the "million dollar" question: "What Should Regional Planners Know?", and fortunately enough, it has been realised in the context of at least decentralised planning and regional development that good research must precede good training Kuklinski (1980).

Select Bibliography

Rationale for Decentralised Planning, Regional Planning and Rural Development.

Ackoff, R.L.:
Re-designing the Future - A Systems Approach to Societal Problems,
(New York: John Wiley) 1974.

Alonso, W.:
"Location Theory"
in Friedman, J. and Alonso, W. (eds.):Regional Development

and Planning: a Reader (Cambridge, Mass: MIT Press) 1964.

Baisya, K.N. and Mali, D.D.:
"Needs for Micro Level Planning" being chapter 4 of Baisya, K.N. and Mali, D.D.: Decentralised Planning Theory and Practice,
(New Delhi: Metropolitan Book Co. Pvt. Ltd.) 1989.

Blackley, E.J.:
Planning Local Economic Development: Theory and Practice,
(Newbury Park: Sage Publications) 1989.

Boudeville, J.R.:
"A Survey of Recent Techniques for Regional Economic Analysis",
in Isard, W. and Cumberland J.H. (eds.):
Regional Economic Planning: Techniques of Analysis
(Paris: OECD) 1961.

Boulding, K.E. & Porter, H.R. (eds.):
General System: Yearbook of the Society for General Systems Research,
Vol. 23, 1978, (Louisville: Society for General Systems Research) 1979.

Brara, J.S.:
The Political Economy of Rural Development: Strategies for Povert, Alleviation
(New Delhi: Allied Publishers Pvt. Ltd.) 1983.

Burehell, Robert, W. and Sternlieb, George (eds.):
Planning Theory in the 1980s
(Newark: Centre for Urban Policy Research, Rutgers University) 1978.

Buchanan, James and Moses, J.E.:
"A Regional Counter Measure to National Wage Standardisation",
American Economic Review, Vol. 50, 1960.

Byres, T.J.:
"Agrarian Transition and the Agrarian Question"
in Harris, J. (ed.):
Rural Development: Theories of Peasant Economy and Agrarian Change,
(London: Hutchinson) 1982.

Carter, Robert:
"The Spatial Basis for Economic Development and Adjustment Policies", in Regions in Transition,
(Canberra: Department of Local Government and Administrative Services) 1984.

Chambers, R.:
Rural Development: Putting the Last First
(London: Longman) 1983.

Chandra, Ramesh:
"Decentralised Planning-Problems and Prospects"
Economic Times, 13th November, 1989.

Clark, Colin:
Population and Land Use
(London: McMillan) 1968.

Dantawala, M.L.:
"Two-Way Planning: Logic and Limitations: A Critical Review of the Asian Experience",
Paper prepared for Food and Agriculture Organisation of the United Nations, Regional Office for Asia and the Pacific, Bangkok, 1981.

Davin, L.:
Economic Regionale et croissance
(Paris: Genin) 1964.

Dunham, D.M. & Hilhorst, J. (eds.):
Issues in Regional Planning
(The Hague: Institute of Social Studies, and Mouton) 1971.

Friedman, J.:
"Regional Planning as a Field of Studies"
in Friedmann, J. & Alonso, W. (eds.):

Regional Development and Planning: a Reader
(Cambridge, Mass.: MIT Press) 1964a.

Friedman, J. & Alonso, W. (eds.):
Regional Development and Planning: A Reader,
(Cambridge, Mass.: MIT Press) 1964b.

Friedman, J. & Douglass, M.:
"Agropolitan Development: Towards a new Strategy for Regional Planning in Asia"
in Lo, F.S. & Salih, K. (eds.):
Growth Pole Strategy and Regional Development Policy: Asian Experiences and Alternative Approaches
(Oxford: Pergamon Press) 1978.

Friedmann, J. & Weaver, C.:
Territory and Function: The Evolution of Regional Planning
(London: Arnold) 1979.

Gant, G.:
"Regional and Local Organization for Development"
in Gant, G.F.:
Development Administration
(Madison: University of Wisconsin Press) 1979.

Government of India:
Report of the Study Group on Training for District Planning
(New Delhi: Planning Commission) June 1989.

Hansen, N.:
'Development from Above: the Centre-down Development Paradigm'
in Stohr, W. & Taylor, R.F. (eds.):
Development From Above or Below? The Dialectics of Regional Planning in Developing Countries
(New York: John Wiley) 1981.

Harriss, J. (ed.):
Rural Development: Theories of Peasant Economy and Agrarian Change
(London: Hutchinson University Library) 1982.

Hilhorst, J.G.M.:
Regional Planning, A Systems Approach
(Rotterdam: Rotterdam University Press) 1971.

Hilhorst, J.G.M.:
"Territory vs Function: a New Paradigm?"
in ISS Occasional Papers, No. 89 (The Hague: Institute of Social Studies) August, 1981.

Higgins, Benjamin:
Economic Development, Principles, Problems and Policies
(Allahabad: Central Book Depot) 1966.

Hirschman, A.:
The Strategy of Economic Development
(New Haven: Yale University Press) 1958.

Holland, S.:
Capital versus the Region
(London: McMillan) 1976.

Hoover, E.:
The Location of Economic Activity
(New York: McGraw-Hill) 1948.

Isard, W.:
Location and Space-Economy
(New York: John Wiley) 1956.

Jayal, B.N.:
Area Development Planning Concept and Technique
Paper read at the workshop on Area Development, Varanasi, 1976.

Jain, L.C.; Krishnamurti, B.V. and Tripathi, P.M.:
Grass Without Roots: Rural Development Under Government Auspices
(New Delhi: Sage Publications) 1985.

Johnston, B.J. & Kilby A.:
"Unimodal' and 'Bimodal' Strategies of Agrarian Change"
in Harriss, J. (ed.):
Rural Development: Theories of Peasant Economy and Agrarian Change
(London: Hutchinson) 1982.

Kuklinski, A.R.:
"Training for Regional Development: Agenda For Future Research"
in Mathur, O.P. (ed.):
Training for Regional Development Planning: Perspectives for the Third Development Decade, Vol. 9,
(Singapore : Marazen, Asia) 1981.

Kuklinski, A.R.:
The Role of Research in Training for Regional Development
(Nagoya, Japan: URCRD) 1980.

Kundu, A. and Raza, M.:
Indian Economy - The Regional Dimension
(New Delhi: Jawaharlal Nehru University) 1982.

Kundu, A.; Misra, G.K. and Maher, R.:
Location of Public Enterprises and Regional Development
(New Delhi: Concept Publishing House) 1986.

Lipton, M.:
"Why Poor People Stay Poor"
in Harriss, J. (ed.):
Rural Development Theories of Peasant Economy and Agrarian Change
(London: Hutchinson) 1982.

Lo, F.C. & Salih, K.: (eds.):
Growth Pole Strategy and Regional Development Policy: Asian Experiences and Alternative Approaches
(Oxford: Pergamon Press) 1978.

Lo, F.C. & Salih, K.:
"Growth Poles, Agropolitan Development and Polrarization Reversal: the Debate and Search for Alternative"
in Stohr W. & Taylor D.R.F. (eds.):
Development from Above or Below? the Dialectics of Regional Planning in developing Countries
(New-York: J. Wiley) 1981.

Losch, August:
"The Nature of Economic Regions",
Southern Economic Journal, Vol. 5, 1938.

Losch, August:
Die raumliche ordung der wirtschaft swaite neu durctrgearbeitate Auflage, Juna 1944,
Translated by Stopler, W.F. as The Economics of Location (New Haven: Yale University Press) 1954. A rare contribution to economics.

Luning, Henk A.:
The Need for Regionalized Agricultural Development
(Laguna: SEARCH) 1981.

Mathur, H.M.:
Training of Development Administrators
(Kuala Lumpur: United Nations Asian and Pacific Development Centre) 1983.

Mathur, O.P. (ed.):
Training for Regional Development Planning: Perspectives for the Third Development Decade, Vol.9.,
(Singapore: Maruzen Asia, UNCRD) 1981.

Mathur, O.P.:
"What Should Regional Planners Know? Reflections of a Trainer",
Paper prepared for conference to be held from 24th to 28 Septem ber 1982 at the School of Urban and Regional Planning, University of South California, Los Angeles, on "Which

Planning Education for Which Planning Practice".

Mathur, P.N. and Hashim, H.R.:
"A Model of Optimum Location and Flows",
in Mathur, P.N. and Venkatramaiah, P. (eds.):
Economic Analysis in Input-Output Framework
(New Delhi: Input-Output Research Association) 1969.

Misra, R.P.:
"Regional Development Planning: Search for Bearings"
in Misra, R.P. (ed.):
Regional Development: Essays in Honour of Masahiko Honjo (Singapore: Maruzen Asia) 1982.

Misra, R.P.; Sundaram, K.V. and Prakasa Rao, V.L.S.:
Regional Development Planning in India: A New Strategy
(Delhi: Vikas Publishing House Pvt. Ltd.) 1974.

Misra, R.P. and Sundaram, K.V.:
Multi-Level Planning for Integrated Rural Development in India
(New Delhi: Heritage Publishers) 1980.

Mukherjee, Amitava:
"District Planning - A Rejoinder",
Economic Times, New Delhi, 13th November, 1989

Mukherjee, Amitava:
"District Planning- Economic Issues",
Economic Times, New Delhi, 14th November 1989.

Myrdal, G.:
Economic Theory and Underdeveloped Regions
(London: Duckworth) 1957.

Needleman, L.:
"What Do We Do About Regional Problem?
Lloyds Bank Review, January 1965.

North, D.C.:
"Location Theory and Regional Economic Growth",
Journal of Political Economy, Vol. LXIII, 1955.

North, D.C.:
"The Spatial and Inter-regional Framework of the United States Economy: A Historical Perspective",
Papers and Proceedings of the Regional Science Association Vol. 2, 1956.

Perroux, F.:
"La Notion de pole de Croissance"
Economie Applique, Vol. 1 No. 2, 1955.

Pal, M.N.:
"Quantitative Delimitation of Regions",
Bombay Geographical Magazine, 1961.

Popovic, B. :
Some Techniques for Regionalised Long Term Planning of the Size and Structure of Employment, Work Employment Programme Workshop on Quantitative Techniques for Employment Planning and their Implicatioins for Labour Market Analysis and Data Base,
ILO Working Paper No. 10, (Geneva: International Labour Organization) 1986.

Raay, H.G.T. Van:
Regional Planning for Integrated Rural Development
(The Hague: ISSAS) 1981.

Richardson, H.W.:
"The Relevance and Applicability of Regional Economics to Developing Countries",
Regional Development Dialogue, Vol. 1, No. 1, Spring 1980.

Rosenberg, Sara A. (ed.):
The Structural Crisis of the 1970s and Beyond: The Need for a New Planning Theory
(Blacksbury, Virginia: Virginia Polytechnic Institute and State University) 1978.

Ruston, G.; Sara, L.M. and Ghosh, A. :
"Equilibrium Locations for Public Services: Individual Preferences and Social Choices",
Geographic Analysis, Vol.13, No. 3, 1981.

Somasekhara, N.:
State's Planning in India, Vols. I & Vol. II
(Bombay: Himalaya Publishing House) 1989.

Sen, A.K.:
Poverty and Famines
(Oxford: The Clarendon Press) 1981.

Sen, Lalit K. (ed.):
Readings in Micro-Level Planning and Rural Growth Centres,
(Hyderabad: NICD) 1972.

Stohr, W. & Taylor, D.R.F. (eds.):
Development from Above or Below? the Dialectics of Regional Planning in Developing Countries
(New York: John Wiley) 1981.

Sundaram, K.V.:
"Multilevel Planning: Concepts, Principles and Some Aspects of its Applications to Sectoral Planning",
in Sundaram, K.V.; Ramesh, A. and Tiwari, P.S. (eds.):
Regional Planning and Development, Essays on Space Society and Development in Honour of Professor R.P. Misra,
Vol.I. (New Delhi: Heritage Publishers) 1989.

Tongyingsire, P:
Training for Regional Development
(Nagoya: United Nations Centre for Regional Development) 1980.

UNDP:
Issues of Tranining and Research in Regional Development, Report on the Inter-regional Workshop for Directors of Centre engaged in Research and Training in Regional Development,
(Nagoya: UNCRD).

Weaver, C.:
"Development Theory and the Regional Question: A Critique to Spatial Planning and its Detractors"
in: Stohr W. & Taylor, D.R.F. (eds.):
Development from Above or Below? the Dialectics of Regional Planning in Developing Countries,
(New York: John Wiley) 1981.

Weaver, C.:
Regional Development and the Local Community: Planning, Politics and Social Context
(London: Wiley) 1984.

Weber, A.:
Theory of the Location of Industries,
Translated from the original in German, by C.J. Friedman in 1909, (Chicago: University of Chicago Press) 1928.

Zonal Planning Team (Zone V), Agro-climatic Regional Planning Unit, Planning Commission:
Upper-Gangetic Plains Regions: Zonal Profile Strategy Action Points: An Approach Paper
(Kanpur: C.S. Azad University of Agriculture and Technology) June 1989.

CHAPTER IV

SPACE AND SPATIAL ORGANISATION, REGIONS AND REGIONALISATION RELEVANT TO DECENTRALISED PLANNING

The concept of Space has been the province of the geographers for a long time and it was only recently that the economists and planners have registered their intrusion into the arena. To begin with, economists held the notion to be a spaceless point as abundantly exemplified by the fact that Richardson (1969) was concerned with spaceless world and Isard (1950) related analysis and theory to a wonderland of no dimensions, and there were authors like Harvey (in Choley & Geggett) 1967, who converted the function of distance into such readily conceivable forms as ten miles being equivalent to ten times one mile.

Von Thunen (1926) laid the early foundations for spatial analysis, followed for other German Scholars like Weber (1979), Losch (1954) and Walter Christaller (1966). More modern contribu tions are by Beckmann (1968), Nijkamp (1981, 1983a, 1983b), Thisse and Zoller (1982), and Nijkamp and Van Pelt (1985). The credit must go to the pioneering work of Berry (1967), and Berry and Pred (1965) in linking the classical models of spatial organisation with the structure of central places to be found in real life situations.

Distinction between the two types of space relation, namely, between the 'banal space or the "geonomical space", and the abstract or relational space, was first made by the frenchman Perroux (1950) in skeleton form, which was clothed in flesh and blood by Boudeville (1977). Perroux subsequently modified his ideas (Perroux 1983) and gave a new dimension to what he called pole of development (Perroux 1988). The spatial relationships, whether political, economic or cultural in nature, or whether established and preserved by individuals, combination of individuals, firms, or institutions, have a crucial role in providing a true and fair account of the development process in an economy. Massey et. al. (1984) provides an interesting conceptualisation of space and its inter-relationships with social, political, cultural and economic currents. Friedman's (1966) seminal work defines the relationship between space and economic growth as "the economy in its spatial dimension", described as either point locations and interacting flows (of goods, capital, labour and information) or as territoral systems of social and economic relations, so that the structural composition of "the space economy is arranged according to social purposes". Johnson (1970) examines the concept of spatial organisation in relation to third world locations in general and Mabogunje (1980), concerns himself with spatial dimensions of development in the context of underdeveloped economies of Africa.

Fortunately, a systematic review of the analytical use made of theories on space and of the numerous issues related to the analysis of spatial organizations exists. A synthesis of selected issues in space economics has been provided in O'Sullivan (1981), and Rhoda (1982) contains reference for regional as well as urban spatial analysis. Evolution of spatial economic theorizing in a historical perspective and an exhaustive bibliography is contained in Ponsard (1983). Mabogunje (1981) made an important distinction between "bureaucratic space" and "people's space", and argues that if one were concerned with people's participation, one ought then to be concerned with people's space thereby implying that smaller planning area vis-a-vis larger ones are preferable.

Regions

The nature of region has been the subject of considerable debate. The region is considered "as a means to an end.... model to help the study of the world..... a device to regregate areal feature". This is the subjective view as opposed to the objective view which considers the region as "an end in itself, a real entity" which can be identified and mapped (Glasson 1974). However, the academic controversy has seemingly been set at rest and the "subjective view" now has a much great general acceptance than its objective counter-part. Entrikin (1981) has ably documented the progress and "proceedings" of this debate.

Perroux (1950) suggests a typology of regions, with a distinction between homogeneous vis-a-vis polarized regions, which was germane to the integration of geographic and non-geographic factors, which amongst themselves, inter se, to a large extent, chart out the character and content of developmental processes in varied territorial settings. Boudville (1966), Kuklinski (1981) and Bocage (1985) and others have contributed significantly to an understanding of the issues at hand. Holland (1976) standing on the top of the cliff of regional development disparities provides a systematic account of the evolution of the concept of regions and their classification.

Hilhorst (1981) by injecting the elements of the perception of individuals of the opportunities and prospects that local resources hold for them, into the definition of regions, has rekindled the dormant debate on the conceptual target. The intrusion of individual perceptions into the realm of defining regions requires the introduction of a mix of social and psycho-cultural considerations in defining a region, which appends a dimension that seems to have quite extensive consequence for developmental process and planning.

Regionalisation for Planning

Regionalisation of any area or country is the acrobatic of partitioning of the country into regions for the purposes of planning, which will generate regions that would be different from regions delimited for an alternative purpose like understanding and having insight into regional problems (rather than intervention) which are for geographic analysis. Delineating regions for planning, programming, implementing, administrating and monitoring developmental plans include consideration of a range of factors, including uniformity and functionality. Consideration of the historical, political, social, cultural and economic forces and forces that have had in the past influenced developmental performance and will continue to have bearing upon developmental performance, both intra-regionally and inter-regionally, in the future, are singularly important. The process of delineating a region should be tempered by consideration of the distribution of environmental and man-made resources that constitutes the repository of resources from which to draw for developmental efforts of the regions. The structure of economic activities, particularly so, the export-oriented activities, the spatial structure with special reference to movements of man and materials, that are the principal determinants of the extent and nature of focal patterns, and the structure of intra-regional and inter- regional decision-making control and its inter-connections with the space economy, should be clearly understood. Rodwin (1963), Smith (1965) and Hilhost (1971) would be useful tools at delineating such regions.

The homogenous region and the polarised region are of particular interest in decentralised planning, especially the latter. Polarised region, rechristened several times over as focal, functional, nodal or interdependent region, is an area displaying an interdependence of parts, within a framework of parameters (Glasson 1974). The direction, volume and intensity of various flows, flow analysis and mapping of spatial interaction, on the basis of gravity analysis, provide abundant tools for the identification of the inter-dependence of parts of a polarized nature.

Because polarised delimitation of region admits of the possibility of making allowance for the vertical dimension of space in terms of the internal structure of, and inter-relationships between, units with horizontal elements and because it defines the spheres of action by defining patterns of spatial organization, polarised regionalisation is of greater operational value in a decentralised planning framework than in other contexts. For development of rural areas the importance of polarised regional delineation is increased all the more.

Techniques for Regional Analysis

Territorial partitioning of a country is crucial in a decentralised set up, for it makes room for clearly demarcating the scenes of actions or various developmental programmes and for demarcation of functions for each territorially partitioned portion of the country. This territorial partitioning is achieved through delineation of regions, on the premise that the regions to be identified will constitute a configuration of peculiar characteristics unique to each territory. These configurations are brought forth by regional analysis, in addition to facilitating the understanding of the features, potentialities and constraints having bearing on a particular area for which planning is directed. Regional analysis can be carried out from various perspectives (Rondinelli 1985) depending upon the priority that the relevant variables, like the socio-political, geographical or economic aspects of regional development and planning have in the study. For instance Rose, Nakamaya and Stevens (1982) thought of "energy region" development as distinct from other regional delineation.

A good exposure to basic mathematics relevant in planning process is provided by Allan (1966), and Wilson and Kirby (1980), which clarifies some of the important issues that concern planners at various levels of planning. Robinson (1971) and Hebden (1983) are useful books in this regard as well. The matrix methods useful for spatial analysis is reviewed in Rogers (1971) and a useful quick glance is provided by the somewhat old but classic books of Isard (1960) and Richardson (1969) and Álagh and Mazumdar (1982) are excellent applications of matrix method in the Indian context in a regional planning framework.

Willemain's (1980) somewhat difficult book treats statistical techniques that are important for spatial analysis and planning. Cole and King (1968), King (1969), Haggett (1972), Yeates (1974) and Hammond and McCullogh (1978) are books on quantitative geography, providing statistical base for the analysis of geographical variables, ranging from index building and description of statistical descriptors to principal components or factor analysis. Hordijk and Paelinck (1973) even talked of spatial econometrics. Cliff and Ord (1981) is a book worth reading and Nijkamp and Rietveld (1982) provides some econometric tools for regional discrepancy analysis.

The methods available to identify homogenous space in quantitative terms and qualitative terms are useful, but which methods to choose depends upon the purpose of the analysis and the degree of complexity (for achieving sophistication) that is required, desired or is permitted by the data base. And naturally enough, the greater the number of variables deployed to achieve sophistication, the greater the complexity introduced in the regionalisation exercise. Haggett (1968), King (1969), and Haggett (1972) discusses the "multi- variate methods", on the basis of "statistical" or "functional distances". Cole and King (1968), Yeates (1974) and Hammond and McCullogh (1978) lay emphasis on "similarity" or "dissimilarity indices", for regionalisation. Delimitation analysis in delineation of regions is provided for in Bunge (1968) and Welman (1980). Nipper and Streit (1982) is an excellent exposition of stochostic methods and autoprojective models of spatial processes.

The nodal region has been identified as a territory whose boundaries are defined by the spatial influence, that a function or combination of "functions", located at a point can exert over other variables or functions spread all over the territory. Small wonder Perroux (1964, called the nodal regions "field of forces". To define nodal region, as a consequence, flow and spatial interaction have to be at the heart of such analyses.

The basis for hinterland demarcation for different types of urban functions is the flow analysis. Losch (1954) and Chistaller (1966), resorted to deductive and theoretical structure of central places. Berry and Garrison (1958); Berry (1964); Berry (1966); Berry and Horton (1970) have proposed a hierarchy of central places in terms of techniques based on transport flows, communication networks, retail trade and other urban functions. Haggett (1968), Haggett and Chorley (1969), and Haggett, Cliff and Frey (1977) provide a systhetical analysis.

Gravitational analysis has also been put to use for identifying nodes and nodal regions, based on the assumption that the interaction between points in space is a function of the mass of economic and social activity located at each point and the distances (transport costs) separating the points or location. Reilly (1931), by generating the famous law of retail gravitation, and its generalisation by Stewart (1974) and Zipf (1949) have enabled the gravitational concept to make significant contributions to analysis in regional urban and transport studies. Isard (1960) and Olson (1965) demonstrates the applicability of the law of retail gravitations. Richardson (1988) has a brief but incisive gravity model discussion. Wilson (1970) and Oppenheimer (1980) have excellent treatments of entropy maximisation. Stewart and Warntz (1958) introduced the concept of gravitational potential, which is highly useful in delineation of regions when the data base is small, and which was subsequently used by Isard (1960), Hilhorst (1971) and others. Incidentally Hoover (1936) was one of the pioneers in the introduction of localization co-efficients, localization quotients, and specialisation indices, to analyse a national system of regions with quantitative techniques that relate regional characteristics to a common denominator.

Forecasting and econometrics have entered regional development planning in a big way. For a long time it was felt that forcasting and modelling will not work because of limited data base at lower territorial levels, but this was later discovered to be not quite true. Isserman, Plane, Rogerson and Beaumont (1985) have resorted to migration forecasting on a limited data base. The pioneering work of Klien and Glickman (1977) and Ledent and Gordon (1980) have demonstrated the possibility of modelling at the regional level.

The technique of comparing the changes in activities occurring in a region (within two points of time) with the national or sub-national average, has been embodied in what is known as the "Shift and Share Analysis". A formidable body of literature has grown around it but the more important ones are Thompson (1957), Dunn (1960), Isard (1960), Perfoff et. al. (1960), Matilla (1964), Berry and Horton (1970), Buck (1970), Hoover (1971), Richardson (1978, 1988), Rondinelli (1980), Bendavid-val (1983), Rondinelli (1985), and Cohen (1986).

For application of the shift and share analysis one could read with profit Blair and Marby (1980), De Boer, Larry and Seeborg (1984) and Green and Allaway (1985). A critique of the shift share models is provided by Houston (1967), Hellman (1976), James and Hughes (1973), and Wilson, (1980). There have been attempts at extending the shift-share analysis of which Arcelus (1984) and Srinath and Ray (1986) are important.

The inter-regional economic flows can be analysed in terms of a different perspective altogather. Isard (1960), Lee Moore and Livis Boisier (1981) and Bendavid-Val (1983) contain authoritative discussions of the methods and techniques of inter-regional economic flows. Blunden et. al. (1973); Armstrong and Taylor 1978, and Boisier (1981) discuss the regional development policy that provides these tools.

Inequalities and disparities between regions are critical elements in thinking and identification of target groups and target regions in a decentralised planning exercise. Needleman (1968) and Smith (1979) provide the analysis of the inter-regional inequalities and their causes. Hewings (1982) discusses inter-regional interdependencies and Clark (1982) talks about inter-regional migration and social justice.

Inter-Regional Analysis

The determination of the exogenous and endogenous forces that have a role in the determination of activity mix of a particular region and its capacity to develop, is possible to a large extent by the export base analysis. Exports and domestic consumption (the two key elements in the export base analysis) are determined by external demand and internal demand respectively, with the latter determined by the inter-industrial relationships between export based activities and those activities that are generated endogenously. Tiebout (1962) developed a technique for calculating the multiplier relating export and domestic activities. Richardson (1969), Berry and Horton (1970), Ledent (1978), Richardson and Gordon (1978), and Bendavid-Val (1983) also made significant contributions in this regard. Isard and Czamanski (1965) have analysed the impacts of government investments in a region by the application of the multiplier and related ideas. Alexander (1954) and Andrews (1956, 1958) are some of the earlier but authoritative activities of a region, to be refined by Massey (1973) and Dacey (1962). The implications of small economies have been analysed threadbare by Weiss and Gooding (1970).

The building up of regional accounts is one of the most difficult areas of regional analysis, because of paucity of data. However, some insights can still be had by building up regional accounts, even if in a simplified form for the measurement of regional income and product, in line with the practices of national social accounting. These are dealt with in detail in Bendavid-Val (1983) which is useful for planning at sub-national level especially for planning at micro or district level. Hirsch (1964), Czamanski (1968), Stone's monumental work (1962) and Hebden (1987) are more advanced treatments of the subject.

Regional-input-output matrices provides glimpses of the inter-linkages between different sectors of a sub-national level economy and it is a very useful planning device, though theoretical and operational limitations are not non-existent. United Nations (1978), Stone (1961), Richardson (1972), Pyatt and Thorbecke (1976) and of course Bendavid-Val (1983) are some of the more lucid discussions of the issues at hand. Miller and Blair (1985) is a fine discussion of the issues relating to input- output analysis, and Richardson (1985) discusses input-output in the context of economic base multipliers. Bossier (1981) contains application of the technique for model building.Alagh and Mazumdar (1983); Alagh, Bhalla and Kashyap (1980) and Subramanyam (1985) are application of input-output techniques in the regional context in India.

Though experts are of the view that nature has not endowed any monopoly to any place over resources, yet differences in natural resource endowment do vary between regions. Assessment of this natural resource endowment is of immense importance for determining the development potentials and constraints to development process of the regional economy (Hoyle 1979), which facilitates the comprehensive assessment of the relative utility of different locations for specific uses (McHarg 1971).

Human resource endowment and human resource development are two of the most important issues in planning at any level whatsoever, more so in a multi-level decentralised set up. Baldwin (1975) in a manual for planning at sub-national levels reviewed the fundamentals of demographic analysis. Isard (1960), and Bougue (1969) contain a more classical approach, while Isard (1960) has useful things to say on projections of the regional population.

While there are some experts who have analysed demographic issues in the African context extensively, there are several United Nations populations studies that are of immediate relevance for sub-national planning. Hauser and Duncan (1959), Clark (1967), Petersen (1969) and Woods (1982) are useful population studies but of a general nature. Woods (1982) has emphasized the inter-relationships between population and socio-economic change and model building. Todaro (1976), is an excellent discussion on importance of internal immigration of people in developing countries. Banerjee (1986) is considered a solid contribution to issues revolving around internal migration and development.

Regional settlement systems are of no mean consequence. Bourne and Simons (1978) provide an overview of the need for analysis of regional settlement systems. The spatial patterns in regional settlement system was first explicitly treated by Losch (1954) and Christaller (1966) as being the outcome of micro-economic equilibrium. Dacey (1962) and King (1969) are discussions on indices of proximity calculated in different areas. Morril (1970) and Smith (1976) have important ideas on regional settlement patterns viewed from socio-economic and geographical perspectives.

Berry (1961) linked rank-size distributions with growth, Vapnarski (1969) held the distribution of city sizes as being de pendent upon the openess of a regional economy and the level of internal integration of their economic activities, which makes private cities concomitant to high levels of external economic dependency. Berry and Horton (1970); Rabson (1973); and Bourne and Simons (1978) all deal with these and related issues. Berry (1967); Berry and Horton (1970) and Johnson (1970) are all important contributions in urban-rural relationships and the urban functions essential for supporting agricultural and non-farm activities, which are of material consequence for sub-national planning. One could also look at Blunden (1973); Cox, Reynolds and Rokkan (1974); UNESCO (1978), Ashe (1979), Rhoda (1982) and Sharma (1980).

Select Bibliography

Space and Spatial Organisation, Regions and Regionalisation

Alagh, Y.K.; Bhalla, G.S. and Kashyap, S.P.:
Structural Analysis of Gujarat, Punjab and Haryana Economies (New Delhi : Allied Publishers)1980.

Alagh, Y.K., and Mazumdar, K.C.:
"Input-Output Model used for 1978-1983 Draft Plan", in Dahiya, S.B.: **Development Planning Models, Vol.I,** (New Delhi: Inter-India Publications)1982.

Alexander, J.W.:
"The Basic Non-Basic Concept of Urban Economic Functions", Economic Geography, Vol.30, July 1954.

Allan, R.G.D.:
Mathematical Economics (London:MacMillan)1966.

Andrews, R.B,:
"Comments: Criticisms of the Economic Base Theory",
Journal of the American Institute of Planners, Vol.24, 1958

Andrews,R.B.:
"Mechanics of the Urban Economic Base",
Land Economics, Vols.29, 30, 31, May 1953 to February 1956.

Arcelus, Francisco Jr.:
"An Extension of Shift-Share Analysis",
Growth & Change, Vol. 15, No. 1, 1984.

Armstrong, H. and Taylor, J:
Regional Economic Policy and its Analysis
(Oxford: Philip Allan) 1978.

Ashe, J.:
Assessing Rural Needs: A Manual for Practitioners
(Cambridge, Mass.: ACCION/ATTEC) 1979.

Baisya, K.N. and Mali, D.D.:
Decentralised Planning
(New Delhi: Metropolitan Book Co. Pvt. Ltd.) 1989.

Baldwin, K.D.S.:
Demography for Agricultural Planners
(Rome: Food and Agriculture Organisation of the United Nations) 1975.

Banerjee, Biswajit:
Rural to Urban Migration and Urban Labour Market,
(Delhi: Himalay Publishing House) 1986.

Beckmann, M.:
Location Theory
(New York: Random House) 1968.

Bendavid-Val, A.:
Regional Economic Analysis for Practitioners: An Introduction to Common Descriptive Methods
(New York: Praeger) 1974, new edition.

Berry, B.:
"City Size Distribution and Economic Development",
Economic Development and Cultural Change, Vol. 9, 1964.

Berry, B.:
Essays in Commodity Flow and the Spatial Structure of the Indian Economy
(Chicago: University of Chicago, Dept. of Geography, Research Papers) 1966.

Berry, B.:
Geography of Market Centres and Retail Distribution
(New York: Prentice Hall) 1967.

Berry, B. & Garrison, W.L.:
"Recent Developments of Central Place Theory", in:
Papers and Proceedings of the Regional Science Association. Vol. 4, 1958.

Berry, B. & Pred, A.:
Central Place Studies: A Bibliography of Theory and Applications
(Philadelphia: Regional Science Research Institute) 1965.

Berry, B. & Horton, F.E.:
Geographic Perspectives of Urban Systems
(Englewood Cliffs: Prentice Hall) 1970.

Blair, D.W. and Marby, R.H.:
"Regional Crime Rate: An Application of the Shift-Share Technique",
Growth & Change, Vol. 11, No. 1, 1980.

Blunden, J. and Brook, C.:
Regional Analysis and Development
(London: Harper and Row) 1973.

Bocage, D.:
General Economics Thoery of Francos Perroux
(New York and London: University Press of America) 1985.

Boisier, S.:
Planning a System of Regions; Methods and Techniques of Inter - regional Planning
(Santiago de Chile: Economic Commission for Latin America) 1981.

Boudeville, J.R.:
Problems of Regional Economic Planning
(Edinburgh:Edinburgh University Press) 1966

Boudeville, J.:
"Functional Regional Analysis: An Elementary Exposition on some Selected Topics",
in Paelinck J.H.P. and Sailaz, A (eds.):
University of Toronto Lectures
(Paris: Association de Science Regional de Langue Francaise) 1977.

Bougue, D.S.:
Principles of Demography
(New York: John Wiley) 1969.

Buck, T.W.:
"Shift Share Analysis: A Guide To Regional Policy",
Regional Studies, Vol. 4, 1970.

Bourne, L.S. & Simmons, J.W. (eds.):
Systems of Cities; Readings on Structure, Growth and Policy (New York: Oxford University Press) 1978.

Bunge, W.:
"Delimitations of Uniform Regions", Theoretical Geography (Lund: C.W.K. Gleerup) 1966.

Chorley, R.J. & Kennedy, B.A.:
Physical Geography; a Systems Approach
(Englewood Cliffs: Prentice Hall) 1971.

Christaller, W.:
Central Places in Southern Germany, translated from original German by Baskin, C.W.,
(Englewood Cliffs: Prentice Hall) 1966.

Clark, C.:
Population Growth and Land Use
(London: McMillan) 1967.

Clark, G.L.:
Inter-regional Migration, National Policy and Social Justice
(Totowa, N.J.: Rowman & Allanhold) 1982.

Cliff, A.D. and Ord, J.K.:
Spatial Processes, Models and Applications
(London: Pion) 1981.

Cohen, Joel E.:
"An Uncertainty Principle in Demography and the Unisex Issue",
The American Statistician, Vol. 40, No. 1, 1986.

Cole, J.P.:
Situations in Human Geography: a Practical Approach
(Oxford: Blackwell) 1975.

Cole, J.P. & King, C.A.M.:
Quantitative Geography: Techniques and Theories in Geography
(London: John Wiley) 1968.

Connell, J. & Lipton, M.:
Assessing Village Labour Situations in Developing Countries
(Delhi: Oxford University Press) 1977.

Cox, K.R.; Reynolds, D.R. and Rokkan, S. (eds.):
Location Approaches to Power and Conflict
(New York: John Wiley) 1974.

Czamanski, S.:
Regional Income and Product Accounts for North-Eastern Nova Scotia
(Halifax: Dalhousie University) 1968.

Dacey, M.F.:
"Analysis of Central Place and Point Patterns by a Nearest Neighbour Method",
Human Geography, Vol. 24, 1962.

De Boer, Larry and Seeborg, Michael:
"The Female-Male Unemployment Differential: Effects of Changes in Industry Employment",
Monthly Labour Review, U.S. Department of Labour, 1984.

Diwan, R. and Lutz, M. (ed.):
Essays in Gandhian Economics
(New Delhi: Gandhi Peace Foundation) 1985.

Dunn, Edgar S.:
"A Statistical and Analytical Technique for Regional Analysis",
Papers and Proceedings of the Regional Science Association, Vol. 6, 1960.

Dziewonski, Kazimierz:
"Theoretical Problems in the Development of Economic Regions",
Papers and Proceedings of the Regional Science Association, Vol. 1, 1955.

Deman, Suresh :
"Region-Regionalisation and Regional Planning: Review of Techniques",
Anvesak, Vol. XIX, No. 2, December, 1984.

Entrikin J.N.:
"Philosophical Issues in the Scientific Study of Regions"
in Herbert, D.T. & Johnston, R.J. (eds.):
Geography and the Urban Environment: Progress in Research and Applications
(London: J. Wiley) 1981.

Friedmann, J.:
Regional Development Policy: a Case Study of Venezuela
(Cambridge, Mass.: M.I.T. Press) 1966.

Glasson, J.:
An Introduction to Regional Planning
(London: Hutchinson) 1974.

Gopal, M.H.:
"Region as Development Concept",
The Indian Economic Journal, Vol. XIX, No. 1, 1971.

Green, Robert T. and Allaway, Arthur W.:
"Identification of Export Opportunities: A Shift-Share Approach",
Journal of Marketing, Vol. 49, 1985.

Greenhut, M.:
Microeconomics and the Space Economy
(Chicago: Scott-Foresman) 1963.

Hagget, P.:
Locational Analysis in Human Geography
(London: Arnold) 1968.

Haggett, P.:
Geography, a Modern Synthesis
(London: Harper & Row) 1972.

Haggett, P. & Chorley, R.J.:
Network Analysis in Geography
(London: Arnold) 1969.

Hammond, R. and McCullogh, P.S.:
Quantitative Techniques in Geography :An Introduction
(Oxford: Oxford University Press)1978.

Hebden, Julia:
Applications of Econometrics
(Oxford: Phillip Allan) 1983.

Hellman, D.A.:
"Shift Share Models as Predictive Tools",
Growth and Change, Vol. 7, No. 3, 1976.

Hewings, G.J.D.:
"Regional and Inter-regional Inter-dependencies; Alternative Accounting Systems",
Environment and Planning, Vol. 14, 1982.

Hilhorst, J.G.M.:
Regional Planning: A Systems Approach

(Rotterdam: Rotterdam University Press) 1971.

Hilhorst, J.G.M.:
"On Unresolved Issues in Regional Development Thinking"
in: Kuklinski, A. (ed.):
Polarized Development and Regional Policies
(The Hague: Mouton & Co.) 1981.

Hirsch, W. (ed.):
Elements of Regional Accounts
(Baltimore: Johns Hopkins University Press) 1964.

Holland, S.:
The Regional Problem
(London: MacMillan) 1976.

Hoover, E.M.:
"The Measurement of Industrial localization",
Review of Economics and Statistics, Vol. 18, 1936.

Hoover, E.M.:
An Introduction to Regional Economics
(New York: A. Knopf) 1971.

Hordijk, L. and Paelinck, J. :
Spatial Econometrics: Some Contributions
(Rotterdam: Netherlands Economic Institute) 1974, mimeographed.

Houston, David B.:
"The Shift and Share Analysis of Regional Growth: A Critique",
The Southern Economic Journal, 1967, pp. 577-581.

Hoyle, B.S. (ed.):
Spatial Aspects of Development
(London: John Wiley) 1979.

Huggett, R.:
Systems Analysis in Geography
(Oxford: Oxford University Press) 1980.

Isard, W. et. al.:
Methods of Regional Analysis
(Cambridge, Mass.: The MIT Press) 1960.

Isard, W. & Cumberland, J.H.:
Regional Economic Planning: Techniques of analysis for Less Developed Areas,
Papers and proceedings of the First Study Conference on Problems of Economic Development organized by E.P.A. Bellagio (Paris:OECD) 1961.

Isard, W. & Czamanski, S.:
"Techniques for Estimating Multiplier Effects of Major Government Programmes",
in Papers of the Peace Research Society, Vol. 3, 1965.

Isserman, A.M.; Plane, D.A.; Rogerson, P.A. and Beaumont, P.M.N.:
"Forecasting Interstate Migration with Limited Data: A Demographic Economic Approach",
Journal of the American Statistical Association, Vol. 80, 1985.

James, Franklin Jr. and Hughes, James:
"A Test of Shift and Share Analysis as a Predictive Device",
Journal of Regional Science, Vol. 13, No. 2, 1973.

Johnson, E.A.J.:
The Organization of Space in Developing Countries
(Cambridge, Mass.: Harvard University Press) 1970.

Kpedackpo, G.M.K.:
Essentials of Demographic Analysis
(London: Heinneman)1982.

King, L.J. :
Statistical Analysis in Geography
(Englewood Cliffs: Prentice Hall) 1969.

Klien, L.R. and Glickman, N.J.:
"Econometric Model Building at the Regional Level",
Regional Science and Urban Economics, Vol. 7, 1977.

Kuklinski, A.:
Polarised Development and Regional Policies: Tribute to Jacques Boudeville
(The Hague, Paris and New York: Mouton) 1981.

Kundu, Amitabh:
"Nodal Regions-Some Conceptual Issues in Measurement and Regionalisation",
Indian Journal of Regional Science, Vol. XIX, No. 1, 1982.

Kundu, Amitabh:
Measurement of Urban Process: A Study in Regionalisation
(Bombay: Popular Prakashan) 1980.

Kundu, Amitabh and Raza, Moonis:
Indian Economy - The Regional Dimension
(New Delhi: Jawaharlal Nehru University) 1981.

Kundu, Amitabh and Sidhu, H.S.:
"Complete and Incomplete Schemes of Regionalisation",
Indian Journal of Geography, Special Issue, University of Jodhpur, 1980.

Ledent, J.:
"Regional Multiplier Analysis: A Deometric Approach",
Environment and Planning, Vol. 10, 1978.

Ledent, J. and Gordon, P.:
"A Deometric Model of Inter - regional Growth Rate differences",
Geographical Analysis, Vol. 12, 1980.

Lee, T.H.; Moore, J.R. & Lewis, D.P.:
Regional and Inter-regional Inter-sectoral Flow Analysis
(Knoxville: University of Tennessee Press) 1973.

Loch, A.:
The Economics of Location,
translated by W.H. Woglom and Stolper W.F., (New Haven: Yale University Press) 1954.

Mabougunje, A.L.:
The Development Process: a Spatial Perspective
(London: Hutchinson University Library) 1980.

Mandal, R.B.:
Introduction to Rural Settlements
(New Delhi: Concept Publishing Company) 1978.

Massam, B.:
Location and Space in Social Administration
(London: Arnold) 1979.

Massey, D.:
"The Basic-Service Categorization in Planning"
Regional Studies, Vol. 7, 1973.

Matilla, J.:
A Methodology of Comparative Analysis of Regional Growth: Some Technical Notes
(Washington D.C.: U.S. Dept. of Commerce) SWP No. 8. 1964.

McHarg, C.:
Design with Nature
(New York: Doubleday) 1971.

Meyer, I.R. and Huggett, R.J.:
Settlements
(London: Harper and Row) 1978.

Miller, R.E. and Blair, P.D.:
Input-Output Analysis: Foundations and Extensions
(Englewood, Cliffs: Prentice Hall) 1985.

Morril, R.L.:
The Spatial Organization of Society
(Belmont: Duxbury Press) 1970.

Needleman, L. (ed.):
Regional Analysis: Selected Readings
(Harmondsworth: Penguin Books) 1968.

Nijkamp, P.:
Urban Impact Analysis in a Spatial Context: Methodology and Case Study

(Amsterdam: Free University) Research Memo, 1981.

Nijkamp, P. :
"Qualitative Impact Assessments of Spatial Policies in Developing Countries",
Regional Development Dialogue, Vol. 4, No. 1, 1983.

Nijkamp, P.:
"Qualitative Spatial Impact Analysis",
in Chatterjee, M. et. al. (eds.): Spatial Environmental and Resource Policy in Developing Countries (Adlershot: Gower) 1983.

Nijkamp, P. and van Pelt, M.:
Spatial Impact Analysis for Developing Countries; A Framework and a Case Study,
mimeographed, 1985.

Nijkamp, P. and Rietveld, P.:
"Soft Econometrics as a Tool for Regional Discrepancy Analysis",
Papers and Proceedings of the Regional Science Association, 1982.

Nipper, J. and Streit, U.:
"A Comparative Study of Some Stochastic Methods and Autoprojective Models for Spatial Processes",
Environment and Planning, Vol. 14, 1982.

Oppenheimer, N. :
Applied Models in Urban and Regional Analysis
(Englewood Cliffs: Prentice Hall) 1980.

O'Sullivan, P. :
Geographical Economics
(Middlesex, England: Penguin Books) 1981.

Perloff, Harvey, S.; Dunn, Edgar S.; Lampard, Eric, E. and Muth, Richard F.:
Regions, Resources and Economic Growth
(Baltimore: Johns Hopkins University Press) 1960.

Perroux, F.:
"Economic Space: Theory and Applications"
in Friedmann, J. & Alonso, W. (eds.): Regional Development and Planning: A Reader (Cambridge, Mass.: MIT Press) 1964.

Perroux, F.:
A New Concept of Development
(Paris: Croom Helm for U.N.E.S.C.O.) 1983.

Perroux, F.:
"The Pole of Development's New Place in a General Theory of Economic Activity",
in Higgins, Benjamin and Savoie, D.J.:
Regional Economic Development,
(Boston: Unwin Hyman) 1988.

Petersen, W.:
Population
(London: McMillan) 1969.

Ponsard, C.:
History of Spatial Economic Theory
(Berlin: Springen-Verlag) 1983.

Pyatt, Graham and Thorbecke, Erik:
Planning Techniques for a Better Future,
(Geneva: I.L.O. and Oxford & IBH, New Delhi) 1976.

Reilly, W.J.:
The Law of Retail Gravitation
(New York: W.J. Reilly, Co.) 1931.

Rhoda, R.:
Urban and Regional Analysis for Developing Planning
(Boulder: Westview Press) 1982.

Richardson, H.W.:
Regional Economics, Location Theory, Urban Structure and Regional Change
(London: Weidenfeld and Nicolson) 1969.

Richardson, H.W.:
Input-Output and Regional Economics
(London: Weidenfeld & Nicolson) 1972.

Richardson, H.W.:
Urban and Regional Economics,
(Harmondsworth: Penguin) 1978.

Richardson, H.W.:
"Input-Output and Economic Base Multipliers: Looking Backward and Forward",
Journal of Regional Science, 1985.

Richardson, H.W. and Gordon, P.:
"A Note on Spatial Multipliers",
Economic Geography, Vol. 54, 1978.

Richardson, H.W.:
"A Review of Techniques for Regional Analysis",
in Higgins, B. and Savoie, D.: Regional Economic Development
(Boston: Unwin Hyman) 1988.

Robinson, J.N.:
Planning and Forecasting Techniques
(London: Weidenfeld and Nicolson) 1971.

Robson, B.T.:
Urban Growth, An Approach
(Cambridge: Cambridge University Press) 1973.

Rodwin, L.:
"Choosing Regions for Development"
in Friedmann, J. and Alonso, W. (eds.):
Regional Development and Planning, A Reader
(Cambridge, Mass.: MIT Press) 1964.

Rogers, A.:
Matrix Methods in Urban and Regional Analysis
(San Francisco: Holden-day) 1971.

Rondinelli, D.A.:
Spatial Analysis for Regional Development: a Case Study in the Bicol River Basin of the Philippines
(Tokyo: United Nations University) 1980.

Rondinelli, D.A.:
Applied Methods of Regional Analysis; the Spatial Dimensions of Development Policy
(London: Westview Press) 1985.

Rose, A.; Nakayama, B. and Stevens, B. :
"Modern-Energy Region Development and Income Distribution: an Input-Output Analysis",
Journal of Environmental Economics and Management Vol.9, 1982.

Sen Gupta, P.:
"Planning Regions for Resource Development in India",
Paper read at the XX International Geographical Congress, New Delhi, 1964.

Sen Gupta, P. :
"The Methodology of Delineating Economic Planning Regions of Different Orders",
Paper read at the Summer School in Applied Geography, Banaras Hindu University, November, 1965.

Sen Gupta, P.:
"The Principles and Techniques of Regional Planning",
The Geographer, Vol.XIX, 1967.

Sharma, A.N. :
Spatial Approach to District Planning
(New Delhi: Concept Publishing House) 1980.

Smith, B.C.:
Regionalism : Its Nature and Purpose
(London: Acton Society Trust) 1965.

Smith, C.A. (ed.):
Regional Analysis Vols. 1 and 2
(New York: Academic Press) 1976.

Smith, D.M.:
Patterns in Human Geography
(New York: Penguin Books) 1975.

Smith, D.M.:
Where the Grass is Greener; Living in An Inequal World
(New York: Penguin Books) 1979.

Srinath, K.P. and Ray, D.M.:
"Multi-Factor Partitioning: A Reformulation of Shift Share Analysis",
paper presented to the International Geographic Union Commissioin on International Division of Labour and Regional Development, Zaregoza, Spain, August 1986.

Steward, J.Q.:
"Empirical Mathematical Rules Concerning the Distribution and Equilibrium of Population",
The Geographical Review, Vol. 37, No. 3, 1947.

Stewart, J.Q. and Warntz, W.:
"Macro-Geography and Social Science"
The Geographical Review, Vol. 48, 1958.

Stone, R.:
A Programme of Growth, 10 Vols.,
in University of Cambridge, Dept. of Applied Economics:
(London: Chapman Hall) 1962.

Subramaniyam, S.:
"Inter-Industry Trasnactions in a District",
Artha Vijnana, June 1985.

Tiebout, C.M.:
The Community Economic Base Study
(New York: Committee for Economic Development, No. 6) 1962.

Thisse, J.F. and Zoller, H.G. (eds.):
Locational Analysis of Public Facilities
(Amsterdam: North Holland) 1982.

Thompson, W.R.:
"The Coefficient of Localization: a Critical Appraisal", Southern Economic Journal, Vol. 23, 1957.

Todaro, M.P. :
Internal Migration in Developing Countries
(Geneva: International Labour Organization) 1976.

Ullman, E.:
Geography as Spatial Interaction
(Seattle: University of Washington) 1980.

Ullman, E. and Dacey, M.:
"The Minimum Requirement Approach to the Urban Economic Base",
Lund Studies in Geography, Vol. 24, 1962.

UNESCO:
Areal Surveys and Integrated Studies
(Paris: UNESCO) 1978.

Vapnarski, C.:
"On Rank-Size Distribution of Cities: An Ecological Approach",
Economic Development and Cultural Change, Vol. 17, 1969.

Von Thunen, J.H.:
The Isolated State, translated from the original German by Wartenberg, C.,
(London: Pergamon Press) 1966.

Weaver, C.:
Regional Development and Local Community: Planning Politics and Social Context
(London: Wiley) 1984

Weber, Alfred:
Theory of Location of Industries, the French version of 1909 translated into English by Wartenberg, C.M.,
(Chicago: University of Chicago Press) 1979.

Weiss, S.J. and Cooding, E.:
"Estimation of Differential Employment Multipliers in Small Regional Economy",
Land Economics, Vol. 44, 1968.

Willemain, T.R.:
Entropy in Urban and Regional Modelling
(London: Pion) 1970.

Wilson, A.C.:
"A Family of Spatial Interaction Models and Associated Developments", Environment and Planning, Vol. 3, 1971.

Wilson, A.G. and Kirby, M.J.:
Mathematics for Geographers and Planners
(Oxford: Clarendon Press) 1980.

Wilson, A.G. and Rees, P.:
Spatial Population Analysis
(New York: Academic Press) 1977.

Woods, R.:
Theoretical Population Geography
(London: Longman) 1982.

Yeats, M.:
An Introduction to Quantitative Analysis in Human Geography (New York: Penguin Books) 1974.

Zipf, G.K.:
Human Behaviour and the Principle of Least Effort
(Cambridge, Mass.: Addison-Wesley) 1949.

CHAPTER V

THEORIES OF REGIONAL DEVELOPMENT AND REGIONAL PLANNING RELEVANT TO DECENTRALISED PLANNING

There is a mass of literature on the theories of regional and sub-national development, and consists of several parts each addressing to the building blocks of the body of knowledge which helps in understanding the process of regional transformation from a state of underdevelopment to one of a developed economy. Theory of regional development and growth and the theoretical foundation of regional development and planning, are of major concern in a decentralised planning set up. Theories of regional growth and development, agrarian transformation of the economy and rural changes and planning, are all, therefore, parts of the landscape for the sub-national planners.

Development : Regional Dimension.

What baffles a student of regional planning and development in his attempt to choose a few readings, is the huge body of literature that has grown on the the subject. The choice of a small number of references, believed to be helpful to an understanding of the purposes and nature of multi-level and regional development planning is by all accounts difficult. Colman and Nixson (1978) is a useful reading, particularly so becuase they discuss the basic approaches and problems of measurement. A review of various conceptualizations can be found in Roxborough (1979) and Smith (1979). Smith in particular stresses the inequality point of view. UNRISD (1970) which is the result of an international Seminar, reviewes a whole range of definitions and forms of measurement. Hirschman (1958) and Myrdal (1957), are also of relevance in understanding regional growth and development.

Theories of regional income determination, regional economic base and of interregional trade are seemingly pertinent. Richardson's clear expositions (1969) and (1979), and Holland's (1976) critique of the plethora of theories, together constitutes a good synthesis of the theoretical strands of thought. Johnson (1970) integrates concepts and processes on economic growth and spatial organization; Perloff (1963) attempts at a reconciliation of different theoretical propositions; Siebert (1969) propounds a two-region growth model; Friedmann and Weaver (1979) gives a review of evolution of thinking in regional growth and Sundaram (1989) recital of the regionalisation dimension of the evolution of the concepts and objectives of planning, are important land marks in this domain of thought.

Massam (1975) Goddard, Boisier and Kuklinski, in Hamilton (1978); and Kundu et. al. (1986) paid attention to locational requirements for decentralization, industrial plant location and the location or allocation of services in the public sector. On development pole and growth pole theory, Darwent (1969), Harmanson (1969), Hermansen, Hansen and Higgins, in the book edited by Kuklinski (1972), and Higgins and Savoic (1988) are main sources. More references will be discussed while dealing with strategies and policies, and more have been included in the General Bibliography.

Socio-Spatial Development: Domination Theory

When the basic imbalances to be faced by regional development planning are generated, a clearer understanding of the process of inter-regional and intra-regional development that emerged in the wake of domination and centre-periphery theorizing is necessary. The pioneering contributions of Friedman and Hilhorst, linked centre-periphery and domination thinking to regional development. Since the socio-spatial dimension is most pertinent to the district identity of regional development plan ning, in a multi-level planning system, we need to deal with the issues involved in some detail, and a number of propositions need clarification.

The reluctance, it has been rightly pointed out, to use the word domination and, hence, several other concepts associated with domination, like power, dependence, periphery and exploitation in relation to modern development stems up because these terms are often seen as attributes of the dominant economic class, in a social milieu where the common belief is that latent interest of a privileged group lurks behind all ideals and values projected in society, including those that are propounded for the amelioration of the conditions of the poor and the downtrodden. Usually these terms also evoke such associations as exploitation, class struggle, class consciousness and perpetual crisis, particularly so in developing countries where deprevation and poverty imbibe in people at large a general under-current of affinity for egalitarian and socialistic ideas. That is an attitude of mind which is understandable because they live in an age where they struggle to etch out a living, but seek to overtake those who are far ahead of them in the race for economic betterment. And then these ideas may contain elements of truth, but the true and fair account of the nature of domination is not revealed, and it is scarcely realised that beneficial effects, in general are just as genuine an aspect of domination as is exploitation. Thus to Hilhorst (1971), "extraction and distribution" appears to be two complementing components of "Domination".

The foregoing together with the realisation that dependency relations cannot be wished away though their structure having considerable bearing upon regional and rural development capacity, explain the revival of great interest that has emerged in the nature and implications of power status-structure. Friedmann (1971) builds upon these ideas and expands on the implications of extractive and distributive components of domination for intra-regional and inter-regional development. Mukherjee (1989) discussed the power-status structure in classical thought. Sharma (1989) brings forth the clamour for participation in the planning process inter alia, as a reaction to domination.

The unequal access to information consistitutes the commercial elements in the emerging situation of dominance, which reduces domination to a condition arising out of the results of relative location within a communication network and the strength of the various filters through which information flows. Greater access to information is an essential pre-requisite for individuals and groups in succeeding to get and keep ahead of others, resulting in a differentiated social structure. If change is accepted in social interaction, it is institutionalized, imparting social validation to inherent powers, and authority becomes socially legitimate power (Friedmann 1972).

Information, communication and domination, can be explicitly inter-linked to the fourth process, viz, polarization. Centrality is the spatially most efficient form and hence is necessary to achieve and retain a position of prominence. Centrality and polarization express central specificity in an occupied space in terms of proximity to the aggregate of facts under consideration, and these have been the unfaltering companions to human efforts at organizing farms, factories, villages, towns, regions and nations. Polarization as human action's logical spatial outcome (van Raay, 1971) impinges upon the spatial structure, on two fronts: one, the centre where the more crucial decisions are made, and two, the surroundings and the periphery, whose inhabitants look to the centre, at least, for the more vital decisions.

If a centre-periphery condition prevails, the existence of a spatial system is usually recognised in so far as integration of a given space is achieved in terms of a pattern of authority- dependent relations with focus on the centre. Since Friedmann (1966) wrote, these concepts have evolved considerably yet seemingly a broad consensus of opinion apparently exists, where the centre and periphery are treated as two sub-systems, with the former typically urban in the regional context and even in the national and, inter-national context (Raul Prebisch). The "centre" and "periphery" nexus is a description of geographic position, and imply" a set of structural relations that hold the periphery in nearly permanent subordination to the urban industrial heartland" (Friedmann & Alonso, 1967) and the very thought of the regional system evokes in mind a picutre of a Regional and Urban System as the Centre. (Mahadev and Kumaran 1989)

Urban Development

The pioneering works of Friedmann (1962, 1966, 1968, 1969a, 1969b) have thoroughly explored the centre-periphery notion in the context of national and regional planning. The city has assumed such an important focus of planning research that it has led to what some have rechristened as "urbanization" of interest, without diverting attention from the regional and rural to the urban context. Deeper insights into urban life, environment, distribution and hierarchy are crucial input for an understanding of region's rural areas and the processes that chart out their transformation. Whenever the city is presented as a prominent point, either in the communication network, or for information exchange,or for innovation generation or for precipitating forces of transformation, it is placed in a regional frame of reference and used in working out a policy. Thus despite sharing urban interest with several other disciplines, regional development planning has adopted its typical pragmatic perspective. The city is envisioned as a centre, whose nature implies that it is not only better served by, but also serves, its surroundings and periphery, to penetrate and transform them. The city is consequently treated as an indispendable medium, whose efficient location and successful operation is absolutely essential for the integration of regional and national economies.

The French economists, notably Perroux (1964), was the first to attempt at a systematic integration of implications of the analysis of economic development in space by conceiving the centre as the growth pole. Boudeville, another French economist concretised Perroux's ideas, which have since become firmly entrenched in regional economic thinking, and there has been a flood of research around the concept. Broadly speaking the growth pole policy attempts at stimulating development generally by controlling the evolving system of urban centres. By implication then the growth pole policy, therefore, involves the manipulation of a whole range of urban levels, functions and service areas. The purposes of the various growth poles and the expanse of space which these growth poles may serve differ considerably (Sen 1971).

The urban development paradigm was extremely influential in the urbanizing countries throughout the sixties and the seventies, has been consolidated by Germani (1973), and by Moseley (1972), Pred (1973), Lamb (1975), Soja and Tobin (1975) - all of whom represent the modernising school of thought. Berry and Pred (1965), Berry et. al. (1966) and Berry (1967) have done remarkable job in the Indian context. Slater (1975) and Massey (1984) perceived peripheral capitalist development to be germane to the relationship between spatial organizations and economic structures, a concept which was elaborated upon by McGee (1976).

It needs to be clearly underpinned that rural aspects of regional development cannot be treated in isolation from urban change. Urban dynamics and the complementarity of urban and rural change, and their interdependence cannot be wished away. Cities are active ingredients of development, and Lampard's (1954) argument that urban concentration of economic activity was the first premise of spatial logic that gradually transforms values and relations, clearly brought forth the creative capacities of cities. Hoselitz (1954) expanded upon the role of cities and Kolb (1954) argued successfully enough the case for a "universalist achievement" spectrum as a strong under-current of being an urban phenomenon in the first place despite inherent socio-economic and environmental disadvantages that flow from modern urban growth (Prakasa Rao & Tiwari 1978a, 1978b). The slogan "Cities First -Rural Development Later" gained usage. Nelson (1973), van Raay and Hilhorst (1981), Renand (1981), and Gilbert and Gugler (1982) backed their plea for urban-rural development continuum with quantitative biases, and Lampard, Morse and Tangri (1964) shed considerable light on the role of cities in development of rural urban nexus. Currie (1976) linked urbanization to transformations of both agricultural and non-agricultural activities. Sinclair (1978) goes deep into the issues of urban industrialisation being dependent upon the flow of "unlimited supply of labour" from the rural to the urban sectors. The issue of growth with unlimited supply of labour was first propounded in the monumental work of Lewis (1954) and issues of flow of labour from rural to urban areas have been examined at length by Ranis and Fie (1964) and Harris and Todaro (1970) in particular. Susequently Todaro and Stilkind (1981) argued that the bias towards urban development has led to the impoverishment of the rural economy. Banerjee (1986) has provided deeper insights into various aspects of internal migration and developmental issues, in the Indian context. Moulik (1989) has moved the other way round to assess the impact of development programmes on migration, instead of the impact of migration on development.

In any event spatial dimension of urbanisation process deserves attention. El-Shanks (1972) found the link between concentrated urbanisation and the levels of economic development. Berry (1964, 1971) ; Vapnarski (1969), Morse (1975), Johnston (1977), Meyer (1980) all provide corroboration to El Shanks. Nagamine and Konno (1989) went a step ahead to argue that the inter-se rank among concentrated urban centres had a "correlation" with their potential for economic development. Morse (19750 and Meyer (1980) had viewed the issues against the backdrop of an historical perspective. One could also read with interest Berry (1973), McGee (1976), Abu-Lughod and Hay (1977), Castells (1977), Gugler and Flannagen (1978a and 1978b) and Safa (1982) McGee (1976), Castell (1977) and Safa (1982) provide the Marxian perspective of the issue. Kundu (1989) and Al-qutub (1989) are of relevance, in this context, particularly Al-qutub, because the complexity of policy issues are clearly dealt with.

Transformation of Rural Landscape

The transformation of the rural landscape transcends agricultural production *perse*, and changes in cultural attitudes, socio-economic and political conditions, organizational issues and relationships, are all integral parts of this transformation process. Harris (1982) identifies three different approaches to rural transformation, viz, neo-classical approach, the systems approach and the structural historical approach, and admittedly the three approaches would generate different inferences about the problems, and the solutions to those problems, of rural transformation. Schultz's (1964) is a brilliant exposition of neo-classical approach to transforming the rural scene, where the farmer is an income maximizer with regard to non-farm allocation, and of the thesis that raising of productivity of agriculture would be a function of such factors as new techniques (newer and better) and more inputs; newer markets and better access to existing markets. Lipton (1968) joined issue with Schultz with regard to peasant behaviour, but provides no specific alter native to Schultz's somewhat general suggestions. Hanumantha Rao (1976 and 1989) have provided significant insights into these discussions and problems.

That higher productivity in, and modernization of, the rural sector is possible through improved technology has long been recognised without demure. Wharton (1969), Collinson (1972) and Upton (1973) all agree on these issues. Bath (1966) and Long (1977), favour decision making approaches to study of rural dimensions.

The influential work of Boserup (1965), is a classic case of systems study with more of macro-orientation. Farmer (1957) Geartz (1963), Allan (1965) and to some extent Prothero (1972) are also amenable to be classified under this class. Farming Systems Research is an adaptive planning approach for a homogenous group (of farmers) and it directly relates to agricultural area based planning. Dillon and Hardeker (1980), Norman et. al. (1980); Ruthenberg (1980) and Shanar (1982a) are important contrubutions in this regard.

The structural-historic approach to rural transformation places the ownership and control of resources at the centre of the analysis, and is basically concerned with inter-relationships between people and combination of peope with focuses on production and environment for production. A historical perspective is provided about commercialisation of production and induction of small scale producers into the world. Palmer and Parsons(1977), Klein (1980), Mobogunje 1980 and Hopkins (1983) are notable contributions. Green revolution as a strategy has worked well in many underdeveloped countries (Tiwari and Sinha 1988) but Griffin (1974), Feder (1976) and Learse (1980) have fiercely criticised it as a technological innovation strategy.

Shanin (1971), Pearse (1975), Berstein (1977) and Helmsing (1985) have added enormously to the continuing debate on peasant agriculture versus capitalist agriculture. Pearse (1971), Sinclair (1978) and Lipton (1972) have contributed much to a better understanding of the rural transformation caused by interaction between rural structures and changing urban industrial economy, and by adoption of technological innovations. Briggs (1973), Cummings (1975), Douglass (1978), Roberts (1978), Butterworth and Chance (1981) and Banerjee (1986) contain graphic description of the dynamics of rural-urban migration in the context of a developmental milieu.

Plan and Plan Implementation

The distinction between process of planning and process of plan implementation (Faludi 1973) has concerned many scholar in the field. Chadrick (1971), Friedman and Hudson (1973), Lichfield (1975), Latsis (1976), Taylor (1980), Hague (1984) and Weaver (1985) are some important writings in the field. On regional, or rural planning or local planning, the principal contributions would be of Bosier (1978), Gillingwater and Hart (1978), Bratton (1980), O'Regan and Bendavid-val (1979), Mobogunje (1981), Dus seldrop (1981), Conyers (1982), Higgins and Savoie (1988) and Blackley (1989).

Decentralised administration is an essential component of decentralised multi-level planning. But decentralisation in administration for decentralised planning is hard to come by. Friedman (1973) saw lack of real power for implementation, weak political will to pursue decentralisation, bias towards developed regions (advocated by Davin and Clark) and low level of co-ordination in the instrumentation of regional decentralisation policies, as the real problems in making decentralisation a success story. Faltas (1977) and United Nations Centre for Regional Studies (1977) corroborate each other that poor co-ordination was the cause of failure of several regional development planning exercises..

Decentralisation automatically means delegation of responsiblities, which is made a useless footnote in the kaliedoscope of developments unless backed by appropriate financial, human and organisational resources. Gant (1979) and Sundaram (1989) have drawn attention to these facts forcefully. But sadly enough Conyers (1982) bear eloquent testimony to the fact that these have not occurred. It is worth mentioning that Cheema (1981), Cheema and Hosake (1983) and Esman and Uphoff (1984) had gone into the problems of decentralization and development in the regional context, with special reference to role of local organisations and institutional aspects involved. Benninger (1983, 1987, 1987b, 1989) has exhaustively examined the institutional arrangements for sub-national development planning which is still not adequate.

International attempts at decentralisation have been documented in Honadle and Klans (1979). Korten and Alfonso (1983), Rondinelli (1983) and Clay and Schaffer (1984) provide excellent cases of decentralisation issues as reflected in policy and planning implementation. Heaver (1982) provides a classic study of how bureacracy hampers implementation of development projects. Lea and Chaudhuri (1983) have provided a number of African and Asian country studies where vested interests affect State intervention in development planning but where State intervention is warranted. Since a separate part is being provided in the study on "decentralised administration for decentralised planning" no further discussion is pursued here of the various issues involved.

Select Bibliography:

Theories of Regional Development and Regional Planning Relevant to Decentralised Planning.

Abu-Lughod, J. and Hay, R. Jr. (eds.):
Third World Urbanization,
(New York: Methuen & Co.) 1977.

Allan, W.:
African Husbandmen
(London: Routledge & Kegan) 1975.

Al-qutub, Ishaaq, Y.:
"The Challenges for Urban Development Policies; The Case of Refugee Camp Cities in Middle East",
in Sundaram, K.V. et. al.:
Regional Planning and Development
(New Delhi: Heritage) 1989.

Baily, J.:
Social Theory in Planning,
(London: Routledge & Kegan) 1975.

Barth, F.:
Models of Social Organization,
(London: Royal Anthropological Institute) Occasional Paper 23, 1966.

Beg, M.A.K.; Anwar, S.M. and Jonathan, H.:
Management for Rural Development in Pakistan, Report of an International Seminar,
January 170-19, 1983 (Peshawar: Pakistan Academy for Rural Development) 1983.

Banerjee, Biswajit:
Rural Urban Migration and Urban Labour Market
(Bombay: Himalaya Publishing House) 1986.

Bendavid-Val, A.:
Regional and Local Economic Analysis for Practitioners
(New York: Praeger) 1983.

Benninger, Christopher, C.:
Spatial Planning, Migration and Human Resources Mobilisation
(Bangkok: ESCAP) 1983.

Benninger, Christopher, C.:
"Institutional Arrangement for Regional (Sub-National) Planning in India",
Paper read at the Expert-Group Meeting on Institutional

Arrangements for Regional (Sub-National) Planning, Nairobi, Kenya in September 1987.

Benninger, Christopher, C.:
"Regional Development Planning Institutions: Issues, Interventions and Deficiencies",
Paper read at the Expert Group Meeting on Institutional arrangements for Regional (Sub-National Planning, Nairobi, in September 1987.

Benninger, Christopher, C.:
"New Institutional Systems for Enhanced Regional Planning and Management",
in Sundaram, K.V.; Ramesh, A. and Tiwari P.S.:
Regional Planning and Development,
Vol. II (New Delhi: Heritage Publishers) 1989.

Bernstein, H.:
"Notes on Capital and Peasantry",
Review of African Political Economy, Vol. 10, 1977.

Berry, B.:
"City Size Distribution and Economic Development",
Friedmann J. and Alonso W. (eds.):
Regional Development and Planning
(Cambridge, Mass.: MIT Press) 1964.

Berry, B.:
"City Size and Economic Development: Conceptual Synthesis and Policy Problems with Special Reference to South-East Asia",
in Jacobson, J. & Prakash, V. (eds.):
Urbanization and National Development,
(Beverly Hills: Sage Publications) 1971.

Berry, B.J.L. and Pred, A.:
Central Place Studies: A Bibliography of Theory and Applications
(Philadelphia: Regional Science Research Institute) 1965.

Berry B.J.L. et. al.:
Essays on Commodity Flows and the Spatial Structure of Indian Economy
(Chicago: University of Chicago, Deptt. of Geography) 1966.

Berry, B.J.L.:
Spatial Analysis: A Reader in Statistical Geography
(New Jersey: Prentice Hall) 1967.

Berry, B.:
The Human Consequences of Urbanisation: Divergent Paths in the Urban Experience of the twentieth century,
(London: McMillan) 1973.

Blackley, Edward, J. :
Planning Local Economic Development: Theory and Practice (Newbury Park: Sage Publications) 1989.

Boisier, S.:
Regional Planning as a Negotiating Process
(Santiago de Chile: ILPES) 1978a, mimeographed.

Boisier, S.:
"Location, Urban Size and Industrial Productivity: A Case Study in Brazil"
Hamilton, F.E.I. (ed.):
Contemporary Industrialization: Spatial Analysis and Regional Development
(London: Longman) 1978b.

Boserup, E.:
The Conditions of Agricultural Growth
(London: Allen & Unwin) 1965.

Bratton, M.:
The Local Politics of Rural Development: Peasant and Party-State in Zambia

(Hanover: University Press of New England) 1980.

Briggs, P.:
Some Economic Interpretations of Case Studies of Urban Migration in Developing Countries
(Washington D.C.: International Bank for Reconstruction and Development) 1973.

Brown, A.J. and Burrows, E.M.:
Regional Economic Problems: Comparative Experiences of Some Market Economies,
(London: Allen & Unwin) 1977.

Casley, D.J. and Lury, D.A.:
Monitoring and Evaluation of Agriculture and Rural Development Projects
(Baltimore: Johns Hopkins University Press) 1982.

Castells, M.:
The Urban Question: A Marxist Approach
(London: Arnold) 1977.

Chadwick, G.:
A Systems' View of Planning
(Oxford: Pergamon) 1971.

Chambers, R.:
Settlements Schemes in Tropical Africa: A Study of Organizations and Development
(London: Arnold) 1969.

Chambers, R.:
Rural Poverty Unperceived: Problems and Remedies
(Washington D.C.: World Bank) Staff Working Paper, No. 400, 1980.

Cheema, G.S. (ed.):
Institutional Dimensions of Regional Development,
(Nagoya: U.N.C.R.D.) Regional Development Series, Vol. 8, 1981.

Cheema, G.S. and Rondinelli, Dennis, A. (eds.):
Decentralization and Development: Policy Implementation in Developing Countries,
(Beverly Hills: Sage) 1983.

Cheema, G.S. and Hosake, M. (eds.):
Administration of Regional and Local Development
(Nagoya: United Nations Centre for Regional Development) 1983.

Clay, E.J. and Schaffer, B.B. (eds.):
Room for Manoeuvre: An Exploration of Public Policy in Agriculture (London: Gower Publications) 1984.

Collinson, M.P. :
Farm Management in Peasant Agriculture: A Handbook for Rural Development Planning in Africa
(London: Praeger) 1972.

Colman, D. and Nixson, F.:
Economics of Change in Less Developed Countries
(Oxford: Philip Allan) 1978.

Conyers, D.:
An Introduction to Social Planning in the Third World
(Chichester: J. Wiley) 1982.

Conyers, D. (ed.):
Organization for Planned Regional Development: A Reader,
(The Hague: Institute of Social Studies) 1982.

Cummings, F.:
"Internal Migration and Regional Development Planning: Thailand, the Philippines and Indonesia",
Journal of Tropical Geography, December, 1975.

Currie, L:
Taming the Megalopolis: A Design For Urban Growth
(Oxford: Pergamon Press) 1976.

Dantwala, M.L. :
"Consistency Between Macro and Micro Planning",
in Dantwala, M.L.; et. al. (eds.):
Asian Seminar on Rural Development
(New Delhi: Oxford & IBH) 1986.

Dantwala, M.L. :
"Rationale and Limitation of Decentralised Planning",
in Dantwala, M.L., et. al. (eds.): Asian Seminar on Rural Development (New Delhi: Oxford & IBH) 1986.

Darwent, D.F. :
"Growth Poles and Growth Centres in Regional Planning: a Review",
in Friedmann, J and Alonso, W. (eds.):
Regional Policy, Readings in Theory and Applications
(Cambridge, Mass.: MIT Press) 1979.

Davey, K.:
Financing Regional Government : International Practices and Their Relevance to the Third World
(Chichester: Wiley) 1983.

Davidoff, P. and Reiner, T.A.:
"A Choice Theory of Planning"
in: Faludi, A. (ed.):
Planning Theory: A Reader
(Oxford: Pergamon Press) 1973.

Deman, Suresh:
"Political Economy of Regional Development - A Review of Theories",
Indian Journal of Regional Science, Vol. XVI, No. 2, 1984.

Desai, Vasant:
Rural Development
(Bombay: Himalaya Publishing House) Vols. I & VII, 1988.

Dillon, J.L. and Hardaker, J.B.:
Farm Management Research for Small Farmer Development
(Rome: Food and Agriculture Organisation of the United Nations) 1980.

Douglass, M.:
"Migration, Employment and Income Study of Rural-Urban Relations in Thailand",
in Pakasam, P. et. al.: Impacts of the Green Revolution and Urban-Industrial Growth in the Bangkok Metropolitan Dominance Sub-region (Bangkok: NESDB/United Nations Centre for Rural Development) 1978.

Douglass, M.:
Rural Regional Development Alternatives: China and Korea as two Asian Success Models,
Development Studies Occasional Paper No. 10,(Norwich: University of East Anglia) 1980.

Douglass, M.:
From Peasant to Migrant Worker: Regional Perspective From the Central Plains of Thailand,
Working Paper Series No. 5, (The Hague: Institute of Social Studies) 1982.

Dusseldorp, D.B.W.M. Van:
"Participation in Planned Development Influenced by Governments of Developing Countries at Local Level in Rural Areas",in Essays in Rural Sociology in Honour of R.A.J. Van Lier,
(Wegeningen: Dept. of Rural Sociology of the Tropics and Sub-tropics, Agricultural University) 1981.

El-Shahks, S.:
"Development, Primacy and Systems of Cities",
Journal of Developing Areas, Vol. 7, 1972.

Esman, M.J. and Uphoff, N.T.:
Local Organisations: Intermediaries in Rural Development
(Ithaca: Cornell University Press) 1984.

Faltas, M.:
The Role of Government in the Regional Development Process,
(Nagoya: United Nations Centre for Regional Development) 1977.

FAO:
Monitoring Systems for Agricultural and Rural development Projects, Development Policy Studies and Training Services, ESDP,
(Rome: Food and Agriculture Organisation of the United Nations) 1981.

Faludi, A.:
Planning Theory
(Oxford: Pergamon Press) 1973.

Faludi, A. (ed.):
Planning Theory: A Reader
(Oxford: Pergamon Press) 1973.

Farmer, B.F.:
Pioneer Peasant Colonization in Ceylon: A Case Study of Asian Agrarian Problem
(London: Oxford University Press) 1957.

Feder, E.:
"McNamara's Little Green Revolution: World Bank Scheme for Self-liquidation of Third World Peasantry"
Economic and Political Weekly, Bombay, 3rd, April, 1976.

Fie, J.C.H. and Ranis, G.:
Development of the Labour Surplus Economy: Theory and Policy
(Homewood, Illinois: Irwin) 1964.

Food and Agriculture Organisation of the U.N.:
Guidelines for a Programme to Improve the Organization and Administration of Agricultural Development
(Rome: FAO) 1979.

Freeman, H.E.; Rossi, P.H. and Wright, S.R.:
Evaluating Social Projects in Developing Countries
(Paris: OECD) 1979.

Friedmann, J.:
"Cities in Social Transformation",
Comparative Studies in Society and History, 1961-1962.

Friedmann, J.:
"Planning as Innovation: the Chilean Case",
Journal of the American Institute of Planners, 1966.

Friedmann, J. :
"Regional Development Policy: A Case Study of Venezuela
(Cambridge, Mass.: MIT Press) 1966.

Friedmann, J.:
"The Strategy for Deliberate Urbanization",
Journal of the American Institute of Planners, 1968.

Friedmann, J.:
"The Role of Cities in National Development",
The American Behavioural Scientist, 1969.

Friedmann, J.:
Urban and Regional Development in Chile: a Case Study of Innovative Planning
(Santiago: Ford Foundation) 1969.

Friedmann, J.:
" A Generalized Theory of Polarized Development",
in Hansen. N.M. (ed.): Growth Centres in Regional Economics Development (New York: Free Press) 1972.

Friedmann, J.:
"The Spatial Organization of Power in the Development of Urban Systems",
Development and Change, Vol. 4, 1973.

Friedmann, J.:
Retracking America; a Theory of Transactive Planning
(Garden City: New York: Anchor Press, Doubleday) 1973.

Friedmann, J. and Alonso, W. (eds.):
Regional Development and Planning
(Cambridge, Mass.: MIT Press) 1964.

Friedmann, J. and Hudson, B.:
Knowledge and Action: a Guide to Planning Theory, Regional Development Planning Course,
(Los Angeles: UCLA, School of Architecture and Urban Planning) Jan. 1973.

Friedmann, J and Alonso, W. (eds.) :
Regional Policy, Readings in Theory and Applications
(Cambridge, Mass.: MIT Press) 1975.

Friedmann, J. and Wulff, R.:
"The Urban Transition: Comparative Studies of Industrializing Societies",
in Progress in Geography, Vol. 8. (London: Arnold) 1976.

Gant, G.F.:
Development Administration,
(Madison: University of Wisconsin Press) 1979.

Geertz, C.:
Agricultural Involution
(Berkeley: University of California Press) 1963.

Germani, G. (ed.) :
Modernization, Urbanization and the Urban Crisis
(Boston: Little, Brown & Co.) 1973.

Gilbert, A.:
"The Arguments for Very Large Cities Reconsidered",
Urban Studies, Vol. 13, 1976.

Gilbert, A. and Gugler, J.:
Cities, Poverty, and Development: Urbanization in the Third World,
(London: Oxford University Press) 1982.

Gillinwater, D.:
Regional Planning and Social Change: A Responsive Approach
(Westmead: Saxon House) 1975.

Gillinwater, D. and Hart, D.A.:
The Regional Planning Process
(Westmead: Saxon House) 1978.

Goodmann, D. and Redcliff, D.:
From Peasant to Proletarian: Capitalist Development and Agrarian Transitions
(Oxford: Blackwell) 1981.

Goddard, J.P.:
"The Location of Non-manufacturing Activities within Manufacturing Industries",
in Hamilton, I. (ed.):
Contemporary Industrialization: Spatial Analysis and Regional Development
(London: Longman) 1978.

Government of India:
Report of the Working Group on Conceptual Framework on Multi-Level Planning and Spatial Analysis
(New Delhi: Planning Commission) 1973.

Gruchman, B.:
"Key Features of Regional Development and Planning in Eastern Europe",
in Kuklinski, A. (ed.):
Social issues in Regional Policy and Regional Planning
(The Hague: Mouton & Co.) 1977.

Gugler, J. and Flannagan, W.G.:
Urbanization and Social Change in West Africa,
(Cambridge: Cambridge University Press) 1978.

Hague, C.:
The Development of Planning Thought: A Critical Perspective
(London: Hutchinson) 1984.

Harris, J.R. and Todaro, M.P.:
"Migration, Unemployment and Development: A Two Sector Analysis",
American Economic Review, Vol. 60, No. 1, 1970.

Hamilton, F.E.I. (ed.):
Contemporary Industrialization: Spatial Analysis and Regional Development (London: Longman) 1978.

Harriss, J. (ed.):
Rural Development Theories of Peasant Economy and Agrarian Change
(London: Hutchinson) 1982.

Hay, (Jr.) R.:
"Patterns of Urbanization and Socio-Economic Development in the Third World: An Overview"
in Abu-Lughod, J. and Hay, R. (eds.):
Third World Urbanization
(New York: Methuen) 1977.

Hayami, Y. and Ruttan, W.:
Agricultural Development: An International Perspective
(Baltimore: Johns Hopkins Press) 1971.

Healey, P.; McDougall, G. and Thomas, M.J. (eds.):
Planning Theory; Prospects for the 1980s
(Oxford: Pergamon Press) 1983.

Heaver, R.:
Bureaucratic Politics and Incentives in the Management of Rural Development,
(Washington D.C.: World Bank) World Bank Staff Working paper No. 537, 1982.

Helmsing, B.:
Firms, Farms and the State: a Study of Rural, Urban and Regional Dimensions of Development
(The Hague: Institute of Social Studies) 1986.

Hermansen, T.:
"Spatial Organisation and Economic Development"
in Kuklinsky, A. (ed.):
Regional Disaggregation of National Policies and Plans
(The Hague: Mouton & Co.) 1975.

Heyer, J.; Roberts, P. and William, G. (eds.):
Rural Development in Tropical Africa
(London: MacMillan) 1981.

Higgins, Benjamin and Savoic, Donalu J. (eds.):
Regional Economic Development: Essays in Honour of Francois Perroux
(Boston: Unwin Hyman) 1988.

Hilhorst, J.G.M.:
Regional Planning: A Systems Approach
(Rotterdam: Rotterdam University Press) 1971.

Hilhorst, J.G.M.:
"National Development Strategies and Regional Planning in Latin America: Some Reflections",
Development and Change, Vol. 12, 1981.

Holland, S.:
Capital versus the Region
(London: MacMillan) 1976.

Honadle, G. and Klauss, R.:
International Development Administration
(London: Praeger) 1979.

Hopkins, A.G.:
An Economic History of West Africa
(London:Longman) 1973.

Hoselitz, B.F.:
"Generative and Parasitic Cities",
Economic Development and Cultural Change, Vol. 2, 1954.

Johnson, E.A.J.:
The Organization of Space in Developing Countries
(Cambridge, Mass.: Harvard University Press) 1970.

Johnston, R.J.:
"Regarding Urban Origins, Urbanization and Urban Patterns", Geography, Vol. 62, 1977.

Khan, M. Baseer Ahmed:
Regional Planning And Economic Development
(Jaipur: Pointer Publishers) 1988

Klaassen, L.H. and Paelinck, J.H.P.:
Integration of Socio-economic and Physical Planning
(New York: United Nations Development Programme) 1974.

Klein, M.A. (ed.):
Peasants in Africa: Historical and Contemporary Perspectives
(Beverly Hills and London : Sag Publications) 1980.

Kolb, W.H.:
"The Social Structure and Function of Cities",
Economic Development and Cultural Change, Vol. 2. 1954.

Korten, D. and Alfonso, F.B. (eds.):
Bureaucracy and the Poor: Closing the Gap
(Delhi: Kumarian Press) 1983.

Knight, C.G.:
Ecology and Changes: Rural Modernisation in an African Community
(New York: Academic Press) 1974.

Kuklinski, A.R. (ed.):
Growth Poles and Growth Centres in Regional Planning
(The Hague: Mouton & Co.) 1972.

Kuklinski, A.R.:
"Industrialization, Location and Regional Development",
in Hamilton, F.E.I. (ed.): ContemporaryIndustrialization: Spatial Analysis and Regional Development
(London: Longman) 1978.

Kuklinski, A. (ed.):
Regional Policies in Nigeria, India and Brazil
(The Hague: Mouton & Co.) 1978.

Kundu, Amitabh:
"The Dynamics of City Hinterland Relationship in India",
in Sundaram, K.V. et. al.:
Regional Planning and Development
(New Delhi: Heritage) 1989.

Lampard, E.E.:
"The History of Cities in the Economically Advanced Areas",
Economic Development and Cultural Change, Vol. 2, 1954.

Latsis, S.J. (ed.):
Method and Appraisal in Economics
(Cambridge: Cambridge University Press) 1976.

Lea, D.A.M., and Chaudhuri, D.P.:
Rural Development and the State: Contradictions and Dilemmas in Developing Countries
(London: Methuen & Co.) 1983.

Lewis, W.A.:
"Economic Development with Unlimited Supply of Labour",
Manchester School, 1954.

Lewis, W.A.
Developmental Planning: The Essentials of Policy
(London: Allen & Unwin) 1966.

Lichfield, N.; Kettle, P. & Whitbread, M. (eds.):
Evaluation in the Planning Process
(Oxford: Pargamon Press), Urban Regional Planning Series, Vol. 10, 1975.

Lipton, M.:
"The Theory of the Optimising Peasant",
Journal of Development Studies, 1968.

Lipton, M.:
Why Poor People Stay Poor? Urban Bias in World Development
(Cambridge, Mass.: Harvard University Press) 1977.

Lipton, M.:
"Why Poor People Stay Poor" in: Harriss, J.(ed.): Rural Development Theories of Peasant Economy and Agrarian Change,
(London: Hutchinson) 1982.

Lipton, M. and Streeten, Paul:
"Introduction: Two Types of Planning",
in Streeten, Paul and Lipton, M.: The Crisis of Indian Planning: Economic Policies in the 1960s (London: Oxford University Press) 1968. A Seminal work on the relevant issues.

Long, N.:
An Introduction to the Sociology of Rural Development
(London: Tavistock) 1977.

Mabogunje, A.L.:
The Development Process: a Spatial Perspective
(London: Hutchinson University Library) 1980.

Mabogunje, A.L.:
Local and Regional Development in Africa: Experiences, Main Issues and Perspectives, International Conference on Local and Regional Development in the 1980s,
(Nagoya: United Nations Centre for Regional Development) 1981.

Mahadev, P.D. and Kumarah, T.V.:
Regional Urban Systems: Operationalising Systems Approach and Basic Needs Strategy for Development",
in Sundaram K.V.; Ramesh, A. and Tiwari, P.S.:
Regional Planning and Development, Vol. II,
(New Delhi: Heritage Publishers) 1989.

Massam, B.:
Location and Space in Social Administration
(London: Edward Arnold) 1975.

Massey, D.:
Spatial Division of Labour: Social Structures and the Geography of Production
(London: MacMillan) 1984.

Mayer, J.P.:
"Regional Employment and Development', The Evolution of Theory and Practice",
International Labour Review, Vol. 123, No. 1, 1984.

McDougall, G.:
"Theory and Practice; A Critique of The Political Economy Approach to Planning"
in Healy, P.; McDougall, G. and Thomas, M.J.:
Planning Theory, Prospects for the 1980s
(London: Pergamon Press), Urban and Regional Planning Series, Vol. 29. 1982.

McGee, T.G.:
"The Persistence of The Proto-proletariat: Occupational Structures and Planning for the Future of Third World Cities",
Progress and Geography, Vol. 9, 1976.

Meyer, D.R.:
"A Dynamic Model of the Integration of Frontier Urban Places into the United States System of Cities",
Economic Geography, 1980.

Misra, R.P. and Sundaram, K.V.:
Multi-Level Planning for Integrated Rural Development in India,
(New Delhi: Heritage Publishers) 1980.

Misra, R.P.; Urs, D.V. and Nataraj, K.V.:
Regional Planning and National Development
(New Delhi: Vikas) 1977.

Misra, V.N.:
"Land Concentration, Agricultural Growth and Rural Poverty in India",
in Sundaram, K.V.; Ramesh, A. and Tiwari, P.S.:
Regional Planning and Development,
Vol. II, (New Delhi: Heritage Publishers) 1989.

Mitra, Asok:
Multi-Level Planning,
Lecture delivered at the Institute of Geography at Moscow, June 1973.

Moseley, M.J.:
The Spatial Impact of Growth Centres: Case Studies in Brittany and East Anglia,
(Reading: Ph.D. Dissertation, University of Reading) 1972.

Morse, R.M.:
"The Development of Urban Systems in the Americas in the Nineteenth Century",
Journal of Inter-American Studies and World Affairs, Vol. 17, 1975.

Moulik, T.K.:
Impact Assessment of Development Programmes on Rural Household Economy and Migration: A Study of Panchmahal District of Gujarat,
(Ahmedabad: Indian Institute of Management) 1989. See also commentary on the study entitled:
"Panchmahals: No let up in *Migration*",
Economic Times, 22nd October 1989.

Nagamine, H. and Konno, M.:
"Rurban Dimensions in Regional Development, Case Studies in Three Asian Countries",
in Sundaram, K.V., Ramesh, A. and Tiwari P.S.: Regional Planning and Development Vol. II (New Delhi: Heritage Publishers) 1989.

Naidu, K. Munirathna (ed.):
Area Planning for Regional Development
(New Delhi: Inter-India Publishers) 1984.
TITLE = Nelson, M.:
The Development of Tropical Lands: Policy Issues in Latin America
(Baltimore: Johns Hopkins University Press) 1973.

O'Regan, F.M. and Bendavid-Val, A.:
Public Participation in Regional Development Planning: A Strategy for Public Involvement with a Case Study of the Bicol River Basin Development Programme
(Washington, D.C.: United States Agency for International Development) 1979.

Palmer, R. and Parsons, N. (ed.):
The Roots of Rural Poverty in Central and Southern Africa
(London: Heinemann) 1977.

Pearse, A.:
"Metropolis and Peasant: the Expansion of the Urban Industrial Complex and the Changing Rural Structures",
in Shanin, T. (ed.):
Peasants and Peasant Societies,
(Harmondsworth: Penguin) 1971.

Pearse, A.:
The Latin American Peasant
(London: Frank Cass) 1975.

Pearse, A.:
Seeds of Plenty, Seeds of Want: A Critical Analysis of the Green Revolution
(London: Oxford University Press) 1980.

Perloff, H.S.; Dunn Jr., E.S. and Lampard, E.E.:
Regions, Resources and Economic Growth
(Baltimore: Johns Hopkins University Press) 1960.

Prakasa Rao, V.L.S. and Tiwari, V.K. :
Urbanisation in India, Spatial Dimensions
(Bangalore: Institute of Economic and Social Change) 1978a.

Prakasa Rao, V.L.S. and Tiwari, V.K.:
Urban System and the Regional Economy,

Papers and proceedings of Indo-French Seminar on Problems of Urban Growth, New Delhi, 16th December 1978b.

Prantilla, B. (ed.):
National Development and Regional Policy,
(Nagoya: United Nations Centre for Rural Development)Regional Development Series, Vol. 3, 1983.

Pred, A.R.:
Urban Growth and the Circulation of Information
(Cambridge, Mass: Harvard University Press) 1973.

Prothero, R.M.:
People and Land in Africa South of the Sahara
(New York: Oxford University Press) 1972.

Raay, H.G.T. Van:
"A Case for Regional Planning",
Development and Change, Vol. 3, 1970-71.

Raay, H.G.T. van and Hilhorst, J.G.M.:
Land Settlement and Regional Development in the Tropics: Results, Prospects and Options
(The Hague: ISSAS) 1981.

Rao, C.H. Hanumantha:
Technological Change and the Distribution of Gains in Indian Agriculture
(Delhi: Macmillan) 1975.

Rao, C.H. Hanumantha:
Technological Change in Indian Agriculture, Emerging Trends and Perspectives
(Bombay: Deptt. of Economics, Bombay University and Indira Gandhi Institute of Development Research) 1989 being the Presidential Address at the Golden Jubilee Conference of Indian Society of Agricultural Economics 4th December to 7th December 1989 at Bombay.

Renaud, B.:
National Urbanisation Policy in Developing Countries,
(Washington D.C.: World Bank) a World Bank Research Publication, 1981.

Reynolds, L.G. (ed.):
Agriculture in Development Theory
(New Haven: Yale University Press) 1975.

Richardson, H.W.:
Regional Economics; Location Theory, Urban Structure and Regional Change
(London: Weidenfield and Nicolson) 1969.

Richardson, H.W.:
Regional Economics
(Urbana: University of Illinois Press) 1979.

Roberts, B.:
Cities of Peasants,
(London: Edward Arnold) 1978.

Rondinelli, D.A.:
"Planning Development Projects: Lessons From Developing Countries",
Long Range Planning, Vol. 12, 1979.

Rondinelli, D.A.:
Development Projects as Policy Experiments: An Adaptive Approach to Development Administration
(London: Methuen & Co.) 1983a.

Rondinelli, D.A.:
"Decentralization of Development Administration in East Africa"
in Cheema, G.S. and Rondinelli, D.A. (eds.):
Decentralization and Development
(Beverly Hills: Sage Publications) 1983.

Rondinelli, D.A. and Ruddle, K.:
Urbanization and Rural Development: A Spatial Policy for Equitable Growth
(New York: Praeger) 1977.

Roxborough, I.:
Theories of Underdevelopment
(London: MacMillan) 1979.

Ruthenberg, H. et. al.:
Farming Systems in the Tropics
(Oxford: Clarendon Press) 1980.

Safa, H.I. (ed.):
Towards a Political Economy of Urbanization in
Third World Countries,
(Oxford: Oxford University Press) 1982.

Schultz, T.:
Transforming Traditional Agriculture
(New Haven: Yale University Press) 1964.

Sen, Amartya:
"Strategies of Economic Development: Feasibility Constraints and Planning",
in Robinson, E.A.G. and Kindron, Michael (eds.):
Economic Development in South Asia
(London: MacMillan) 1970.

Shaner, W.W.; Phillipp, P.F. and Schmehl W.R. (eds.):
Reading in Farming Systems Research and Development
(Boulder: Westview Press) 1982.

Shaner, W.W.; Phillipp, P.F.and Schmehl W.R. (eds.):
Farming Systems Research and Development: Guidelines for Developing Countries
(Boulder: Westview Press) 1982.

Shanin, T. (ed.):
Peasants and Peasant Society,
(Harmondsworth: Penguin) 1971.

Shanin, T.:
"The Nature of the Peasant Economy",
Journal of Peasant Studies, Vol. 1, Nos. 1 and 2, 1973-74.

Siebert, H.:
Regional Economic Growth: Theory and Policy
(Scranton: International Textbooks Co.) 1969.

Sinclair, S.W.:
Urbanization and Labour Markets in Developing Countries, (London: Croom Helm) 1978.

Slater, D.:
"Underdevelopment and Spatial Inequality Approaches to the Problem of Regional Planning in the Third World",
Progress in Planning, Vol. 4, 1975.

Slater, D.:
"Colonialism and the Spatial Structure of Underdevelopment: Outlines of an Alternative Approach, with Special Reference to Tanzania", in :
Abu-Lughod, J.R. & Hay Jr., R. (eds.):
Third World Urbanization
(New York: Methuen & Co.) 1977.

Smith, D.M.:
Where the Grass is Greener: Living in An Unequal World
(Harmondworth: Penguin Books) 1979.

Smith, W.E.:
The Design of Organisations for Rural Development Projects
(Washington D.C.: World Bank) Staff Working Paper, 1980.

Soja, E.W. and Tobin, R.J.:
"The Geography of Modernization: Paths. Patterns and Processes of Spatial Change
in Developing Countries in: Brewer, G.D. and Brunner, R.O. (eds.):
Political Development and Change
(New York: Free Press) 1975.

Stevens, B.H.; Bower, J.R. and Ehrlich, D.J.:
Effects of Neighbourhood Economic Development on the

Economic Health of the Central Business District
(Peace Dale, Virginia: Regional Science Research Institute) Discussion Paper No. 127, October 1981.

Sundaram, K.V.:
"Multi-Level Planning: Concept Principles and Some Aspects of its Application to Sectoral Planning",
in Sundaram, K.V.; Ramesh, A. and Tiwari, P.S.:
Space, Society and Development,
(New Delhi: Heritage Publishers) 1989.

Taylor, N.:
"Planning Theory and the Philosophy of Planning",
Urban Studies, Vol. 17, 1980.

Tewari, R.T. and Sinha, R.C.:
Rural Development in India
(New Delhi: Ashis Publishing House) 1988.

Tilakaratna, S.:
Participatory Rural Development: Two Case Studies
(Konnad Adenauer Foundation) 1981.

Todaro, M.P.:
Internal Migration in Development Countries: A Review of Theory, Evidence, Methodology and Research Priorities
(Geneva: I.L.O.) 1976.

Todaro, M.P. and Stilkind, J.L.:
City Bias and Rural Neglect: The Dilemma of Urban Development
(New York: Population Council) 1981.

United Nation Centre for Regional Development:
First Seminar on the Implementation of Regional Plans: Recommendations
(Nagoya: United Nations Centre for Regional Development) 1973, mimeographed.

United Nations Research Institute for Social Development :
Content and Measurement of Socio-Economic Development
(Geneva: United Nations Research Institute for Social Development) 1970.

Upton, M:
Farm Management in Africa
(London: Oxford University Press) 1973

Ushijima, T. and Hosaka, M.:
Institutional Aspects: Administrative and Financial System for Regional Development
(Nagoya: United Nations Centre for Regional Development) 1981.

Vapnarski, C.:
"On Rank Size Distribution of Cities: An Ecological Approach",
Economic Development and Cultural Change, Vol. 17. 1969.

Weaver,C.:
"Development Theory and The Regional Question: A Critique of Spatial Planning and Its Detractors"
in Stohr, W. and Taylor, D.R.F. (eds.):
Development From Above or Below? The Dialectics of Regional Planning in Developing Countries
(London: John Wiley) 1981.

Weaver, C.:
Regional Development and The Local Community: Planning Politics and Social Context
(Chichester: John Wiley) 1984.

Wharton, C.R. (eds.):
Subsistence Agriculture and Economic Development
(London: Frank Cass) 1969.

CHAPTER VI

APPROACHES TO DECENTRALISED PLANNING WITH SPECIAL REFERENCE TO LOCAL/DISTRICT PLANNING

Articulation of planning approaches that help link and integrate the rural and regional dimensions of development and planning is central to developmental planning for the upliftment of the poor. Friedmann and Weaver (1979) emphasized the importance of the dichotomy between 'territory' and 'function' and clarified different interpretations of decentralised planning for rural development. Cepede (1964) summarized the distinct strategic choices as, one, those that consist of the establishment of pilot zones, where all activities contributory to the technical, economic, social and human development of the zone were introduced vertically and horizontally; two, those that specifically restrict the agricultural sector and 'tends to provoke an outward flow of produce', which brings the regions to have interface with the general economic life, 'causing an inward flow of income'.

Granted the foregoing, planning approaches can be evaluated in terms of either horizontal or vertical integration or some sort of combination of the two. The mid-course between these could be one that is a compromise of various approaches which attempt at synthesizing production, consumption and organisation, programmes top-down and bottom-up planning, outward and inward flows, rural and urban development, as well as growth and distribution. There are, therefore, in terms of planning style and breath, a wide variety of approaches. A distinction between the comprehensive approaches, the action-oriented approach and disjointed incrementalism, embodied in planning approach which produces no more than isolated initiatives and actions, is useful.

While no approach is complete or relevant irrespective of environmental and socio-spatial systems, the concepts and procedures put forward in van Raay's micro-regional p4-approach appears to provide particularly helpful guidelines for effective rural and backward area developmental planning. van Staveren and van Dusseldorp, eds. (1980) describe how a concerted effort in an inter-disciplinary framework for the planning of the rural economy can be realized, indicating the methodology thereof and the procedures to be followed. Planning is made a purely profes sional affair and a blueprint orientation appears to pervade the six stages of planning that have been suggested: preparation - reconnaissance - main field studies - additional field studies- plan drafting- and final planning, with no room for the formulation of objectives and straetgies; and issues appertaining to identification of people's needs and their problems and the participation of target groups, left unclear.

Growth-Pole and Small City Development

The growth-pole approach was initially conceived as a policy-instrument for promoting regional growth through the establishment and promotion of typically large-scale industrial activity in a few large urban centres. Promotion of a city with more than a million inhabitants to act as a counter-magnet to the metropolitan capital, was inadequately separated conceptually from the stimulation of rural service centres and small towns. It is doubtful if large urban-industrial growth-poles clearly qualify for inclusion in a review of regional development planning approach. Even as earnest an advocate as Richardson of the original growth-pole strategy, modified his position in his successive works (1976), (1978), (1982a), (1982b)and (1988) to come to a position, where we are seemingly defeated by the evidence against it, to hold that growth pole strategy is relevant to development process, but with limitations, but the imperative that strategies for small city development be conceived within the framework of a national urban hierarchy is nonetheless stressed, as important. The pioneering contribution in India has been by Sen (1971a, 1971b, 1972a, 1972b) which has triggered a long chain of research in this area but the results do not show clearly that the growth pole strategy works (Misra et. al. 1974 and Mukherjee).

Johnson (1960) influenced considerably the ideas on small cities, intermediate cities or towns, rural centres and other terms that may be used to describe the urbanization of the rural areas. Johnson's thesis was that development requires agrarian commercialization, which made the existence of a network of small market towns essential for integrating farmers into the market- economy. Johnson had already foreseen the need to establish some form of planning authority at the local and regional level, but he seemingly underrated the issues pertaining to equity and distribution.

The United States Agency for International Development Planning Approach

Johnson's ideas influenced Rondinelli and Ruddle (1978) who outlined the USAID approach to decentralised planning for integrated regional development. Rondinelli and Ruddle were all in favour of urban centres as an essential pre-requisite to stimulate the growth of rural economies. Rondinelli (1983) presented a comprehensive study of secondary city development, showed the critical importance of secondary cities for national development and dealt with the planning for, and management of, secondary cities.

The USAID planning approach can be further assessed in terms of Rondinelli (1979), version where the approach has been considered a process of analysis and a package of analytical techniques and planning methods that can strengthen rural and urban centres, satisfying a critical need for exploiting fully rural development potential for meeting minimum human requirements, for articulating the settlement system, and for accelerating the tempo of regional economic development.

ESCAP (1979) planning procedures and techniques, have a striking similarity with those of USAID. Additionally, they include a bird's-eye view of theoretical considerations, sectoral planning in water supply, rural electrification, transport and communication, health and nutrition, physical planning and rural resource management. Hoselitz, (1971), Taylor (1975), USAID (1976a, 1976b, 1978) and Chetwyndo (1980) deal with these issues. Dusseldorp (1971), Funnel (1978), Southall (1979) and Sen et.al (1976) deal with applied aspects of these issues. Clearly these planning techniques could be operationalised with regard to the bigger infrastructural projects such as river basin development, colonization and resettlement. A mass of the literature by Gaitskell (1973); Aradeon, et al. (1980); Siann (1981); Watt (1981); Winid (1981); and Majid (1983), all deal with settlement planning.

Reduced Planning Approach and Themes-Strategies-Projects Approach

Bendavid-val and Waller (1975), presented an outline of two closely-related planning approaches: Reduced Planning and Themes-Strategies-Projects (TSP). They opted for a mid path for regional development planning, placed "between the unacceptable primitiveness of an isolated project approach and the widely demonstrated futility of the conventional planning approach", and then held that the two approaches aim "at a reduction of the time consuming process of data collection and they truly try to direct it toward those data, that are really needed for the decisions to be made", with some implementable projects on which immediate action can be intelligible to decision-makers and executers of proposed activities. They, therefore, disfavour complicated quantitative models.

The Reduced Planning Approach, developed in Germany reduces work at three points: reduction of sectors, reduction of work within sectors and elimination of feasibility studies in the planning phase. For certain key sectors, key projects are to be identified, followed by support projects, together forming a project complex.

Six planning steps are distinguished. The first four steps are: (1) delineation of the region, (2) regional analysis, (3) goal analysis and (4) sector and project analysis. All steps should be covered but any one can be taken as the point of departure. Once the first four steps are completed, project complexes can be constructed based on spatial inter-connections, through the movement of food, migration of people, and the like, while a qualitative goal-achievement matrix will facilitate ultimate choices and determine the integrated development programme. Step six constitutes the implementation of this integrated development programme, where, significantly enough for the first time mention is made of local level participation. van Raay (1981), commenting on the practical examples of reduced planning approaches remarked that "The choice of and justification for certain priority areas vis-a-vis others appear underrepresented in the urge to initiate action quickly, as do matters as social control structures, structural change, long-term perspectives and comprehensive orientation".

The core of the Themes-Strategies-Projects approach is that several rounds of investigation are to be resorted to, the first being the preliminary round for only identifying potential themes of local development, which are then investigated in greater depth for identification of specific categories of potential activities, that together forms a generalized strategy. This strategy and the specific categories of potential activities identified are then minutely examined to identify potential projects. Themes-Strategies-Projects provides, not a plan per se, but a well articulated framework for decision-making, of every description, without employing the formal optimization techniques.

Multilevel Planning

Misra and Sundaram (1980) outline the framework of their Planning for Integrated Rural Development -approach. Multilevel planning is an integrated area-based rural development approach. Misra and Sundaram's multilevel operation represents a systems approach in planning, with an area-based system made up of sub-systems, which are parts of an interdependent system, yet relatively decentralized and independent. The underlying principle is that proper decision-making is possible at any level provided the strategy at each level is decided upon "after a careful consideration of the potentials, needs and limitations of the next higher as well as the next lower levels of planning. The higher level should give all macro-framework indicators and guidelines for planning. The lower level must feed the higher level with information and has also to prepare the plan from below".

Six steps are involved in multi-level planning approach of Misra and Sundaram:-

i) Identification of levels and the functions to be performed at each level of planning
ii) Establishment of planning machinery at each level with professional staff.
iii) Indication of outlays available for planning at each level.
iv) Delegation of powers, matching of resources and responsibilities in consonance with the tasks assigned.
v) Well-defined procedures for plan formulation, execution and monitoring
vi) Set time frames for various stages of planning to be accomplished has to be laid down.

Multilevel planning for rural development at and below the district level, at any of five geographical levels: farm, village, sub-block, block and district. A specificity and focus of planning is claimed for each level with about 16 planning fields distinguished and distributed over these levels.

Misra (1979), discusses changes in Indian policies from block level planning to district level planning etc. and the relevance of local and block plans. Misra makes decentralization and people's participation critical components of the process, and he holds at once that, "the centre must remain strong in order that the country survives the external and internal pressures, but the local agencies must have adequate autonomy and power to strengthen the local and thus the regional and national economy", and the difficulty of reconciling the conflicting claims is also clearly mirrored. Reference is also invited to Tripathy (1979), Misra and Natraj (1981), Yang-Boo-Choe (1981) for Korea; and Singh (1982) for Nepal.

Rurban Development Approach

The "top-down, bottom-up" debate is also relevant in the context of urban functions. Richardson (1982b) held that investment to promote the larger cities in the national rurban hierarchy, particularly so regional megapolises and metropolises, will lead to stability and improvement in the lower order centres in the urban hierarchy, but Misra and Bhooshan (1981), rejected development models based on dichotomies, because rather than conceiving rural or urban as discrete entities, it is more appropriate to "think of rurban or rural towns or urban villages as an integrated continuum". Misra (1974) used the term 'rural growth centre', and by so doing, it may be mentioned in passing, this time he contributed his mite to the semantic confusion revolving around the growth pole concepts. By arguing that in place "of thinking of a hierarchy of settlements, we should perhaps think of regional settlement complexes, wherein size, spacing and the ordering of settlements are determined not by the theory of central places, but by the dynamic need of national and local societies", Misra et.al. argued for the creation of rurban centres planned at the regional level, conceived of as a district in the Indian context.

At the district level, Misra and Bhooshan (1981) argued, that the focus should be on productive activities as the basis for settlement development, and not on services, rejecting Christallers' hierarchy for ignoring "productivity as an ordering factor". Misra's thinking on rurban centres forms part of his multilevel planning approach to integrated rural development where small town development constitutes a sub-strategy to be fitted into a broader developmental framework.

Bhooshan, (ed. 1980) provides an operationalisation of Misra's thinking in terms of four pilot studies on the role of the small towns in integrated rural development. Incidentally Park (1982) is an interesting case of small town development from below in the Republic of Korea, and the emerging approach aims to harmonize the regionalization of a local rural development programme called "Sacmal Undung" and the small town revitalization programme.

Rehovot Approach

Weitz (1979), elaborated the Rehovot approach, developed at the Rehovot-Development Centre in Israel. Development is envisioned as a gradual process, "a process of transformation, which occurs in definite sequences and is not erratic: from subsistence farming to diversified (and later to specialized) and automated farming".

The six main areas of emphasis of the Rehovot approach are:

i) The existence of a supporting system of services, without which no growth in agriculture is possible.

ii) The existence of a diversified regional economic resource base because rural development will not come about without non-agricultural employment generation and rural industrialization.

iii) The existence of the mechanism of decentralised planning and decision-making for mobilization of human resources in intermediate level regional planning, implying that priority setting is not predominantly a vertical affair.

iv) The possiblity of coordination of planning at various territorial tiers like farm, village, and planning area.

v) The existence of a machinery for coordination of inter-sector planning including agriculture, industry and services sectors.

vi) The coordination of intra-sector planning at the project level.

And the planning process itself generally has five steps:

i) basic data collection, collation and processing; delineation of regions and areas and diagnosis of the malady;

ii) approximation of the regions, and the drawing up of a rural region macro-plan in consonance with the overall national plan;

iii) micro level planning and planning from below;

iv) transformation of economic and social programmes into a spatial and physical plan for the region; and finally

v) preparation of concrete projects.

The Israeli regional planning exercise has been successful as it was not constrained by paucity of human and financial resources, while in most under-developed countries, in contrast, the approach may not succeed, because of scarcity of human and material capital, despite the fact that the applicability of the approach is not dependent on a specific political system, but on the effectiveness of governmental organizations and available institutional arrangements. Landau & Rokach (1971); Weitz (1971); Boguslawski (1978); Weitz, Peley & Applebaum (1980), and Arnon, (1981) all quite extensively deal with the Rehovot approach and related matters.

P4-Micro-Regional Approach

Van Raay (1981) elaborated his so - called P4-approach, where regional development planning for rural upliftment is perceived of as a normative art of stressing the need for making use of existing organizational arrangements and socio-cultural resources.

For van Raay's scheme the planner should be ready to make full use of regional potentials to address changing needs. In developing countries the sub-national planning approach should provide for, inter alia, eight things:

i) a long-term perspective plan providing the contours of direction;

ii) a modest time-horizon for the actual planning effort to fructify into implementation;

iii) active participation of the local populace for whom planning is undertaken, in both the preparation and implementation of the plans;

iv) recognition that resources (both human and financial) are scarce in developing countries, and therefore, only a few of the most pressing problems can be tackled at one go;

v) quick action for resolving urgent problems as reflected in short-term action programmes, having due regard for recurring expenditure and maintenance requirements;

vi) because the scope for the application of sophisticated and quantitative measurements is limited, heavy dependence on common sense, intuition, imagination and popular participation;

vii) due allowance for the likelihood of serious errors creeping in explanations and recommendations; and

viii) need for continuous evaluation, monitoring and corrective action on an on-going basis.

The P4-approach attempts at putting into motion a rolling planning process, starting with the early identification of an initial focus based on a first encounter with immediate problems, potentials, and possible long-term needs, to be followed by a gradual expansion of the sphere of activity and intervention with progressive attention to the long-term perspective. The aim of sub-national planning can be conceived of as the rational and efficient allocation of scarce resources over time and space, for achieving ends in the broad field of economic growth, social justice, environmental quality and spatial organization. Therefore, a continuous prospective process of comprehensive analytical orientation and selective action is obviously one of the methodological choices for engaging in sub-national planning attempting at the promotion of integrated rural development.

There are four main components around which the outlined approach of this interactive and mutually reinforcing process is structured, namely, "policy environment" (p3), "problems and potentialities" (p2), "priority clusters" (p1) and "project complexes" (p4). The basic understanding, recommendations, action-evaluation and future perspectives are treated as synchronic and equally important elements of a flexible process of learning, intervention and adaptation. Initially, a method is offered for facilitating comprehensive analysis of the pertinent policy areas and strategic choices (P1) and then shown how regional and rural issues and problems can be structured in a five to five matrix (P2) focussing on:

a) growth, number, density, age, sex composition and activity structure, of population;

b) macro-organizational arrangements, such as relative position of socio-political power of various power-status-structure;

c) the socio-cultural environment including the social and psycho-cultural attributes of the population and of the prevailing production systems and technological means and practices, and

d) the natural and physical environment.

Priority setting (P3), commences with a "recommended reconnaissance survey". A method for quickly selecting feasible priority-areas for regional rural planning is provided, where control, urgency, financial burden, manpower burden, recurrent commitment, spatial demand, time lag and coherence are the criteria applied in selecting the feasible priority areas. Similarly for the nature and contents of action programme (P4) projects considered most critical to the stated objectives are listed and subsequently clustered by timeframe, space and requirements.

van Raay (1982), and van Raay & Hilhorst, (1981) depict cases of applications of P4 approach apart from those mentioned in the select bibliography on Regional Plans. The P4-approach has a clear identity vis-a-vis the so-called 'pure-action oriented' or reduced planning approaches and it insists on examination of both the original reference points and initiated actions regularly, against the backdrop of the overall context, whereby ensuring that the principle of purely temporary sub-ordination of certain priority areas vis-a-vis others remains valid. With the flux of time, functional micro-regions tend to come about characterized by both a rural and urban component. van Raay is of the view that these functional micro-regions are the basic building blocks of the larger social-spatial system, and constitute the intermediate level at which rural developmental planning at the sub-national level can be meaningfully applied. The distinct identity of rural developmental planning at the sub-national level is determined jointly by the two opposing yet complementary forces of spatial structuring are dealt with in analysis for the intervention.

In sub-regional planning terms, an urgent need exists for a dual perspective, i.e. community and micro-regions. Self-reliance, resource-orientation, and self-control are all imperative for survival of the community, but any scheme for improving the lot of the rural poor cannot be separated from the changing values and norms of society in which they are born, bred, live and die. The community and its associated territory can normally no longer be the exclusive sphere of life in a modernizing rural society and hence an integrated micro-approach to rural development should be designed to serve several communities concurrently and to take account of the inter-relationships and complementarities in an area that is progressively organized as a functional unit. This functional unit or minimal basic building block is called the micro-region which is an integrated whole, for the purpose of development planning at the sub-national level, encompassing a population base of about 25,000 to 50,000 people with a preference for 50,000 as the sets of services and provisions that can be considered critical for the attainment of self-reliance and viability is for anything between 5,000 to 10,000 families. And development should be planned in terms of the micro -regions as a whole, so that several rural centres and their hinterlands are looked after concurrently, this will also eliminate the possibility of arbitrary project planning (van Raay,1984).

Selective Spatial Closure

Stohr and Todtling (1978) developed the concept of selective spatial closure but they neither advocated the closer integration of localities and regions into the national and world economy, nor local, regional or national autarky. Stohr and Todtling based their argument not on the mere dependent position of poor countries within the world economy, but on an evaluation of regional policies in both developing and developed countries (Stohr & Todtling, 1977). The world-wide trend towards centralization was found to have intensified the "backwash effects" (economic, social, cultural and political) but on specific regional communities. The foundation of Selective Spatial Closure has deep roots into neo-populist notions of development, incorporating the neo-populists concern for the ill-effects of centralization and large-scale organization (Gore, 1984).

Selective Spatial Closure is taken as synonymous with "selective self-reliance and endogenous regional development", which requires the territorial communities to moblize to their fullest extent the "internal resources and endogenous development potential in economic, socio-cultural, environmental and political terms" (Stohr, 1984), but the execution of Selective Spatial Closure concept as a regional planning approach for rural development will be neither easy nor straight forward, as is manifest from Stohr's own summary of a plethora of political, social, cultural, and economic and ecological preconditions, and constraints, ranging from a decentralized power structure and provision of broad access to scarce resources through the promotion of a broad autochthonous intellectual elite and their integration into the regional society, to self-regulating mechanism and restriction of 'territorial expansionist tendencies', to which Selective Spatial Closure approach is subject to.

This approach does not commend itself unquestioningly in that what are taken as pre-conditions and constraints are in fact the common range of objectives which the sub-national planning exercise sets out to achieve and therefore, if such preconditions were fulfilled before planning for rural development starts, such an exercise would be unnecessary or the entire gamut of rural development would have to adopt a different perspective. There is no assessment of the feasibility or the desirable preconditions and the empirical foundation on which the Selective Spatial Closure in grounded is extremely narrow.

These concepts and ideas were, however, contributory factors in initiating a paradigm shift in sub-national planning which was the foundation of the so-called "Agropolitan District Approach" of Friedmann, Weaver and Douglass, stated in the late seventies. Since these proposals, at least in part, warrant considerable changes in institutional and, power-status-structures, and new alliances of social and territorial groups, "they may broadly be considered as medium or long-term alternatives to existing policies" (Stohr 1983), which also, by and large holds true for the Selective Spatial Closure Approach of which Stohr is a great proponent.

The Agropolitan District Approach

Friedman & Douglass (1978), Suggested the Agropolitan District Approach as their translation into operational language of a stragety of rapid rural development. Gore (1984) deals with this Agropolitan District Approach to planning for rural development admirably. "The formation of small politically empowered urban-agrarian-districts, which should solve the impending crisis of development and the designing of development processes, which respond to local needs" (Douglass, 1981) is at the base of the Agropolitan District Approach, which is built on the conviction that rural development is possible "empowering regions with the means of controlling institutional arrangements and ownership patterns internally and bargaining externally for allocation of national resources" on an equal footing with metropolitan and other regions (Douglass, 1981).

There are more than one version of the Agropolitan District Approach. Its initial version involved the creation of local government units, network within a country: the agropolitan districts, which requires, inter-alia:

(i) a devolution of power and change in "federal" taxation arrangements,

(ii) land reforms, and

(iii) the commitment of the government at the Centre to support locally initiated developments with financial, material and technical resources.

Agropolitan districts were conceived of as rural areas with densities of a minimum of 200 per km., and a town of between 10,000 to 25,000 inhabitants would generally be located within the district, where district boundaries would be defined by a commuting radius of between five to ten kilometers. These would imply that an Agropolitan District would have an overall size of population ranging from 50,000 to 150,000, a majority of whom would be initially engaged in the agricultural sector (Friedmann & Douglass, 1978).

In geographic area, the Agropolitan District would be roughly the Community Development Blocks in India or the Asstt. Government Agency Divisions in Sri Lanka and Uppa Zilla Parishad in Bangladesh. What is refreshing in this approach is the emphasis on effective political power and self-government, implying that identification with so-called field administration units must be avoided (Friedmann, 1981). Friedmann and Douglass, not unlike Johnson, argue that the development efforts of agropolitan districts would involve social facilities, infrastructure, agricultual improvements and light labour-intensive industry.

Originally the agropolitan development strategy was thought of as being particularly suitable for developing countries of Asia because it was specifically designed in the context of areas with less than 20 percent urbanization, with more than 200 people per square kilometer, rising rural population density patterns, having a settlement pattern of clustered villages and towns, and conditions of extreme poverty. Subsequently it was transformed from "the spatial correlate of a strategy of accelerated rural development" to "a basic-needs strategy of territorial development", which involved changes that bring into sharp focus the shift in thinking from functional to territorial regional planning (Friedmann and Weaver (1979).

The Agropolitan District is still defined as a unit of local government, where development programmes will be formulated and implemented, but the stress is now on the district boundaries as being co-terminous with a local community or interest, or a 'primordial unit of territorial integration', (Friedmann and Weaver 1979) with Agropolitan Districts as the smallest territorial units capable of providing the basic needs of their inhabitants with virtually no important resource transfers from outside.

The expansion of production within the agropolitan district, should follow the principles of self-reliant development, with the aim of creating a diversified local economy, so that local demands are answered from local production to the maximum extent possible and developments should be self-financed by local territorial communities as far as practicable, which implies that mobilization of local natural resources, without disturbing the ecosystem and reliance on local knowledge, must be emphasized.

The concept elaborated by Stohr (1984) resembles initial formulation of Agropolitan District Development, which relies on transactive planning and not on mathematical and econometric techniques. Interpersonal dialogue, marked by mutual learning (Friedmann, 1973) is the strategy for formulation of policies and implementation of action programme.

Skeptics argue that Agropolitan District thinking reinforces false consciousness by concealing real class interests under the veil of an ideology of community. It is also argued that village and regional elites are invested with strong vested interests, making it unlikely that the interest of weaker sections in society or the region will be adequately looked after. Implicitly, protagonists of Agropolitan District Planning are depicted as being overly optimistic in assuming that agropolitan districts would break through priomordial power status structures and associated interests (Friedmann, 1981), and new organisational structures would emerge.

Individual interests and territorial interests need not obviously be co-terminous, and development in the aggregate sense will not benefit each individual equally, as a consequence of which emphasis on the pursuit of greater social equity in sub-national planning is unattainable by the Agropolitan District Planning approaches. It is, nonetheless, a logically necessary condition for the application of the approach.

It needs to be added also that it is unrealistic to plan to eradicate the existing metropoles in developing countries. The necessity of projects of national significance, of small-scale projects, basic-needs oriented projects within the agropolitan districts has to be recognized. There will be national investments in industries which can complement the development programmes formulated and implemented within the agropolitan districts. Thus alongwith the cellular economy of the districts there will be an urban-based corporate economy (Friedmann and Weaver 1979) and the industries within this "parallel economy", should develop "backward and forward linkages with the thousands of small industries in agropolitan localities", and not set up as competitors to agropolitan industries. It has even been argued that the agropolitan development programme "would be complemented with a policy of selective basic materials" (Friedmann and Douglass 1978) whereby implying that this encourages planned "industrial dualism" with small-scale, technologically appropriate, labour-intensive agropolitan industries co-existing with technologically advanced, capital-intensive large-scale industries, which can achieve agglomeration economies and are thus best located in close proximity to one another, forming industrial complexes or growth poles. But the agropolitan industries, however, have to be protected from competition generated by larger, technologically advanced industries. Such poles therefore, would have to be regional enclave economies at major ports or in other suitable locations and need not necessarily be spatially integrated with agropolitan development.

The co-existence of the parallel economy and an agropolitan development strategy raises additional theoretical questions of basic question is how basic and intermediate industries and projects of national significance will be financed and operated when one of the objectives of the strategy is to avoid increasing dependence on the outside world, which is left unexplained by the protagonists of this approach. The formulation of agropolitan development strategy is weakest at precisely the point where neo-populist development theory requires the most careful argument (Gore, 1983).

Select Bibliography

Approaches Relevant To Decentralised Planning With Special Reference To Local District Planning

Abt, Y.:
"Types of Agricultural Projects Used in Developing Countries"
in Weitz, R. (ed.):
Rural Development in a Changing World
(Cambridge, Mass: MIT Press) 1971.

Appabiajie, J. and Safier, M.:
"Growth-Centre Strategies in Less Developed Countries",
in Gilbert, A. (ed.):
Development Planning and Spatial Structure
(Chichester: John Wiley) 1978.

Aradeon, D.; Tomori, S. and Gandonu, A.:
"Medium and Small Size Settlement in Development Strategy, Portonovo Region"
in Bhooshan, B.S. (ed.):
Towards Alternative Settlement Strategies, the Role of Small and Intermediate Centres in the Development Process
(New Delhi: Heritage Publishers) 1980.

Arnon, I.:
Modernization of Agriculture in Developing Countries: Resources, Potentials and Problems
(Chichester: John Wiley) 1981.

Acklebesove, M.; Anderson, A.K. and Smickers, Folke:
Regional Development Modelling: Theory and Practice,
(Amsterdam: North Holland Publishing Co.) 1982.

Belshaw, D.G.R.:
"Rural development Planning: Concepts and Techniques",
Journal of Agriculture Economics, Vol. 28, 1977.

Belshaw, D.G.R. and Chambers, R.:
"A Management Systems Approach to Rural Development", Discussion Paper, No. 161
(Nairobi: Institute of Development Studies) 1973.

Bendavid-val, A. and Waller, P. (eds.):
Action-Oriented Approaches to Regional Development Planning (New York: Praeger) 1975.

Bhooshan, B.S. (ed.):
Towards Alternative Settlement Strategies
(New Delhi: Heritage Publishers) 1980.

Boisier, S.:
"Regional Planning : What Can We Do Before Midnight Strikes",
CEPAL Review, No. 7, April 1979.

Blackley, E.J.:
Planning Local Economic Development
(Newbury Park: Sage Publications) 1988.

Cambell, M. (ed.):
"Integrated Approach to Local Rural Development",
in Report of an Interdisciplinary Seminar Makti, Philippines, 31st March -3rd April 1975.

Cepede, M.:
"The Implementation of Rural Areas Development Programmes and Coordination Between the Different Services",
in
OECD Regional Rural Development Programme with Special Emphasis on Depressed Agricultural Areas Including Mountain Regions
(Paris: OECD) Documentation in Agriculture and Food, No. 66, 1964.

Chetwyndo, E. Jr.:
"Regional Planning to Strengthen the Contribution of Urban Centres to Development"
Development Digest, Vol. 18, No. 4, 1980.

Choe, Y.B.:
"Dynamics of Rural-Urban Relations and Rural Underdevelopment in the Republic of Korea"in
Misra, R.P. (ed.):
Rural Development: National Policies and Experiences
(Singapore: Maruzen Asia) United Nations Centre for Regional Development Series, Vol. 4, 1981.

Cloke, P.J.:
An Introduction to Rural Settlement Planning
(London: Methuen & Co.) 1983.

Damas, T. (ed.):
Integrated Rural Regional Development: a Workshop Report
(Munchen, Grunewald: Mainz and Kaiser) 1982.

Dhar, Ranjit and Rao, M. Rammohan:
The Empov Model (A Supply Model for Rapid Employment Promotion and Removal of Poverty in Developing Countries), with an Experiment in Bangalore
(Nagoya: United Nations Centre for Regional Development) UNCRD Working Paper No. 83-7, April 1983.

Douglass, M.:
"Territorial Dissolution and Alternative Regional Development for the Central Plains of Thailand",
in Stohr, W.B. and Taylor, D.R.F. (eds.):
Development from Above or Below: the Dialectics of Regional Planning in Developing Countries
(Chichester: John Wiley) 1981.

Dusseldorp, D.B.W.M., van:
Planning of Service Centres in Rural Areas of Development
(Wageningen: Agricultural University) 1971.

ESCAP:
Guidelines for Rural Centre Planning
(New York: United Nations) 1979.

Friedmann, J.:
Retracking America: A Theory of Transactive Planning
(New York: Doubleday Anchor) 1973.

Friedmann, J.:
"The Active Community: Towards a Political Territorial Framework",
Economic Development and Cultural Change, Vol. 29, 1981.

Friedmann, J. and Douglass, M.:
"The Agropolitan District Approach"
in Lo, F.C. and Salih, K. (eds.):
Growth pole Strategy and Regional Development Policy: Asian Experiences and Alternative Approaches
(Oxford: Pergamon Press) 1978.

Friedmann, J. and Weaver, C.:
Territory and Function: the Evolution of Regional Planning
(London: Pergamon Press) 1978.

Funnel, D.C. :
"The Role of Small Service-Centres in Regional and Rural Development, with Special Reference to Eastern Africa",
in Gilbert, A. (ed.):
Development Planning and Spatial Structure
(Chichester: John Wiley) 1978.

Gaitskell, A.:
"Alternative Choices in Development Strategy and Tactics: The Mekong River Project as a Case Study",
World Development, Vol. 1, No. 10, 1973.

Gilbert, A. (ed.):
Development Planning and Spatial Structure
(Chichester: John Wiley) 1978.

Gore, C.:
Regions in Question, Space, Development Theory and Regional Policy
(London: Methuen & Co.) 1984.

Government of India:
Various Reports. For details see at the end of the General Bibliography.

Higgins, B.:
"The Unified Approach to Development Planning at the Regional Level, the Case of Pahang Tenggara",
in: Kuklinski, A. (ed.):
Regional Development and Planning
(Leyden: Sijthoff) 1975.

Higgins, B.:
"Welfare Economics and Unified Approach to Development Planning",
in Kuklinski, A. (ed.):
Social Issues in Regional Policy and Regional Planning
(The Hague: Mouton) 1977.

Higgins, B.:
"Economics and Ethics in the New Approach to Development",
Philosophy in Context, Vol. 7, 1978.

Higgins, B.:
"Growth Poles: Do They Exist?",
in Kuklinski, A. (ed.):
Polarized Development and Regional Policies
(The Hague & New York: Mouton) 1981.

Higgins, B. and Savoie, D.J. :
Regional Economic Development, Essays in Honour of Francois Perroux
(Boston: Unwin Hyman) 1988.

Hajnal, A. and Kiss, I:
"Systems Approach to Planning Integrated Development",
in UNESCO: Innovative Approaches to Development Planning (Paris: UNESCO) 1988.

Hilhorst, J.G.M.:
Integrated Rural Regional Development - Another Search for the Stone of Wisdom?
(The Hague: Institute for Social Studies - Paper) undated

Janki, V.A.:
Economic Geography: Factors Influencing the Location of Economic Activity
(New Delhi: Concept Publishing Co.) 1987.

Hoselitz, B.F.:
"Rural-Urban Relationships and the Development of Rural Areas in Developing Countries"
in Weitz, R. (ed.):
Rural Development in a Changing World
(Cambridge, Mass.: MIT Press) 1971.

Johnson, E.A.J.:
The Organisation of Space in Developing Countries
(Cambridge: Harvard University Press) 1970.

Landau, Y.H. and Rokach, A.:
"Rural development in Israel"
in Weitz, R. (ed.):
Rural Development in a Changing World
(Cambridge, Mass.: MIT Press) 1971.

Lakshmanan, T.R. :
"Role of Infrastructure in Economic Transformation",
in Sundaram, K.V.; Ramesh, A. and Tiwari, P.S.:
Space Society and Development, Vol.I
(New-Delhi: Heritage Publishers) 1989.

Lea, A.M.D. and Chaudhri, A.D.P.:
Rural Development and the State: Contradictions and Dilemmas in Developing Countries
(London: Methuen & Co.) 1983.

Leupett, M.:
"Re-orientation of Objectives and Approaches to Rural Development", Land Reform, Land Settlement and Cooperatives, No. 2
(Rome: Food & Agriculture Organisation of the U.N.) 1975.

Limcaoco, J. and Andres A.:
"Integrated Area Development Approach to Regional Development",
Philippines Planning Journal, Vol. XV, No. 2, April 1984.

Lisk, F. (ed.):
Popular Participation in Planning for Basic Needs: Concepts, Methods and Practices
(Aldershot, Hampshire: Gower) 1985.

Livingstone, I.:
"On the Concept of "Integrated Rural Development Planning", in Less Developed Countries",
Journal of Agriculture Economics, Vol. 30, 1979.

Lo, F.K. and Salih, K.:
"Growth Poles, Agropolitan Development and Polarization Reversal: the Debate and Search for Alternatives"
in Stohr, W.B. and Taylor, D.R.F. (eds.):
Development from Above or Below, the Dialectics of Regional Planning in Developing Countries
(Chichester: John Wiley) 1981.

Luning, H.A.:
The Need for Regionalized Agricultural Development Planning; Experiences from Western Visayas, Philippinas
(Philippinnas: South East Asian Regional Centre for Graduate, College Laguna) 1981.

Mahadev, P.D. and Kumarah, T.V.:
"Regional Urban Systems: Operationalizing Systems Approach and Basic Needs Strategy for Development",
in Sundaram, K.V.; Ramesh A. and Tiwari, P.S. :
Regional Planning and Development, Vol II
(New-Delhi: Heritage Publishers) 1989.

Malizia, E.:
"Contingency Planning: A New Approach to Local Economic Development Planning"
(North Carolina: Department of Natural Resources and Community Development) manuscript, 1981.

Malizia, E.:
"Planning Economic Development in Small Communities and Rural Areas",
(Charlotte, North Carolina: Division of Community Assistance, North Carolina, Department of Natural Resources and Community Development) 1981.

Majid, S. and Majid, A.:
"Public Sector Land Settlement: Rural Development in West Malaysia"
in Lea, A.M.D. and Chaudhri, A.D.P. (eds.):
Rural Development and the State: Contradictions and Dilemmas in Developing Countries
(London: Methuen & Co.) 1983.

Manne, A.S.:
"DINAMICO, A Dynamic Multi Sector, Multi Skill Model",
in Goreax L.M. and Manne A.S. (eds.):
Multi-Level Planning: Case Studies in Mexico
(Amsterdam: North Holland Publishing Co.) 1973.

McLaughlin, J.B.:
Urban and Regional Planning: A Systems Approach,
(London: Faber and Faber) 1970.

Mehta, Meera:
"Service Centres for Area Planning Towards An Integrative Approach",
Indian Journal of Regional Science, Vol. XIX, No.2, 1982.

Misra, R.P.:
Block level Planning: Experiments in Local Level Planning in India, Seminar on National Development and Regional Policy
(Nagoya: United Nations Centre for Regional Development) 1979.

Misra, R.P. et. al.:
Regional Development Planning in India: A New Strategy
(New-Delhi: Vikas) 1974.

Misra, R.P. and Sundaram, K.V.:
"Area Approach to Rural Development Planning",
being chapter 5, in their
Multi-Level Planning for Integrated Rural Development in India
(New-Delhi: Heritage Publishers) 1980.

Misra, R.P. and Bhooshan, B.S.:
"Rural development: National Policies and Experiences",
Misra, R.P. (eds.):
Rural Development: National Policies and Experiences
(Singapore: Maruzen Asia) United Nations Centre for Regional Development, 1981.

Misra, R.P. and Natraj, V.K.:
"India: Blending Central and Grass-roots Planning",
in Stohr, W.B. and Taylor, D.R.F. (eds.):
Development from Above or Below, the Dialectics of Regional Planning in Developing Countries
(Chichester: John Wiley) 1981.

Misra, R.P. and Sundaram, K.V.:
Multi-Level Planning, Integrated Rural Development and District Planning and Implementation in India
(New Delhi: Heritage Publishers) 1980.

Mukherjee, Amitabha:
"Growth Centre Approach: The Need for Change in Strategy" Economic Times, 8th January 1990.

Nanjundappa, D.M.:
Area Planning and Rural Development
(New Delhi: Associated Publishing House) 1981.

OECD:
Regional Rural Development Programmes, with Special Emphasis on Depressed Agricultural Areas Including Mountain Regions
(Paris: OECD) 1964.

O'Regan, F.M. and Bendavid-Val, A.:
Public Participation in Regional Development Planning: A Strategy for Public Involvement with a Case Study of the Bicol River Basin Development Programme
(Washington D.C.: United States Agency for International Development) 1979.

O'Regan, F.M.; Walker, E.Y. and Hellinger, D. :
Public Participation in Regional Devlopment Planning: a Strategy for Popular Involvement
(Washington, D.C.: The Development Group for Alternative Policies) 1980.

Penouil, M.:
"Ivory Coast: An Adaptive Centre-Down Approach in Transition" in Stohr, W.B. and Taylor, D.R.F.:
Development from Above or Below? The Dialectics of Regional Planning in Developing Countries
(Chichester: John Wiley) 1981.

Pescatore, G.:
"The Role of Industry in the Development of Rural Areas",
in Weitz, R. (ed.):
Rural development in a Changing World
(Cambridge, Mass.: MIT Press) 1971.

Pantilla, E.B.:
"On the Functional Capability of Local Development Bodies in the Philippines",
in Misra, R.P. (ed.):
Regional Development: Essays in Honour of Masahiko Honjo (Singapore: Maruzen Asia) 1982.

Preston, Andrade:
"A Graphical Approach to Settlement Planning for Integrated Area Development",
Urban and Rural Planning Thought, July 1974.

Raay, H.G.T. van:
Regional Planning for Integrated Rural Development
(The Hague: ISSAS) 1981.

Raay, H.G.T. van:
Rural Development Planning, an Action Oriented Approach (The Hague: ISSAS) 1982.

Raay, H.G.T. van:
Integrated Development of Dedah Region, Malaysia
(The Hague: ISSAS) 1984.

Raay, H.G.T. van and Hilhorst, J.G.M.:
Land Settlement and Regional Development in the Tropics; Results, Prospects and Options
(The Hague: ISSAS) 1981.

Richardson, H.W.:
"Growth Pole Spillovers: The Dynamics of Backwash and Spread",
Regional Studies, Vol. 10, 1976.

Richardson, H.W.:
"Growth Centres, Rural Development and National Urban Policy: A Defense",
International Regional Science Review, Vol. 3, No. 2, 1978.

Richardson, H.W.:
"Policies for Strengthening Small Cities in Developing Countries" in Mathur, O.P. (ed.):
Small Cities and National Development
(Nagoya: United Nations Centre for Regional Development) 1982.

Richardson, H.W.:
"Towards a National Urban Development Strategy for Thailand" in Misra, R.P. (ed.):
Regional Development: Essays in Honour of Masahiko Honjo (Singapore: Maruzen Asia) 1982.

Rondinelli, D.A.:
"Applied Policy Analysis for Integrated Regional Development Planning in the Philippines",
Third World Planning Review, Vol. 1, No. 2, 1979.

Rondinelli, D.A.:
Secondary Cities in Developing Countries, Policy for Diffusing Urbanisation
(Beverly Hills: Sage Publications) 1983.

Rondinelli, D.A. and Ruddle, K.:
Urbanization and Rural Development: A Spatial Policy for Equitable Growth
(New York: Praeger) 1978.

Sachs, Ignacy:
Development and Planning
(Cambridge: Cambridge University Press) 1987, translated to English from original French by Peter Fawcett.

Sapru, R.K.:
Management and Planning of Rural Development,
(New-Delhi: Ashis Publishing House) 1989.

Schumer, M. :
"The Application of Social Planning Methods in Regional Palnning: South Gwembe, Zambia"
in Bendavid-Val, A. and Waller, P. (eds.):
Action-Oriented Approaches to Regional Development Planning
(New-York: Praeger) 1975.

Schneider, J.B. and Symons, J.G.:
Regional Health Facility System Planning: An Areas Opportunity Approach
(Peace Dale, Virginia: Regional Science Research Institute) Discussion Paper No. 48, July 1971.

Sen, Lalit K.:
"The Growth Centre and Its Application to Development Planning",
ASCI Journal of Management, Hyderabad, 1971a.

Sen Lalit, K.:
Planning Rural Growth Centres for Integrated Area Development,
(Hyderabad: National Institute of Community Development) 1971b.

Sen Lalit, K.:
Planning Rural Growth Centres for an Integrated Area Development: A Study in Miryalgude Taluka
(Hyderabad: National Institute of Community Development 1972a.

Sen Lalit, K.:
Integrated Area Development Concepts and Methods
(New-Delhi: Department of Personnel, Cabinet Secretariate, Government of India) 1972b.

Sharma, Prem Narain:
Project Planning for IRDP
(Integrated Rural Development Programme) (Lucknow: Print House) 1989.

Siann, J.M.:
"Conflicting Interests in River Basin Planning: A Nigerian Case Study",
in Saha, S.K. and Barrow, C.J.:
River Basin Planning, Theory and Practice
(Chichester: John Wiley) 1981.

Singh, N.N.:
"Regional Approach to Development in Nepal",
in Misra, R.P. (ed.):

Regional Development; Essays in Honour of Masahiko Honjo
(Singapore: Maruzen Asia) 1982.

Sinha, R.L.P.:
"Rural Development Approach: Its Application at Taluk Level" in Singh, L.R. (ed.): New Perspectives in Geography
(Allahabad: Thinkers Library) 1981.

Southall, A. (ed.):
Small Urban Centres in Rural Development in Africa
(Madison: University of Wisconsin) 1979.

Sundaram, K.V.:
"Experience of Area Development Planning in India: Alternative Approaches"
in Misra, R.P. (ed.):
Rural Development: National Policies and Experiences
(Singapore: Maruzen Asia)1981.

Staveren, J.M. van & van Dusseldorp, D.B.W.M. (eds):
Framework for Regional Planning in the Developing Countries
(Wageningen: ILRI) 1980.

Stohr, W.B.:
"Changing External Conditions and a Paradigm Shift in Regional Development Strategies"
(Wien: Wirtschafts Universitat) IIR-Discussion 17, 1983.

Stohr, W.B.:
Selective Self-reliance and Endogenous Regional Development Pre-conditions and Constraints,
(Wien: Wirtschafts Universitat) IIR Discussion No.19, 1984.

Stohr, W.B. and Todtling, F.:
"An Evaluation of Regional Policies - Experiences in Market and Mixed Economies",
in Hansen, N.M. (ed.)
Human Settlement Systems: International Perspectives on Structure, Change and Public Policy
(Cambridge, Mass.: Ballinger Publishers) 1977.

Stohr, W.B. and Todtling, F.:
"Spatial Equity: Some Antitheses to Current Regional Development Doctrine",
in Folmer, H. and Oosterhaven, J. (eds.):
Spatial Inequalities and Regional Development
(Leyden: Nijhoff) 1978.

Taylor, D.R.F.:
"Growth Centres and Rural Development in Africa",
in Kuklinski, A. (ed.):
Regional Development and Planning
(The Hague: Mouton & Co.) 1975.

Thomas, H. Logan, C.:
Mondragon: An Economic Analysis
(London: Allen & Unwin) 1982.

Todaro, Michael, P.:
Development Planning: Models and Methods
(Nairobi: Oxford University Press) 1971.

Todaro, Michael P.:
Economic Development in the Third World
(Delhi: Orient Longmans) 1985.

Tripathi, B.L.:
Block-level Planning; An Approach to Local Development, Seminar on National Development and Regional Policy
(Nagoya: United Nations Centre for Regional Development) 1979

UNCRD:
Project on Regional Development Documentation: An Annotated Bibliography:
Country Bibliography **Series:**
Vol. 1, Japan: **Annotated** Bibiliography **on** Regional Development,(Nagoya: UNCRD) 1976.

Vol. 2, India: Annotated Bibliography on Rural Regional Development (Nagoya: UNCRD)1978.

Vol. 3, Philippines: Annotated Bibliography on Regional Development (Nagoya: UNCRD) 1979.

Vol. 4, Sri Lanka: Annotated Bibliography on Regional Development (Nagoya: UNCRD) 1981.

Vol. 5, Pakistan: Annotated Bibliography on Local and Regional Development (Nagoya: UNCRD) 1981.

Vol. 6, Thailand: Annotated Bibliography on Local and Regional Development (Nagoya: UNCRD) 1982.

Vol. 7, Indonesia: Annotated Bibliography on Local and Regional Development (Nagoya: UNCRD) 1983.

UNESCO:
Innovative Approaches to Development Planning
(Paris: UNESCO) 1988.

Uphoff, Norman:
Approaches to Community Participation in Agriculture and Rural Development
(Ithaca: Cornell University, Rural Development Committe Review Paper) 1987.

USAID:
Urban Functions in Rural Development: An analysis of integrated development policy
(Washington: United States Agency for International Development) 1976.

USAID:
Working Paper on Regional Planning for Rural Development
(Washington: United States Agency for International Development) 1976.

USAID:
Bicol River Basin Urban Functions in Rural Development Project: Summary and Evaluation
(Washington: United States Agency for International Development) 1978.

Vicinelli, P.:
"Rural Areas Development Programme in Italy",
in OECD:
Regional Rural Development Programmes with Special Emphasis on Depressed Agricultural Areas including Mountain Regions
(Paris: OECD) 1964.

Waller, P.:
"The Application of a Reduced Planning Approach: South Madagascar",
in Bendavid-Val, A. and Waller, P.:
Action Oriented Approaches to Regional Development Planning (New-York: Praeger) 1975.

Vatt, S.B.:
"Peripheral Problems in the Senegal Valley",
in Saha, S.K. and Barrow, C.J. (eds.):
River Basin Planning, Theory and Practice
(Chichester: John Wiley) 1981.

Weiss, D.:
"Socio-Economic Analysis and Identification of a Priority Project in the Kosi-Region, Nepal"
in Bendavid- Val, A. and Waller, P. (eds.):
Action oriented Approaches to Regional Development Planning
(New-York: Praeger) 1975.

Weitz, R.:
From Peasant to Farmer; A Revolutionary Strategy for Development
(New York: Columbia University Press) 1971.

Weitz, R.:
"Regional Planning for Rural Development in Developing Countries" in Weitz, R. (ed.): Rural Development in a Changing World (Cambridge, Mass.: MIT Press) 1971.

Weitz, R.:
Integrated Rural Development: The Rehovot Approach
(Rehovot: Settlement Study Centre) Publications on Problems of Regional Development No. 28, 1979.

Weitz, R. and Rokach, A.:
Agricultural Development Planning and Implementation
(Dordrecht, Holland: Reidel Publishing Co.) 1968.

Weitz, R.; Peley, D. and Applebaum, L.:
" A Model for the Planning of New Settlement Projects",
World Development, Vol. 8, No. 9, 1980.

William, Thomas (ed.):
Keys to Rural Community Development: The 1890 Land Grant Universities Approach",
in Proceedings of the Forty Fifth Annual Professional Agricultural Workers Conference, 1987 (Alabama: Tuskegee Institute Alabama) 1988.

Wood, Harold A.:
"Regional Planning and Rural Development in Latin America"
in Kuklinski, A. (ed.):
Regional Development and Planning
(Leyden: Sijthoff) 1975.

Ziolhowski, J.A.:
"The Integrated Social Science Approach to Regional Planning in the Developing Countries",
in Kuklinski, A. (ed.):
Social Issues in Regional Policy and Regional Planning
(The Hague: Mouton & Co.) 1977.

CHAPTER VII

STRATEGIES RELEVANT FOR DECENTRALISED PLANNING WITH SPECIAL REFERENCE TO LOCAL DISTRICT PLANNING

Regional Planning Orientation

The regional disaggregation of national strategies, policies and plans have been in existence for a long time and to that extent a regional planning of sorts at the national level can be said to have also existed for a long time, which has helped in maximising sub-national contributions to national economic growth; which has helped in defining the role that each sub-national region should play in achieving specific national targets and goals; and which has been of great use in defining an optimal framework wherein to fit the interregional allocation of investments for development.

Cases of significant regional intervention where activities are entirely dependent on objectives, initiatives and decision-making powers at the national level are not infrequent. When a central government decides to make its presence felt in a particular region, or when it decides that a regional problem is sufficiently acute to force central government's intervention, but which being inter-state or inter-province in character cannot be dealt with at provincial level or state level, or when the central government is tempted to take advantage of the resource potentials of a region, etc., it resorts to sub-national planning.

The "river basin" approach to regional planning is a typical example in point. First applied by the Tenesse Valley Authority by the United States (Moore 1967) in the 30's, it found adherents all over the world; for instance, in Ghana (Volta River), in India (Damodar Valley), in Chile (the Bio-bio region), and in Brazil (the Northeast) were all inspired and framed in line with the pioneering work done by the Tenesse Valley Authority. These sub-national plans were started as national activities with profound regional impacts, with the expectation that eventually a more autonomous process of regional development and planning would come about following a first effort towards "deconcentration", but experience has shown that this has been achieved only in part. Hansen & Perloff (1942); Robock (1963); Moore, ed. (1967); Owen (1973); Gilbert et. al. (1976); Ayeni (1976); Friedmann & Weaver (1979) and Misra et. al. (1977) could be read with profit.

Regional policy formulation and strategy-building subsequently was imparted an interregional perspective which in several respects meant a response to actually felt interregional inequalities in income and disparity in distribution of wealth. Concepts, theories and policies revolving around import substitution and 'development from inside', created an adequate political and social climate (Gilbert, 1974) to question the policies focussing entirely towards economic growth. This led to the adoption of strategies increasingly aimed at regional redistribution and economic decentralization (Boisier, 1981b) and hence the emerging strategies had the dual orientation, of favouring both intra-regional and inter-regional vertical and horizontal integration. Vertical or functional integration was attempted at through the mobilization and articulation of the region's comparative advantages, which has increasingly been combined with institutional changes to make room for decentralized decision-making, with active people's participation. Studies and assessment of such experiences make valuable reading given their impact on the reorientation of regional planning thinking generally though they may be country specific studies, (Gilbert, 1974). Sub-national development planning has gained greatly from the benefits of the decentralization of the planning function, and sub-regional development planning has been professionalized quickly (Boisier, 1981b). Highly sophisticated techniques and models were sometimes applied to help maximize growth, minimize social costs and reduce political tensions (Richardson 1988). Occasions when decisions were based on the application of mathematical models aiming at harmonizing the sectoral or regional or sub-national allocation of financial resources with a quantified set of national goals are not rare. A reading of Carrillo-Arronte (1970); Boisier (1975); Waardenburg (1975), Bloomstein (1983) and Chatterjee (1983) would be quite rewarding.

Stohr (1975); Stohr & Todling (1978); Friedmann (1973); and Hilhorst (1981), represent the other variety where detailed regional or sub-national economies' reviews and appraisals were undertaken, leading to the formulation of sub-national policy by central planners or by centrally controlled sub-national planners, which has often been considered a more realistic approach as it allows diagnosis of the major problems faced by a region and permits need based investments to be made by the central governments. This evolution of planning style and practice has received a good deal of attention on account of its relevance for regional strategy formulation and policy making generally.

A whole range of strategies and applications have been generated by the regional dimension of polarization reversal thinking. Galtung (1978) in an interesting paper poses the question of what is a strategy and then answers it. Many countries who have resorted to sub-national regional development planning have contemplated, have initiated, or are presently engaged in polarization reversal strategy of sorts. Industrialization, crises in rural areas, etc. have forced many developing countries to suffer the pangs of extremely rapid urbanization rates with all its complex problems.. Megapolises and metropolises have grown rapidly, abeting the process of a highly concentrated and much more imbalanced spatial pattern of growth and population distribution, than would be desirable, while the rural towns have had no such comparable expansion.

The concept of growth pole is an important element in all polarization reversal strategies. Induced and shaped by macro decision and allocations, development poles were assumed to have the potential of mobilizing regional resources and entrepreneurial capabilities, and forward and backward linkages were supposed to evolve, setting in motion a spiral of regional economic development. With flux of time, growth poles were expected to turn into 'poles d'equilibre', counter-balancing their earlier pull in so far as locational alternatives would be offered to new industrial and service undertakings.

The expected deconcentration is many cases were found not up to the expected mark, possibly because the growth pole was conceived of as exclusively being one single urban or industrial node that was capable of pushing industrial and service activities in particular. The growth pole growth-centre doctrine has, therefore, been extended and is progressively associated with the urban settlement system as a whole. Granted that any region, and the urban centres within it, are confronted with problems but at once have potentials of their own, the focus of applications of growth pole-growth centre thinking has been shifted to assigning roles and functions to each urban centre over and above certain population or economic activity thresholds. Thus the urban contribution to polarization reversal is progressively cast in terms of national and regional settlement policy and planning. On the foundation of hierarchical structure of central places within a region, this interpretation is of consequence to multilevel decentralised planning framework. Out of the staggering amount of literature covering polarization reversal and growth centre-growth pole strategies, it is difficult to select a few. The most important references are Darwent (1969); Baeyens (1977); Friedman and Douglass (1978); O'Regan and Bendavid-val (1979); Baeyens and Dolman (1981); Boisier (1980, 1981a); Conyers (1981); Hilhorst (1981, 1985); Lo & Salih (1981); Lundquist (1981); Mabogunje

(1981); Richardson (1978, 1980, 1982); Stohr (1981); Stohr & Taylor (1981); Taylor (1981); and Tendler (1981); Rondinelli (1983); Riddell (1985), and Perroux (1988), Polenske (1988) and Higgins and Savoie (1988).

Any discussion on the evolution of regional policy orientation, must pay attention to the intra-regional dimension that is at the heart of regional development policy and philosophy, particularly the rural sector. Many reasons can be assigned for the failure of the macro policies and strategies, including inter-regional ones, to produce the anticipated results, in terms of development of the rural sector, which includes inadequate planning and inadequate monitoring and co-ordination of sub-national planning. The state of the art in the field of regional planning still leaves much to be desired.

The new approaches to development significantly enough has brought the micro-regional level into sharp focuss in contra-distinction to earlier macro- level approach. The new interest in the micro-regional perspective is not exclusively on account of the failure or incompleteness of macro prescriptions, because over two decades back an intra-regional perspective was viewed as a logical spatial extension to the sphere of local urban planning (Hermansen, 1969) in an effort to incorporate the rural and/or suburban hinterland into the folds of planning process. Additionally, some regional development corporations, endowed with special funds and ad-hoc legal charters, have been effective in dealing with depressed micro-regions. Stohr (1975) discusses the Cauca Valley Development Corporation (CVC), and others in Columbia; the Superintendencias for the Amazon Region and the North East in Brazil; the Junta de Adelanto de Africa and the Corporation for the Development of Magallanes in Chile; CONZUPLAN in Zulia, Venezuela; The Development Corporation of Guyana; The Chittagong Hill Tracts Development Board in Bangladesh, (Ali, 1981); and the Regional Development Authorities of Malaysia (Mat, 1981) are also examples in point.

Three Clusters of Strategic Choices

Development of backward areas aims at making rural society economically less vulnerable, the agricultural system more productive and the people better off. While during the fifties the most typical agricultural objectives were dominant employment creation as (we have seen) was the case with the community development blocks in India. Reduction of income disparities were progressively emphasized in subsequent years. Rural development was defined as a strategy for improving the economic and social life of the rural poor: small farmers, tenants and the landless (World Bank 1975). It was also believed that rural development entailed an improvement of the living standards of the mass of the low-income population residing in rural areas through a self-sustaining process (Lele 1975), and the objective of all planning would be to bring the mass of people below the poverty line, to lives where minimum requirements were at least met (Government of India 1989).

Thus, in the seventies, the satisfaction of basic needs had become a critical issue, emphasising both standard of living and quality of life as being dependent on levels of agricultural production, on employment diversification, on improvements in the field of health and education, on active participation in the development process etc. (Arnon 1981). Spatial dimension to this was added by Mabogujhe (1980), enjoning that a broad-based reorganization and mobilization of the rural masses should go together with a transformation of the socio-political structures of productive activities. In terms of their relevance to rural development planning at sub-national level, three distinct clusters of strategic choices have been distinguished:

(a) the technocratic cluster;

(b) the radical cluster; and

(c) the reformist cluster.

Griffin (1973); Stavenhagen (1975); Arnon (1981); and Lea and Chaudhri (1983), make it abundantly clear that different emphases might be applied within these strategic clusters, while at the same time different, even contradictory, planning approaches may be adopted. Moreover, the policy environment in most countries is likely to change profoundly over time which might warrant switching, swapping or combining of strategies. Though admittedly, the distinction of only three strategic clusters is an over-simplication, yet it does help in bringing out pertinent differences that are of material consequence in the context of sub-national planning for economic development of rural and backward areas. The differences so delineated emphasise the fact that no single development strategy, particularly so far rural development can be relevant to a whole range of problems, contexts and policy environments, and they require substantive innovation, adaptation and modification.

The Technocratic Cluster

Technocratic cluster of strategies assumes that rural development can be achieved by introducing technological change, and often on the the conviction that such technological changes can be introduced without simultaneously tampering with the structure of rural society and often without taking cognizance of the existing power status-structure, customs and culture, traditional land tenure arrangements, and the like. Field applications were predominantly micro-level in nature and based on decision - making models of agrarian change. Bunting, ed. (1970); Hayami & Ruttan (1971), Stevens, ed. (1977), and Binswanger and Ruttan (1978) all belong to this genre.

The principal objective of technocratic cluster is to increase agricultural output through technological improvements, the operation of free market forces, competition, and private property rights. This strategy has also been denoted as the "crash-modernization strategy" or the "spearhead" approach, which appellations suggest that technocratic clusters' experts are of the opinion that trickle - down effects would occur, eventually extending the benefits to all.

Advocates of the technocratic strategies call for a "big push" or transformation of rural society, as does the radical school although in a different fashion. In so far as the radicals favour a complete restructuring of the space economy by state intervention, technocrats emphasise efficiency and place a low degree of reliance on public intervention in free market forces. The three strategies have been aptly rechristened as the "low intervention-productivity" model, the "medium intervention-solidarity" model, and the "high intervention-equality" model (Inayatulla 1979). Clayton (1983), one of the most outspoken exponents of the "low intervention-productivity" model, attacks the redistributive and basic needs ideologies, and attempts at the establishment and rehabilitation of a technocratic approach, that is usually discarded in development literature as being a premature and largely ineffective attempt to achieve rural economic development.

The Radical Cluster

Radical strategies grounded in Marxist ideology emphasise social ownership and control of the means of production, rejecting gradualism, so that traditional forms do not reassert themselves (Mabogunje, 1980). Implicitly, the radical critiques reject the so-called modernization strategies of national governments and aid organizations, for these are at best capable of producing only marginal changes in rural power structure, the main beneficiaries being the big and medium landowners, while the smaller peasants are affected negatively. Judith Meyer, et. al. (1981) argue that modernization strategies tend to ascribe the failure of most rural development programmes to such factors as rural environments, to the resource base, to population to land ratios, and to the delivery system, thus detracting attention from the real cause, namely, the conflicting interests of the poor and those who control them. Howard (1978), Ghose and Griffin (1980); Sen (1981); Payer (1982); Saith (1982); Bello, et. al. (1982) and Hart (1983) and Sharma (1989) are critical about modernisation strategies.

Countries which have applied radical strategies to rural development include Russia, Vietnam and China. In view of its alleged achievements, the Chinese model of rural development evinced a good deal of interest in the West. Elvin (1973); Gray (1973); Blair (1976) and Aziz (1978) are examples in point. But the recent events in the Chinese political scenario has cast a spell of shadow upon the efficacy of the Chinese model of economic development. We have to wait before passing the final judgment.

Tanzania has received a good deal of attention and admiration for her philosophy of rural socialism and self-reliance derived from the belief that the traditional African extended family is an indigenous form of socialism, which unique social and cultural heritage provided a framework for development along socialist lines (Nyerere, 1967 and Connell 1977). As food production and industrial investments have stagnated, and dependence on the state and on foreign aid have increased, the Tanzanian model has been bitterly criticised. The bibliography on Ujamaa by Mellenry (1981) and Hyden (1980), shows that the Tanzania experiment has been extensively documented. Chung et. al. (1985) is an excellent study of comparison between the Chinese and Tanzanian rural development story. It is worth reading.

The Reformist Cluster

The reformist cluster includes a group of strategic choices which is a mid course between the technocratic and radical clusters, and could be called progressive modernization strategies, and a majority of rural development policy makers and practitioners employed by governments and international organizations are adherents of these modernization strategies. Johnston & Kilby (1975), advocated a uni-model approach and so focussed exclusively on small holders. Morse, et. al., ed. (1976) followed suit. Lipton (1977) introduced his analysis of the urban bias and Lele (1975) emphasised a broad-based minimal package of servies and institutional developments. Hunter, ed. (1978) spelled out guidelines for action. Harvey et. al. (1979) drew attention to the inter-relationships that existed between institutional structure, technological innovations, scale, redistribution and employment. Chambers (1983) is an important contribution. Ruttan, (1975) dealt with question of whether redistribution of income and wealth will lead to shared poverty, and whether welfare is more a function of output level than of distribution question with equity. The 18th Conference of Agricultural Economists (1983) and Hayami & Kikuchi (1982) are interesting readings in this area.

The group of intermediate strategies between the technocratic and radical strategies includes Integrated Rural Development Programme. Despite universal usage, there is no general definition for Integrated Rural Development Programme which has been agreed upon, and skeptics even argue that the word 'integrated' was largely superfluous, although the phrase Integrated Rural Development was coined in the belief that development planning directed towards a single goal, discipline or segment of the economy was not likely to bring forth the desired alleviation of poverty and the required economic development of the region, which is why Integrated Rural Development is multisectoral, multilevel and multi-dimensional approach, atleast theoretically, concerned with both social and economic objectives on a low key. It, theoretically atleast, identifies the beneficiaries and seeks to involve target group(s) and to secure political sanction for the developmental and planning process. The principles and nature of integrated rural development has been documented extensively, by at least: Kotter (1974); Leupolt (1975), Ruttan (1975), Waterstone (1975), UNAPDI (1975), Hunter et. al. (1976), Anker (1977), Hunter (1978), Bouguslavski (1979) Livingston (1979); Morse & Gow (1981) and Desai (1988). Johnston & Klard (1982) significantly distinguished between three integrated rural development sub-programmes: the production programme, the consumption programme, and the organization programme. Whereas production programmes focussed attention on agricultural production and the transformation of crops and natural resources through agro-industry; consumption programmes focussed on elementary services to satisfy minimum needs of the rural population and providing rural employment; organization programmes were mostly concerned with organization of beneficiaries and their participation in planned development projects. ILO (1976); Ghai et. al. (1977); Schwefel (1978); German Development Institute (1980); Beg et. al. (1980); Leipziger, (1981) and Epstein et. al.; (1983); Lest (1962), Belshaw and Chambers (1973); Chambers (1974); FAO (1978); Schneider (1978); O'Regan and Bendavid-Val (1979); Bryant and White (1980); Lassen (1980); Smith (1980); Dusseldorp (1980) and Korten and Uphoff (1981), all deal with organization programmes.

Integrated Rural Development and Development Planning at the Sub-National Level/Local Level

The integrated rural development so far did not consider spatial aspect of the problem implying that no allowance has been made for the urban and rural fields at several levels, like communities, districts, micro-regions and provinces. It is curious that authors like Hunter (1978) UNAPDI (1980) and Johnston and Clark (1982) seemingly ignored the spatial dimension. Others provided only a fleeting mention of the need for a regional planning level, but fail to come up with an operational scheme. The World Bank (1975) states that the planning and implementation of integrated rural development should ideally involve adequate regional planning, strong central coordination, and effective local level participation. Regional planning is desirable both because rural development cuts across all sectors and because rural programmes need to be framed to meet regional conditions. Lea and Chaudhri (1983), held that the word "integrated" implied that planning had to take place in defined areas, but at several different scales, "varying from local communities, administrative districts or geographically defined regions, such as a river basin...." Leupolt (1975) pointing out that integrated rural development has regional, social and sectoral dimensions, emphasizes the needs for an area systems level and a regional level of coordination. Arnon (1981) argued that the micro-planning at village and farm levels and macro-planning at regional and national levels must be a harmonious whole, particularly so because of the interdependence of agriculture and other sectors. Sundaram, K.V. (1989) has made this harmonization inherent in the prinicples of decentralised planning that he discusses. Schickele (1971); Yitzhask; Pescatore and Weitz in Weitz, ed. (1971), and Howes (1974) deal with the issues competently and at length.

To Belshaw (1977) the potential value of rural development planning lay in improving the problem-solving capacity of regional and rural planning. The integration of urban development is considered essential for any course of action for both rural and regional development and requires intimate understanding of area-specific conditions and problems which are both spatial and non-spatial in nature (Bouguslavski, 1979).

Land Tenure and Land Settlement

In the face of pressure upon resources, common strategic choices have been to either intensify production within the existing agrarian structure or to bring forward structural changes (e.g. land reform) and additionally or alternatively increase agricultural land. Land reforms are often partial, fragmented, incomplete and concentrated in certain areas to the exclusion of others, in most underdeveloped countries, including India. Practical action can be hampered because political power is applied to block implementation by vested interests operating in society. Baraclough (1973), Kuitenbrouwer (1973), Walinsky, ed. (1977),, and Griffin (1981) deal with these issues. The Indian scenario is well documented in Khusro (1973) Joshi (1975) and Eashvaraiah (1985). Eashvariah (1985) and Gupta (1986) amongst others deal with the dynamics of political economy of land reforms in India.

Van Raay and Hilhorst (1981) is a summary of the results of and options for land settlement in the humid tropics. They stressed the absence of integration within overall regional and rural development planning efforts in several of the countries in their zone of study. Integrated rural development and regional rural development planning have largely remained abstract aspirations, and have suggested no ways to translate aspirations into concrete and manageable field approaches. The document of van Raay and Hilhorst (1981) contains an impressive list of more than one hundered relevant publications, including Farmer (1957); Chambers (1969); Nelson (1973); Katzman (1978); Klempin (1979); McAntews (1979); and Hardjono (1979).

Participation Development Approach

In the context of economic development people's participation in development process in very important : people's participation is at the heart of decentralised planning at lower levels of planning. As a matter of fact Swaminathan (1989) maintains that participatory development was central to human culture of the past. Chopra, Kadekodi and Murty (1990) deals with participatory development for development of common property rights.

Bhaduri and Rahman (1982) made a very incisive study of participation of the rural masses in the process of development. Peoples participation in various regional planning has been documented extensively. Dhuvanarayan et. al. (1986) examined the issues pertaining to people's participation in watershed management and Singh (1986) talks about resource management through peoples participation. Esman (1987) concerns himself with social development. Gow and Van Sant (1983) and Graaff (1984) address themselves to larger issues of people's participation in the development process as an approach to cause development. Hirchman (1984) documents the success of participatory planning in the Latin American countries, and Korten (1985) deals with Asian experience in community management. Richardson (1983) talks about the impact and efficacy of particaption in development. Cernea (1985, 1987) could be read with interest particularly for the sociological dimensions of the problem.

Select Bibliography

Strategies Relevant For Decentralised Planning

Allen, K. and Maclennan, M.C.:
Regional Problems and Policy in Italy and France, (Beverly Hills: Sage Publications) 1970.

Ali, S.M.:
"Organisation for Local Development: the Case of Bangladesh",
Cheema, G.S. (ed.):
Institutional Dimensions of Regional Development, United Nations Centre for Regional Development, Regional Development Series,
Vol. 8, (Singapore: Maruzen Asia) 1981.

Anker, D.L.W.:
"Rural Development Problems and Strategies",
International Labour Review, Vol. 108, 1973.

Apthorpe, R.:
"Agriculture and Strategies: the Language of Development Policy",
in Clay, E.J. and Schaffer, B.B. (eds.):
Room for 'Manoeuvre': An Exploration of Public Policy in Agriculture and Rural development
(London: Gower Publications) 1984.

Armstrong, H. and Taylor, J.:
Regional Economic Policy and its Analysis
(Oxford: Philip Allan) 1978.

Arnon, I.:
Modernization of Agriculture in Developing Countries: Resources, Potentials and Problems
(Chichester: John Wiley) 1981.

Asian Centre for Development Administration:
Approaches to Rural Development in Asia
(Kualaumur: Asian Centre for Development Administration) 1975.

Asian Centre for Development Administration:
Strategies for Rural Development in Asia: A Dimension
(Kuala Lumpur: Asian Centre for Development Administration) 1976.

Asian Development Bank:
Rural Asia
(Singapore: Federal Publications) 1977.

Ayeni, M.A.O.:
A Regional Plan for Lagos State: Planning Lagos Metropolitan Area
(Nigeria: University of Ibadan) 1976.

Aziz, Sartaz:
Rural Development Learning from China
(London: MacMillan Press) 1978.

Baeyens, H.:
"The Sociological Failure in Regional Planning: Comment on Some Recent Publications in the Field of Sociology and Planning", in Kuklinski, A. (ed.):
Social Issues in Regional Policy and Planning
(The Hague: Mouton) 1977.

Baeyens, H. and Domain, A.:
"Design of a Development Pole in Malaysia: Planning in a Pluriethnical Society",
in Kuklinski, A. (ed.): Polarized Development and Regional Policy (The Hague: Mouton & Co.) 1981.

Baisya, K.N.:
"Rural Reconstruction Block-Level Planning",
paper read at a seminar organised by the National Institute of Small Industry Extension Training, North-East Regional Centre, Guwahati, 21st-22nd August 1986.

Bandopadhaya, D.:
"An Evaluation of Policies and Programmes for the Alleviation of Rural Poverty in India",
in Isla, R.(ed.):
Strategies for Alleviating Poverty in Rural Asia
(Geneva: ILO/ARTREP) 1985.

Barraclough, S.L.:
"Rural Development and Agrarian Reform",
in Gotsch, G. (ed.): Rural Development and Employment (Ibadan: Ford Foundation) 1973.

Beg, M.A.K.; Anwar, S.M. and Azim, M.(eds.):
Basic Needs and Rural Development
(Peshawar: Pakistan Academy of Rural Development) 1980.

Belshaw, D.G.R.:
"Rural Development Planning: Concepts and Techniques",
Journal of Agricultural Economics, Vol. 28, 1977.

Bhaduri, A. and Rahman, M.D. (eds.):
Studies in Rural Particiaption
(Delhi: Oxford and IBH Publishing Co.) 1982.

Benninger, Christopher, C.:
"New Institutional Systems for Enhanced Regional Planning and Management",
in Sundaram, K.V.; Ramesh, A. and Tiwari P.S.:
Regional Planning and Development,
Vol. II, (New Delhi: Heritage Publishers) 1989.

Bernstein, H.:
"Notes on Capital and Peasantry"
in Harriss, J. (ed.):
Rural Development: Theories of Peasant Economy and Agrarian Change
(London: Hutchinson University Library) 1982.

Bhoduria, B.P.S. and Dua, S.C.:
Rural Development Strategy and Perspective
(New-Delhi: Anmol Publishers) 1986.

Binswanger, H. and Ruttan, V.W.:
Induced Innovation: Technology, Institutions and Development
(Baltimore: John Hopkins University Press) 1978.

Blair, P.:
Development in the People's Republic of China: A Selected Bibliography
(Washington, D.C.: Overseas Development Council) 1976.

Blackley, E.J.:
Planning Local Economic Development
(Newbury Park: Sage Publications) 1988.

Bloomstein, H. and Nijkamp, P.:
"Multivariate Methods for Soft Data in Development Planning: A Case Study in Natural Resources",
in Chatterjee, M. et. al. (eds.):
Spatial Environmental and Resource Policy in Developing Countries
(Aldershot: Gower) 1983.

Bouguslavski, M. von (ed.):
Principles and Limitations of Integrated Rural Development: A Workshop Report
(Giessen:) 1979.

Boisier, S.:
"Regional Disaggregation of National Plans: Some Comments on the Rotterdam and Warsaw Models",
in Kuklinski, A. (ed.):
Regional Disaggregation of National Policies and Plans
(The Hague: Mouton & Co.) 1975.

Boisier, S.:
Growth Poles: Are They Dead? UN Latin American Institute for Economic and Social Planning
(Santiago de Chile: ILPES) 1980.

Boisier, S.:
"Continuity and Change: Variations of Centre Down Strategies Under Different Political Regimes",
in Stohr, W.B. and Taylor, D.R.F. (eds.):

Development from Above or Below? The Dialectics of Regional Planning in Developing Countries
(Chichester: John Wiley) 1981.

Brara, J.S.:
The Political Economy of Rural Development: Strategies for Poverty Alleviation
(New Delhi: Allied Publishing & Co.) 1983.

Brown, L.R.:
Seeds of Change
(New York: Praeger) 1970.

Bryant, C. and White, L.:
Managing Rural Development: Peasant Participation in Rural Development
(West Hartford: Kumarian Press) 1980.

Carrillo-Arronte, R.:
An Empirical Test for Inter-regional Planning: a Linear Programming Model for Mexico
(Rotterdam: University Press)1970.

Centre for the Study of Science Technology and Development:
Rural Development and Technology: A bibliography
(New Delhi: Centre for Study of Science and Technology Development) 1980.

Central Treaty Organization:
Seminar on Integrated Rural Development
held at Islamabad, 1975 (Ankara: Central Treaty Organisation) 1975.

Cernea, M.M. (ed.):
Putting People First: Sociological Variables in Rural Development
(New York: Oxford University Press) 1985.

Cernea, M.M. (ed.):
"Farmer Organisations and Institution Building for Sustainable Development",
Regional Development Dialogue, Vol. 8, No. 2, 1987.

Chambers, R.:
Managing Rural Development: Idea and Experiences from East Africa,
(Uppsala: The Scandinavian Institute of African Studies) 1974.

Chambers, Robert:
Two Frontiers in Rural Management: Agricultural Extension and Managing the Exploitation of Communal Natural Resources
(Brighton: University of Sussex, Institute of Development Studies) 1975.

Chambers, R.:
Rural Development: Putting the Last Thing First
(London: Longman) 1983.

Chee, S.:
"Rural Development in the Plural Society of West-Malaysia", in Inayatullah (ed.): Approaches to Rural Development: Some Asian Experiences
(Kuala Lumpur: APDAC) 1979.

Chaterjee, M. et. al. (eds.):
Spatial, Environmental and Resource Policy in Developing Countries
(Aldershot: Gower) 1983.

Cheema, G.S.:
Institutional Dimensions of Regional Development,
United Nations Centre for Rural Development, Regional Development Series, Vol. 8, (Singapore: Maurzen Asia) 1981.

Chopra, K.; Kadekodi, G.K. and Murty, M.N.:
Participatory Development: People and Common Property Resources
(New Delhi: Sage Publications) 1990.

Chung, Tong Wu; David, F.I.P. and Maeda, J.H.J.:
China and Tanzania
(New Delhi: Concept Publishing Co.) 1985, being vol. V of Misra,

R.P. (General Editor): Rural Development: Capitalist and Socialist Paths, 1985.

Clay, E.J. and Schaffer, B.B. (eds.):
Room for Manoeuvre: An exploration of Public Policy in Agriculture and Rural Development,
(London: Gower Publications) 1984.

Clayton, E.:
Agriculture, Poverty and Freedom in Developing Countries (London: McMillan) 1983.

Connell, John:
The Evolution of Tanzania Rural Development
(Brighton: University of Sussex, Institute of Development Studies) 1973.

Conyers, D.:
"Decentralization for Regional Development: A Comparative Study of Tanzania, Zambia and Papua New Guinea",
Public Administration and Development, Vol. 1, 1981.

Coraggio, J.S.:
"Polarisation, Development and Integration",
in Kuklinski, A. (ed.): Regional Development and Planning: International Perspectives (Leyden: Sijthoff) 1975.

Daniels, B. and Tilly, C.:
"Community Economic Development: Seven Guiding Principles", Resources, Vol. 11,
(Washington D.C.: Congress for Community Economic Development) 1985.

Darwent, D.F.:
"Growth Poles and Growth Centres in Regional Planning: A Review",
Environment and Planning, Vol. 1, 1969.

Desai, Vasant:
Rural Development
(Bombay: Himalaya Publishing House) 1988, Vols. I & II.

Dhar, P.N.:
"Strategy to Industrialise Rural and Backward Areas",
Kurukshetra, 1st December, 1973.

Dhruvanarayana, V.V. et. al.:
"People's Participation in Watershed Management - A Good Means",
paper read at a Seminar on Environmental Security - Watershed Management: Relevance of People's Participation, Pantnagar, June 1986.

Dusseldorp, D.B.W.M.van:
"Participation in Planned Development Influenced by Governments of Developing countries" in Essays in Rural Sociology in Honour of R.A.J. van Lier,
(Wageningen: Deptt. of Rural Sociology in the Tropics and Sub-tropics, Agricultural University) 1981.

Dutt, Ashok K.:
"The Ultimate Planning Tool and the Green Heart of Netherlands",
in Sundaram, K.V.; Ramesh, A. and Tiwari, P.S.:
Regional Planning and Development Vol. II.
(New Delhi: Heritage Publishers) 1989.

Eashvaraiah, P.:
Political Dimensions of Land Reforms in India
(New Delhi: Ashish Publishing House) 1985.

Elvin, M.:
Quantitative Growth, Qualitative Standstill: The Pattern of the Chinese Past
(Palo Alto: Stanford University Press) 1973.

Epstein, T.S.; Panini, M.W. and Srinivas, M.W.:
Basic Needs Viewed from Above and from Below: The Case of Karnataka State, India
(Paris: OECD) 1983.

ESCAP:
Poverty, Productivity and Participation: Contours of an Alternative Strategy for Poverty Eradication
(Bangkok: ESCAP) 1985.

Essman, M.J.:
"Methodologies for Planning and Managing Social Development Activities",
Regional Development Dialogue, Vol. 8, No. 2, 1987.

European Free Trade Association:
National Settlement Strategies: A Framework For Regional Development
(Geneva: European Free Trade Association Secretariate) 1974.

Evans, M:
"Policy and Change, the Asian Development Bank",
in Clay, E.J. and Schaffer, B.B. (eds.):
Room for Manoeuvre: An Exploration of Public Policy in Agriculture and Rural Development
(London: Gower) 1984.

Food and Agriculture Organisation of the United Nations:
Report of the Expert Group Meeting on Agrarian Reform and Rural Development
(Bangkok: Food and Agriculture Organization) 1978.

Food and Agriculture Organization of the United Nations:
Learning from China; A Report on Agriculture and Chinese People's Communes
(Bangkok: Food and Agriculture Organization of the United Nations, Regional Office for Asia and the Far East) 1977.

Food and Agriculture Organization of the United Nations, and Swedish International Development Agency:
Expert Consultations on Policies and Institutions for Integrated Rural Development, at Nairobi, in 1976
(Rome: Food and Agriculture Organization of the United Nations) 1977.

Food and Agriculture Organisation of the United Nations:
Small Farmers Development Manual: Field Action for Small Farmers, Small Fishermen and Peasants
(Bangkok: Food and Agriculture Organisation) 1978.

Farmers, B.F.:
Pioneer Peasant Colonization in Ceylon: A Case Study of Asian Agrarian Problems
(London: Oxford University Press for the Royal Institution of International Affairs) 1957.

Folmer, H. and Oosterhover, J. (eds.):
Spatial Inequalities and Regional Development
(Boston: Martinus Nijhoff) 1979.

Friedmann, J.:
Retracking America: A Theory of Transactive Planning
(New York: Garden City: Anchor Press Doubleday) 1973.

Friedmann, J. and Alonso, W. (eds.):
Regional Policy: Readings in Theory and Applications
(Cambridge, Mass: MIT Press) 1975.

Friedmann, J. and Weaver, C.:
Territory and Function: The Evolution of Regional Planning
(London: Arnold) 1979.

Friedman, John and Forest, Yvon:
"The Politics of Place: Toward a Political Economy of Territorial Planning",
in Higgins, Benjamin and Savoie, D.J.:

Regional Economic Development
(Boston: Unwin Hyman) 1988.

Friedmann, J. and Douglass, M.:
"The Agropolitan District Approach"
in Lo, F.C. and Salih, K. (eds.):
Growth Pole Strategy and Regional Development Policy: Asian Experiences and Alternative Approaches
(Oxford: Pergamon Press) 1978.

Friedmann, J. and Douglass, M.:
"Agropolitan Development - Towards a New Strategy for Regional Planning in Asia"
in Growth Pole Strategy and Regional Development Planning in Asia (Nagoya : United Nations Centre for Regional Development) 1985.

Gaikwad, V.R.:
"Rural Development Strategies: Evaluation of Some Early Experiments in India",
in Dantwala, M.L., et. al. (ed.):
Asian Seminar on Rural Development,
(New Delhi: Oxford & IBH) 1986.

Gaitskell, A.:
"Importance of Agriculture in Economic Development",
in Metherson, W.W. (ed.): Economic Development of Tropical Agriculture (Gainesville, Florida: University of Florida Press) 1968.

Galtung, J.:
"The New International Economic Order and The Basic Needs Approach",
Alternatives, Vol. 4, 1978-79

German Development Institute:
Basic Needs Oriented Rural Development: Analysis, Structural Conditions and Policy Measures
(Berlin: German Development Institute) 1980.

Ghai, D.P.; Kahn, A.R. and Lee, E.L.H.:
The Basic Needs Approach to Development: Some Issues Regarding Concepts and Methodology
(Geneva: International Labour Organization) 1977.

Ghai, D. and Radwan, S. (eds.):
African Policies and Rural Poverty in Africa
(Geneva: International Labour Organization) 1982.

Ghai, D.:
"Stagnation and Inequality in African Agriculture",
in International Association of Agricultural Economists: Growth and Equity in Agriculture Development
(London: Gower) 1983.

Ghonemy, M. (ed.):
How Development Strategies Benefit the Rural Poor: Analysis of Country Experiences in the Implementation of the WCARRD Programme of Action
(Rome: Food and Agricultural Organisation of the U.N.) 1984.

Ghosh, A. and Griffin, K.:
" Rural Poverty and Development Alternatives in South and South East Asia",
Development and Change, Vol. II, No. 4. 1980.

Gilbert, A.G.:
Latin American Development: A Geographical Perspective
(Hamonsworth: Penguin Books) 1974.

Gilbert, A.G. and Goodman, D.E.:
"Regional Income Disparities and Economic Development; A Critique",
in Gilbert, A. (ed.):
Development Planning and Spatial Structure
(Chichester: John Wiley) 1976.

Gilder, I.M.:
"Rural Planning Policies: An Economic Appraisal",
Progress in Planning, Vol. 11, No. 3, 1979.

Gow, D.D. and Vansant, J.:
Beyond the Rhetoric of Rural Development Participation: How can It be Done?
(Washington, D.C.: Development Alternatives Inc.) 1981.

Gray, J.:
"The Two Roads: Alternative Strategies of Social Change and Economic Growth in China",
in Schram, S.R. (ed.):
Authority, Participation and Cultural Change in China
(Cambridge: Cambridge University Press) 1973.

Griffin, K.:
"Policy Options for Rural Development",
in Gostsch, C. (ed.):
Rural Development and Employment
(Ibadan, Nigeria: Ford Foundation) 1973.

Griffin, K.:
Land Concentration and Rural Poverty
(London: McMillan) 1981.

Government of India:
Economic Survey (1988-89),
(New Delhi: Ministry of Finance) and various issues of earlier years.

Gow, D.D. and Van Sant, J.:
"Beyond the Rhetoric of Rural Development Participation: How Can It Be Done?
World Development, Vol. 11, No. 5, May 1983.

Gupta, Amit Kumar (ed.):
Agrarian Structure and Peasant Revolt in India
(New Delhi: Criterion Publications) 1986.

Gurley, J.:
"Rural Development in China (1949-1975) and The Lessons to be Learned from It",
in Maxwell, N. (ed.): China' Road to Development (Oxford: Pergamon Press) 1979.

Guzman, E.C.:
"Rural Development in Mexico: Problems, Policies and Issues",
in Misra, R.P. (ed.):
Rural Development: National Policies and Experiences
(Singapore: Maruzen Asia) UNCRD Regional Development Series, No. 4, 1980.

Hansen, A.H. and Perloff, H.S.:
Regional Resource Development
(Washington D.C.: National Planning Association) 1942.

Hansen, N.M.:
"Development Pole Theory in a Regional Context",
Kyklos, Vol. 20, 1967.

Hansen, N.M. (ed.):
Growth Centers in Regional Economic Development
(New York: Free Press) 1972.

Hansen, N.M.:
"Criteria for a Growth Centre Policy",
in Friedmann, J. and Alonso, W. (eds.):
Regional Policy: Readings in Theory and Applications
(Cambridge, Mass.: MIT Press) 1975.

Hansen, N.M. (ed.):
Human Settlement Systems
(Cambridge, Mass.: Ballinger Publishers) 1978.

Hansen, N.M.:
"Development From Above: The Centre-Down Paradigm",
in Stohr, W.B. and Taylor, D.R.F. (eds.):
Development from Above or Below? the Dialectics of Regional Planning in Developing Countries
(Chichester: John Wiley) 1981.

Hardjono, J.:
Transmigration in Indonesia
(Kuala Lumpur: Oxford University Press) 1983.

Harris, J.:
Rural Development: Theories of Peasant Economy and Agrarian Change (London: Hutchinson) 1982.

Hart, K.:
The Political Economy of Agriculture in West Africa
(Cambridge: University Press) 1983.

Harvey, C.; Jacobs, J.; Lamb, G. and Schaffer, B.:
Rural Employment and Administration in the Third World: Development Methods and Alternative Strategies
(Farnborough: Saxon House) 1979.

Hayami, Y.:
"Growth and Equity: Is There a Trade Off?"
in
Growth and Equity in Agricultural Development
(London: Gower) 1983.

Hayami, Y. and Kikuchi, M.:
Asian Village Economy at the Crossroads
(Baltimore: Johns Hopkins University Press) 1982.

Hayami, Y. and Ruttan, V.W.:
Agricultural Development: An International Perspective
(Baltimore: Johns Hopkins University Press) 1982.

Hermansen, Tormod, (1969):
"Regional Disaggregation of National Plans with the Context of National, Sectoral and Regional Planning",
in Kuklinski, A.(eds.):
Regional Disaggregation of National Policies and Plan
(The Hague: Mouton & Co.) 1975.

Hermansen, Tormod:
Interregional Allocation of Investments for Social and Economic Development: An Elementary Model Approach to Analysis
(Geneva: United Nations Research Institute for Social Development) 1970.

Hewes, L.:
Rural Development: World Frontiers
(Ames, Iowa: Iowa State University Press) 1974.

Heyers, J.; Roberts, P. and Williams, G. (eds.):
Rural Development in Tropical Africa
(London: MacMillan Press) 1981.

Hilhorst, J.G.M.:
"National Development Strategies and Regional Planning in Latin America: Some Reflections",
Development and Change, Vol. 12, No. 4, 1981.

Hilhorst, J.G.M.:
"On the Effects of Certain Policies upon Regional Development",
in Misra, R.P. (ed.):
Humanizing Development
(Hongkong: Maruzen Asia) 1981.

Hilhorst, J.G.M.:
Regional Development Policies
(The Hague: Institute of Social Studies) 1985.

Holland, S.:
Regional Development Policies
(The Hague: Institute of Social Studies) 1985.

Holland, S.:
Beyond Capitalist Planning
(London: MacMillan) 1978.

Hove, N. and Klassen, L.H.:
Regional Policy: A European Approach,
(Farnborough: Saxon House) 1980.

Howard, R.:
Colonialism and Underdevelopment in Ghana
(London: Croom Helm) 1978.

Hirschman, A.O. :
Getting Ahead Collectively: Grass-Roots Experience in Latin America
(New York: Pergamon Press) 1984.

Hunt, D.:
"Policy Implementation: IFAD and Rural Poverty in Kenya",
in Clay E.J. and Schaffer, B.B. (eds.):
Room for Manoeuvre: An Exploration of Public Policy in Agriculture And Rural Development
(London: Gower Publications) 1984.

Hunter, G.:
The Administration of Agricultural Development: Lessons from India
(London: Oxford University Press) 1970.

Hunter, G. (ed.):
Agricultural Development and the Rural Poor: Declaration of Policy and Guidelines for Action
(London: Overseas Development Institute) 1978.

Hunter, G.; Bunting, H. and Bottrall, A. (eds.):
Policy and Practice in Rural Development
(London: Overseas Development Institute) 1976.

Hyden, G.:
Beyond Ujamaa in Tanzania: Underdevelopment and an Uncaptured Peasantry
(London: Heinemann) 1980.

Inayatullah (ed.):
Approaches to Rural Development: Some Asian Experiences
(Kuala Lumpur: Asian and Pacific Development Administration Centre) 1979.

International Labour Organization:
Employment,Growth and Basic Needs: A One World Problem
(Geneva: International Labour Organisation) 1976.

International Labour Organisation:
Towards Full Employment: A Programme for Columbia
(Geneva: International Labour Organisation) 1970.

Institute for International Cooperation:
Rural Development in the Third World: Selected Bibliography
(Ottawa, Ontario: University of Ottawa) 1977.

Islam, R. (ed.):
Strategies for Alleviating Poverty in Rural Asia,
(Bangkok: Bangladesh Institute of Development Studies, Dhaka and ARTREP) 1985.

Jain , L.C.:
"Panchayati Raj and Decentralisation"
Kurukshetra, February 1989.

Johnston, B.F. and Clark, W.C.:
Redesigning Rural Development: A Strategic Perspective
(Baltimore: Johns Hopkins University Press) 1982.

Johnston, B.F. and Kilby, P.:
Agriculture and Structural Transformation: Economic Strategies in Late Developing Countries
(Oxford: Oxford University Press) 1975.

Johnston, B.G. and Kilby, P.:
"'Unimodal' and 'Bimodal' Strategies of Agrarian Change", in Harriss, J.:
Rural Development: Theories of Peasant Economy and Agrarian Change
(London: Hutchinson) 1982.

Joshi, P.C.:
Land Reforms in India: Trends and Perspectives
(Bombay: Allied Publishers Private Ltd.) 1975.

Junankar, P.N.:
"Land Tenure and Indian Agricultural Policy",
The Journal of Development Studies, Vol. 13, No. 1, 1976.

Katzman, M.T.:
Colonisation as an Approach to Regional Development,
(Heidelberg: Research Centre for International Agrarian Development) 1979.

Kao, Anthony, Y.C.:
"An Economic Justification for Land Reformation",
Economic Development and Cultural Change, Vol. 25, No. 3, 1977.

Korten, D.C. and Uphoff, N.:
Bureaucratic Reorientation for Participatory Rural Development
(Washington D.C.: National Association of Schools of Public Affairs and Administration) Working Paper, 1981.

Khusro, A.M.:
The Economics of Land Reforms and Farm Size in India
(Madras: Macmillan Co. of India Ltd.) 1973.

Kothari, R.:
"India: An Alternative Framework for Rural Development",
in Nerfin, M. (ed.):
Another Development: Approaches and Strategies
(Uppsala: Dag Hammarskjold Foundation) 1977.

Kotter, H.R.:
"Some Observations on the Basic Principles and General Strategy Underlying Integrated Rural Development",
Monthly Bulletin of Agricultural Economics and Statistics, Vol. 23, 1974.

Korton, F.F. (ed.):
Community Management: Asian Experiences and Perspectives
(Connecticut, West Hartford: Kumarian Press) 1985.

Kuitenbrower, J.:
The Dynamics of Land Reform in Japan, Taiwan and South Korea
(The Hague: Institute for Social Studies) 1984.

Kuklinski, A. (ed.):
Growth Poles and Growth Centres in Regional Planning
(The Hague: Mouton & Co.) 1972.

Kuklinski, A. :
"Regional Development, Regional Policies and Regional Planning"
in Kuklinski, A. (ed.):
Regional Disaggregation of National Policies and Plans
(The Hague: Mouton & Co.) 1975.

Kuklinski, A. (ed.):
Regional Disaggregation of National Policies and Plans
(The Hague: Mouton & Co.)1975.

Kuklinski, A. (ed.):
Regional Development and Planning: International Perspectives
(Leyden: Sijthoff) 1975.

Kuklinski, A. (ed.):
Social Issues in Regional Policy and Planning
(The Hague: Mouton, & Co.) 1981.

Kuklinski, A. (ed.):
Polarized Development and Regional Policy
(The Hague: Mouton & Co.) 1981.

Kuklinski, A. and Petrella, R. (eds.):
Growth Poles and Regional Policies
(The Hague: Mouton) 1972

Laar, A.J.M. van de:
The World Bank and the Poor
(Boston: Martinus Nijhoff) 1980.

Leagans, J. Paul and Loomis, C.P. (ed.):
Behavioural Change in Agriculture: Concepts and Strategies for Influencing Transition
(Ithaca: Cornell University Press) 1971.

Lassen, Ch.:
Reaching The Assetsless Poor: Projects and Strategies for Their Self-reliant Development
(Ithaca: Cornell University) Rural Development Committee, Special Series on Landlessness and Near- landlessness, No. 6. 1980.

Lea, D.A.M. and Chaudhri, D.P. (eds.):
Rural Development and the State: Contradictions and Dilemmas in Developing Countries
(London: Methuen & Co.) 1983.

Lee, E.:
"Basic Needs Strategies: A Frustrated Response to Development from Below?"
in Stohr, W.B. and Taylor, D.R.F. (eds.):
Development from Above or Below? : The Dialectics of Regional Planning in Developing Countries
(Chichester: John Wiley) 1981.

Lefeber, L. and Dutta Choudhuri, M.:
Regional Development: Experiences and Prospects,
Report No. 70.21 (Geneva: UNRISD) 1970.

Leipziger, D.M. (ed.):
Basic Needs and Development
(Cambridge, Mass.: Harvard University Press) 1981.

Lele, Uma:
The Design of Rural Development: Lessons from Africa
(Baltimore: Johns Hopkins University Press) 1975.

Leupolt, M.:
"Reorientation of Objectives and Approaches to Rural Development" Land Reform, Food and Agriculture Organisation of the United Nations, No. 2, 1975.

Lipton, M.:
Why Poor People Stay Poor: Urban Bias in World Development
(Cambridge, Mass: Harvard University Press) 1977.

Livingstone, I.:
"On the Concept of "Integrated Rural Development Planning", in Less Developed Countries",
Journal of Agricultural Economy, Vol. 30. 1979.

Lo, F.C. and Salih, K. (eds.):
Growth Pole Strategy and Regional Development Policy: Asian Experiences and Alternative Approaches
(Oxford: Pergamon Press) 1978.

Lo, F.C. and Salih, K.:
"Growth Poles, Agropolitan Development and Polarisation Reversal: The Debate and Search for Alternatives"
in Stohr, W.B. and Taylor, D.R.F. (eds.):
Development from Above or Below?: The Dialectics of Regional Planning in Developing Countries
(Chichester: John Wiley) 1981.

Lundquist, J.:
"Tanzanian Socialist Ideology Bureaucratic Reality and Development From Below",
in Stohr, W.B. and Taylor, D.R.F. (eds.):
Development from Above or Below? The Dialectics of Regional Planning in Developing Countries,
(Chicester: John Wiley) 1981.

Luning, H.A.:
The Need for Regionalized Agricultural Development Planning: Experiences From Western Visaya, Philippines

(Philippines: College Laguna) South East Asian Regional Center for Graduate Study and Research in Agriculture, 1981.

Mabogunje, A.L.:
The Development Process: A Spatial Perspective
(London: Hutchinson University Library) 1980.

Mabogunje, A.L.:
Local and Regional Development in Africa: Experiences, Main Issues and Perspectives
(Nagoya: United Nations Centre for Regional Development) 1981.

MacArthur, J.D.:
"Appraising the Distributional Aspects of Rural Development Projects: A Kenya Case Study",
World Development, Vol. 6, No. 2, 1978.

Mallet, J.A. :
Planning for Agricultural Development
(New York: St. Martin's Press) 1984.

Mat, J.H.B.:
"Coordination, Institutional Capability and Development Performance in Malaysia"
in Cheema, G.S. (ed.):
Institutional Dimensions of Regional Development
(Singapore: Maruzen, Asia) UNCRD Regional Development Series, Vol.8, 1981.

McAndrews, C.:
"The Role of Potential Use of Land Settlements in Development Policies: Lessons from Past Experience",
Sociologia Ruralis, Vol. 19, No. 2-3, 1979.

McCoy, A.:
"Land Reform as Counter Revolution",
Bulletin of Concerned Asian Scholars, Vol. 3, No. 1, 1971.

Mellenry, D.E. Jr.:
Ujamaa Villages in Tanzania: A Bibliography
(Uppsala: Scandinavian Institute of African Studies) 1981.

Mellor, J.:
The New Economics of Growth
(Ithaca: Cornell University Press) 1976.

Misra, R.P. and Sundaram, K.V.:
Rural Area Development
(New Delhi: Sterling) 1977.

Misra, R.P. (ed.):
Humanizing Development
(Hongkong: Maruzen Asia) 1981.

Misra, R.P. (ed.):
Rural Development: National Policies and Experiences
(Singapore: Maruzen Asia) UNCRD Regional Development Series; 1981.

Misra, R.P. (ed.):
Regional Development: Essays in Honour of Masahiko Honjo
(Singapore: Maruzen Asia) 1982.

Morse, E.R.:
Strategies for Small Farmer Development
(Washington: Westview Press) 1976.

Moore, J.R. (ed.):
The Economic Impact of the TVA
(Knoxville: University of Tennessee Press) 1967.

Morse, E.R. and Cow, D.:
Integrated Rural Development: Nine Critical Implementation Problems
(Washington, D.C.: Development Alternatives Inc.) 1981.

Mosely, M.J.:
Growth Centers in Spatial Planning
(Oxford; Pergamon Press) 1974.

Nagamine, H. and Konno, M.:
"'Rurban' Dimensions in Regional Development, Case

Studies in Three Asian Countries",
in Sundaram, K.V.; Ramesh, A. and Tiwari, P.S.:
Regional Planning and Development,
Vol. II, (New-Delhi: Heritage Publishers) 1989.

Nelson, M.:
The Development of Tropical Lands: Policy Issues in Latin America
(Baltimore: Johns Hopkins University Press) 1973.

Nerfin, M.(ed.):
Another Development: Approaches and Strategies
(Uppsala: Dag Hammarskjold Foundation) 1977.

Nyerere, J.K.:
Socialism and Rural Development
(Dar es Salaam: Tanzania: Government Printers Office) 1967.

Obudho, R.A. and Taylor, D.R.F. (eds.):
The Spatial Structure of Development: A Study of Kenya
(Boulder: Westview Press) 1979.

OECD:
Regional Rural Development Programmes; with Special Emphasis on Depressed Agricultural Areas Including Mountain Regions
(Paris: OECD) 1964.

Ojala, E.M.:
"The Programming of Agricultural Development",
in Southworth, H.M. and Johnston, B.F. (eds.):
Agricultural Development and Economic Growth
(Ithaca: Cornell University Press) 1967.

O'Regan, F.M. and Bendavid val, A.:
Public Participation in Regional development Planning: A Strategy For Public Involvement with a Case Study of the Bicol River Basin Development Programme
(Washington, D.C.: United States Agency for International development) 1979.

Owen, M.:
The Tennessee Valley Authority
(New York: Praeger) 1973.

Perroux, Francois:
"The Pole of Development's New Place in a General Theory of Economic Activity",
in Higgins, B. and Savoie, D.J.:
Regional Economic Development
(Boston: Unwin Hyman) 1988.

Pescatore, G.:
"The Role of Industry in the Development of Rural Areas",
in Weitz, R. (ed.):
Rural Development in a Changing World
(Cambridge, Mass.: MIT Press) 1971.

Pioro, Z.:
"Growth Centres in Regional Development in Tropical Africa",
in Kuklinski, A. (ed.):
Regional Development and Planning: International Perspectives
(Leyden: Sijthoff) 1975.

Polenske, K.R. :
"Growth Pole Theory and Strategy Reconsidered: Domination, Linkages and Distribution",
in Higgins, B. and Savoie, D.J.:
Regional Economic Development
(Boston: Unwin Hyman) 1988.

Proceedings:
18th International Conference of Agricultural Economists: Growth and Equity in Agricultural Development, in Proceedings of the XVII International Conference of Agricultural Economists,
(London: Gower) 1983.

Qureshi, M.H. and Mathur, Ashok:
A Geo-Economic Evaluation Micro Level Planning
(New Delhi: Concept Publishing Co.) 1985.

Raay, H.G.T. van and Hilhorst, J.G.M.:
Land Settlement and Regional Development in the Tropics: Results, Prospects and Options,
(The Hague: ISSAS) 1981.

Rau, S.L.:
"Strategies of Rural Development",
Kurukshetra, Vol. XXVIII, No. 11, March 2, 1980.

Rayudu, C.S.:
Management of Rural Development
(New Delhi: Discovery Publishing House) 1989.

Rapoport, R.N.:
"Three Dilemmas in Action Research",
Human Relations, Vol. 23, No. 6, 1970.

Richardson, A.:
Participation
(London: Routledge Kegan Paul) 1983.

Richardson, H.W.:
"Growth Centres, Rural Development and National Urban Policy: A Defense',
International Regional Science Review, Vol. 3, No. 2, 1978.

Richardson, H.W.:
"The Relevance and Applicability of Regional Economics to Developing Countries",
Regional Development Dialogue, Vol. 1, No. 1, Spring 1980.

Richardson, H.W.:
"Towards a National Urban Development Strategy for Thailand",
in Misra, R.P. (ed.):
Regional Development: Essays in honour of Masahiko Honjo
(Singapore: Maruzen Asia) United Nations Centre for Regional Development, 1982.

Richardson, H.W. :
"A Review of Techniques for Regional Policy Analysis",
in Higgins, B. and Savoie, D.J.:
Regional Economic Development,
(Boston: Unwyn Hyman) 1988.

Riddell, R.:
Regional Development Policy: The Struggle for Rural Progress in Low-income Nations
(New York: St. Martin's Press) 1985.

Robock, S.:
Brazil's Developing Northeast: A Study of Regional Planning and Foreign Aid
(Washington, D.C.: Brookings Institution) 1963.

Rokkan, Stein (ed.):
A Quarter Century of Inter-national Social Science: Papers and Reports on Development: 1952-1977
(New Delhi: Concept Publishing Co.) 1979.

Rondinelli, D.:
Secondary Cities in Developing Countries: Policies for Diffusing Urbanisation
(Beverly Hills: Sage Publications) 1983.

Ruttan, V.W.:
"Integrated Rural Development Programmes: A Skeptical Perspective", International Development Review, No. 4, 1975.

Saith, A.:
"Processes Generating Rural Poverty: Parables and Empirical Analysis"
in Rural Poverty Processes in LDCs: A General Analysis (The Hague: Institute for Social Studies) 1982.

Schickele, R.:
"National Policies for Rural Development in Developing Countries",
in Weitz, R. (ed.):
Rural Development in a Changing World
(Cambridge, Mass.: MIT Press) 1971.

Scheneider, H.:
Promoting Rural Development Through Institution Building: A Case from the Congo, Experiences in Rural Development
(Paris: OECD Development Centre), Occasional Paper No. 7, 1978.

Schwefel, D.:
Basic Needs, Planning and Evaluation
(Berlin: German Development Institute) 1978.

Seldon, M. (ed.):
The People's Republic of China: A Documentary History of Revolutionary Change
(New York: Monthly Review Press) 1979.

Seidman, A.:
Comparative Development Strategies in East Africa
(Nairobi: East African Publishing House) 1972.

Sen, A.:
Poverty and Famines
(Oxford: Clarendon Press) 1981.

Singh, Bhupinder:
"People's Participation in Resource Management for Eco-Development",
paper read at seminar on People's Participation in Resource Management for Eco-Development, on 20th November 1986, at Institute of Economic Growth, New Delhi.

Sharma, A.N.:
Spatial Approach to District Planning
(New Delhi: Concept Publishing House) 1980.

Sharma, B.D.:
"Towards a Strategy"
being Chapter 4 of B.D. Sharma:
The Web of Poverty,
(Shillong: North Eastern Hill University and New Delhi: Prachi Publishers) 1989.

Sharma, P.N.:
"Participation of the Rural Poor in the Planning Process",
in Sundaram, K.V.; Ramesh, A. and Tiwari, P.S.:
Regional Planning and Development, Vol. II,
(New Delhi: Heritage Publishers 1989.

Sinha, S.:
Planning for Rural Industrialization: A Review of Developing Country Programmes
(London: Intermediate Technology Development Group) 1983.

Smith, W.E.:
The Design of Organisations for Rural Development Projects
(Washington D.C.: World Bank) Staff Working Paper No. 375, 1980.

Stavenhagen, R.:
"Basic Needs, Peasants and the Strategy for Rural Development",
in Nerfin, M. (ed.):
Another Development: Approaches and Strategies
(Uppsala: Dag Hammarskjold Foundation) 1977.

Stevens, R.D. (ed.):
Tradition and Dynamics in Small Farm Agriculture
(Ames: Iowa State University Press) 1977.

Stoer, W.:
"Towards 'another' Regional Development? In Search of Strategy of Truly Integrated Regional Development",

in Misra, R.P. and Honjo, M.(eds.):
Changing Perceptions of Development Problems
(Singapore: Maruzen Asia) 1971.

Stohr, W.B.:
Regional Development: Experiences and Prospects in Latin America
(The Hague: Mouton & Co.) 1975.

Stohr, W.B. and Todtling, F.:
"An Evaluation of Regional Policies: Experiences in Market and Mixed Economies",
in Hansen, N. (ed.):
Human Settlement Systems
(Cambridge, Mass.: Ballinger Publishers) 1978.

Stohr, W.B.and Todtling, F.:
"Spatial Equity: Some Antitheses to Current Regional Development Doctrine",
in Folmer, H. and Oosterhovern, J. (eds.):
Spatial Inequalities and Regional Development
(Boston: Martinus Nijhoff) 1979.

Swaminathan, M.S.:
"Foreword"
dated May, 1989, in Chopra, K. et. al.:
Participatory Development, People and Common Property Resources, (New Delhi: Sage Publications) 1990.

Sundaram, K.V. and Palanidurai, K.V.:
"Development of Hill Areas in India - Some Lessons for Strategy Formulation and Planning",
Indian Journal of Regional Science, Vol. XX, No. 1, 1988.

Swan, B.:
"Sri Lanka: Constraints and Prospects in the Pursuit of Rural Development",
in Lea, D.A.M. and Chaudhri, A.D.P.:
Rural Development and the State: Contradictions and Dilemmas in Developing Countries
(London: Methuen & Co.) 1983.

Taylor, D.R.F.:
"Some Observations on Theory and Practice in Regional Development in Africa",
Kuklinski, A. (ed.):
Polarized Development and Regional policy
(The Hague: Mouton & Co.) 1981.

Tendler, J.:
Rural Projects Through Urban Eyes: An Interpretation of the World Bank's New-Style Rural Development Projects
(Washington D.C.: World Bank), World Bank Staff Working Papers No. 532, 1982.

United Nations:
An Approach to Evolving Guidelines for Rural Development
(Bangkok: The United Nations Development Institute) Discussion Paper No. 1, 1975.

United Nations Asian and Pacific Development Institute, Bangkok:
Local Level Planning and Rural Development - Alternative Strategies
(New-Delhi: Concept Publishing Co.) 1980.

Vyas, V.S.:
"Growth and Equity in Asian Agriculture",
in International Association of Agricultural Economists: Growth and Equity in Agricultural Development, Proceedings of the XVIII Conference of Agricultural Economists, (London: Gower Publications) 1983.

Wardenburg, J.G.:
"Regional Disaggregation of National Development Planning: a Regional Framework",
in Kuklinski, A. (ed.):

Regional Disaggregation of National Policies
(The Hague: Mouton & Co.) 1975.

Walinsky, L. (ed.):
Agrarian Reform as Unfinished Business:
Selected Papers of Wolf Ladejinsky (New York: Oxford University Press) 1977.

Waterstone, A.:
"A Viable Model for Rural Development",
in Integrated Rural Development, Vol. 1, No. 1.

Weitz, R. (ed.):
Rural Development in a Changing World
(Cambridge,Mass.: MIT Press) 1971.

Weitz, R.:
"Regional Planning for Rural Development in Developing Countries" being chapter 5 of

Weitz, R. (ed.):
Rural Development in a Changing World,
(Cambridge, Mass.: MIT Press) 1971.

Wen, G.:
"Ten Years"
Effort in Promoting Regional Development: A Review of the Progress of the United Nations Programme of Research and Training in Regional Development",
in Kuklinski, A. (ed.):
Regional Development and Planing: International Perspectives
(Leyden: Sijithoff) 1975.

World Bank:
Rural Development Sector Policy Paper, International Bank for Reconstruction and Development
(Washington, D.C.: World Bank) 1975.

APPENDIX A

SELECT BIBLIOGRAPHY

DECENTRALISED ADMINISTRATION & DECENTRALISED PLANNING

Ahmad, M.:
Unfinished Revolution: Studies in Local Government and Rural Development in Pakistan
(Karachi: Bookland) 1976.

Ahmed, F.:
"Administrative Reforms for Decentralized Development in Bangladesh",
in Sacena, A.P. (ed.):
Administrative Reforms for Decentralized Development
(Kuala Lumpur: Asian and Pacific Development Administration Centre) 1980, pp. 43-48.

Akuoko-Frimpong, H.:
"The Need For an Effective Decentralized Framework to Promote Development from Below",
Greenhill Journal of Administration (Ghana), Vol. 1, No. 1, 1974.

Al Assam, M.:
Decentralization for Development
(Dacca: National Institute of Public Administration) 1978.

Ali, S.M.:
"Organization for Local Development: the Case of Bangladesh",
in Cheema, G.S. (ed.):
Institutional Dimensions of Regional Development
(Singapore: Naruzen Asia for United Nations Centre for Rural Development) 1981.

Allan, B. and Hinchilifee, K.:
National Planning plus Decentralization Regional Planning? Papua New Guinea's Experience
(Norwich: University of East Anglia, School of Development Studies) Discussion paper 76, 1980.

Aqua, R.:
Local Institutions and Rural Development in Japan
(Ithaca: Cornell University, Center for International Studies) Special Series on Rural Local Government 8, 1974.

Aqua, R.:
Local Institutions and Rural Development in South Korea
(Ithaca: Cornell University, Center for International Studies) Special Series on Rural Local Government, 13, 1974.

Bamberger, M.:
The Role of Country Participation in Development Planning and Project Management
(Washington D.C. World Bank) 1988.

Beaglehole, J.H.:
The District: A Study of Decentralization in West Malaysia
(London: Oxford University Press) Hull Monographs of South-East Asia 6, 1976.

Bhaduri, A. and Rahman, M.D. (eds.):
Studies in Rural Participation
(Delhi: Oxford & IBH Publishing Co.) 1982.

Bhalerao, C.N.:
"Changing Patterns of Development Administration in the District",

The Indian Journal of Public Administration, Vol. XII, No. 1, 1966.

Bhargava, B.S.:
Panchayati Raj Institutions: An Analysis of Issues, Problems and Recommendations of Asoka Mehta Committee
(Delhi: Ashish Publishing House) 1979.

Bhattacherjee, J.:
Administration Organisation for Development
(Brussels: International Institute of Administrative Sciences) 1973.

Bhatnagar, S.C.; et. al.:
"Decision Support System for District Administration",
Rural Regional Development network Newsletter, No. 6,(Bangkok: Asian Institute of Technology) April 1987.

Blair, H.W.:
The Elusiveness of Equity: Institutional Approaches to Rural Development in Bangladesh
(Ithaca: Cornell University, Center for International Studies) Special Series on Rural Local Government, 1, 1974.

Blair, H.W.:
"Re-orienting Development Administration",
Journal of Development Studies, April 1985.

Blau, P.M. and Schoenherr, R.A.:
The Structure of Organizations
(New York: Basic Books) 1971.

Bonsu, G.A.K.:
"The Role of Local Authorities in National Development Planning and Implementation in Ghana",
Planning and Administration (The Hague), Vol. 3, No. 1, 1976.

Bowden, P.:
"The Administration of Regional Development",
Journal of Administration Overseas, Vol. 18, 1979.

Bratton, M.:
Beyond Community Development; The Political Economy of Rural Administration in Zimbabwe
(London: Catholic Institute for International Relations) 1977.

Bryant, C.:
Managing Rural Development: Peasant Participation in Rural Development
(Conn. : Kumarian Press) 1980.

Bruton, M.J.:
The Malaysian Planning System: a Review,
Third World Planning Review, Vol. 4, 1982.

Budhraja, J.C.:
"Organisational Framework for District Planning and Involvement of People in Development Process",
Indian Journal of Regional Science, Vol. XIX, No. 2, 1987.

Campbell, M. :
"Towards a Classification of Decentralized Systems",
Studies in Comparative Local Government
(The Hague) No. 2 (Winter 1968), pp. 33-40.

Chambers, R.:
Managing Rural Development: Ideas and Experience from East Africa
(Uppsala: Scandinavian Institute of African Studies, 1974).

Chaturvedi, H.R.:
Bureaucracy and the Local Community: Dynamics of Rural Development
(Bombay: Allied Publishers) 1977.

Chaturvedi, T.N.:
"Institutional Machinery, Coordination and Development Performance in India",
in Cheema, G.S.(ed.):

Institutional Dimensions of Regional Development
(Singapore, Maruzen Asia, for UNCRD) 1981.

Chee, S.:
Rural Local Government and Rural Development in Malaysia
(Ithaca: Cornell University, Center for International Studies, Special Series on Rural Local Government, 9) 1974.

Cheema, G.S.:
"People's Communes, Panchayati Raj and Basic Democracies: a Comparative Analysis",
in Inayatullah (ed.):
Approaches to Rural Development: Some Asian Experiences
(Kuala Lumpur, Asian and Pacific Development Administration Centre) 1979.

Cheema, G.S. (ed.):
Institutional Dimensions of Regional Development
(Singapore: Maruzen Asia, for United Nations Centre for Regional Development, 1981).

Cheema, G.S. and Rondinelli, D.A. (eds.):
Decentralization and Development: Policy Implementation in Developing Countries
(Beverly Hills and London: Sage Publications) 1983.

Christensen, K.S. and Weber, M.M.:
On Styles of Non-Centralized Planning
(Berkeley: University of California at Berkeley, Project on Managing Decentralization) 1981.

Cliffe, L.; Coleman, J.S. and Doornbos, M.R. (eds.):
Government and Rural Development in East Africa: Essays on Political Penetration
(The Hague: Martinus Nijhoff) 1977.

Cohen, J.M. and Uphoff, N.T.:
Rural Development Participation: Concepts and Measures for Project Design, Implementation and Evaluation
(Ithaca: Cornell University, Center for International Studies, Monograph 2) 1977.

Cohen, J.M. and Uphoff, N.T.:
"Participation's Place in Rural Development: Seeking Clarity Through Specificity",
World Development, Vol. 8, 1980.

Chopra, R.N.:
"Administrative Organization for Regional Development",
Indian Journal of Public Administration, Vol. XI, No. 4, Oct-December 1965.

Cohen, S. (ed.):
Debaters' Comments on 'Inquiry into Participation: A Research Approach' by A. Pearse and M. Stiefel
(Geneva: United Nations Research Institute for Social Development) 1980.

Colebatch, H.:
Policy, Process and Outcome in Government: A Study of the Rural Improvement Programme
(Port Moresby: Institute of Applied Social and Economic Research) Monograph 10, 1979.

Collins, P.D.:
"Local Government and Community Development in Tanzania",
Community Development Journal, Vo. 7, 1972.

Collins, P.D.:
"Decentralization and Local Administration for Development in Tanzania",
Africa Today, Vol. 21, 1974.

Collins, P.D.:
Decentralization and Local Administration for Development in Tanzania,

(Sussex: University of Sussex, Institute of Development Studies) 1976.

Collins, P.D.:
The Institutionalization of Basic Needs for Rural Development: Lessons from an African Experience
(The Hague: Institute of Social Studies) Occasional Papers 93, 1981.

Conyers, D.:
"Organization for Development: the Tanzanian Experience",
Journal of Administration Overseas, Vol. 8, 1974.

Conyers, D.:
Decentralized Planning in Papua New Guinea
(Geneva, International Labour Office) World Employment Programme Research, Working Paper WEP 2-23/WP 107, 1981.

Conyers, D.:
"Papua New Guinea: Decentralization and Development from the Middle",
in Stohr, W.B. and Taylor, D.R.F. (eds.):
Development from Above of Below?
(Chichester: Wiley) 1981.

Conyers, D.:
"Decentralization for Regional Development: a Comparative Study of Tanzania, Zambia and Papua New Guinea",
Public Administration and Development, Vol. 1, 1981.

Conyers, D.:
"The Role of Decentralization in National Development Policies",
Development Policy Seminar for UNDP Executives (The Hague: Institute of Social Studies) November 1982.

Conyers, D.:
"Decentralization: the Latest Fashion in Development Administration?",
Public Administration and Development, Vol. 3, 1983.

Das, R.B. (ed.):
Urban Planning and Local Authorities
(Lucknow: Lucknow University) Administrative Series 4, 1970.

Davey, D.J.:
Financing Regional Government
(Chichester: Wiley, 1983)

Davies, B.V.:
"Administration of the Rural Development Programme in Fiji",
Journal of Administration Overseas, Vol. 10, 1971.

Dawson, P.:
"Decentralization in Sri Lanka: the Significance of District Ministers",
in Institute of Commonwealth Studies, A Revival of Local Government and Administration? (London: University of London, Institute of Commonwealth Studies) Collected seminar papers 23, 1978.

DeMello, L.:
"Decentralization for Development -I",
Journal of Local Administration Overseas, Vol. 2,

Deng, A.:
"Political Power and Decentralization in the Sudan",
Decentralization and Development Review (Berkeley: University of California at Berkeley Press) Project on Managing Decentralization, No. I, Spring 1981.

Deogaonkar, S.G.:
Rural Development Administration in India,
(New Delhi: Concept Publishing Co.) 1980.

Desai, D.K. and Prakash, H.:
Planning and Implementation of Financing Agriculture through Area Approach (A Case Study in Bihar State)
(Ahmedabad: Indian Institute of Management) 1973.

Dochen, M. and Deutsch, K.W.:
Decentralization: Sketches Towards a Rational Theory
(Cambridge, Mass.: Oelgeschlager, Gunn & Hain) 1980.

Domingo-Tapales, P.:
"Administering Regional Development",
Philippine Planning Journal, Vol. 6, 1974.

Donge, J.K. van:
"Politicians, Bureaucrats and Farmers: a Zambian Case Study",
Journal of Development Studies, Vol. 19, 1982.

Douglass, M.:
Agropolitan Development: An Alternative for Regional Development in Asia
(Norwich: University of East Anglia, School of Development Studies) Discussion Paper 59, 1979.

Due, J.D.:
Report on Financial Aspects of Decentralization in the Democratic Republic of the Sudan
(Washington D.C.: United States Agency for International Development) 1981.

Due, J.D. (ed.):
Institution Building and Development: From Concepts to Application (Beverly Hills: Sage) 1972.

El-Arifi, S.A.:
Local Government and Local Participation in Rural Development in Sudan
(Khartoum: University of Khartoum , Development Studies and Research Centre) Monograph 10, 1978.

Escobar, A.:
"Decentralization and Community Participation in Nutrition Planning",
Decentralization and Development Review (Berkeley: University of California at Berkeley) project on Managing Decentralization, No. 1, Spring 1981.

Esman, M.J. and Uphoff, N.T.:
Local Organization: Intermediaries in Rural Development
(Ithaca, Cornell University Press) 1984.

Esman, M.J.:
"Development Administration and Constituency Organization",
Public Administration Review, Vol. 38, 1978.

Esman, M.J.:
"Methodologies for Planning and Managing social Development Activities",
Regional Development Dialogue, Vol. 8, No. 2, 1987.

Fabella, A.V.:
"Regionalizing for Administration and Development: the Philippine Experience",
in Cheema, G.S. (ed.):
Institutional Dimensions of Regional Development
(Singapore: Maruzen Asia, for United Nations Centre for Regional Development) 1981.

Faltas, M.:
Role of Governments in the Regional Development Process
(Nagoya: Japan, United Nations Centre for Regional Development) 1977.

Faltas, M.:
"Decentralization and the Design of Planning Systems",
Development Studies Association, Regional Development and Planning Study Group Meeting, Nottingham: March 1982.

Fernandes, A.J.:
Central Coordination for Effective Rural Development: A Case Study of Tanzania
(Buea, Cameroon: Pan-African Institute for Development) 1979, mimeographed.

Fernandes, W.:
Development for People
(New Delhi: Indian Social Institute) 1985.

Fisk, D.M.:
"Issues in local Government Productivity Measurement",
Public Management, Vol. 56, No. 6, 1974.

Food and Agriculture Organization of the U.N.:
Administering Agricultural Development for Small Farmers: Issues in Decentralization and People's Participation,
(Rome: Food and Agriculture Organisation of the United Nations) Economic and Social Development Paper No. 20, 1981.

Fortmann, L.:
Peasants, Officials and Participation in Rural Tanzania: Experience with Villagization and Decentralization
(Ithaca: Cornell University, Center for International Studies) Special Series on Rural Local Organization, No. 1, 1980.

Friedman, H.J.:
"Decentralized Development in Asia: Local Political Alternative",
in Cheema, G.S. and Rondinelli, D.A. (eds.):
Decentralization and Development: Policy Implementation in Developing Countries
(Beverley Hills and London: Sage) 1983.

Friedmann, J. and Weaver, C.:
Territory and Function: The Evolution of Regional Planning
(London: Arnold) 1979.

Furniss, N.:
"The practical Significance of Decentralization",
Journal of Politics, Vol. 37, 1974.

Gant, G.F.:
"Regional and Local Organisation for Development",
being Chapter 7 of his
Development Administration
(Madison: University of Wisconsin Press) 1979.

Garcia-Zarmor, J.C. (ed.):
Public Participation in Development Planning and Management
(Boulder: Westview Press) 1985.

Garzon, J.M.:
"Public Works, Decentralization and Linkages",
Decentralization and Development Review (Berkeley: University of California at Berkeley Press) Project on Managing Decentralization, No. 2, Summer 1981.

Gow, D.D. and Van Sant, J.:
Beyond the Rhetoric of Rural Development Participation: How Can it be Done?
(Washington D.C.: Development Alternatives Inc., for United States Agency for International Development) 1981.

Grayson, L.E.:
"Decentralization in Planning and Economic Decision-Making in Ghana",
Journal of Modern African Studies, Vol. 13, 1975.

Gran, Guy:
Development by People: Citizen Construction of a Just World
(New York: Praeger) 1983.

Guzman, R.P. de:
"Administrative Reforms for Decentralized Development",(Philippines),
in Saxena, A.P. (ed.):
Administrative Reforms for Decentralized Development
(Kuala Lumpur: Asian and Pacific Administration Centre) 1980.

Hadden, S.G.:
Rural Electrification and Decentralized Decision-making in Rajasthan, India
(Ithaca: Corneil University, Center for International Studies) Special series on Rural Local Government, 6, 1974.

Hadden, S.G.:
"Controlled Decentralization and Policy Implementation: the Case of rural Electrification in Rajasthan",
in Grindle, M.S. (eds.):
Politics and Policy Implementation in the Third World,
(Princeton: Princeton University Press) 1980.

Hansen, G.E.:
Rural Local Government and Agricultural Development in Java, Indonesia
(Ithaca: Cornell University, Center for International Studies) Special Series on Rural Local Government, No.7, 1974.

Harris, J. and Hermans Q.:
Thailand: Options for Decentralization
(Washington D.C.: World Bank Development Management Review Mission, Working Paper) 1980, mimeographed.

Harris, R.L.:
"Decentralization and Strengthening of Local Government",
Decentralization and Development Review (Berkeley: University of California at Berkeley, Project on Managing Decentralization), no. 2, Summer 1981.

Hart, D.K.:
"Theories of Government Related to Decentralization and Citizen Participation",
Public Administration Review, Vol. 32, 1972.

Heeger, G.A. :
"The Search for Political Stability",
being Chapter 3 in his:
Politics of Under-Development,
(New York and London: Macmillan) 1974.

Heyer, J.; Ireri, J. and Moris, J.:
Rural Development in Kenya
(Nairobi: East African Publishing House) 1971.

Hicks, U.K.:
Development from Below: Local Government and Finance in Developing Countries of the Commonwealth
(Oxford: Oxford University Press) 1961.

Hicks, U.K.:
Intergovernmental Relations with Special Reference to the Less Developed Countries
(Syracuse: Syracuse University Maxwell School of Citizenship and Public Affairs) Occasional Paper 29, 1976.

Hill,F.:
"Administrative Decentralization for Development, Participation and Control in Tanzania",
Journal of African Studies, Vol. 6, No. 4, (Winter 1979-80)

Hirschman, A.O.:
Getting Ahead Collectively: Grass-Roots Experiences in Latin America
(New York: Pergamon Press) 1984.

Hirschman, David:
"Six District Administrators Talk",
Planning and Administration, Vol. 10, No. 1, Spring 1983.

Howell, J.:
"Assessing Management and Organizations For Agricultural Development Projects",
in Overseas Development Institute: Institutions, Management and Agricultural Development (London: ODI Agricultural Administration Unit) Occasional Paper No.3, 979.

Humes, S.:
"The Role of Local Government in Economic Development in Africa",
Journal of Administration Overseas, Vol. 12, 1973.

Hunter, G.:
"Introduction: Reflection on The Management of Rural Services",
Agricultural Administration, Vol. 11, 1982, pp. 253-58.

Inayatullah:
"An analysis of the Emergence of a Rural Development Innovation in Comilla, Bangaladesh",
Journal of Developing Areas, Vol. 11, No. 1, October 1976.

Institute of Planning Studies:
Report of a Workshop on Decentralization
(Nottingham: University of Nottingham) 1981, mimeographed.

Islam, N. and Renault, G.M.:
Changing Notions of Development, Development Administration and Administrative Development: Prologues, Paradoxes and Perspectives
(Ottawa: Institute for International Co-operation, University of Ottawa) 1979.

Johl, S.S. and Mudahar, M.S.:
The Dynamics of Institutional Change and Rural Development in Punjab, India
(Ithaca: Cornell University) Center for International Studies, Special Series on Rural Local Government, No.5, 1974.

Johnston, J.G.:
"Local Government as a Tool for Development",
Workshop on the Management of Large Cities in Africa (Bonn: DSE) 1973.

Jong, L. de:
Organization for Participation in Rural Development in Zambia
(Lusaka: National Institute of Public Administration) 1978.

Kaushmanan, T.R.:
"A System Model of Rural Development"
World Development, Vol. 10, 1982.

Kenya, Office of the President:
District Focus for Rural Development
(Nairobi: Government Printer) 1983.

Khan, A.R.:
"The Comilla Model and the Integrated Rural Development Programme of Bangladesh: An Experiment in "Cooperative Capitalism",
World Development, Vol. 7, 1979.

Kingsland, J.L.:
"Divisional Development Planning in Gambia: the Early Stage",
Planning and Administration (The Hague) Vol. 4, No. 1, 1977.

Kinsey, B.:
Planning and Implementation: Problems of Parallel Hierarchies in Local Development in Zambia
(Norwich : University of East Anglia, School of Development Studies) Discussion paper No. 99, 1981.

Kochen, M. and Deutsch, K.W.:
"Toward a Rational Theory of Decentralization: Some Implications of Mathematical Approach",
American Political Science Review, Vol. 63, 1969.

Kolawole, A.:
"The Role of Grass-Roots Participation in National Development: Lessons from the Kwara State of Nigeria"
Community Development Journal, Vol. 17, 1982.

Korten, D.C. and Uphoff, U.T.:
Bureaucratic Reorientation for Participatory Rural Development
(Washington, D.C.: National Association of Schools of Public Affairs and Administration) Working Paper 1, 1981.

Korten, F.F.:
"Community Participation: A Management Perspective on Obstacles and Options",
in Korten, D.C. and Alfonso, F.B. (eds.):
Bureaucracy and the Poor: Closing the Gap
(Singapore: McGraw-Hill) 1981.

Korton, D.C. and Alfanso, F.B. (eds.):
Bureaucracy and the Poor: Closing the Gap
(Connecticut, West Hartford: Kumarian Press) 1983.

Leach, J.:
"Managing Rural Development in Botswana",
Public Administration and Development, Vol. 1, 1981.

Leach, J.:
"Administrative Co-ordination in African Rural Development",
Agricultural Administration, Vol. 11, 1982.

Leonard, D.K. (ed.):
Rural Administration in Kenya
(Nairobi: East African Literature Bureau) 1973.

Leonard, D.D. and Marshall, D.R. (ed.):
Institutions of Rural Development for the Poor: Decentralization and Organizational Linkages
(Berkeley : University of California at Berkeley) Institute of International Studies, Research Series, 49, 1982.

Levy, F. and Truman, E.M.:
"Toward a Rational Theory of Decentralization: Another View",
American Political Science Review, Vol. 65, 1971.

Lo, F. and Salih, K. (eds.):
Growth Pole Strategy and Regional Development Policy
(Oxford: Pergamon) 1978.

Mabogunje, A.L.:
"Critique of the Concept of Popular Participation"
in Mabogunje, A.L.(ed.):
Regional Development Alternatives: International Perspectives
(Singapore: Maruzen Asia, for United Nations Centre for Regional Development) 1981. The author maintains that most approaches to spatial planning focus on 'ureaucratic space' rather than 'people's space'.

McLoughlin, P.F.M.:
The Farmer, the Politician and the Bureaucrat: Local Government and Agricultural Development in Independent Africa
(New Brunswick: Peter McLoughlin Association) 1972.

Macjahon, A.W.:
Delegation and Autonomy
(Bombay: Asia Publishing House) 1961.

Maddick, H.:
Democracy, Decentralization and Development
(Bombay: Asia Publishing House) 1963. This is a 'classic' text on decentralization.

Maddick, H.:
Panchayati Raj: A Study of Rural Local Government in India
(London: Longman) 1970. This is a detailed study of the Panchayati Raj system from its origins to 1966.

Maro, P.S.:
"Decentralization and the Organization of Space in Tanzania",
Africa, Vol. 49, 1979.

Mat, J.bin:
"Coordination, Institutional Capability and Development Performance in Malaysia",
in Cheema, G.S. (ed.):
Institutional Dimensions of Regional Development
(Singapore: Maruzen Asia, for United Nations Centre for Rural Development) 1981.

Mathur, B.C.:
"Administrative Reforms For Decentralised Development: the Indian Experience",
in Saxena, A.P. (ed.): Administrative Reforms for Decentralized Development (Kuala Lumpur: Asian and Pacific Development Administration Centre) 1980.

Mathur, K.:
"Administrative Decentralization in Asia",
in Cheema, G.S. and Rondinelli, .A. (eds.):
Decentralization and Development:Policy Implementation in Developing Countries,
(London and Beverley Hills: Sage Publications) 1983.

Mauzy, D.K.:
"Two Rural Development Strategies: Organization, Administrative Performance and Political Priorities in India and Malaysia",
Philippine Journal of Public Administration, Vol. 19, 1975.

Mawhood, P.:
"Decentralization for Development - a Lost Cause",
in Bruhns, F.C. et. al. (eds.):
Local Politics, Development and Participation
(Pittsburg: University of Pittsburg, Centre for International Studies) 1974.

Mawhood, P.:
"Stage of Development" and The Model for Local Government Reform in Africa",
in Mlinar, Z. and Teune, H. (eds.): The Social Ecology of Change (London: Sage Publications) 1978.

Mayers, J.M.:
"Administering Agricultural Development Through a Public Corporation: The Case of Barbados",
Agricultural Administration, Vol. 12, 1983.

Mayfied, J.B.:
Local Institutions and Egyptian Rural Development
(Ithaca: Cornell University) 1974.

Mehta, Prayag:
Bureaucracy, Organizational Behaviour and Development
(New Delhi: Sage Publications) 1989.

Minocha, A.C.:
"Decentralised Planning in India And the Role of Administration",
Indian Journal of Regional Science, Vol. XIX, No. 1, 1987.

Mekpaiboon, S.:
"Administrative Reforms For Decentralized Development: Some Experiments in Thailand,
in Saxena, A.P. (ed.):
Administrative Reforms for Decentralized Development
(Kuala Lumpur: Asian and Pacific Development Administration Center) 1980.

Midgley, J.; Hall, A.; Hardiman, M. and Narine, D.:
Community Participation, Social Development and the State
(New York: Metheun) 1986

Minns, Richard and Thoornley, Jennifer:
"Do Local Authorities have a Role in Economic Planning?"
Planner, Vol. 63, No. 3, May 1977.

Morgan, T.E.:
Decentralization for Development: The Form and Substance of International Development Strategies
(Madison: University of Wisconsin) Regional Planning and Area Development Project Occasional paper No.3, 1981.

Murthi, K.L.N.:
Planning for Integrated Area Development
(New Delhi : B.R. Publishing Company) 1986.

Mushi, S.S.:
"Popular Participation and Regional Development Planning: the Politics of Decentralized Administration",
Tanzania Notes and Records, No. 83, Dares Salaam, 1978.

Mutahaba, G.:
"Local Autonomy And National Planning: Complementary or Otherwise? Case Study from Tanzania",
The African Review, Vol. 4, 1974.

Negi, S.S.:
Tribal Welfare, Development and Administration
(Dehradun: International Book Distribution) 1986.

Neale, W.C.:
"Indian Community Development: Local Government, Local Planning and Rural Policy Since 1950",
Economic Development and Cultural Change, Vol. 33, No. 4, 1985.

Nicholson, N. and Khan, D.A.:
Basic Democracies and Rural Development in Pakistan
(Ithaca: Cornell University, Center for International Studies) Special Series on Rural Local Government, No. 10, 1974.

Nicholson, N.K.:
"Application of Public Choice Theory to Rural Development",
in Russell, S. and Nicholson, N.K. (eds.):
Public Choice and Rural Development
(Washington D.C.: Resources for Future) 1981.

Noranitipadungkarn, C.:
"Decentralization, Coordination and Development in Thailand",
in Cheema .S. (ed.):
Institutional Dimensions of Regional Development
(Singapore: Maruzen Asia, for United Nations Centre for Rural Development) 1981.

Okafor, F.C.:
"Administrative Problems of Integrated Rural Development: Some Lessons From Nigeria",
Planning and Administration, 1980-2, (The Hague).

Olisa, M.:
"Local Government and Community Development in East-Central State",
in Collins, P. (ed.):
Administration for Development in Nigeria
(Lagos: African Education Press) 1980.

Omari, C.K.:
Strategy for Rural Development: Tanzania Experience
(Nairobi: East African Literature Bureau) 1976.

Onokerhoraye, A.G.:
"Urban and Regional Planning and Development Administration in Nigeria",
International Review of Administrative Sciences, Vol. 42, 1976.

Opoku - Afriyie, Y.:
"Popular Participation in Regional Development in Ghana",
Greenhill Journal of Administration (Ghana) Vol. 2, No. 3, 1975.

Owens, E. and Shaw, R.:
Development Reconsidered: Bridging the Gap Between Government and People,
(Lexington: D.C. Heath & Co.) 1972.

Panandiker, V.A.; Pai, R.N. and Sharma, O.P.:
Development Bureaucracy
(New Delhi: Oxford and IBH Publishing Co.) 1983.

Panandiker, V.A.P.:
Development Administration in India
(Delhi: McMillan,(1974.)

Passmore, G.C.:
The National Policy of Community Development in Rhodesia, with Special reference to Local Government in the African Rural Areas
(University of Rhodesia, Department of Political Science) Source Book No.5, 1972.

Philippines, University of, Local Government Centre:
Survey of Training Needs of Local Government
(Manila: University of Philippines) 1974.

Picard, L.A. and Endresen, K.:
Report on A Study of the Manpower and Training Needs of the Unified Local Government Service, 1982-1992,
2 Vols., (Gaborone Botswana: Government Printer) 1981.

Project on Managing Decentralization:
Decentralized Models of Agricultural Administration
(Report of a Conference organized by the University of California at Berkeley and USAID, at Lake Naivasha, Kenya, December 1981)

Rao, K.V.N.:
Panchayati Raj: an Analytical Survey
(Hyderabad: National Institute of Community Development) 1977.

Rao, M.V.:
"People's Participation: Myths and Realities",
paper presented at a Seminar on People Participation in Resource Management, Institute of Economic Growth, Delhi, 20th November 1986.

Raup, P.M.:
"Some Interrelationships Between Public Administration and Agricultural Development",
in Uphoff, N. and Ilchman, W.F. (eds.):
The Political Economy of Development: Theoretical and Empirical Contributions
(Berkeley: University of California press) 1972.

Reddy, G.R.:
Panchayati Raj and Rural Development in Andhra Pradesh, India
(Ithaca: Cornell University, Center for International Studies) Special Series on Rural Local Government, No.4, 1974.

Reilly, W.:
"District Development Planning in Botswana",
in Studies in Decentralization: Papua New Guinea, Botswana, Sri Lanka (Manchester: University of Manchester) Manchester Papers in Development, No. 3, 1981.

Reggs, F.W.:
Administration in Developing Countries, The Theory of Prismatic Society
(Boston: Houghton Mifflin) 1964.

Rondinelli, D.A.:
"National Investment Planning and Equity Policy in Developing Countries: The Challenge of Decentralized Administration",
Policy Sciences, Vol. 10, 1978.

Rondinelli, D.A.:
"Administration of Integrated Rural Development Policy: the Politics of Agrarian Reform in Developing Countries",
World Politics, Vol. 31, 1979.

Rondinelli, D.A.:
"Government Decentralization in Comparative Perspective: Theory and Practice in Developing Countries",
International Review of Administrative Sciences, Vol. 47, 1981. This article provides a comprehensive overview of the role of decentralization in development and alternative forms of decentralization.

Rondinelli, D.A.:
"Administrative Decentralization and Economic Development: The Sudan's Experiment with Decentralization",
Journal of Modern African Studies, Vol. 19, 1981.

Rondinelli, D.A.:
"Dilemma of Development Administration Complexity and Uncertainty in Central Oriented Bureaucracies",
World Politics, Vol. 35, No. 1, 1982.

Rondinelli, D.A.:
"Decentralization of development administration in East Africa",
in Cheema, G.S. and Rondinelli D.A. (eds.):
Decentralization and Development: Policy Implementation in Developing Countries
(Beverly Hills and London: Sage Publications) 1983.

Rondinelli, D.A.:
"Administrative Decentralisation for Agricultural and Rural Development Programmes in Asia",
in Rivera, W.M. and Schram, S.G. (eds.):
Agricultural Extension Worldwide
(London: Croom Helm) 1987.

Rondinelli, D.A.; McCullough, James S. and Johnson, R.W.:
"Analysing Decentralisation Policies in Developing Countries: A Political Economy Framework",
Development and Change, Vol. 20, No. 1, 1989.

Rondinelli, D.A.:
" The Dilemma of Development Administration Complexity and Uncertainty in Central Oriented Bureaucracies",
World Politics, Vol. 35, No. 1, 1982.

Rondinelli, D.A. and Mandell, M.B.:
"Meeting Basic Needs in Asia, Government Capacity and Performance",
Public Administration and Development, Vol. I, 1981.

Rondinelli, D.A.; Nellis, J.R. and Cheema, G.S.:
Decentralization in Developing Countries: A Review of Recent Experience

(Washington D.C.: World Bank Staff Working Paper) 1983.

Rondinelli, D.A. and Nellis, J.R.:
"Assessing Decentralisation Policies in Developing Countries",
Development Review, Vol. 4, No. 1, 1986.

Rondinelli, D.A. and Ruddle, K.:
Urbanization and Rural Development: A Spatial Policy for Equitable Growth
(New York: Praeger) 1978.

Rondinelli, D.A. and Ruddle, K.:
"Coping with Poverty in International Assistance Policy: An Evaluation of Spatially Integrated Investment Strategies",
World Development, Vol. 6, 1978.

Saha, S.K. and Srivastava, K.:
"Federalism and inter-regional resource allocation policy in India",
Third World Planning Review, Vo. 5 1983, pp. 37-56.

Sanda, A.O. (ed.):
Planning with the People: The Place of the Local Governments in Nigeria's Development Planning Process
(Ibadan: Nigerian Institute of Social and Economic Research) 1980.

Sanwal, Mukul (ed.):
Computer Application in District Administration
(Nainital: Administrative Training Institute) 1986.

Saxena, A.P. (ed.):
Administrative Reforms for Decentralized Development,
(Kuala Lumpur: Asian and Pacific Development Administration Centre) 1980.

Schroeder, L.:
An Assessment of the Revenue Generation Capabilities of Villages, Districts and Arusha Region: Some Policy Options
(Syracuse: Syracuse University, Maxwell School) 1981.

Sharma, Prem Narain:
Project Planning for IRDP Integrated Rural Development
(Lucknow: Print House) 1989.

Shepherd, A.W. and El Neima, A.M.:
Popular Participation in Decentralized Water Supply Planning: A Case Study on the Western District of Northern Kordofan Province, Sudan
(Geneva: International Labour Office, World Employment Programme Research) Working Paper No. WEP 2-32/WP 42, 1982.

Sherwin, W.J.:
Decentralisation for Development: The Concept and its Application in Ghana and Tanzania
(Washington DC: United States Agency for International Development) Development Studies Program, Occasional Paper No.2, 1977.

Simpas, S.S.; Carino, L and Pacho, G.:
Local Government and Rural Development in the Philippines
(Ithaca: Cornell University) Centre for International Studies, Special Series on Rural Local Government, No. 12, 1974.

Smith, B.C.:
"The Measurement of Decentralization",
International Review of Administrative Sciences, Vol. 45, 1979.

Smith, B.C.:
"Measuring Decentralisation",
in Jones, G.W. (ed.):
New Approaches to the Study of Central Local Government Relationship
(Aldershot: Gower) 1980.

Smith, B.C.:
Decentralisation-The Territorial Dimension of the State
(London: George Allen & Unwin) 1985.

Smith, B.C.:
" Spatial Ambiguities: Decentralisation within the State",
Public Administration and Development, Vol. 6, No. 4, 1986.

Slater, D.:
"Territorial Power and the Peripheral State: The Issue of Decentralisation",
Development and Change, Vol. 20, No. 3, July 1989.

Stavis, B.:
Rural Local Government and Agricultural Development in Taiwan
(Ithaca: Cornell University, Center for International Studis) Special Series on Rural Local Government, No.15, 1974.

Stohr, W.B. and Taylor, D.R.F.:
Development from Above or Below? The Dialectics of Regional Planning in Developing Countries
(Chichester: Wiley) 1981.

Stubbings, B.J.J.:
"Integrated Rural Development in Pakistan",
Journal of Administration Overseas, Vol. 13, 1975.

Taylor, L.:
Decentralized Planning: A Case Study of Zambia
(Geneva: International Labour Office, World Employment Programme Research) Working Paper No. WEP 2-32/WP 43, 1982.

Ubogu, R.E. :
"Urbanization, Fiscal Decentralization and Economic Development: A Time Series Evidence",
Socio-Economic Planning Sciences, Vol. 17, 1983, pp. 191-98.

United Nations:
Decentralisation for National and Local Development
(New York: United Nations) 1962.

United Nations:
Interregional Seminar on Major Administrative Reforms in Developing Countries,
October - November 1971, 3 Vols. (New York: United Nations) 1971.

United Nations:
Credit Institutions for Local Authorities
(New York: United Nations) 1972.

United Nations :
Proceedings of the Interregional Seminar on Organization and Administration of Development Planning Agencies,
Kiev, 1972 (New York: United Nations) 1974.

United Nations, Asian and Pacific Development Institute:
Local Level Planning and Rural Development (Asia): Alternative Strategies
(Delhi: Concept Publishing Co.) 1980.

United Nations Centre for Regional Development :
India: An Annotated Bibliography on Rural Regional Development
(Nagoya: UNCRD Project on Regional Development Documentation, No. 2) 1978.

United Nations:
Report of Interregional Seminar on Decentralization for Development,
Khartoum , September 1981 (New York: Department of Technical Cooperation for Development, United Nations 1981) mimeographed.

United Nations:
Popular Participation as a Strategy for Promoting Community-Level Action and National Development
(New York: United Nations) 1981.

United Nations:
"Do local Needs Need Local Powers?",
Development Forum, (Joint UN Information Committee) Vol. 11, No. 5 (June/July) 1983.

United Nations Centre for Regional Development:
Implementing Decentralization Policies and Programmes,
Report of Workshop, (Nagoya: United Nations Centre for Regional Development) 1981.

United Nations, Economic Commission for Asia and Far East:
Role of Governments, Cooperatives and Voluntary Agencies in Community Development
(Bangkok: Economic Commission for Asian and Far East) 1973.

United Nations Educational, Scientific & Cultural Organization:
Eleven Experiences of Innovations in Decentralization of Educational Administration and Management of Local Resources
(Paris: U.N.E.S.C.O.; Division of Educational Policy and Planning) 1980.

Uphoff, N.T. and Esman, M.J.:
Local Organization for Rural Development: Analysis of Asian Experience
(Ithaca: Cornell University, Center for International Studies) 1974.

Thoung, U.:
"Decentralization for development -II",
Journal of Administration Overseas, Vol. 2, 1963.

Wanasinghe, S.:
"Administrative Reforms For Decentralized Development: the Sri Lankan Experience",
in Saxena, A.P. (ed.):
Administrative Reforms for Decentralized Development
(Kuala Lumpur: Asian and Pacific Development Administration Centre) 1980.

Warren, D.M.:
"The Role of Communication Training for District and Regional Level Officials in Ghana's Decentralization Program",
African Studies Association Meeting, Los Angeles, 1979.

Wassem, M.:
"Local Power Structures and the Relevance of Rural Development Strategies: A Case Study of Pakistan",
Community Development Journal, Vol. 17, 1982.

Vyasalu, Vinod:
Development of Backward Areas: Decentralised Production and Regional Development
(New Delhi: Yatan Publishers) 1987.

Williams, G.:
"Promoting the Rural Economy: The Role of the Developmental Agencies in Remote Rural Areas",
Regional Studies, Vol. 18, No. 1, 1984.

Wijayapala, W.A.L. (ed.):
Local Level Planning and Development in Sri Lanka
(Colombo: Government of Sri Lanka, Ministry of Plan Implementation) 1981.

World Bank:
The Design of Organizations for Rural Development Projects: A Progress Report

(Washington D.C.: World Bank) Staff Working Paper 375, 1980.

Wu, C.T. and Ip, D.F.:
"China: Rural Development - Alternating Combinations of Top-down and Bottom-up Strategies",
in Stohr, W.B. and Taylor D.R.F. (eds.):
Development From Above cr Below?.
(Chichester: Wiley, 1981)

APPENDIX B

PROJECT PLANNING AND PROJECT APPRAISAL

Bruce, C.M.F. :
The States of Project Planning - An Introduction to Project Planning
(Washington, D.C. : International Bank for Reconstruction and Development) 1980.

Baldwin, G.B. :
"Discounted cash-flow. What does it mean ?",
Finance and Development, 1969, p. 33

Baum, Warren C. and Stokes M, Tolbert :
Investing in Development Lessons of World Bank Experience
(Washington, D.C : International Bank for Reconstruction and Development/The World Bank) 1985.

Bussery, Andre :
Methods of Project Appraisal in Developing Countries
(Paris : Organisation for Economic Cooperation and Development) 1973

Chambers, Robert :
"Project Selection for Poverty-Focussed Rural Development: Simple is Optimal",
in : World Development, 1978. Vol. 6, No.2, pp.209. 219

Cohen, John M. and Uphoff, Norman T. :
Rural Development Participation : Concepts and Measures for Project Design, Implementation and Evaluation.
(Ithaca, N.Y. : Cornell University) (Monograph Series No. 2), 1977

Dasgupta, Ajit K. and Pearce, D.W. :
Cost-Benefit Analysis : Theory and Practice,
(London : Macmillan) 1978

Dias, Hiran D. and Wickramanayake, B.W.E. :
Manual for Training in rural Development Planning
(Bangkok : Division of Human Settlements Developments, Asian Institute of Technology) 1983

Dias, Hiran D. and Wickramanayaka, B.W.E.; Nanda Rajapakse, and Weber, Karl E.:
Training Course on Rural Development Planning
(Habantota, Sri Lanka) Course Handbook (Bangkok : Division of Human Settlements Development, Asian Institute of Technology) 1983.

F.A.O. :
Guidelines for the Cooperation of Feasibility Studies: Rural Development Projects
(Rome : Food and Agriculture Organization) FAO/World Bank Cooperative Programs, 1975.

F.A.O. :
General Guidelines to the Analysis of Agricultural Projects
(Rome : Food and Agricultural Organization of the United Nations) 1971

Goodman, Louis J. and Ralph N. Love (eds) :
Project Planning and Management.
in Integrated Approach, (New York :Pergamon Press) 1983, p. 11

Gittinger, J.P :
The Economic Analysis of Agricultural Projects,
(Baltimore The Johns Hopkins University Press) 1972, p. 2

Irvin, George :
Modern Cost-Benefit Methods. An Introduction to Financial, Economic and Social Appraisal of Development Projects,
(London : Macmillan Press) 1978.

King, Josh Andrews :
Economic Development Projects and their Appraisal: Cases and Principles from the Experience of the World Bank,
(Baltimore, The Johns Hopkins University Press,) 1967.

Iglesias, Gabriel U. and Romeo B. Ocampo (eds):
Studies in the Management of Rural Development Projects. Cases from Asian Experiences
(Kuala Lumpur : Asian and Pacific Development Centre,) Vol. 1, 1984.

Little, I.M.D,. and Mirrless, J.A. :
Manual of Industrial Project Analysis in Developing Countries. Social Cost-Benefit Analysis.
(Paris : Organization for Economic Cooperation and Development) Vol. 2,1969.

Little, I.M.D. and Mirrless, J.A.:
Project Appraisal and Planning for Developing Countries
(London : Heinemann) 1977

Lal, Deepak :
Methods of Project Analysis : A Review
(Washington, D.C. : The World Bank,) 1974 World Bank Occasional Papers, No. 16.

Luft, Harold S.:
"Benefit-Cost Analysis and Public Policy Implementation From Normative to Positive Analysis",
Public Policy, 1976, Vol. 4 no. 4,p.437.

Levin, Richard I.; Charles, A. Kirkpatrick et al. :
Quantitative Approaches to Management
(London : McGraw-Hill) 1982, p.643.

Rozani, Reza:
"Implementation",
In : Louis J. Goodman and Ralph N. Love (eds):
Project Planning and Management. An Integrated Approach,
(New York : Pergamon Press), 1983.

Lockyer, K.G. :
An Introduction to Critical Path Analysis
(London : Pitman) 1981

Carmichael, David G.:
Construction Engineering Network Techniques
(Bangkok : Asian Institute of Technology), 1985 (Mimeograph), p. 42.

Michael, Standord B. and Linn C. Stuckenbruck :
"Project Planning"
in Linn C. Stuckenbruck (ed.):
The Implementation of Project Management: The Professional's Handbook,
(Reading, Mass. : Addison-Wesley) 1982, .99

Niyabara, Tetsuo:
"Feasibility, Appraisal, and Design",
in Louis J. Goodman and Ralph N. Love(eds) :
Project Planning and Management. An Integrated Approach
(New York : Pergamon Press) 1983, pp, 82-83

Meredith, Jack R. and Mantel Jr. Samuel J.: Project Management.
Managerial Approach,
(New York : John Wiley and Sons) 1985, p. 56.

Miller, Duncan (ed.):
Studies on Project Design, Implementation and Valuation
(Paris : Development Centre of the Organization for Economic

Cooperation and Development 1980.

Merrett, A.J. and Sykes, Allen:
The Finance and Analysis of Capital Projects,
(London : Longman,) 1963.

Miyabara, Totsuo:
"Feasibility, Appraisal and Design",
in Louis J. Goodman and Ralph N. Love (eds) :
Project Planning and Management. An Integrated Approach,
(New York : Pergamon Press) 1983.

Miller, Duncan (ed.) :
Studies on Rural Development : Studies on Project Design, Implementation and Evaluation,
(Paris : Organization for Economic Cooperation and Development) 1980.

Mishan, Edward J. L.:
Cost-Benefit Analysis : An Introduction,
(New York : Praeger) 1971.

Miyan, Khalil :
" The Formulation of Horticultural Projects in Nepal",
Paper presented at the Agricultural Project Analysis and Rural Development Planning Course, Kathmandu, Nepal, Jan. 27-Feb. 29, 1980.

O.E.C.D. :
Manual of Industrial Project Analysis in Developing Countries
(Paris : Organization for Economic Cooperation and Development) 1968.

Seasone, Peter G. :
Cost-Benefit Analysis, A Handbook
(New York: Academic) 1978.

Ogander, Mats (ed) :
The Practical Application of Project Planning by Network Techniques
(New York : John Wiley and Sons,) 1972.

Packward, Philip C. :
Project Appraisal for Development Administration
(The Hague : Mouton,) 1974.

Pouliquen, Louis Y. :
Risk Analysis in Project Appraisal,
(Baltimore : The Johns Hopkins University Press) 1970.

Prest, A.R. and Turrey, R. :
"Cost-Benefit Analysis : A Survey"
Economic Theory, The American Economic Association & the Royal Economic Society, 1966, pp. 155-207.

Rondinelli, Dennis A.:
"Why Development Projects Fail. Problems of Project Management in Developing Countries",
Project Management Quarterly, vol. 3,no. 1, 1976 , pp. 10-15.

Reutlinger, Shlomo :
Techniques for Project Appraisal Under Uncertainty.
(Baltimore : Johns Hopkins University Press) 1970.

Roemer, Michel and Stern, Joseph J. :
The Appraisal of Development Projects : A Practical Guide to Project Analysis with Case Studies and Solutions.
(New York : Praeger) 1975.

Rozani, Reza :
"Implementation",
in Louis J. Goodman and Ralph N.Love (eds):
Project Planning and Management. An Integrated Approach
(New York : Pergamon Press) 1983, p. 135.

Salapatas, James N. :
"Project Management : How much is Enough ?"
in Stuckenbruck, Linn C. (ed.):

The Implementation of Project Management : The Professional's Hand book
(Reading, Mass, : Addison-Wesley) 1982. p. 179.

Seasone, Peter G. and William A. Schaffer :
Cost-Benefit Analysis. Handbook
(New York : Academic Press) 1978.

Squire, Lyn and Van der Tak, Herman G. :
Economic Analysis of Projects
(Baltimore, : The Johns Hopkins University Press) 1975.

tuckenbruck, Linn C. :
"The Implementation of Project Management Getting Off on The Right Foot"
in Stuckenbruck, Linn C. (ed.):
The Implementation of Project Management : The Professional's Handbook
(Reading, Mass, : Addison-Wesley) 1982. pp. 41-42.

Spinner, M. :
Elements of Project Management : Plan, Schedule and Control
(Englewood Cliffs, N.J. : Prentice-Hall) 1981.

Wilson, F.A. :
"The Planning and Appraisal of Rural Development Projects. An Approach Towards an Operational Basis for Determining Viability",
Savings and Development, Vol. 11, No. 2, 1978. pp. 144-152.

Wickramanayake, B.W.E. :
Manual for Training in Rural Development Planning,
(Bangkok : Asian Institute of Technology) 1983, pp. 180-194.

United States Agency for International Development:
Project Evaluation Guidelines,
(Washington, D.C. : Office of Development Programme Review and Evaluation, Agency for International Development) 1974

Vokes, R.W.A.:
"Introduction to Project Planning",
in Karl E. Weber et. al.: Rural Development Planning in Nepal : Course Handbook and Survey Report, (Bangkok : Division of Human Settlements Development, Asian Institute of Technology) 1985, (HSD Manual, 3)

II. Net Work Analysis

Carmichael, David G. :
" Construction Engineering Network Techniques"
(Bangkok Asian Institute of Technology,) 1985 (mimeograph)

Ralph, Diaz :
Organizational Responsibility Charting Technique and Network Analysis As Applied to Regional Planning Organizations
(Nagoya United Nations Centre for Regional Development) 1979.

Elimaghraby, Saleh Eldin; Activity Networks :
Project Planning and Control by Network Models
(New York : John Wiley and Sons) 1977.

Garzia, Maurizio :
Project Planning and Monitoring Using Network Analysis Technique : Theoretical Aspects and Some Applications to Agricultural and Rural Development Projects in Nepal
(Kathmandu : Agricultural projects Services Centre (APROSC) Project Planning Series- Nepal No. NP 2, 1980.

Goodman, Louis J. and Ralph N. Love (eds),
Project Planning and Management. An Integrated Approach.
(New York : Pergamon Press) 1983.

Levin, Richard I.; Kirkpatrick, Charles A. et.al.:
Quantitative Approaches to Management
(London : McGraw-Hill) 1982.

Lombaers, H.J.M. (ed.) :
Project Planning by Network Analysis, Proceedings of the Second International Congress on Network Analysis
(Amsterdam North- Holland) 1969.

Mandl, Christoph :
Applied Network Optimization.
(London : Academic Press,) 1979.

Ogander, Mats :
The Practical Application of Project Planning by Network Techniques
(Stockholm : Almquist and Wiksell) 1972.

Phillips, Don T. and Diaz, Albert Garcia :
Fundamentals of Network Analysis
(Englewood Cliffs, N.J. : Prentice - Hall) 1981.

Simms, Alfred G. and Britten, John R.:
Project Network Analysis and Critical Path
(Brighton, Sussex : The Machinery Publishing Co.) 969.

Smith, David Kendall:
Network Optimization Practice : A Comparative Guide.
(Chichester, West Sussex : Ellis Harwood) 1982.

Klingman, D. and J.M. Mulvey (eds) :
Network Models and Associated applications
(Amsterdam : North - Holland) 1981.

Abeyrama, Tilakasena and Weber, Karl E.:
Evaluating NGO Sponsored Income Generating Projects, Review and Recommendations
(Bangkok : Division of Human Settlements Development, Asian Institute of Technology) 1986 ("HSD Working Paper", No. 22), pp. 40-41.

Abeyrama, Tilakasena and Weber, Karl E.:
Evaluation of IGPs : Observations of Current Procedure, Assessment of Methods and Techniques, and Recommendations for a Unified Approach
(Bangkok : Division of Human settlements Development, Asian Institute of Technology) A Report Prepared for Foster Parents Plan International, December, 1986 (Revised April, 1987).

Bamberger, Michael and Hewitt, Eleanor.:
Monitoring and Evaluating Urban Development Programs : A Handbook for Programme Managers and Researchers, Discussion Paper on Water Supply and Urban Development, Operation Policy Staff
(Washington, D.C. : The World Bank) Report No. UDD-67, 1985, p. 1-10.

Cain, Glen G. and Hollister, Robinson G.:
"The Methodology of Evaluating Social Action Programs",
in Evaluating Social Programs : Theory, Practice, and Politics, edited by Peter H. Rossi and Walter Williams (New York : Seminar Press) 1972, pp. 109-112.

Casley, D.J. and Lury, D.A.:
A Handbook on Monitoring and Evaluation of Agriculture and Rural Development Projects, Monitoring and Evaluation Unit,

Agriculture and Rural Development Department, CPS,
(Washington, D.C. : World Bank) 1981 p.8.

Casley, Dennis J. and Lury, Denis A.:
Monitoring and Evaluation of Agriculture and Rural Development Projects
Baltimore, Md : The Johns Hopkins University Press, 1982.

Freeman, Howard E.; and Rossi, Peter H. Sonia R. Wright, Sonia R.:
Evaluating Social Projects in Developing Countries,
(Paris : Development Centre of the Organization for Economic Cooperation and Development) 1979, p. 20.

Guttentag, Marcia and Elmer L. Struening (eds),
Handbook of Evaluation Research Vol. 2.
(Beverley Hills, Calf : Sage Publications) 1975.

Goldmark, Susan and Rosengard, Jay:
A Manual for Evaluation of small-scale Enterprise Development Projects,
A.I.D Programme Design and Evaluation Methods, Report No. 6, Washington, D.C. USAID) 1985

III. Project Evaluation and Monitoring

Madaus, George F.; Stufflebeam, Daniel; Scriven, Michael S.:
"Program Evaluation : A Historical Overview"
in
Evaluation Models : Viewpoints in Educational and Human Services Evaluation,
edited by George F. Madaus, Michael S. Scriven and Daniel L. Stufflemeam, (Boston : Kluwer-Nijhoff 1983) fourth printing 1986, pp. 3-22.

Morrell, Jonathan A.,
Program Evaluation in Social Research,
(New York : Pergamon Press) 1979, pp. 6-25.

Madaus, George G.F. Scriven, Michael and Stufflebeam, Daniel L. (eds).:
Evaluation Models : Viewpoints on Educational and Human services Evaluation,
Boston : Kluwer-Nijhoff Publishing, 1983.

Patton, Michael Quinn:
Qualitative Evaluation Methods,
(Beverley Hills, Calf, : Sage Publications) 1980.

Rossi, Peter H. and Williams, Walter (eds.):
Evaluating Social Programs. Theory, Practice and Politics
(New York : Seminar Press) 1972.

Sweet, Charles F. and Rosengard, Jay:
Guidelines for the Design and Use of Monitoring and Evaluation Systems in Managing Rural Development.
(Washington, D.C. : Development Alternatives Inc.) 1983.

Weber, Karl E. and Md. Rafiq Azimi, Samart Nitsmer, Christoph Schneller, Abdul Majid Tantray:
Baseline Survey
(Bangkok : The Asian Institute of Technology) June 1981.

Weber, Karl E.; Md. Rafiq Azimi; Samart Nitsmer; Christoph Schneller; Abdul Majid Tantray:
First Monitoring Survey
(Bangkok: The Asian Institute of Technology) July 1981.

Weber, Karl E.; Md. Rafiq Azimi; Samart Nitsmer; Christoph Schneller; and Abdul Majid Tantray:
Second Monitoring Survey
(Bangkok : The Asian Institute of Technology) March 1982.

Weber, Karl E.; Md. Rafiq Azimi, Chintana Chantachaeng, Samart Nitsmer, Christoph Schneller and Abdul Majid Tantray:
Research Design and Survey Organization,
Phase I (1980-1981) (Bangkok : The Asian Institute of Technology) July 1982.

Weber, Karl E.; Chintana Chantachaeng; Srisaang Kaojarern; Christoph Schneller and Danai Turongruang:
Synopsis and Summary of Findings through Monitoring Project Implementation
Phase III March, 1979 until 1 October, 1981, (Bangkok: The Asian Institute of Technology) August 984.

Weber, Karl E.; Chintana Chantachaeng, and Schneller Christoph:
Farm Management Survey Manual (FMSM).
(Bangkok : The Asian Institute of Technology). June 1984, xiv., 73 p.

Weber, Karl E. and Songpol Jetanavanich:
Final Report on Monitoring Methods and Techniques
March 1985, xiv. 219 p. 2 Charts, appendices.

IV. Evaluation Research

Franklin, J.L. and J.H. Trasher :
An Introduction to Program Evaluation
(New York : Wiley) 1976.

Hoole, F.W. :
Evaluation Research and Development Activities
(London : Sage Publications) 1978.

Suchman, E. :
Evaluative Research.
(New York : Russel Sage) 1967.

Weiss, C.H. :
Evaluation Research
(Englewood Cliffs, N.J. : Prentice Hall) 1972.

Morris, Lynn Lyons and Fits-Gibbon, Carol Taylor:
How to Deal with Coals and Objectives
(Beverly Hills & London : Sage) 1976

Morris, Lynn and Fitz-Gibbon, Carol Taylor:
How to Measure Program Implementation
(Beverly Hills & London : Sage) 1978

Morris, Lynn Lyons and Fitz-Gibbon, Carol Taylor:
How to Measure Achievement.
(Beverly Hills & London : Sage)1978.

Fitz-Gibbon, Carol Taylor and Morris, Lynn Lyons:
How to Design and Program Evaluation
(Beverly Hills & London : Sage)1978.

Morris, Lynn Lyons and Fitz-Gibbon, Carol Taylor:
How to Present an Evaluation Report.
(Beverly Hills & London : Sage)1978.

Henerson, Marlene, Morris, Lynn Lyons and Fitz-Gibbon, Carol Taylor:
How to Measure Attitudes
(Beverly Hills & London : Sage)1978.

Morris, Lynn Lyons, and Fitz-Gibbon, Carol Taylor:
Evaluator's Handbook
(Beverly Hills & London : Sage)1978.

Fitz-Gibbon, Carol Taylor and Morris, Lynn Lyons:
How to Calculate Statistics.
(Beverly Hills & London : Sage).

V. Monitoring Methods and Economic Project Appraisal

Abeyrama Tilakasena and Weber, Karl E. :
Monitoring in Retrospect : Reflections on Practical Experience and Recommendations
(Bangkok : Division of Human Settlements Development, Asian Institute of Technology) HSD Working Paper, No. 25.

Cenera and Tepping, B.J. :
A System for Monitoring and Evaluating Agricultural Extension Projects,
(Washington, D.C. : World Bank 1977.

Murphy Josette and Leendert II, Sprey :
Monitoring and Evaluation of Agricultural Change.
(Wageningen : International Institute for Reclamation and Improvement/IIRI) 1982.

Imboden, N. A:
Management Approach to Project Appraisal and Evaluation.
(Paris : OECD) 1978.

Lal, Deepak :
Wells and Welfare : An Exploratory Cost-Benefit Analysis of the Economics of Small-Scale Irrigation in Maharashtra.
(Paris : OECD) 1972.

Little, dan M.D. and Mirrless, James A. :
Project Appraisal and Planning of Developing Countries
(London : Heinemann Educational Books) 1974.

Overseas Development Administration :
A Guide to Project Appraisal in Developing Countries
(London : Her Majesty's Stationery Office) 1972.

Schneider, Harmut :
National Objectives and Project Appraisal in developing Countries,
(Paris : OECD.) 1975.

Squire, Lyn and van der tak, Herman G. :
Economic Analysis of Projects,
(Baltimore : The Johns Hopkins University Press, for World Bank), 1975.

United Nations Industrial Development Organisation (UNIDO):
Guidelines or Project Evaluation.
(New York : United Nations) 1972.

Burton, Thomas L. and Cherry, Gordon E. :
Social Research Techniques for Planners
(London : Allen and Unwin) 1970, Publication of the University of Birmingham, Centre for Urban and Regional Studies.

Miller, Delbert C. :
Handbook of Research Design and Social Measurement
(New York : Longman, 4th edition) 1983.

Sanders William B. and Pinhey, Thomas K. :
The Conduct of Social Research
(Rinehart and Winston) 1983.

Wright, S.R. :
Quantitative Methods and Statistics : A Guide to Social research.
(London : Sage Publications) 1979.

Webb. Eugene J.; Campbell; Donald T. Schwartz, Richard D.; Lee Sechrest :
Unobstrusive Measures : Nonreactive Research in the Social Science.
(London : Chicago : Rand McNally) 1972.

Maxwell, A.E. :
Analysing Qualitative Data
(London : Champman & Hall Science Paperbacks, No. 118) 1971.

Schatzman, L. and Strauss, A.A. :
Field Research : Strategies for a Natural Sociology
(Englewood Cliffs, N.J. : Prentice - Hall) 1973.

Weber, Karl E. and Abeyrama, Tilakasena. :
Observation - An Effective Alternative to Oral Communication: Nine Topical Survey Schedules.
(Bangkok : Division of Human Settlements Development, Asian Institute of Technology) HSD Reference Material, No. 9.

Hunt, K.E. :
Agricultural Statistics for Developing countries.
(Oxford : Institute of Agrarian Affairs, University of Oxford) 1969.

Hursh, Gerald D. :
Survey Research Methods in Developing Countries.
(New Delhi : Longmans-Orient) 1976.

Lynch, S.J. (ed.) :
Field Data Collection in Developing Countries :Experiences in Asia.
(New York : Agricultural Development Council) 1976.

Bennet, C.A. and Lumsdaine, A.A. (eds.) :
Evaluation and Experiment
(New York : Academic Press) 1975.

Campbell, D.T. and Stanley, J.C. :
Experimental and Quasi-Experimental designs for Research
(Chicago : Rand McNally) 1966.

Cook, Thomas D. and Campbell, Donals T. :
Quasi-Experimentation : Design and Analysis Issues for Field Settings.
(Chicago : Rand McNally, 979.

Riecken, H.W. and Boruch, R.F. (eds) :
Social Experimentation : A Method for Planning and Evaluating Social Intervention
(New York : Academic Press) 1974.

Rossi, P.H.; Freeman, H.E. and S.R. Wright :
Evaluation : A Systematic Approach
(London : Sage Publications) 1979.

Fisher, R.A. :
The Design of Experiments
New York : Hafner, 1951, 6th ed.

Flanagan, J.C. :
"General Considerations in the Selection of Test Items and a Short Method of Estimating the Product-moment Coefficient From Data at the Tails of the Distribution,"
Journal of Educational Psychology, 1939, 30, pp. 674-80.

Glass, G.V., and Maquire, T.O. :
Analysis of Time-Series Quasi-Experiments, S. Office of Education Report No. 6-8329.
(Boulder, Colorado : Laboratory of Educational Research University of Colorado) 1968.

Hammond, R.L. :
Evaluation at the Local Level
(Tucson, Arizona : EPIC Evaluation Centre) 1972 Mimeograph.

Kalpan, A. :
The Conduct of Inquiry
(San Francisco, California : Chandler) 1964.

Rippey, R.M. (ed.):
Studies in Transactional Evaluation
(Berkeley, California : McCutcheon,) 1973.

Stake, R.E. :
"Objectives, Priorities and Other Judgement Data,"

Review of Educational Research, 1970, 40.

Suchman, E.A. :
Evaluative Research
(New York : Russell Sage Foundation) 967.

Taylor, J.P. :
An Administrator's Perspective of Evaluation,
(Kalamazoo, Michigan : Western Michigan University) 1974.

APPENDIX C

REGIONAL STUDIES AND REGIONAL DEVELOPMENT PLANS

AFGHANISTAN

Conditions of and Possiblilities for the Economic Development of the City of Kabul (Frankfurt\m. ; K.H. Hendrikshon), 1961.

Study of the Economic Development of Paktia Province - Special Report on Agriculture,(Frankfurt/m. ; K.H. Hendrikshon), 1964.

AUSTRALIA

The Pilbara Study : Report on the Industrial Development of the Pilbara, (Canberra : Australian Government, Department of Northern Development, & Government of Western Australia, Department of Industrial Development), 1974.

Industrial Potential of the Bowen Basin Region-Queensland,(Canberra: Australian Government Publishing Service),1974.

Resources and Industry of the Mackay Region, (Canberra : Australian Government Publishing Service) 1974.

Regional Planning in Victoria - Papers From a Symposium Held to Consider the Theory, Practice and Need for Regional Planning in Victoria, (Victoria: National Trust of Australia) 1976.

"Reckhampton-a Growth Centre of Tomorrow" (Rockhampton : Rockhampton Regional Promotion Bureau) 1973.

BELIZE

Feasibility Study of a Regional Agricultural Project Production and Marketing of Grain/Oil Seeds in the Belize River Valley of Belize (Michael: Carribbean Development Bank) 1975.

BOLIVIA

Report on Village and Irrigation Management Research in the Abapo-Izozog Project, (Rehovot : Israel : Ministry of Agriculture, Centre for International Agricultural Cooperation) 1978.

BOTSWANA

Appraisal of the Francistown Urban Development Project, (Washington D.C. : International Bank for Reconstruction) 1974.

Land Usage in Barotseland, (Lusaka: The Rhodes-Livingstone Institute, D.U. Peters) 1959.

A Study of Constraints on Agricultural Development in The Republic of Botswana, (Rome : Division of Planning and Statistics, Ministry of Agriculture, and The FAO of the U.N) 1974.

Kgalagadi District Development Plan 1977-1982, (Kgalagadi, Botswana : Kgalagadi District Council, Kgalagadi District Development Committee) 1977.

Central District Development Plan 1977=1982 (Central District, Botswana: Central District Council, Central District Development Committee) 1977

Ngamiland District Development Plan 1977-1982,(Ngamiland : Botswana ; North West District Council, Ngamiland District Development Committee) 1972.

Ghanzi District Development Plan 1977-1982, (Ghanzi: Ghanzi District Council, Ghanzi District Development Committee) 1977.

Kweneng District Development Plan 1977-1982 (Kweneng : Kweneng District Council, Kweneng District Development Committee) 1977.

Kgatleng District Development Plan 1977-1982,(Kgatleng : Kgatleng District Council, Kgatleng District Development Committee) 1977.

South-East District Development Plan 1977-1982, (South East District : South East District Council, South East District Development Committee) 1977.

Chobe District Development Plan 1977-1982, (Chobe : North West District Council, Chobe District Development Committee) 1977.

BANGLADESH

Minimum Package Programme (Phase I) - Project : North West Division: Preparation Mission. Vol. I : Main Report (Rome : FAO of the U.N.) 1976.

BURMA

The Namsang Resettlement Project-A Pioneering Task of the Defence Services, An Introduction (Namsang : Resettlement Unit) 1961.

Dry Zone Development Project, (Jerusalem: Water Resources Development International Ltd., Agricultural Department) 1962.

Report on Water Resources Investigation in Part of The Dry Zone (Tel Aviv : TAHAL Water Planning Ltd.) 1963.

COOK ISLANDS

Project Formulation and Evaluation Cook Islands Pineapple Scheme, (Rarotonga : UN Advisory Team for the Pacific) 1973.

CAMEROON

Report and Recommendation of the President to the Executive Directors on a Proposed Credit to the Federal Republic of Cameroon for a Rice Irrigation Project (Washington, D.C. : International Development Agency) 1972.

CHAD

Multipurpose Herder Support Project of the USAID Financed Chad Range and Livestock Development Project 201, (Chad : AID; Ministry of Agriculture) 1976.

CHILE

Proposal for an Integrated Research Programme on Watershed, Pasture and Animal Husbandry Development in the Norte Chico of Chile (Rehovot : Centre for International Agricultural Cooperation,) 1976.

COLOMBIA

Atlantico No. 3 Irrigation Project Colombia (Washington D.C. : International Bank for Reconstruction and Development) 1967.

Plan for Operations for the Design and Implementation of Atlantico Project No. 3 , First Phase (Tel Aviv : TAHAL Consulting Engineers) 1967.

Atlantico Project No. 3, South Sector-Feasibility Study, Stage II, Phase I : Non Irrigated Farming (Bogota : INCORA;TAHAL Consulting Eng. Ltd. (Israel), 1970.

Second Atlantico Development Project (Washington D.C. : Interntional Bank for Reconstruction and Development) 1972.

Report and Recommendation of the President to the Executive Directors on a proposed Loan to the Republic of Colombia for the Second Atlantico Development Project (Washington D.C. : International Bank for Reconstruction and Development) 1972.

Atlantico No. 3. - Irrigation Project, Quarterly Report December, 1969. (Bogota : Instituto Colombiano de la Reforma Agraria) 1969.

Atlantico No.3- International Project, Halfyearly Report December 31,1970. (Bogota : Instituto Colombiano de la Reforma Agraria)1969.

Special Physical and Chemical Studies South Sector Atlantico Project No.3 (Bogota : Instituto Colombiano de la Reforma Agraria) 1965.

Agrologic Study of the South Sector of the Department of Atlantico, Part IV (Bogota : Instituto Colombiano de la Reforma Agraria) 1965.

Atlantico No. 3 Project - Plan of Operations 1974. Second Phase (Draft) (Bogota : Instituto Colombiano de la Reforma Agraria) 1973.

Bogota Urban Development Study, Phase II, Vol. I (Bogota : International Bank for Reconstruction and Development) 1973.

Caqueta Land Colonization Project (Washington D.C. : International Bank for Reconstruction and Development and International Development Agency) 1971.

Appraisal of the Caqueta Rural Settlement Project (Phase II) (Washington D.C. : International Bank for Reconstruction & Development, and International Development Agency)1975.

The Autonomous Regional Corporation of the Cauca and the Development of the Upper Cauca Valley (Washington, D.C. : International Bank for Reconstruction and Development) 1955.

Reconnaissance Report on Groundwater Development Possibilites in the Gujira Region (Tel Aviv : TAHAL Consulting Engiaeers Ltd., and Institut Colombino de la Reforma Agraria) 1973.

Urba : A Study for a Region in Colombia, (Retterdam: Bouwecentrum Internatioanal Education) 1968.

Cesar No. 1 Project-Feasibility Study, Quarterly Report (Bogota : INCORA ; TAHAL Consulting Engineers Ltd., Israel and Instituto Colombiao de la Reforma Agraria) 1969.

Cesar Project No. 1 Feasibility Study, Quarterly Report No. 5-August to October, 1970 (Bogota : TAHAL Consulting Engineers Ltd., Israel, and Instituto Colombiano de la Reforma Agraria) 1970.

Cesar Project No. 1 - Feasibility Study, Progress Report No. 6 November to December 1970 (Bogota : Instituto Colombiano de la Reforma Agraria, and TAHAL Consulting Enginner Ltd., Israel) 1970.

Agriguani Agricultural Feasibility Study-Progress Report April to June 1971. (Bogota : Instituto Colombiano de la Reforma Agraria and Montreal Engineering Company Ltd., Canada) 1971.

Report of the Colombia Integrated Rural Development Project (Rome : Food and Agriculture Organisation of the U.N., The World Bank Cooperative Programme) 1975.

Staff Project Report-Colombia Integrated Rural Development Project (Bogota : The World Bank, Latin America and the Caribbean Regional Office) 1976.

An Appraisal of the Corodoba 2 Agricultural Development Project (Washington, D.C.: International Bank for Reconstruction and Development) 1974.

DOMINICAN REPUBLIC

El Sisal Development Project (Rehovot : Centre for International Agricultural Cooperation) 1973.

Integrated Rural Development Projects, an Evaluation of their Generational Effects - II. Small holder Settlement Project "Alexander Dothan" (El Sisal, Azua Province) (Rehovot : Centre for International Agricultural Cooperation) 1974.

ECUADOR

Project for the Irrigation Plan of the Loja Province (Quito : Subcommission Ecuatoriana, Programma Regional para Desarrollo del Sur del Ecuador) 1979.

Feasibility Study for the Irrigation Project Santiago in the Loja Province (Quito : Subcommission Ecuatoriana, Programma Regional para Desarrollo del Sur del Ecuador) 1975.

Socio Economic Diagnosis of the Rio Nangaritza Valley, Provincia de Zamora-Chinchipe (Quito : Subcommission Ecuatoriana, Programma Regional para Desarrallo del Sur del Ecuador) 1977.

Integrated Rural Development - Provincia de /Zamora - Chichipe, Canton Zamora (Quito : Subcommission Ecuatoriana, Programma Regional para Desarrollo del Sur del Ecuador) 1977.

Socio-Economic Survey of the Zamora and Nangaritza Valleys (Quito: Subcommission Ecuatoriana, Progaramma Regional para Desarrollo del Sur del Ecuador) 1977.

Proposal for Regional Planning in the Southern Region Of Ecuador (Quito: Subcommission Ecuatoriana, Programma Regional para Desarrollo del Sur del Ecuador) 1976.

CONGO - POOL

Rural Development Programme in the Region of Pool-Plan of Operation, (New - York : UNDP, Special Fund) 1970.

EGYPT

Water Resources and Soil Potential Development in the New Valley-Mission Report Vol. I to IV. (Cairo : Arab Republic of Egypt; German Agency for Technical Cooperation Ltd., Bundesanstalt fur Geowissenschaften und Rohstoffe; Geographisches Institut der Universitat Wurzburg; Salzgitter Consult GmbH,) 1976.

The Study and Evaluation of the Rehabilitation Process in the Newly Settled Communities in Land Reclamation Areas, Vol. I & II (Cairo : American University) 1975.

Appraisal of Agricultural Development Project, (Washington, D.C.: International Bank for Reconstruction and Development) 1978.

ETHIOPIA

Report on Survey of the Awash River Basin, Vols. I to V, (Rome : Food and Agriculture Organisation of the United Nations) 1965.

Report No. 1 on the Establishment of a Regional Development Project in Ethiopia Part II : Project Outline, (Asela : Swedish International Development Agency) 1966.

Report No. 11 on the Establishment of a Regional Development Project in Ethiopia (Chilalo) (Addis Ababa : Swedish International Development Agency) 1967.

The Changing Rural Society in Arussi Land : Some Findings From a Field Study 1967-68 (Addis Ababa : Chilalo Agricultural Development Unit) 1968.

A Master Plan for Water Resources and Supplies Within CADU's First Project Area, (Addis Ababa : Chilalo Agricultural Development Agency) 1970.

Survey of the Consumption of Coffee, Tea, Tobacco and Alcohol in a Market Town (Sagure) Especially with Regard to the Cost (Addis Ababa : Chilalo Agricultural Development Unit) 1971.

Chilalo Agricultural Development Unit (CADU)- Collection of Papers No. 1 to No. 4. (Addis Ababa : Chilalo Agrticultural Development Unit) 1969 to 1971.

Diffusion of Agricultural Innovations in Chilalo Awraja (Addis Ababa : Institute of Development Research, Haile Selassie University) 1975.

Metahara Project - Masterplan for the Development and Management of the Estates (Tel Aviv : Water Resources Development International Ltd.) 1961.

Wolamo Agricultural Development Project (Washington, D.C. : International Bank for Reconstruction and Development; International Development Agency) 1969.

Appraisal of Second Wolamo Agricultural Development Project (Washington, D.C.: International Bank for Reconstruction and Development; International Development Agency) 1974.

Appraisal of an Agricultural Minimum Pakage Project Ethiopia (Washington, D.C. : International Bank for Reconstruction and Development) 1973.

Development of the Awash Valley Project-Interim Report (Rome : Food and Agriculture Organisation of the United Nations; UNDP and The Government of Ethiopia) 1974.

Third Development Programme 1971/72 to 1973/74 (Bathurst : Government Printer) 1971.

Preliminary Survey on Possiblilities of Rural Development in The Gambia (Rehovot : Settlement Study Centre) 1972.

Report of the Gambia Rice Development Project (FAO./IRBD Cooperative Program) (Rome: Food and Agriculture Organisation of the United Nations) 1971.

Appraisal of an agricultural Development Project (Washington D.C.: International Bank for Reconstruction and Development ; International Development Agency) 1972.

Proposals for a Land Resources Development Project in The Gambia (Land Resources Division; Foreign and Commonwealth Office, Overseas Development Administration, Survey) 1971.

Report of a Mission on Gambia River Basin (Foreign and Commonwealth Office Overseas Development Administration) 1970.

GHANA

A Socio-Economic Survey (Accra : Ministry of Social and Rural Development, Rural Planning Department) 1969.

Development of the South Eastern Coastal Savannah Accra Plains and the Dawhweny Dam Projects (Accra : Ministry of Food and Agriculture, Soil, Water and Land-Use Branch) 1959.

Abstract of the Peki Blengo Agricultural Development Project (Frankfurt: Bundesministerium fur Wirtschaftliche Zusammenarbeit) 1968.

Feasibility Study on Development of a Commercial Plantation with Smallholders for the Production Of Oil Palms in Central Region, Ghana (London : Commonwealth Development Corporation) 1976.

Feasibility Study Report on Wood Complex Project to be Sited in the Central Region Ghana by Assin Foso Wood Complex Ltd. (Central Regional Development Corporation) 1978.

GILBERT AND ELLICE ISLANDS

Physical Planning in the Gilbert Islands with Particular Reference to the Islands of Abemama and Butaritari,(Suva : U.N. Development Advisory Team) 1975.

The Integration and Colonization of the Brazilian Portion of the Amazon Basin (Nijmegen : Geografisch en Planologisch Institute, Katholieke Universitiet) 1975.

Five Year Plan for the Development of the Brazilian Northeast

(Nordeste : Presidencia de Republica ; Superintendencia de Desenvolvimento do Nordeste) 1961.

The Third Master Plan for the Social and Economic Development of the Northeast 1966-1968, (Racife : United States Agency for International Development/Brazil) 1965.

Northeast Brazil-Rio Grtande do Norte Rural Development Project Report (Washington D.C. : The World Bank, Rural Development Division, Agriculture and Rural Development Department) 1975.

Report on a Mission to the Northeast of Brazil (Rome and Rehovot : Gabriele Pescatore, Raanan Weitz,) 1966.

Proposal for the Establishment of the Central Semi-Arid Zone Research Institute for Northeastern Brazil (Beer-Sheva : Research Institute for Northeastern Brazil, Ben-Gurion University of the Negev) 1975.

Appraisal of the Alto Turi Settlement Project (Washington D.C. : IRBD; International Development Agency) 1972.

Land Use and Cultural Influences in the Itaguai Colonization Project-In Land Tenure Conditions and Socio-economic Development of the Agricultural Sector-Brazil (Washington : Pan American Union) 1966.

Appraisal of the Lower San Francisco Polder Project (Washington D.C. : IRBD; International Development Agency,)1975 .

HAITI

Feasibility of Expanding the Integrated Cooperative Project of Bas Boen (The Organisation of American States in Haiti) 1972

Integrated Planning for the Integrated Agricultural Development Proejct of the Plaine de Cul-De-Sac Bas Boen (Rehovot : Organisation do Estados Americanos Israel) 1973

Development of the Trois Rivieres Valley (Port-de-Paix : UNDP) 1975

HONDURAS

Integrated Agricultural Development in Selected Zones (Tegucigalpa : Programa de las Naciones Unidas para el Desarrollo) 1974

INDIA

The Musahri Plan (New Delhi : Association of Voluntary Agencies for Rural Development) 1971.

Musahri Industrial Development Programme-A Schematic Lay-out of the Musahri Plan (New Delhi : Association of Voluntary Agencies for Rural Development) 1972.

The Musahri Whole Village Development Project-Project Report on Whole Village Development Programme in Bihar (New Delhi : Association of Voluntary Agencies for Rural Development) 1972.

Haldia Region-Interim Strategy Plan (Calcutta : Calcutta Metropolitan Planning Organization) 1971.

Development of a Tribal Region-Banpur Block, District Puri, Orissa (Interim Report) (New Delhi : Association of Voluntary Agencies for Rural Development) 1974.

Integrated Development Programme of Bolepur Block (West Bengal) - Interim Report (New Delhi : Association of Voluntary Agencies for Rural Development) 1974.

Planned Rehabilitation and Economic Change- A Case Study of Tungabhadra River Project Rehabilitation Colonies at H.B. Halli (Poona : Gokhale Institute of Politics and Economics) 1970.

Land and Water Use Potentials : Tungabhadra Irrigation Project, Mysore State (Knoxville : University of Tennesse) 1972.

Report and Recommendation of the President to the Executive Directors on a Proposed Development Credit to the Government of India for the Kadana Irrigation Project (Washington : IDA) 1970.

Tamil Nadu Agricultural Credit Project (Washington D.C. : International bank for Reconstruction and Development, International Development Agency) 1971.

Regional Planning : A Case Study of Marathwada Region (Poona : Gokhale Institute of Politics and Economics) 1975.

Sundarban Region Interim Devlopment Plan (Calcutta : Government of West Bengal, Development and Planning Department, Sundarban Development Board) 1973.

Appraisal of the Calcutta Urban Development Project (Washington D.C. : International Bank for Reconstruction and Development) 1973.

Fringe Areas of Calcutta-Development of Three Rural Situation (New Delhi : Association of Voluntary Agencies for Rural Development) 1978.

The Structure of the Bihar Economy in the Fifth Plan : Implication for the Banking Industry (Bombay : National Institute of Bank Management) 1974.

Conference on Bihar Banking Plan Held at Patna 3rd-5th October, 1974 (Bombay : National Institute of Bank Management) 1974.

Plan for Integrated Area Development in Pauri Garhwal (Hyderabad : National Institute of Community Development) 1975.

Plan for Integrated Area Development in West District (Hyderabad : National Institute of Community Development) 1975.

Rural Development for Rural Poor Dharampur Project-Part I : The Setting (Ahemedabad : Centre for Management in Agriculture ; Indian Institute of Management) 1975.

Soil and Water Management Project - Agricultural Engineering Aspects of Command Area Development (Working Paper) (Kota : United Nations Development Programme and Food and Agriculture Organization of the United Nations/UN) 1973.

Soil and Water Management Project-Command Area Development : Social and Institutional Aspects (Kota : United Nations Development Programme and Food & Agriculture Organization of the United Nations) 1974.

Rural Development in Indian Environment : Assessment and Prospects-A Case Study of Chamaon Gram Sabha near Varanasi City, U.P. (Varanasi : National Geographical Society of India, Banaras Hindu University) 1977.

Andhra Pradesh Composite C.A.D. Project-Typical Land Development Situations and Estimated Costs (Food and Agriculture Organization of the United Nations ; World Bank Cooperative Programme) 1975.

Resettlement Planning-Socio-Economic Implications of Kabini Reservoir Project (Mysore : Institute of Development Studies, University of Mysore) 1976.

Techno-Economic Survey of Rajasthan (New Delhi : National Council of Applied Economic Research) 1963. Techno-Economic Survey of Andaman & Nicobar Islands (New Delhi : National Council of Applied Economic Research) 1972

Integrated Area Development Programme Etawah (Pune : Centre for Development Studies) undated. One of the best known regional studies of India.

Regional Planning : A Case Study of Marathwada Region (Poona : Gokhale Institute of Economics & Politics), Arth Vijnana, March-June 1975.

Planning for a Debt Ridden Society-Adhara Block, District Rohtas, Bihar (New Delhi : Association of Voluntary Agencies for Rural Development) 1976.

Development of a Dacoit Affected Area-Joura Block, Chambal Valley, Morena District, M.P. (New Delhi : Association of Voluntary Agencies for Rural Development) 1976.

Meiti Village Imphal East Block Manipur-Rural Development Plan (New Delhi : Association of Voluntary Agencies for Rural Development) 1976.

Design of a Panchayat Plan Kumarikata Kamrup Assam (New Delhi : Association of Voluntary Agencies for Rural Development) 1978

Planning for Integrated Rural Development Yelburga Block (Hyderabad : National Institute of Rural Development) 1976.

Development Plan for Hosur (Madras : Anna University) 1987.

Development through Industrialisation : A Case Study of Hosur (Madras : Madras Institute of Development Studies) 1981.

Govt of Uttar Pradesh : Integrated Watershed Management Project:Amlawa - Saligad Projects, Uttar Pradesh (Dehradun : LandSurvey Directorate, Forest Department) March 1988.

Planning for Integrated Rural Development P. Gannavaram Block, East Godavari District (Hyderabad : National Institute of Rural Development) September 1986.

Programmes and Potentialities of Industrial Development and Growth of Small and Medium Towns in Tarai Region of Eastern Uttar Pradesh, being Chapter 6 of Bhadouria, B.P.S and Dua, S.C.: Rural Development Strategy and Perspective (New Delhi : Anmol Publications) 1986.

Note: More Regional Plans are given in Chapter II and in General Bibliography.

INDONESIA

Development Plan for West Pasaman/Sumatra (Bukittinggi : Institute for Development Research) 1975.

Evaluation of the Agricultural Development Project in West Sumatra (ADS/ADP) and of the Regional Planning Study in West Pasaman (Hamburg: HWWA-Institute for Wirtschaftaforschung-Hamburg) 1975.

Development Plan for West Pasaman/Sumatra, Vols I & II, (Bukittinggi : Institute of Development Research; Agricultural Development Project; German Technical Assistance; Ministry of Public Works and Electric Power-Directorate General of Housing, Building, Planning and Urban Development; Directorate of City and Regional Planning) 1975.

West Pasaman Development Planning (WPDP) - Agricultural Development Project (ADP). Final Report (Padang : Institute for Development Research) 1976

Citanduy Basin Development Project Paper-Proposal and Recommendations for the Review of the Development Loan Committee (Washington D.C. : United States Agency for International Development) 1975.

Interim Evaluation Report on Lampung Tani Makmur Project (Jakarta: Japanese and Indonesian Joint Evaluation Team) 1976.

Luwu Agricultural Development Loan-Proposal and Recommendation for the review of the Development Loan Committee (Washington D.C.: United States Agency for International Development) 1975.

Pematang Panggang Transmigration Study-Prepared for the FAO of the U.N Acting as Executing Agency for the UNDP (Nottingham : Huszar Brammah and Associates) 1975.

Regional Development of Yogyakarta - A Comprehensive Planning Report (A Summary) (Jakarta : Department of Public Works and Electric Power: Directorate General of Housing, Building, Planning and Urban Development; United Nations Centre for Regional Development) 1975.

Economic Aspects of Rubber Research at Bogor and Sembawa (Canberra : Australian National University) 1975.

Report on Recommendation of the President to the Executive Directors on a proposed Credit to the Republic of Indonesia for a Third Irrigation Rehabilitation Project (Washington D.C. : International Bank for Reconstruction and Development) 1970.

East Indonesia Regional Development Study, Vols I & II (Bate : Ministry of Public Works and Electric Power; Directorate General of Housing, Building, Planning and Urban Development-Directorate of City and Regional Planning; Canadian International Development Agency) 1974.

Appraisal of Smallholder Development Project North Sumatra (Washington D.C. : International Bank for Reconstruction and Development, International Development Agency) 1973.

The Design of a Regional Development Planning and Action Programme for the Northern Sumatra Region (Jakarta : Planning and Development Collaborative International (PADCO), Northern Sumatra Study Design Team) 1974.

Way Abung Transmigration Project (Honolulu : East-West Centre, East-West Technology and Development Institute) 1977.

Regional Agricultural Development Planning East Kalimantan-Preliminary Results of the Project Identification Mission (Jakarta : German Agency for Technical Cooperation Gmbh) 1976.

East Kalimantan Transmigration Area Development Project

Tad-Report No. 12 : An Outline of Regional Planning and Project Identification.

Tad-Report No. 14 : Regional Outline Plan.

Tad-Report No. 19 : Outline for Industrial Development

Department of Manpower, Transmigration and Cooperatives, Jakarta; German Agency for Technical Cooperation (GTZ) GmbH; HWWA - Institute for International Economics, Hamburg, 1978.

Java Regional Study-Phase I, Part A, East Java-Final Report (Japan : Japan International Cooperation Agency, International Development Centre of Japan) 1975.

Southern Coast Development Plan East Java-Draft Report Java Regional Study, Phase II, Part A, East Java (Japan : Japan International Cooperation Agency) 1979.

Memorandum on Community Based Integrated Rural Development (Jakarta : Department of Social Affairs) 1977.

Sumatra Regional Planning Study, Part B, Prepared for Directorate General of Housing, Building, Planning and Urban Development, Final Report Washington D.C. : Ministry of Public Works and Electric Power, Government of Indonesia ; Robert R. Nathan Associates.

IRAN

Ghazvin Development Project, Proposal for Five Year Development Plan 1967-1971 (Tel Aviv : TAHAL Water Planning Ltd.) 1967.

Ghazvin Area Development Project Plan of Operation for the Year 1347 (1968/69) - The Agriculture Development Project (Ghazvin : TAHAL Consulting Engineers Ltd.) 1968.

Ghazvin Area Development Project . Plan of Operations for the year 1347 (1968/69) The water Development Project(Ghazvin : TAHAL Consulting Engineers Ltd.), 1968.

Village Planning and Reconstruction of the Earthquake Zone in the Ghazvin Area(Tel Aviv : Institute for Planning and Development 1968).

JAMAICA

Report on the Kingston-St.Andrew-St. Catherine Planning Region (Kingston : United State Agency for International Development, Mission to Jamaica), 1963.

Appraisal of a Sites and Services Project (Washington : International Bank for Reconstruction and Development) 1974.

Planning for Montego Bay-Retirement Urban-Region Development Project (Kingston : National Planning Agency)1974.

Summary of the Hanover, St. James, Trelawny Regional Plan (Kingston : Ministry of Mining and Natural Resources, Town Planning Division) 1974.

Summary of the Westmoreland/St. Elizabeth Regional Plan (Kingston: Ministry of Mining and Natural Resources, Town Planning Division) 1974.

First Rural Development Project (Kingston : Government of Jamaica) 1975.

Summary of Jamaica : A Regional Division (Kingston : Ministry of Mining and Natural Resources, Town Planning Division) 1973.

Oasis Project-Rural Youth Settlement and Training in Jamaica, A Pilot Project (Washington : Organisation of American States) 1977.

JAPAN

A Case Study of the Comprehensive Development of the Kitakami River Basin (Bangkok : UN Economic Commission for Asia and the Far East) 1962.

Report on Survey for Development of Mountain District-Adjustment to Provide New Living Environments in Mountain Villages (Nagoya : Aichi Prefecture Planning Department) 1968.Aichi Prefecture : Its Vitality and Growth (Nagoya : Aichi Trade Centre) 1970.

KHMER REPUBLIC

Irrigation and Drainage Project in the Prek Thnot Region-Vol. I (Tel Aviv : Tahal Consulting Engineers Ltd) 1965.

KENYA

Report and Recommendation of the President to the Executive Directors on a Proposed Loan to the Colony and Protectorate of Kenya (Washington D.C. : International Bank for Reconstruction and Development) 1961.

Project for the Development and Settlement of Land in the Scheduled Areas (Washington D.C. : International Bank for Reconstruction and Development) 1961.

Kenya-Proposed Changes in the Land Settlement Project and Loan Documents (Washington D.C. : International Bank for Reconstruction and Development) 1964.

Some Experiences with Smallholder Settlement in Kenya 1963/64 to 1966\67 (Munchen : Weltforum Verlag) 1970.

Upper Tana Catchment Water Resources Survey 1958-59 (Nairobi : Sir Alexander Gibb & Partners (Africa) Consulting Engineers) 1959.

Survey of the Irrigation Potential of the Lower Tana River Basin-Interim Report Vol.I: Text (Nairobi : Acres International Ltd., Canada ; Koninklijke Nederlandse Heidemaatschappij) 1965.

The Socio-economic Problems of the Ahero Pilot Resettlement Scheme Area in the Kano Plains of Western Kenya (Nairobi : University College Nairobi, Department of Sociology).

Kakamega Plan - 1970 (Nairobi : Ministry of Lands and Settlement) 1970.

Kakamega District Development Plan 1975-1978, Western Province Kenya, Draft (Kakamega, Nairobi : Provincial Planning Officer) 1976.

Appraisal of a Sigar Roads Project (Miwani-Chemelil-Mukoroni Regional Development Program) (Washington D.C. : International Bank for Reconstruction and Development) 1967.

Kisii District Planning - Draft Plan

Vol. I : Part A: Analysis of the Socio-Economic Situation,

Part B: Development Strategy,

Vol. II: Part C: Project Proposals,

(Kissii : Kisii District Development Committee, District Commissioner's Office) 1973.

District Development Plan 1975-78, Busia-Western Province Kenya-Draft (Kakamega: Provincal Planning Office) 1976.

Busia-District Development Plan 1974-1978 (Nairobi : Republic of Kenya, Busia District Development Committee) 1976

North Eastern Province- Regional Physical Development Plan (Nairobi : Ministry of Lands and Settlement, Town Planning Department) 1971.

Rift Valley Province-Regional Physical Development Plan (Nairobi : Ministry of Lands and Settlement, Physical Planning Department, Regional Planning Section) 1973.

Central Province-Regional Physical Development Plan (Nairobi : Ministry of Lands and Settlement, Physical Planning Department) 1973.

Integrated Agricultural Development Programme-Phase I, Loan Application Report (Nairobi : Republic of Kenya, Ministry of Agriculture) 1975.

An Overall Evaluation of the Special Rural Development Programme (Nairobi : Ministry of Finance and Planning, University of Nairobi, Institute for Development Studies) 1972.

Second Overall Evaluation of the Special Rural Development Programme (Nairobi : Ministry of Finance and Planning, University of nairobi, Institute for Development Studies) 1975, Provisional text.

Special Rural Development Programme (SRDP) in Migori/Kihancha : Report of the Mid-Term Review (Nairobi : Swedish International Development Agency) 1973.

District Development Plan 1974-1978-Meru, Draft (Meru Kenya : District Planning Office) 1974.

District Development Plan-South Nyanza, Draft (Kisumu Kenya : District Planning Office) 1975.

District Development Plan 1975-1978-Bugoma, Draft (Kakamega, Kenya : Provincial Planning Office) 1976.

The Planning Phase of an Integrated Rural Development Programme in Miqori-Kuria-Report to the Government of Kenya (Rome : Food and Agriculture Organization and Swedish International Development Agency Planning Team, Swedish Funds-in-Trust) 1972.

Embu Municipality - A Development Study (Nairobi : Highlands Field Station, Department of Urban + Regional Planning, University of Nairobi,) 1978.The Hindi-Magogoni Settlement Scheme in Lamu District, Coastal Province of Kenya, Pre-Feasibility Study (Berlin : Post-Graduate Training Centre for Agricultural Development, Institute of Socio-Economics of Agricultural Development, Technical University of Berlin) 1978

KOREA

Han River Basin-Reconnaissance Report- Water Resources Study (Washington : Republic of Korea, Ministry of Construction; Water Resources Development Corporation; USA: Department of the Interior, Bureau of Reclamation and Geological Survey) 1971.

Appraisal of Yound San Gang Irrigation Project-Stage 1 (Washington D.C. : International Bank for Reconstruction and Development; International Development Agency) 1971.

Appraisal of the Secondary Cities Regional Project in Korea (Washington D.C. : International Bank for Reconstruction and Development) 1974.

Master Plan of Seoul 1972-1981 (Seoul : Seoul Metropolitan Government) 1972.

LESOTHO

Development of a Pilot Agricultural Scheme in the Leribe Area, Lesotho-Project Findings and Recommendations (Rome : United nations Development Programme and Food & Agriculture Organisation of the United Nation) 1975.

Farm Management and Production Economics Report-Development of a Pilot Agricultural Scheme in the Leribe Area, Lesotho (Leribe : Food and Agriculture Organisation of the United Nations and United Nations Development Programme) 1975.

Proposals for a Basic Agricultural Service Development Programme in Lesotho (London : Ministry of Overseas Development) 1976.

Lesotho Appraisal of Basic Agricultural Services Program (BASP), Draft (World Bank, Regional Projects, Eastern Africa Regional Office) 1977.

Lesotho Appraisal of the Basic Agricultural Services Project (Washington D.C. : World Bank; IDA mission of experts and Consultants) 1978.

Basic Agricultural Services Project Lesotho-Credit and Project Summary (Washington D.C. : International Development Agency) 1978

Basic Agricultural Services Programme (BASP) Lesotho (Frankfurt : Kreditanstalt fur Wiederfufbau,) 1978.Basic Agricultural Services Programme(BSAP) Lesotho-Survey (Eschborn : Deutsche Gesellschaft fur Technishe Zusammenarbeit (GTZ) GmbH) 1978.

LIBERIA

Rural - Regional Development Planning in Liberia (Monrovia : Ministry of Planning and Economic Affairs) 1973

Methodological Outline and Guidelines for Preparing a Regional Development Plan for Upper Lofa and Bong Areas (Monrovia : Ministry of Planning and Economic Affairs, Regional Planning Division) 1974

Regional Development Planning-Project Findings and Recommendations, Report Prepared for the Government of Liberia (New York : United Nations Executing Agency for the UNDP) 1975

Mano River Basin (Monrovia : United Nations Development Programme) 1975

LIBYA

National Physical Perspective Plan 1981-2000(Draft) (Tripoli : Secretariat of Municipalities, Secretariat of Planning ; UN Technical Co-operation Physical Planning Projects) 1979

LAOS

Integrated Agricultural Development Programme for the Vientiane Plain (The Hague : Asian Development Bank, Technical Assistance Mission ; NEDECO) 1969

Action Plan for 6,000 ha in the Vientiane Plain (Rehovot : Israel : Centre Pour la Cooperation Agricole Avec les Pays an Voie de Development) 1970

The Planning of the Regional Area (6,000ha) in the Vientiane Plan Project-A Synopsis of the Rural Development Plan (Rehovot : Israel : Ministry of Agriculture, Centre for Agricultural Cooperation with Developing Countries) 1971

Feasibility Report on Casier Sud Pioneer Agricultural Project in Laos (Tokyo : Japan Engineering Consultants Co. Ltd.) 1974

MALAYSIA

The Jengka Triangle Report (Kuala Lumpur : Federal Land Development Authority; Hunting Technical Services Ltd.) 1967

Report and Recommendation of the President to the Executive Directors on a Proposed Loan to the Federal Land Development Authority for a Land Settlement Project (Washington D.C. : International Bank for Reconstruction and Development) 1968

Jengka Triangle Project (Washington D.C. : International Bank for Reconstruction and Development ; International Development Agency) 1968

Report and Recommendation of the President to the Executive Directors on a Proposed Loan to Malaysia for the Third Jengka Triangle Project (Washington D.C : International Bank for Reconstruction and Development) 1973

Second Jengka Triangle Project (Washington D.C. : International Bank for Reconstruction and Development ; International Development Agency) 1970

Appraisal of the Third Jengka Triangle Project (Washington D.C. : International Bank for Reconstruction and Development; International Development Agency) 1973

The Jenga Triangle Report - The Outline Master Plan (New York : Tippetts-Abbett-McCarthy-Stratton/Hunting Technical Services Ltd. for Federal Land Development Authority, Malaysia) 1967

Appraisal of the Johore Land Settlement Project (Washington D.C.: International Bank for Reconstruction and Development International Development Agency) 1974

Kemubu Irrigation Project (Washington D.C. : International Bank for Reconstruction and Development; International Development Agency) 1974

Regional Planning Study of the First Division Sarawak- Vol. II: Main Report (Wageningen : Agricultural University) 1971

Organization and Administration of Agricultural Development, Sarawak (Rome : Food & Agriculture Organization of the United Nations) 1975

Appraisal of the North Kelantan Rural Development Project (Washington D.C. : The World Bank, East Asia and Pacific Project Department) 1976

Evaluation of a Plan to Increase the Employment Potential for Rural People (Baton Rouge : South University and A & M College) 1974

Appraisal of the Western Johore Agricultural Development Project (Washington D.C. : International Bank for Reconstruction and Development International Development Agency) 1974

Hohor tenggara Regional Masterplan Johor Tengah and Tanjong Penggerang (Kuala Lampur : The Government of Malaysia and the State of Johor; Hunding Technical Services Ltd.) 1971

Trengganu Tengah - Regional Planning and Developent Study (Kuala Lampur The Government of Malaysia; Hunting Technical Services, Ltd.,) 1974 Land Capability Classification Report, West Malaysia First Malaysi Plan (Kuala Lampur : Prime Minister,s Department, Economic Planning Unit) 1971

MADAGASCAR

Report and Recommendation of the President to the Executive Directors on a Proposed Development Credit to the Malagasy Republic for an Irrigation Project (Washington D.C. : International Development Agency) 1970

Appraisal Report Morondava Irrigation and Rural Development Project-Malagasy Republic (Washington D.C. : International Bank for Reconstruction and Development; International Development Agency) 1972

Report au Government de la Republique Malgache-Development Rural de la Zone D Androvakely, Morondava, et Mahobo Report to the Government of the Republic of Malagasy-Rural Development of the D Andr ovakely, morondava and mahobo Region, (Rome : Food and Agriculture Organisation of the United Nations) 1975

Rural Development in the D'Androvakely, Morondava and Mahobo Zones-Final Report (Rome : World Health Organisations Food and Agriculture Organisation of the United Nations) 1975

The Samangoky Settlement Scheme on the lower Mangoky River in South West Madagascar-An Appraisal for the World Food Programme (Berlin : Institute) 1966

Regional Development Aid Programme- Southwest Region Madagascar-Part A : Concept and Results (Berlin) 1974

MALAWI

Appraisal of Karonga Rural Development Project (Washington D.C. : International Bank for Reconstruction and Development; International Development Agency) 1971

Report and Recommendation of the President to the Executive Directors on a Proposed Development Credit to the Republic of Malawi for the Karonga Rural Development Project (Washington D.C. : International Bank for Reconstruction and Development) 1972

Lilongwe Agricultural Development Project, Phase II (Washington D.C. : International Bank for Reconstruction and Development) 1971

A Working Atlas of the Lilongwe Land Development Programme (Lilongwe : Lilongwe Land Development Program) 1971

A Planning Survey of the Northern Region-Report Prepared for Town Planning Department, Ministry of Works and Supplies (University of Utrecht, Department of Geography) 1975

Upper Shire Valley Development Project (Kasupe-Mwanza)-A Prefeasibility Study (The Netherland : International Technical Assistance Department, Minstry of Foreign Affairs; Rehovot Israel: International Cooperation Division, Ministry of Foreign Affairs) 1976

Central Region Lakeshore Development Project - Revised Additional Loan Application (Zomba : Agriculture Advisory Group of German Technical Assistance and Minsitry of Agriculture and Natural Resources, Planning Unit) Zomba, 1970

Central Region Lakeshore Development Project-Joint Project Evaluation 1973/74 Final Report, Vol I & II (Salima : Central Region Lakeshore Development Project) 1974

Central Region Lakeshore Development Project - Revised Submission Phase II (Zomba : Ministry of Agriculture and Natural Resources) Zomba, 1970

Regional Project SALIMA - Report No. 6 (Hamburg : Afrika-Verein) May 1971

MAURITIUS

Land and Water Resources Survey, Final Report, Volume II : Feasibility Report on the Western Coastal Region Irrigation Scheme - Annex : Engineering Data (Rome : Food and Agriculture Organisation of the United Nations) 1970

4- Year Plan for Social and Economic Development 1971-1975,Vol I & II (Port Louis : Government Printer) 1971

MEXICO

Regional Planning In Mexico : Experiment of the Lerma Plan (Paris: Organization for Economic Cooperation and Development), 1967.

Lerma Plan : Technical Assistance- Industrial Development Programme in the Lerma Region Plan Lerma, (Paris: Organisation for Economic Co-operation and Development) 1968.

Agriculture in the State of the California (Mexico City : Banco National de Mexico), 1970.

The Puebla Project-Seven Years of Experience : 1967--1973 (Mexico City : International Maize and Wheat Improvement Centre), 1974.

The Peubla Project - Paper Presented to a Meeting on Social Science Research in Rural Development, April 29 - 30, 1975 (New York : Rockefeller Foundation) 1975.

Draft Report on the Upper Papaloapan Rural Development Identification Mission (Rome : Food and Agriculture Organisation of the United Nations) 1972.

Report and Recommendations of the President to the Executive Directors on a Proposed Loan to Nacional Financiera, S.A. in Mexico - Second Irrigation Rehabilitation Project Mexico (Washington D.C. : International Bank for Reconstruction and Development) 1963.

Report and Recommendation of the President to the Executive Directors on a Proposed Loan to Nacional Financiera S.A. of Mexico for the Third Irrigation Project (Washington D.C.: International Bank for Reconstruction and Development) 1966.

Report and Recommendation of the President to the Executive Directors in a Proposed Loan to Nacional Financiera, S.A. of Mexico for the Rio Colorado Irrigation Project (Washington D.C. : International Bank for Reconstruction and Development)1978.

Synopsis of the Report on the Pilot Project E1 Limon, La Chontalpa, Tabasco (Mexico City : Banco Interamericano de Desarrollo) 1963.

Pilot Project E1 Limon, La Chontalpa, Tabasco (Mexico City : Bano Interamericano de Desarrollo) 1963.

Plan of Operations - Programme for the Agricultural and Livestock and Industrial Development of the "Ejidos Colectivos" in the Valles del Yaqui and Mayo (Mexico City : Banco Nacional de Mexico) 1971.

The Agricultural and Livestock Structure of the State of Nuevo Leon (Mexico City : Banco Nacional de Mexico) 1971.

The Socio-economic Structure of the State of Sonora (Mexico City : Banco Nacional de Mexico) 1970.

MOROCCO

The Economic Development of the Sebou Basin-Water Management (Rome : Food and Agriculture Organisation of the United Nations) 1970.

The Economic Development of the Sebou Basin, Morocco-Rural Economy and Agricultural Activities (Rome : Food and Agriculture Organisation) 1970.

Report and Recommendation of the President to the Executive Directors on a Proposed Loan to the Kingdom of Morocco for the Development of the Sebou Basin (Rharb Irrigation Project (Washington, D.C. : International Bank for Reconstruction and Development) 1969.

NEPAL

Appraisal of the Birganj Irrigation Project (Narayani Zone) (Washington D.C. : International Bank for Reconstruction and Development : International Development Agency) 1973.

Gandaki / Lumbini Region Planning Project Phase I (Kathmandu : United Nations Development Programme) 1974.

Nawalpur Settlement Project (Jerusalem, Israel : Ministry for Foreign Affairs, Department for International Cooperation) 1964.

Two Development Projects in the Terai of Nepal (Rehovot, Israel : Ministry of Agriculture, Centre for International Agricultural Cooperation) 1977.

Blueprint : Integrated Hill Development Project - Activities for the Fifth Plan Period 1975/76-1980-81 (Kathmandu : His Majesty's Government of Nepal; Swiss Association for Technical Assistance) 1974.

Integrated Hill Development Project : Sun Kosi - Khimti Khola (Kathmandu : Swiss Association for Technical Assistance) 1974.

Integrated Hill Development Project : Sun-Kosi - Khola, Eastern Nepal- The Role of Energy Resource Management and Alternative Energy Sources for the Hilly Regions of Nepal (Zurich : Swiss Association for Technical Assistance) 1975.

Integrated Hill Development Project - The Existing Fruit Tree Cultivation Along the Planned Lamosangu-Jiri Road-Results of a Preliminary Survey and Some Suggestions For an improvement of the Situation (Kathmandu : Swiss Association for Technical Assistance) 1975.

Dharapani-Kakani Village Panchayat Development Project - Prepared by Dutch-Israeli Survey Team, Nov.4 - Dec. 10 1976. (Rehovot, Israel : The Royal Netherlands Government : International Technical Assistance Department, Ministry for Foreign Affairs; State of Israel : Ministry for Foreign Affairs, International Division) 1977.

Regional Development Planning for Nepal (Kathmandu : National Planning Commision) 1969.

Preliminary Report on Regional Development Areas in Nepal (Kathmandu : National Planning Commission) 1969.

Final Report for Aug./Sep. 1978 on Agricultural Development in the Bhairawa-Lumbini Groundwater Project in the Rupandahi District Nepal (Tel Aviv : TAHAL Consulting Engineers Ltd.) 1978.

Integrated Rural Development Project in Nepal, ICIMOD occasional Paer No. 2, Kathmandu, 1985.

Rapti Zone Rural Area Development Project Final Situation (PADCO Inc.) Kathmandu, No. 367-0129) 31st October, 1985.

Rapti Zone Regional Assessment, Rapti Integrated Rural Development Project, (PADCO, Inc. Kathmandu), Sept., 1985.

NICARAGUA

Report - A General Concept for the Rehabilitation of the Persons Resettled from Managua to Neighbouring Towns, as a Consequence of the Earthquake (Managua : La Mission de Israel,) 1977.

Cuenca del Rio Escondido : Colonization Based on Cattle Development (Managua; MEIC; Banco Interamericano de Desarrollo) 1976.

PANAMA

Project Agricultural Development Planning, Report No. 3 : Comparative Evaluation of the Provinces of Panama, According to Priorities for Agricultural Development (Panama : Gobierno de Panama; Food and Agriculture Organisation; United States Agency for International Development) 1975.

Administrative Aspects of Planification and Regional and Provincial Development in Panama (Ciudad de Panama : United Nations) 1974.

Panama - Integrated Rural Development - Proposal and Recommendations for the Review of the Development Loan Committees (Washington D.C. : United States Agency for International Development) 1977.

Analysis, Comments and Preliminary Recommendations on the Census of Tonosi (Ciudad de Panama : United States Agency for International Development) 1978.

Interim Report - Integrated Rural Development (impact Areas) (Washington D.C. : United States Agency for International Development.

PARAGUAY

Land Settlement and Rural Development Project in Itapua, Preparation Mission (Rome : Food and Agriculture Organisation of the United Nations,) 1976.

PAKISTAN

Daudzai Project - A Case Study (Peshawar, Pakistan : Pakistan Academy for Rural Development) 1975.

Reflections on the Comilla Rural Development Projects (Washington D.C. : Overseas Liaison Committee American Councl on Education) 1974. Note - At the time of publication of this document Commilla is in Bangladesh.

Karachi Development Plan 1974-1976-National Pilot Project 3 for the Government of Pakistan, Master Plan for Karachi Metropolitan Region (Karachi : Master Plan Department, Karachi Development Authority) 1974.

Report of the Punjab Barani Commission - Summary (Lahore : Government of the Punjab) 1976.

Evaluation of Swanirvar Programme in Five Villages of Mithapukur Thana Pangpur (Bogra : Rural Development Academy) 1976.

Report on Ulashi - A Self-help Project (Bogra : Rural Development Academy) 1978.

Regional Development in Sind - A Comprehensive Planning Report (Nagoya : United Nations Centre for Regional Development) 1976.

PAPUA NEW GUINEA

Comprehensive River Basin Development (Purari) (New York : UNDP ; Tippetts - Abbett-McCarthy-Stratton) 1974.

Western District Development Study (Second Draft) (Waigani : Fly River Area Authority and Central Planning Office) 1975.

Madang District - Draft Economic Development Programme (Port Moresby: Office of the Economic Advisor) 1969.

East Sepik District Growth Centre Study (Waigani : Central Planning Office) 1973.

Gulf District-Area Improvement Study (Waigani : Central lPlanning Office) 1973.

Growth Centres and Area Improvement in the Eastern Highlands District (Canberra : The Australian National University, Department of Human Geography, Research School of Pacific Studies) 1974.

Papua New Guinea's Improvement Plan 1973-74, District Supplement (Port Moresby : Central Planning Office) 1973.

PERU

Reconnaissance Report of the Chavimochic Project Area (Tel Aviv : Corporacion de Fomento Economico Y Social de la Libertad ; Consulting Engineers Ltd.,) 1968.

Inventory, Evaluation and Rational Use of the Natural Resources of the Costa, Valle Chancay-Huaral(Lima : Officina Nacional de Evaluacion de Recursos Naturales) 1969.

Inventory of Projects : Subregion Piura-Tumbes (Chiclayo : Officina Regional de Desarrolla del Norte) 1973.

Data Systematization for Alto Piura (Lima : Centro Nacional de Capacitacion Investigacion para la Reforma Agraria) 1975.

Socio-Economic Indicators : Frontier Integration Zone Peru-Ecuador (Piura : Officina Regional de Desarrolla del Norte) 1973.

Integrated Regional Planning Model-Piura-Tumbes (Rehovot Israel : Settlement Study Centre, Course in Comprehensive Regional Development Planning) 1976

The Structural and Spatial Problems of Northern Peru (Chiclayo : Officina Regional de Desarrolla del Norte) 1972.

Chira-Piura Storage and Diversion Project-Feasibility Study (San Fransisco, USA : International Engineering Co.) 1968.

Summary Report-Integrated Development of Resources in the Tumbes-Chira-Piura River Basins (San Fransisco, USA : Oficina Regional de Desarrolla del Norte ; International Engineering Company, Inc.) 1968.

Rehabilitation and Development Plan for the Zone Affected by the Earthquake (Chiclayo : Commision de Reconstrucion & Rehabilitacion de la Zona : Officina Regional de Desarrollo del Norte) 1971.

Study of the Housing Market-Summary and Methodological Annex (Lima : Comision de Reconstruccion & Rehabilitacion de la Zona Afectada por el Terremto del 31 de Mayo 1970) 1973.

National Development Plan 1971-1975 -Vol.XII - Development Plan for the Zone Affected by the Earthquake (Huaraz : Comicion de Reconstruccion & Rehabilitacion de la Zona Afectada por el Terremto del 31 de Mayo 1970) 1973.

Evaluation of the Budget No. 28 of ORDEZA- First Quarter, January - March., 1977 (Huaraz : Organismo Regional para el Desarrollo de la Zona Affectada) 1977.

Lambaveque-Jayanca Groundwater Development Project - Feasibility Report (Tel Aviv : TAHAL (Water Planning Ltd.), 1964.

Operation Tocahe (Lima : Enrique Ferreyros Y Cia,) 1968.

Study of the Housing Market in Huaraz (Lima : Comicion de Reconstruccion Rehabilitacion de la zona Afectada por el Terremto del 31 de Mayo 1970; Banco de la Vivienda del Peru) 1972.

Study of the Housing Market in Carza (Lima : Comicion de Reconstruccion & Rehabilitacion de la zona Afectada por el Terremto del 31 de Mayo1970; Banco de la Vivienda del Peru) 1972.

Study of the Housing Market in Carhuaz (Lima : Commicion de Reconstruccion & Rehavilitacion de la zona Afecta por el Terremto del 31 de Mayo 1970; Banco de la Vivienda del Peru) 1972.

Study of the Housing Market in Recuay (Lima : Comicion de Reconstruccion & Rehabilitacion de la zona Afecta por el Terremto del 31 de Mayo 1970; Banco de la Vivienda del Peru) 1972.

Study of the Housing Market in Yungay (Lima : Comicion Reconstruccion & Rehabilitacion de la zona Afecta por el Terremto del 31 de Mayo 1970; Banco de la Vivienda del Peru) 1972.

Study of the Housing Market in Chimbote (Lima : Comicion de Reconstruccion & Rehabilitacion de la zona Afecta por el Terremto del 31 de Mayo 1970; Banco de la Vivienda del Peru) 1972.

Study of the Housing Market in Casma (Lima : Comicion de Reconstruccion & Rehabilitatcion de la zona Afecta por el Terremto del 31 de Mayo 1970; Banco de la Vivienda del Peru) 1972.

Study of the Housing Market in Huarmey (Lima : Comicion de Reconstruction & Rehabilitacion de la zona Afecta por el Terremto del 31 de May 1970; Banco de la Vivienda del Peru) 1972.

Study of the Housing Market in Pativilca (Lima Comicion de Reconstruccion de la zona Afecta por el Terremto del 31 de Mayo 1970; Banco de la Vivienda de Peru) 1972.

Study of the Housing Market in Barranca (Lima: Comicion de Reconstrucion & Rehabilitacion de la zona Afecta por el Terremto del 31 de Mayo 1970; Banco de la Vivienda del Peru) 1972.

Study of the Housing Market in Huacho (Lima : Comicion de Reconstrucion & Rehabilitacion de la zona Afecta por el Terremto del 31 de la Vivienda del Peru) 1972.

Study of the Housing Market in Trujillo (Lima : Comicion de Reconstruccion & Rehabilitacion de la zona Afecta por el Terremto del 31 de Mayo 1970; Banco de la Vivienda del Peru) 1972.

Study of the Housing Market in Casa Grande (Lima : Comicion de Reconstruccion & Rehabilitacion de la zona Afecta por el Terrremto del 31 de Mayo 1970; Banco de la Vivienda del Peru) 1972.

Study of the Housing Market in Cartayio (Lima : Comicion de Reconstruccion & Rehabilitacion de la zona Afecta poer el Terremto del 31 de Mayo 1970; Banco de la Vivienda del Peru) 1972.

Study of the Housing Market in Paramonga (Lima : Comicion de Reconstruccion & Rehabilitacion de la zona Afecta por el Terremto del 31 de Mayo 1970; Banco de la Vivienda del Peru)1972.

Soil Investigation in the Callejon de Huavlas (Half-Detailed) (Lima : Officiana Nacional del Evaluacion de Recursos Naturales) 1973.

Soil Investigation in the Collejo n de Conchucos (Lima : Officina Nacional del Evluacion de Recursos Naturales; Organisms Regional para el Desarrollo de la Zona Afectada) 1975.

National Development Plan 1977-78 Plan de Desarrollo Regional Ancash & La Libertad (Huaraz : Organisms Regional para el Desarrollo de la Zona Afectada) 1977.

General Analysis of the Situation in the Northern Region (Lima : Officina Regional de Dessarrollo del Norte) 1969/70.

Report on the Development Programme for the Subregion Cajamarca (Chiclayo : Officina Regional de Dessarrollo del Norte) 1972.

LIvestock Development Project Jaen-San Ignacio : Socio-economic Study (Lima : Centre Nacional de Capacitacione Investigacion para la Reforma Agraria) 1975.

Socio-economic Study Alto Marannon (Lima : Centre Nacional de Capacitacione Investigacion para la Reforma Agraria) 1974.

Report of the Socio-Economic Aspects of the Settlement Project Jenaro Herrera (Lima : Centre Nacion al de Capacitacione Investigacion para la Reforma Agraria) 1974.

Significance of the Socio-economic Study of the Pucallpa Zone (Lima : Centre Nacional de Capacitacione Investigacion para la Reforma Agraria)

Community Development Programme for the Cooperatives Associated to SATS Tupac Amru : Chalhuas-Canchaillo-Chacapalpa-Pachachaca(Huancayo : Co-operation Tecnica en Planificacion Peruano-Alemana- Sistema Nacional de Empresas de propiedad Social) 1976.

Identification Study of an Agriculture/Livestock and irrigation Project for Canchaillo, a Cooperative of SATS Tupac Amaru Ltd., No.1 (Panchacayo/Huancayo/Lima : Centro Nacional de Capacitaciane Investigacion para del Ferorma Agraria) 1972.

Pilot Project : Sheep Fattening on Exotic Pastures Based On Rotating Grazing in the Higher Andean Mountains - Technical and Financial Data (Huancayo : Co-operacion Tecnica enplanificacion Peruans - Alemana - Sistema Nacional de Empresas de propiedad Social) 1977)

Intermediate Report and Perspectives of Activities for the Communal Enterprise of Usibamba (Huancayo/Lima : Co-operacion Tecnica en planificacion Peruans - Alemana - sistema Naciónal de Empresas de propiedad Social)1975.

Survey, Evaluation and Rational Use of the Natural Resources of the Costa-Moche River Basin (Lima : Officina Nacional de Evaluacion de Recurso Naturales) 1973.

Survey, Evaluation and Rational Use of the Natural Resources of the Costa-Santa, Lacramarca and Napenna River Basins (Lima : Officina Nacional de Evluacion de Recursos Naturales) 1972.

Survey, Evaluation and Rational Use of the Natural Resources of the Costa-Viru and Chao River Baisns (Lima : Officina Nacional de Evaluacion de Recursos Naturales) 1973.

Survey, Evaluation and Rational Use of the Natural Resources of the Costa-Chicama River Basin (Lima : Officina Nacional de Evaluacion de Recursos Naturales) 1973.

Survey, Evaluation and Rational Use of the Natural Resources of the Costa-Casma, Culebras Y Huarmey River Basins (Lima : Officina Nacional de Evaluacion de Recursos Naturales) 1972.

Survey, Evaluation and Rational Use of the Natural Resources of the Costa-Ica River Basin (Lima : Officina Nacional de Evaluacion de Recursos Naturales 1971.)

Survey, Evaluation and Rational Use of the Natural Resources of the Costa-Fortaleza, Pativilca and Supe River Basins (Lima : Officina Nacional de Evaluation de Recursos Naturales) 1972.

Survey, Evaluation and Rational Use of the Natural Resources of the Costa-Moquegua, Locumba, Sama and Caplina River Basins (Lima : Officina. Nacional de Evaluacion de Recursos Naturales) 1972.

Survey, Evaluation and Rational Use of the Natural Resources of the Costa-Quilca and Tambo River Basins (Lima : Officina Nacional de Evaluacion de Recursos Naturales) 1974.

PHILIPPINES

Magat River Project Feasibility Report (Washington D.C. : United States Agency for International Development, Bureau of Reclamation) 1973.

An Indicative Plan of Agricultural Development for the Minsupala Area (Manila : National Economic and Development Authority) 1973.

Mindanao Regional Development Study : Mindanao and Sulu : Guidelines for Regional Planning - A Summary of Project Findings and Recommendations (Manila : United Nations Development Programme) 1975.

The Regional Cooperative Development Programme for Cagayan Valley-A Project Proposal (Quezon City : Bureau fof Cooperatives Development) 1973.

The Framework Physical Development Plan for Tarlac (Manila : University of the Philippines, Institute of Planning) 1973.

Magalang Rural Settlement Project (Manila : State of Israel, Ministry for Foreign Affairs and Ministry of Agriculture Submitted to Phillipinas Foundations Inc.) 1970.

Magalang Cooperative Settlement Project (Moshav-Type) San Augustin, Magalang, Pampanga-Feasibility Study (Pampanga : Regional Planning and Project Development Staff, Region III) 1974.

Description, Analysis and Tentative Evaluation of the Project in Barrio Ricarte (Rehovot, Israel : Centre for International Agricultural Cooperation) 1974.

A Development Scheme for a 50-Barrio Complex in Laguna (Nueva Ecija : Philippine Rural Reconstruction Movement, Nieves, San Leonardo) 1972).

Bicol River Basin Development Proposal (Manila : Development of Public Works, Transportations and Communications) 1973.

Bicol River Basin Council Annual Report 1974-75 (Manila : Bicol River Basin Council) 1975.

The Bicol River Basin Development Program (Baras : Bicol River Basin Programme Office) 1976.

Comprehensive Operational Plan (Proposed Projects) 1976-77 (Baras : Bicol River Basin Programme Office) 1976.

Bicol River Basin Urban Functions in Rural Development Project : Summary and Evaluation (Washington D.C. : U.S. Department of State, Office of Urban Development) 1978.

Angat Magat Integrated Agricultural Development Project (Quezon City : National Irrigation Administration, Diliman) 1974.

Land Consolidation and Development Projects Supportive of Agrarian Reform-Yulo Estate, Floridablanca, Pampanga (San Fernsando : Regional Project Development Team, Region III) 1974.

Mindoro Rural Development Project (Rome : Food and Agriculture Organisation of the United Nations) 1974.

Imelda Settlement Development Plan (Quezon City : United Nations Development Programme; Food and Agriculture Organisation, Department of Agrarian Reform) 1978.

SIERRA-LEONE

Appraisal of Integrated Agricultural Development Project (Washington, D.C. : International Bank for Reconstruction and Development ; International Development Agency) 1972.

Feasibility Study of an Inland Swamp Development Programme Unit in the Northern Province of Sierra Leone - Report to the Republic of Sierra Leone (Berlin : German Development Institute) 1973.

National Urbanization Plan : Survey for Planning (Magburaka : Institute for Planning and Development) 1965.

SOMALIA

Juba Valley Development Programme (Mogadishu : Demogratic Republic of Somalia) 1976.

Strengthening of Forestry and Wildlife Managment Project-Seasonal Distributions of Wildlife and Livestock in Relation to Development and Human Settlement in the Southern Trans-juba Area of Somalia (Mogadishu : United Nations Development Programme ; Food and Agriculture Organisation of the United Nations) 1976.

SRI LANKA

Report of the Gal Oya Project Evaluation Committee (Colombo : Government Publications Bureau) 1971.

A Proposal for the Establishment of Family Farms in the Uda-Walawe Scheme Ceylon (Tel Aviv : Israel : Ministry for Foreign Affairs, Department for International Cooperation) 1968.

Appraisal of the Walawe Development Project in Ceylon (Manila : Asian Development Bank) 1969.

Report of a Mission to the Dry Zone of Ceylon in Connection with Irrigation and Drainage April/May 1970 (Rehovot, Israel : Jewish Agency, Land Settlement Department) 1970.

Uda Walawe Project Ceylon - A Comparative Study of Two Regional Planning Alternatives (Rehovot, Israel : Settlement Study Centre) 1971.

The Process of Dynamisation in Rural Ceylon with special Reference to a Kandyan Village in Transition (Bern : University of Fribourg) 1965.

Sri Lanka Catchment Development Project-Integrated Rural Development of Nilambe, Atabage and Gurugoda-Ritigaha River Catchments (Colombo : Ministry of Plantation Industries; United Nations Development Programme; Food and Agriculture Organisation) 1976.

Participation of Rural Poor in Local Level Planning : A Case Study of Local Level Planning in Katuwana AGA Division in Hambontota Division (Bangkok : Asian Institute of Technology) 1985.

Implementation of Rural Development Programames Within a Framework of Limited Decentralization : A Case Study of Nuwara Eliya Integrated Rural Development Project, Sri Lanka by Amarasinghe, P.D. (Bangkok : Asian Institute of Technology) 1986.

SUDAN

Sudan : Appraisal of the Southern Region Agricultural Rehabilitation Development Project (Washington D.C. : International Bank for Reconstruction and Development) 1979.

Appraisal of the Managil Irrigation Project (Washington, D.C. : International Bank for Reconstruction and Development) 1960.

The Managil South-Western Extension, an Extension to the Gezira Scheme (Washington D.C. : International Institute for Land Reclamation and Improvement) 1965.

Some Socio-economic Characteristics of Gezira Tenants (Khartoum : Faculty of Agriculture, University of Khartoum) 1967.

Report on a Reconnaissance Mission of June 1976 to the Khashm el Girba Irrigation Scheme (Washington, D.C. : IRBD, Eastern Africa Projects Department) 1976.

Proposed Change in Roseires Irrigation-Project Bank Loan and IDA Development Credit (Washington, D.C. : International Bank for Reconstruction and Development) 1964.

Appraisal of Second Mechanized Farming Project Sudan (Umm Seinat in Kassala Province and Habila in Kordofan Province (Washington, D.C. : International Bank for Reconstruction and Development) 1975.

Increase of Agricultureal Production in the Sudan (Khartoum : The Democratic Republic of the Sudan and Essen ; German Agency for Technical Coopeation Ltd., Agrar-und Hydrotechnik GmbH, Consulting Engineers) 1975.

Nuba Mountain Region Development Potential Survey, Vol. I : Main Report (Khartoum : The Democratic Republic of the Sudan and Essen : German Agency for Technical Cooperation Ltd. ; Agrar-und Hydrotechnik GmbH, Consulting Engineer,) 1977.

Southern Darfur Land-use Planning Survey - Development Plan Annex 5 : Organisation (Khartoum : Ministry of Agrticulture, Food and Natural Resources; Hunting Technical Services Ltd. ; and London : Sir MacDonald & Partners) 1974.

An Agricultural Development Plan fort Southern Darfur (Khartoum : Economic and Social Reserach Council, National Council for Research; Hunting Technical Services) 1976.

Sag el Na'am Evaluation and Pre-investment Study Khartoum : Government of the Democratic Republic of Sudan, Ministry of Agriculture, Food, and Natural Resources, Hunting Technical Services Ltd.) 1976.

Study of Agricultural Development in the Sudan Central Rain Lands (Leeds : University of Leeds) 1975.

South Kordofan Agricultural Development (Nairobi : The World Bank, Regional Mission in Eastern Africa) 1976.

Project Performance Audit Report - Sudan First Mechanized Farming Report (Wahsington, D.C. : IBRD, Operations Evaluation Department) 1975.

Nomadism and Settlement - General Issues with an Example from The Sudan (England : Agriculture Extension and Rural Development Centre, Reading University) 1976.

Sudan's Desert Encroachment Control Rehabilitation Programme (DECARP) (Khartoum : Ministry of Agriculture Food and Natural Resources, The General Administration for Natural Resources, The Agricultural Research Council ; Food and Agriculture Organisation of the United Nations, Regional Office for the Near East, Khartoum) 1976.

Integrated Rural Development Project for Ingessana Hills, Blue Nile Province, Sudan, (Draft) Vols. I,II & III, (Khartoum : Food and Agriculture Organisation of the United Nations, Regional Office for the Near East ; and Cairo : Regional Office of Food and Agriculture Organisation & World Health Organisation, Joint Mission to the Sudan) 1976.

Rahad Irrigation Project (Khartoum : The Democratic Republic of the Sudan) 1977.

Rahad Corporation Social Survey of Rahad Project First Stage (Khartoum : Ministry of Agriculture, Food and Natural Resources) 1974.

Jonglei kProject (Phase One) (Khartoum : Executive Organ for the Development Project in Jonglei Area) 1975.

SWAZILAND

Survey of Army Operated Farms _ Report of a Mission, Sept. 24-Oct. 22, 1976 (Rehovot, Israel : Ministry of Agriculture, Centre for International Agricultural Cooperation) 1977.

TANGANYIKA

The Rufiji Basin Tanganyika - Report to the Government of Tanganyika on the Preliminary Reconnaissance Survey of the Rufiji Basin (Rome : Food and Agriculture Organisation of the United Nations) 1960.

An Outline Plan for the Development of the Ruvu Basin - Report to the Government of Tanganyika (Rome : Food and Agricultural Organisation of the United Nations) 1961.

New Settlement and Agricultural Development in Tanganyika (Jerusalem, Israel : Ministry for Foreign Affairs, Department for International Cooperation) 1961.

TANZANIA

Regional Settlement Plan in the Lake Territory Tanzania (Agricultural Development Company International Ltd.) 1966.

Iringa Region - Integrated Rural Development Proposals for the Third 5 - year Plan, 1976-81, Vols. I & II, (Rural Development Bank, Tanzania; Rome : Food and Agriculture Organisation of the United Nations and United Nations Development Programme, Overseas Development Group Norwich University of East Anglia, UK) 1976.

Tanga Regional Development Plan 1975 - 1980 Vols. I,II & III, (Tanga, Tanzania : Tanga Integrated Rural Development Programme, Regional Development Director's Office) 1975.

Tanga Integrated Rural Development Programme (TIRDEP) - Annual Report 1975 (Tang, Tanzania : Tanga Integrated Rural Development Programme Project Coordinator)1976.

Tanga Integrated Rural Development Programme Annual Report 1976 (Tanga, Tanzania : Tanga Integrated Rural Development Programme Project Coordinator) 1977.

Tanga Integrated Rural Development Programme - Programme Report January -June 1977 (Tanga, Tanzania : Tanga Integrated Rural Development Programme Project Coordinator) 1977.

Tanga Regional Development Plan 1975-1980 - Establishment of an Agricultural Mechanical Service Centre (Tanga, Tanzania : Tanga Integrated Rural Development Programme, Tanga) 1975.

Report : Feasibility and Backstopping - Tanga Integrated Rural Development Programme (Giessen : German Agency for Technical Cooperation Ltd.; Centre for Regional Development Research) 1977.

Development Problems and a Proposed Strategy for Development Planning in West Lake Region (Bukoba, Karagwe, Ngara Districts) (Copenhagen : Institute for Development Research, Copenhagen) 1972.

Study of Six Ujamaa Villages in Karagwe District - West Lake Region (Copenhagen : Institute for Development Research, Copenhagen) 1972.

Mpainduzi Majani : The Bukoba Tea Scheme (Copenhagen : Institute for Development Research) 1972.

Integrated Development Plan for Morogoro Region, Tanzania (In : IILRI Annual) Report 1974 (Wageningen : InternationalInstitute for Land Reclamation and Improvement, Wageningen)

Report to the Government of Tanzania on Village Settlement Scheme and Farmers Training Centre at Male (FFHC Project) (Rome : Food and Agriculture Organisation, Freedom from Hunger Campaign) 1968.

Shinyanga Regional Integrated Development Plan - First Report (Amersfoot/Arnheim :Dwars, Heederiken Verhey, Consulting Engineers; and International Land Development Consultants) 1975.

Shinyanga Regional Development Plan - Phase II (Amersfoot\Arnhein Dwars: Heederik en Verhey, Consulting Engineers,and Interanational Land Development Consultants in Cooperation with World Bank Mission, Mwanza, Amersfoort/Arnheim) 1976.

Shinyanga Water Supply Survey - Water Master-Plan Study for Shinyanga Region, Final Report, Vols I & II, : (United Republic of Tanzania : Ministry of Water Development and Power ; and the Hague; The Netherlands: Ministry of Foreign Affairs, NEDECO) 1974.

Shallow Wells Project Shinyanga - Evaluation and Fifth Progress Report (Dwars, Heederik en Verhey; International Land Development Consultants ; and Amersfoort : Organization of Netherlands Volunteers) 1977.

Feasibility Study Kilimangaro Area, Vols I to IV (London & Copenhagen : COWI Consult ; The Economic Intelligence Unit Ltd.) 1975.

THAILAND

Pa Mong Stage one, Feasibility Report Supplement : Optimization Study and Interest Rate Sensitivity Analysis(Washjington, D.C. : US Department of the Interior, Bureau of Reclamation) 1970.

Socio- Cultural Conditions in the Pa Mong Study Area of North East Thailand (Bangkok : Agency for International Development) 1969.

Pa Mong Reservoir - Area and Capacity Tables and Curves (Washington D.C. : US Department of the Interior, Bureau of Reclamation) 1971.

Pa Mong Phase II (Washington. D.C. : US Department of the Interior, Bureau of Reclamation) 1972.

Pa Mong Phase II, Supplement to Main Report (Hydraulics and Sediment Studies) Vol. I + II (Washington, D.C. : Department of the Interior, Bureau of Reclamation, Washington) 1973.

Northern Region of Thailand, Regional Planning Study (Tel Aviv : Institute for Planning and Development) 1973.

Planning for the Northern Region - Project Findings and Recommendations (New York : The United Nations) 1974.

Report on Thailand - Northern Natural Resources Survey (Vancouver : Royal Thai Government, National Economic and Social Development Board; Canadian International Development Agency under Assignment to Underwood, McLellan & Asso. Ltd.,) 1975.

Northern Region Planning- Progress Report (Tel Aviv : Institute for Planning and Development) 1971.

A Case Study of Forest Village System in Northern Thailand (Chiang Mai : Chiang Mai University, Faculty of Social Sciences) 1971.

Selected Indicators for Northern Region (Bangkok : Office of the National Economic and Social Development Board) 1973.

Report of Industrial Survey for Northern Region Development, 1971 (Bangkok : National Statistical Office, Office of the Prime Minister) 1972.

Irrigated Agriculture in Northern Thailand- March 17 - 19, 1974 (Chiang Mai : Ching Mai University, Faculty of Agriculture) 1977

Optimal Multiple Cropping Systems for the Chiang Mai Valley- Agricultural Economics Report No. 1 (Chiang Mai : Chiang Mai University, Faculty of Agriculture) 1974.

Northern Region of Thailand- Development Plan Chiang Mai Sub - Region (Tel Aviv : Institute for Planning and Development) 1974.

Regional Development Planning in Northern Thailand (Phase II)- Preparatory Assistance Report on Subregion IV : Chiang Mai (New York : The United Nations,)1974.

Detailed Reconnaissance Soil Survey of the Northern Part of Chiang Mai Province (Bangkok : Ministry of National Development) 1971

Regional Development of North-East Thailand (San Mateo, Calif : URS Company) 1968.

Planning Report - A Basic Framework for Planning Strategies in North-East Thailand, State - I (Bangkok : Northeast Economic Development Planning Advisory Group; Louis Berqer Inc. - Systems Associates, Inc.)1969.

Crop Labour Time and Motion Study of Selected Crops in North-East Thailand (Bangkok : Department of Land Development, Ministry of National Development) 1969.

Report on the Resettlement Study and Planning Project (Bangkok : Committee for coordination of Investigations of the Lower Mekong Basin,) 1976.

A Review of Land and Water Resource Development in the Lower Mekong Basin (Washington. D.C. : International Bank for Reconstruction & Development), 1972.

Proposals for the Introduction of Multicropping, New Agrotechniques, Improved Implements in Irrigated Agriculture in the Lower Mekong Basin (Jerusalem : Ministry of Agriculture, Centre for International Agricultural Cooperation) 1973.

Feasibility Study on Pilot Fish Farm Project in the Mekong Basin (Tel Aviv : SKR International Consultants Ltd.; Israel : Ministry for Foreign Affairs, International Cooperation Division) 1974.

Report on Indicative Basin Plan-A Proposed Framework for the Development of Water and Related Resources of the Lower Mekong Basin (Bangkok : Committee for the Coordination of Investigations of the Lower Mekong Basin,) 1970.

Agricultural Periodical No. 1 (Bangkok : Committee for the Coordination of Investigations of the Lower Mekong Basin,)1975.

Agricultural Periodical No. 2 (Bangkok : Committee for the Coordination of Investigations of the Lower Mekong Basin,)1975.

The Saraphi Project 1966 -1970 (London : Shell International Petroleum Company Ltd.) 1972.

Experts' Opinion on the Settlement Activities of the Government of Thailand (Bonn : Gesellschaft Fur Agrarische Entwicklungshilfe) 1962.

Hup-Kapong- Me Thai-Israeli Joint Venture in Rural Development - Summary of Five Years of Cooperation 1966-1971 (Jerusalem : Israel : Ministry of Foreign Affairs, International Cooperation Division; Ministry of Agriculture, Centre for International Agricultural Cooperation; Kingdom of Thailand : Ministry of National Development) 1972.

Feasibility Report Me Tang Project (Colorado : ECI International S.A., Denver) 1961.

Feasibility Report on the Greater Me Klong Multi-Purpose Project, First Stage : Development for Irrigation and Flood Protection (Bangkok : Royal Irrigation Department, Technical Division) 1962.

Experimental and Demonstration Farm for Irrigated Agriculture, Kalasin, Final Report(Bangkok : Royal Thai Government; United Nations Development Programme and Food and Agriculture Organisation of the United Nations) 1973.

A Systems Analysis of Development Alternatives Lam Pao Project-Experimental and Demonstration Farm for Irrigated Agriculture, Kalasin (Bangkok : Royal Thai Government, United Nations Development Programme; and Food and Agriculture Organisation of United Nations) 1975.

Experimental and Demonstration Farm for Irrigated Agriculture, Kalasin(Rome : United Nations Development Programme; and Food and Agriculture Organisation of the United Nations) 1975.

Nan River Basin Development (Bangkok : Royal Irrigation Department, Ministry of National Development) 1970.

Draft Proposal for the Establishment of the Thai-Israeli Pioneer Resettlement Project at Tak-Fa (Jerusalem : Israel: Ministry for Foreign Affairs, International Cooperation Division; Ministry of Agriculture, Centre for International Agricultural Cooperation) 1972.

Economic Evaluation of the Development of Water Control in the Northern Chao Phya Region: Some Preliminary Results (Bangkok : Kasetsart University, Department of Agricultural Economics, Faculty of Economics and Business Management) 1971.

South Thailand-Regional Planning Study (London : Government of the Kingdom of Thailand, National Economic and Social Development Board; Ministry of Overseas Development, London; Hunting Technical Services, Ltd.) 1975.

Report of the Thailand Southern Land Settlement Preparation Mission (Rome : Food and Agriculture Organisation of the United Nations)1975.

Land Classification and Master Planning of Sorthern Land Settlements (Redecon : Resources and Development Consultants Ltd.) 1974.

Draft Development Plan Ubol Ratchathani 1977-1981 (Bangkok : US Asian Development Institute) 1976.

Bangkok Traffic Study-Final Report Sept. 1975, Summary(Technical Cooperation Federal Republic of Germany and Kingdom of Thailand; Consultants : Kocks, Rhein-Ruhr-Ing. GmbH) 1975.

Recommendations Concerning Agricultural Development with Improved Water Control in the Mekong Delta (Bangkok : Kingdom of the Netherlands, Ministry of Foreign Affairs, International Technical Assistance Department, The Netherlands Delta Development Team) 1974.

Economic Planning Studies and Studies on Coordination of National and Basin Planning (Rotterdam : Committee for the Coordination of Investigations of the Lower Mekong Basin, Kingdom of the Netherlands, International Technical Assistance Department, Netherlands Economic Institute) 1975.

Preliminary Observations on the Production of New High Yielding Rice Varieties and Traditional Rice Varieties in Suphan Buri (Ithaca : Cornell University, Department of Agricultural Economics) 1972.

Chianat Province : A Social-Economic Study of the Four Villages under the TRRM Reconstruction and Development Programme (Bangkok : Social Science Research Institute, Chulalogkorn University) 1974.

Exploration of Application of the National Rural Development Village Data System for Rural-Regional Development Planning at Local Level : A Case Study of Nakorn Ratchasima Province, North East Thailand (Bangkok : Asian Institute of Technology) Thesis No. 86-12, 1986.

Regional Integration on the Capitalist Periphery : The Chentral Plains of Thailand Institute of Social Studies Research Report Series No. 15, 1984,

TOGO

Complementary Integrated Rural Development Project in the Kara Region (Paris : Food and Agriculture Organisation of the United Nations & United Nations Development Programme)1975.

TRINIDAD AND TOBAGO

Coordinated Agricultural Development Project for Trinidad and Tobago (Washington D.C. : Food and Agriculture Organisation of the United National,/ IBD Cooperative Programme,)1974.

TURKEY

Central Anatolia Integrated Rural Development Project- (Draft Report) (Rome : Food and Agriculture Organisation of the United Nation and International Bank for Reconstruction and Development) 1973.

Planning for the Zongulda Region(Ministry of Reconstruction and Settlement, Regional Planning Development), 1964.

Under-Underdevelopment - A Regional Case Study of the Aurdish Area in Turkey (Helsinki : Social Policy Association,) 1976.

Appraisal of Corum-Cankiri Rural Development Project (Washington D.C. : International Bank for Reconstruction and Development) 1975.

Report and Recommendation of the President to the Executive Directors on a Proposed Loan to the Republic of Turkey for the Corum-Cankiri Rural Development Project (Washington D.C.: International Bank for Reconstruction and Development) 1975.

The Antalya Region (Rehovot Israel : Settlement Study Centre, Work Project in Comprehensive Rural Planning) 1965.

Appraisal of an Irrigation, Rehabilitation and Completion Project (Washington D.C. : International Bank for Reconstruction and Development; International Development Agency) 1972.

Report and Recommendations of the President to the Executive Directors on a proposed Cridit to Turkey for an Irrigation Rehabilitation and Completion Project (Washington D.C.: International Development Agency) 1972.

Production, Sensibility and Evolution of the Vegetation and Environment in the Pre-Sahara of Tunisia - Consequences for Planning the Regional Development of the Area of Oglat Merteba) (Montpalliar : Centre d'Etudes Phytosociologiques et Ecologiques Louis Emberger) 1973.

Potential Agricultural Development Zones in Uganda (Entebbe : Ministry of Agriculture and Forestry)1973.

Upper Volta - Integrated Rural Development Project (Washington, D.C. : United States Agency for International Development) 1974

An Analysis of the Eastern ORD Rural Development Project in Upper Volta : Report of the Michigan State University Mission (East Lansing : Michigan State University, Department of Agricultural Economics) 1976.

A Proposed Structure for the Medium-term Credit - Programme in the Eastern ORD of Upper Volta (East Lansing : Michigan State University, Department of Agricultural Economics) 1976.

The Development of the Volta Valleys and the Example of Kaibo (Grenoble : Universite Scientifique et Medicale de Grenoble, Institut de Geographie Alpine) 1976.

URUGUAY

La Plata River Basin : Inventory of Hydrological and Climatological Data-study on its Planning and Development (Washington D.C : Organisation of American States) 1969.

La Plata River Basin : Study on its Planning and Development Inventory and Analysis of Basic Information on Natural Resources (Washington D.C.: Organisation of American States) 1971.

La Plata River Basin-Study on Its Planning and Development Eastern Republic of Uruguay, Santa Lucia River Basin (Washington D.C. : Organisation of American States) 1971.

Summary Version of the Pre - Feasibility Study of the Regional Agro-Industrial Project Known as Colonia Dr. Eduardo Acevedo in the Province of Artigas, Eastern Republic of Uruguay (Jerusalem : Israel : Ministry for Foreign Affairs, International Cooperation Division,) 1972.

The North of Uruguay Moving Towards Integrated Development (Bella Union : CALNU) 1968.

VENEZUELA

Zuliana Region-Study on the Rational Use of the Natural Resources (Washington D.C.: Organisation of American States) 1975.

Caicaraade Maturin-Case Study of an Agrarian Reform Settlement in Venezuela (Washington : Pan American Union) 1967.

Leonardo Ruiz Pineda - A Case Study of a Venezuelan Agrarian Reform Settlement (Washington : Pan American Union) 1968.

UNITED ARAB EMIRATES

Survey of Soils and Agricultural Potential in the Trucial States : Mileiha Development Project Hamraniyah Development Area 1967. (Durham : University of Durham, Department of Geography) 1967

YEMEN

Proposals for the Agricultural Project "Central and Northern Highland") (Eschborn : Deutsche Gesellschaft Fur Technische Zusammenarbeit (GTZ) GmbH,) 1975.

Appraisal of Southern Uplands Rural Development Project (Washington, D.C. : International Bank for Reconstruction and Development) 1975.

Mission Report on "Al Baun Agricultural Programme" - Yemen Arab Republic, 2-17. Dec., 1977(Eschborn : Deutsche Gesellschaft fur Technische Zusammenarbeit (GTZ) GmbH,) 1977.

Appraisal of the Tihama Development Project (Washington, D.C. : International Development Agency)

ZAMBIA

The Southern Province of Zambia - Prospects of Regional Development) Vols. I & II (Bonn : Gesellschaft fur regionale Strukturentwicklung) (GRS) 1971.

Report on the Development Possibilities of Gwembe South Region, Vols. I,II, & III, (Berlin : German Development Institute) 1973.

Gwembe South Development Project - Planning Paper II Cattle Development in Gwembe South (Lusaka : Ministry of Rural Development) 1975.

North-Western Province, Vols. I & II, Indicative Development Plan, and Provincial Development Plan (Lusaka : Ministry of Planning and Finance; Ministry of Rural Development) 1975.

Regional Development North-Western Province Zambia- Intensive Development Zone-Kabompt (Eschborn : Deutsche Gesellschaft fur Technische Zusammenarbeit (GTZ) GmbH) 1977.

Supply of Productive inputs 1978 - Integrated Rural Development North -Western Province Zambia (Giessen : German Agency for Technical Cooperation Ltd, GmbH) 1978.

Preliminary Survey Report of the Israel Mission to the Western Province of Zambia (Nov. 1969) (Jerusalem, Israel : Ministry for Foreign Affairs, International Cooperation Division) 1970.

The Kafulafuta and Kafubu Cooperative Settlement Project(Rehovot : Israel : The Centre for Agricultural Cooperation with Development Countries; Republic of Zambia : Ministry of Rural Development, Department of Cooperative Societies) 1970.

The Kafulafuta and Kafubu Cooperative Settlement Scheme- A Synopsis of the Rural Development Plan (Rehovot, Israel : Ministry of Agriculture, Centre for Agricultural Cooperation with Developing Countries) 1970.

A Project in Zambia - Integrated Area Settlement in the Copperbelt- an Evaluative Description) (Rehovot, Israel : Centre for International Copoperation) 1974.

Report of the Zambia Identification Mission on Agricultural, Technical and Health Education and Training (Rome : Food and Agriculture Organisation of the United Nations and International Bank for Reconstruction and Development, Cooperative Programme), 1972.

Land Resources of the Northern and Luapula Provinces, A Reconnaissance Assessment, Vols. I, II, III and IV.

(Surrey U.K.: Foreign and Commonwealth Office, Overseas Development Administration) 1973.

Eastern Province IDZ, Phase II - Final Proposals (Lusaka : Government of the Republic of Zambia : and IBRD Regional Mission in Eastern Africa, Lusaka), 1974.

Ikumbi Coffee Development Plan - Intensive Development Zone Programme Northern Province (Lusaka : Ministry of Rural Development, Central Unit IDG), 1974.

Mambwe IDZ Area - Mbala District - Development Plan 1975-1976 (Kasama : Ministry of Rural Development, Northern Province IDZ Programme) 1975.

Multipurpose Survey of the Kafue River Basin - Vol IV : Ecology of the Kafue Flats (Rome : Food and Agriculture Organisation and United Nations Development Programme) 1968.

Multi-purpose River Basin Study - Progress Report of July 1970 (Lusaka : Government of the Republic of Zambia, Ministry of Finance; and Rome : Italconsult) 1970.

Multipurpose River Basin Surveys and Studies - Vol. IV : Market and Commodity Analysis (Lusaka : Government of the Republic of Zambia, Ministry of Finance; and Rome : Italconsult) 1970.

Local Effects of Two Large-Scale Industrial Projects in the Kafue--Mazabuka Area in Zambia : Kafue Estate and Nakambala Sugar Estate, Final Report (Nijmegen : Geografisch en Planologisch Institut, Kath, Universiteit Nijmegen) 1977.

Report of the Mazabuka Resettlement Project - Vol. II : Appendices (Rome : Food and Agriculture Organisation of the United Nations,Investment,Centre)1972.

APPENDIX D

GOVERNMENT REPORTS

Government of India:
Report of the Team for the Study of Community Projects and National Extension Service,
Vols. I, II and III, (New Delhi: Planning Commission) 1957.

Government of India:
Report of the Study Team on Rural-cum-Urban Township at the Headquarters Community Development Blocks,
(New Delhi: Ministry of Community Development and Co-operation) 1960. This is an indepth study of the deficicncies in the quantity and quality of services provided at the block level to meet the needs of component villages under the Community Development Programme.

Government of Maharashtra:
Report of the Committee on Democratic Decentralisation, Co-operation and Rural Development
(Ahmedabad, 1960)

Government of India:
Report of the Committee on Special Multi-purpose Tribal Blocks,
(New Delhi: Government of India, Ministry of Home Affairs) 1960.

Government of India:
Report of the Committee on the Dispersal of Industries Board
(New Delhi: Small Scale Industries Board) 1962-63.

Government of West Bengal:
Perspective of Development: 1961-1976, Implications of Planning for and Minimum Level Of Living
(New Delhi: Planning Commission) 1962.

Government of India:
Guidelines for Intensive Development of Blocks under the Programme of Integrated Rural Development, Vols. I and II.
(New Delhi: Government of India, Deptt. of Rural Development, Ministry of Agriculture and Irrigation) 1978.

Committee on Plan Projects:
Report on Planning Commission, Industrial Township
(New Delhi : Government oi India) 1963. Mimeographed.

Government of India:
Rural Health Services in India
(New Delhi: Central Health Education Bureau, Ministry of Health, Govt. of India) 1963.

Government of India:
Notes on Perspectives of Development in India: 1960-61,
(New Delhi: Planning Commission) April 1964.

Government of India:
Resource Development Regional and Division of India
(New Delhi: Planning Commission) 1964. An early document which emphasises that while the District as the primary unit of decentralised planning process continues to hold its own, optimal change is possible if regions as units of planning are selected scientifically.

Government of India:
Report of the Industrial Licensing Policies Enquiry Committee,
(Govt. of India: Ministry of Industrial Development) July

1969. The report interestingly enough shows that licencing has not helped by and large in bringing about regional dispersal.

Government of India:
Report of the Working Group on Ravine Reclamation for Areas in U.P., M.P. and Rajasthan
(New Delhi: Ministry of Agriculture & Irrigation) 1966.

Government of India:
Formulation of Area Development Plan
(New Delhi : Committee on Plan Projects, Government of India) 1966, mimeographed.

Government of Maharashtra:
Report on Metropolitan Regional Planning in Bombay & Poona
(Bombay: Govt. of Maharashtra) 1967.

Government of India:
Report of the Study Team on Metropolitan Traffic and Transport
(New Delhi: Planning Commission) 1967.

Government of India:
Administrative Reforms Commission, Study Team on the Machinery for Planning: Final Report
(New Delhi: Govt. of India) 1967.

Government of India: Programme Evaluation Organization:
Regional Variations in Social Development and Levels of Living
(New Delhi: Planning Commission) 1968.

Government of India:
Report on Machinery for Planning
(New Delhi: Manager of Publications, Administrative Reforms Commission, Ministry of Health, Govt. of India) 1968.

Government of India:
Annual Evaluation Reports on the Working of the Community Projects and NES Blocks, Vol I to Vol. VIII
(New Delhi: Planning Commission, Programme Evaluation Organisation) 1968.

Government of India:
Formulation of Area Development Plan
(New Delhi: Planning Commission) 1968, mimeographed.

Government of Gujarat:
Classification of Economically Backward Areas
(Gandhinagar: Govt. of Gujarat) 1968.

Government of Gujarat:
Report of the Backward Area Study Team
(Gandhinagar: Govt. of Gujarat) 1969.

Government of India:
Identification of Backward Areas
(New Delhi: Planning Commission) 1969.

Government of India:
Fiscal and Financial Incentives for Starting New Industries in Backward Areas Report of the Working Group
(New Delhi: Government of India, Ministry of Industrial Development) April 1969.

Government of India:
Guidelines for the Formulation of District Plans,
(New Delhi: Planning Commission) 1969. This also contains a valuable analysis of the concept of District as a useful unit for decentralised planning.

Government of India: Development Commissioner (Small Scale Industries):
Fiscal and Financial Incentives for Starting Industries,
(New Delhi : Government of India) 1969.

Government of India:
Report of the Rural-Urban Relationship Committee
(New Delhi: Ministry of Health Govt. of India) 1969. They have concluded that where establishment of one administrative machinery is not possbile for urban-rural development, special statutory authority should tackle the problem of metropolitan areas by performing area wide functions and local authorities should tackle local problems. (Vols. I & II).

Government of India:
Modernising Indian Agriculture,
(New Delhi: Govt. of India) 1969. This is a thorough evaluation of Intensive Agricultural Area Development Programme (IADP).

Government of India:
Identification of Backward Areas Report of the Working Group
(New Delhi: Planning Commission) 1969. (Also known as B.D. Pande Report).

Government of India:
Report of the Working Group to Recommend Fiscal and Financial Incentives for Starting Industries in Backward Areas
(New Delhi: Govt. of India) 1969.

Government of India:
Report the Study Team on Tribal Development Programmes
(New Delhi: Planning Commission) 1969.

Government of India:
Report of the Committee on Tribal Economy in Forest Areas
(New Delhi: Government of India, Deptt. of Social Welfare) 1970.

Government of India:
Case Studies in Indian Community Development Programme
(New Delhi: The Programme Evaluation Organisation, Planning Commission) 1970.

Government of India:
Report of the Committee of Experts on Unemployment Estimates
(New Delhi: Government of India) 1970.

Government of India: Planning Commission:
Perspective Planning Division: "Perspective of Development 1971-76, Implication of Planning for a Minimum Level of Living: A Decade of Development",
Sankhya Series C, Vol. 36, 1971.

Government of India:
Report of the Steering Group on Development of Backward Classes and Social Welfare for the Fifth Five Year Plan
(New Delhi: Planning Commission) 1973.

Government of India:
Report of the Steering Group on Development of Backward Classes and Social Welfare for the Fifth Five Year Plan
(New Delhi: Planning Commission) 1973.

Government of India:
Report of the Task Force on Development of Tribal Areas
(New Delhi: Planning Commission) 1973.

Government of India:
Report of the Working Group on Conceptual Framework on Multi-Level Planning & Spatial Analysis
(New Delhi: Planning Commission) 1973 mimeographed. Planning Commission Circular No. PC (P) 9/46/WG/ cf) 72-MLP dt. 22.1.73.

Government of India:
Guidelines for intensive Development of Blocks under the programme of Integrated Rural Development, Vol. I and II,
(New Delhi : Government of India, Deptt. of Rural Development, Ministry of Agriculture and Irrigation) 1978.

Government of India:
Report of the Working Group on Block Level Planning, 1978.
(New Delhi: Planning Commission) (Dantwala Committee Report).

Government of India:
Report of the Committee on Panchayati Raj Institutions
(New Delhi: Ministry of Rural Reconstruction) 1978. (Ashok Mehta Committee Report).

Government of India:
Report of the Working Group on Tribal Development During Medium Term Plan (1978-83)
(New Delhi: Ministry of Home Affairs, Government of India) 1978.

Government of India:
"Integrated Rural Development in India",
paper presented to the ESCAP Seminar on Integrated Regional Development for Asia and The Pacific, at Bangkok, (New Delhi: Ministry of Agriculture and Irrigation) Mimeographed, 1978.

Government of India:
Manual on Integrated Rural Development Programme
(New Delhi: Government of India, Ministry of Rural Development) 1979.

Government of India:
National Committee on Development of Backward Areas: Report on Development of Backward Hill Areas
(New Delhi: Government of India) 1981.

Government of Uttar Pradesh:
Guidelines for Formulation of District Plans
(Lucknow: Planning Department, Govt. of U.P.) 1981.

Government of India:
Guidelines for Scheme for Strengthening of Planning Machinery at the District Level
(New Delhi: Planning Commission) (mimeographed) paper No. 10, of Planning Commission, Multi-Level Planning Division.

Planning Commission:
Report of the Working Group on Hill Area Development for the VII Plan
(New Delhi: Government of India) 1982.

Government of India:
Report of the Working Group on District Planning
(New Delhi: Planning Commission) 1984. Vol I & Vol. II.

Government of India:
First Report of "Decentralisation of Development Planning and Implementation in the States",
The Economic, Advisory Council to the Prime-Minister, 4th October 1983, Text Published in Economic Times, 14th January 1984.

Government of India:
Towards Improved Local Level Planning for Rural Development: Case Study of Kundrakudi, Tamil Nadu
(New Delhi: Planning Commission) 1985, mimeographed.

Government of Uttar Pradesh:
Decentralised Planning In Uttar Pradesh: A Case Study of Barabanki

(Lucknow: Area Planning Division, State Planning Institute) 1985.

Government of West Bengal:
Village Based District Planning Process: An Outline of Methodology,
(Midnapore: District Planning Committee) 1985 September, mimeographed.

Government of India:
Report of the Study Group on Agricultural Strategies for Eastern Region of India
(Delhi: Planning Commission) 1985.

Government of India, Ministry of Agriculture:
Report of the Committee to Review Existing Administrative Arrangements for Rural Development and Poverty Alleviation Programmes (CAARD)
December 1985.

Government of India:
Integrated Rural Development And Allied Programmes - A Manual,
(New Delhi: Department of Rural Development) 1986.

Government of India:
Towards Improved Local Level Planning for Rural Development
(New Delhi: Government of India) 1986.

Government of India:
Evaluation Report on Integrated Rural Development Programme
(New Delhi: Govt. of India) 1986.

Government of India:
Towards Improved Local Level Planning for Rural Development,-
Lessons from Some Experiences
(New Delhi: Planning Commission) 1986.

Government of India:
Report of the Commission on Centre - state Relations, Parts I & II,
(New Delhi : Government of India) 1988

Government of India:
Report of the Fourth Workshop of Collectors/District Magistrates on Responsive Administration,
April 30-May 3, 1988, Jaipur Group III,
Context & Methodology of District Planning.
(New Delhi: Government of India, Ministry of Personnel, Public Grievances and Pensions) 1988.

Government of India:
Report of the Study on Training for District Planning
(New Delhi: Planning Commission) June 1989.

Government of India:
Report of the Committee of the Study Group on Information Gap
(New Delhi: Planning Commission) July 1989.

Other Reports

Government of India:
Ninety-Seventh Report of the Estimates Committee of the Lok Sabha (Second),
(New Delhi: Lok Sabha Secretariate) 1960-61.

Government of India:
Seventy-Second Report of the Estimates Committee of the Lok Sabha (Third),
(New Delhi: Lok Sabha, Secretariate) 1964-65.

Government of India:
Estimates Committee (1974-75), Fifth Lok Sabha, Sixty-Ninth Report: Development of Backward Areas
(New Delhi: Lok Sabha Secretariate) 1974.

Government of Rajasthan:
The Report of the High Power Committee on Panchayati Raj, Institutions
(Jaipur: Govt. of Rajasthan) 1973. This report clearly discerned two types of Panchayati Raj structures - "The Maharastra Model", and "The Rajasthan Model": the former has Zilla Parishad as operative body, while the latter has Block Development Officer, Pradhan and Panchayat Samiti as the main functional unit.

Government of Uttar Pradesh:
A Tentative Framework for Balanced Regional Economic Development of Uttar Pradesh,
(Lucknow: Area Planning Division, State Planning Institute, Planning Deptt.) 1979 May.

Government of Uttar Pradesh:
Report of the Task Force on Decentralised Planning
(Lucknow: Deptt. of Planning, Govt. of Uttar Pradesh) 1986. [Chairman T.P. Tiwari]

Government of U.P.:
A Compilation of the Government Orders Under Decentralised Planning Schemes
(Lucknow: State Planning Commission, Govt. of Uttar Pradesh) 1986 (July).

Government of U.P.:
Report of the State District Level Administration Commission.
(Lucknow: Deptt. of Revenue, Govt. of U.P.) August 1986 [Chairman: T.N. Dhar].

General Bibliography

A

Abeydeera, W.P.P. :
Participation of Rural Poor in Local Level Planning : A Case Study of Local Level Planning in Katuwana AGA Division in Hambontota Division, Sri Lanka
(Bangkok : Asian Institute of Technology, Division of Human Settlements Development) M.Sc, Thesis No. 85-3, 1985.

Abeyrama, T. :
Monitoring in Retrospect : Reflections on Practical Experience and Recommendations
(Bangkok : Division of Human Settlements Development, Asian Institute of Technology) 1988.

Abhyankar, N.G. :
"Essays of District Planning Approach",
Industrial India 26th July 1975.

Abiodun, Josephine Olu :
"Spatial Impact of Growth Firms : Case Studies From Ondo State, South Western Nigeria",
Indian Journal of Regional Science, Vol. XIV, No. 1, 1987.

Abraham, C.M. :
"District Planning",
Madras Development Seminar Series Bulletin, October 1974.

Absan, Qamar :
Planning from Below : A Review of the District Planning Strategy in India
Manuscript, (Patna : Deptt. of Economics, A.N. College) 1988.

Acharya, S.S. :
"Rural Growth Centres",
Paper read at the Workshop on Project Formulation organised by special schemes organization, Govt. of Rajasthan at Jaipur from January 22 to 24, 1980.

Acharya, S.S.:
Rural Growth Centres,
Training memorandum circulated at the Workshop on Project Formulation, January 22-24, 1979, at Jaipur organised by Special Schemes Organisation (since renamed Special Schemes and Integrated Rural Development Department) Govt. of Rajasthan.

Acklebesove, M.; Anderson, A.K. and Snickars, Folke :
Regional Development Modelling: Theory and Practice
(Amsterdam : North Holland Publishing Co.) 1982.

Ackoff, R.L. :
Redesigning the Future- A Systems Approach to Societal Problems (New-York: John Wiley) 1964.

Acquino, Behindo A. :
"Dimensions of Decentralisation and Development",
unpublished Ph.D. dissertation, Cornell University, Ithaca, 1974.

Adams, J. and Bumb, B. :
"Economic, Political and Social Dimensions of an Indian State : A Factor Analysis of District Data For Rajasthan",
Journal of Asian Studies Vol. XXXI, No. 1, Nov. 1973.

Adelman, I. and Robinson, S.:
A Wage and Price Endogenous General Equilibrium Model of a Developing Country: Factors Affecting the Distribution of

Income in the Short Run
(Washington D.C. : World Bank Development Research Centre) 1975 Mimeographed. This is a pioneering study of Korea based on a completed I/O Model.

Adrezej, W. :
Perspectives and Limitations of the Application of Mathematical Methods in Economic Regionalisation,
in the Proceedings of the 4th General Meeting of the Commission on Methods of Economic Regionalisation of the International Geographical Union, Prague, 1967.

Agajanian, S. :
California Planner
(Sacramento: California Chapter, American Planning Association) 1987.

Agarwal, S.R. :
Reorganisation of Economic Structure for Decentralised Planning
(Jhansi : Bundelkhand University, Deptt. of Economics and Co-operation) manuscript, 1988.

Agro Economic Research Centre :
Falna (Pali District Rajasthan): Socio-Economic Profile of a Village
(Vallabh Vidyanagar: Agro-Economic Research Centre) 1967. Similar Studies by the Agro-Economic Research Centre are available for Nargol (Bulsar District); Moti-Khadol (Kaira District, Gujarat) Oan (Surat District).

Ahmad, Q.K. and Hossain, M.:
"Economic Development Through People's Participation on a Self Help Basis : Lessons from Bangladesh",
in Friedman, J. and Weaver, C.:
Territory and Function
(Oxford : Pergamon Press) 1979.

Ahmad, Yusuf J. :
"Administration of Integrated Rural Development Programmes : A Note on Methodology",
Integrated Labour Review, February 1955.

Ahmed, A.G. and Rahman, M.A. :
"Small Urban Centres: Vanguards of Exploitation : Two Cases from Sudan",
Africa, Vol. 49, No. 3, 1979.

Ahmed, S.M. Humair and Quadir, Abdul:
"Decentralised Planning in India", Conference Volume,
Indian Economic Association, December 1988, Calcutta.

Ahuja, Kanta (ed.):
District Planning in Rajasthan
(Jaipur : H.C.M. State Institute of Public Administration) 1977.

Ahuja, Kanta :
Block Development Plan Sikrai (Jaipur)
Mimeographed.

Ahuja, Kanta :
"Determination of Plan Priorities : The Need for a Regional Approach",
Prashasnika, Vol. II, No. 2, April-June 1973.

Airov, J. :
"Fiscal Policy Theory in an Inter-Regional Economy : General Inter-Regional Multipliers and Their Application",
Papers and Proceedings of the Regional Science Association, Vol. 19, 1967.

Akinchan, S. :
"Regional Development of Backward Areas in a Federation",
in Noorami, A.G. (ed.):
Central-State Relations in India
(Bombay : Lislie Sawhney Programme on Training for Democracy) 1972.

Akinchan, S. :
"Regional Development of Backward Areas in a Federation" in Noorani, A.G. (ed.): **Central State Relations in India** (Bombay: Leslie Sawhney Programme of Training For Democracy) 1972.

Akthar, R. Majeed (ed.) :
Regionalism : Developmental Tensions in India (New- Delhi : Cosmo Publications) 1984.

Alagh, Y.K. :
"District Planning in India : Some Issues", Journal of the Lal Bahadur Shastri National Academy of Administration, Vol XX, No. 1, 1973.

Alagh, Y.K. :
"Formulation of State Plan-Rajasthan A Case Study", Economic Weekly, July 7th, 1962 contains an account of the state of district planning during the Third Five Year Plan period.

Alagh, Y.K.:
Regional Aspects of Indian Industrialisation (Bombay: University of Bombay, Economic Series No. 21) 1972.

Alagh, Y.K.:
"District Planning, New Technology and Panchayati Raj", Yojana, New-Delhi, January 26, 1989. An authoritative work on water-delivery system, pricing strategies, subsidies and supply of inputs for the agricultural sector.

Alagh, Y.K.; Bhalla, G.S. and Kashyap, S.P.:
Structural Analysis of Gujarat Punjab and Haryana Economies, (New-Delhi:Allied Publishers) 1980.

Alagh, Y.K.; Subramaniam, K.K. and Kashyap, S.P.:
"Inter-Industrial Structure in a Developing Economy : A Conceptual Frame with A Case Study", Indian Journal of Regional Science, Vol. 3, No. 2, 1971.

Alagh, Yoginder and Kashyap, S.P.:
"Problems and Uses of the Regional Input-Output Tables", Anvesak, June 1971.

Alam, K. :
"Decentralized Planning - An Assesment of Assam Model", Conference Volume, Indian Economic Association, Calcutta 1988, Part III pp. 89-99.

Alam, K.:
"Decentralised Planning - The Indian Experience", The Indian Economic Association Conference Volume, Calcutta (1988).

Alam, Manzoor A.:
"Metropolitan Planning - A Trend Report", in A Survey of Research in Geography, ICSSR Project (Bombay: Popular Prakashan) 1972.

Alampieu, Feter M.:
"Practical Applications of the Work of Economic Regionalisation in the USSR", in Polish Academy of Sciences, Methods of Economic Regionalization (Warsaw: Institute of Geography, Polish Academy of Sciences) 1964. This is a good discussion of homogenity approach and functional integration approach to Regionalisation.

Allan, A. :
"The Goals of Comprehensive Planning", Journal of American Institute of Planners, 1965.

Albegov, M.; Anderson, A.E. and Snickars, F.: (eds.) :
Regional Development Modeling : Theory and Practice

(Amsterdam : North Holland) 1982.

Alderfer, H.F. :
Local Government in a Developing Country
(New-York : McGraw Hill) 1964.

Alexander, E.R. :
"Implementation : Does a Literature Add upto a Theory",
Journal of American Planning Association, Vol. 48, No.1, 1982.

Ali, Mansoor :
"Problem of People's Participation with Reference to Water Resource Utilisation",
Manuscript, (Roorkee: Deptt. of Humanities and Social Sciences, University of Roorkee) 1988.

Ali, Mansoor :
"Problems of People's Involvement in Developmental Plans in India",
in Papers in the Proceedings of Seminar on the Sixth Five Year Plan (Lucknow : Govt. of Uttar Pradesh) 1979.

Ali, Nasir S. :
"Plan Implementation Through District Administration",
Indian Journal of Politics, July-December 1972.

Allen, H.B. :
Rural Reconstruction in Action: Experiences in Near and Middle East,
(Ithaca : Cornell University Press) 1953.

Allen, K. and Hermansen, T. :
Economic Growth : Regional Problems and Growth Centre India
(Geneva : European Free Trade Association) 1968.

Almendinger, V.V. :
Topics in Regional Growth Model,
Penn-Jersey Study Paper No. 4, Philadelphia, 1961.

Alonso, W :
Location Theory, in Friedman, J. and Alonso, W. : Regional Development & Planning : A Reader,
(Cambridge, Mass : M.I.T. Press) 1964.

Alonso, W.:
Industrial Location and Regional Policy in Economic Development, Working Paper 14,
(Berkeley: Centre for Planning and Development Research; Institute of Urban and Regional Development, University of California at Berkeley; and Deptt. of City and Regional Planning) 1968. This study demonstrates that even in western economies use of capital investment inducements as instruments for development in depressed regions has not been effective.

Altimir, O.:
Income Distribution Estimates from Household Survey and Population Census in Latin America : An Assessment of Reliability
(United Nations Economic Commission for Latin America and World Bank Development Research Centre) 1975 Mimeographed. This indicates the real difficulties that may arise while reconciling information on distribution of Income and National Accounts.

Amiran, David H.K. :
"Regional Planning: Some Geographical Consideration of Objectives and Procedures",
Indian Journal of Regional Science, Vol.5, No. 2, 1973.

Ampuero, Ramos; Luis, A. and Fletcher, L.B. :
Planning For Rural Development with Popular Participation, (Ames, Iowa : University of Iowa) 1982.

Andrede, Preston and Roy, Prodipto:
Pilot Projects for Integrated Area Development,
(New-Delhi: Govt. of India, Ministry of Agriculture) 1969.

Angrish, A.C. (ed.) :
Regional Economic Planning in India
(Meerut : Twentieth Century Publishers) 1987.

Appalraju, Jaya and Safier, Micheal :
"Growth-Centre Strategies in Less Developed Countries",
in Gilbert, Alan G. :
Development Planning and Spatial Structure
(London: John Wiley) 1979.

Appleby, P.H. :
Public Administration in a Welfare State
(Bombay : Asia Publishing House) 1961.

Aputheraj, C. and Rajayan, E.C. :
Future Decentralised Agricultural Planning in India,
Manuscript, (Madras: University of Madras, Agricultural Economics Research Centre) 1988.

Aravindakshan, K.:
"Rolling Plan: Some Reflections",
Mainstream, Vol. 16, No. 20, January 1978.

Arif, M.; Ahmed, B. and Jannisar, M. :
Expansion of Employment and Income through Local Resource Mobilisation
(Bangkok : ARTEP) 1985.

Arora, S.K.:
"Policy Making and Social Indicators",
Economic and Political Weekly, Special Number, Vol. 6, No. 30-32, July 1971, stresses the importance of building geometry of regional development , sociology of distribution of income and ecology of environmental development into data matrix to be used for framing short-run and medium-run goals and strategies.

Arrow, K.J. and Hurwicz, L. :
"Decentralization and Computation in Resource Allocation",
in Pfouts R. (ed.):
Essays in Economics and Econometrics, in Honour of Harold Hotelling.
(Chapel Hill: University of North Carolina Press) 1960.

Arrow, K.J.; Karlin, S. and Suppes P. (ed.):
Mathematical Methods in the Social Sciences
(Stanford : Stanford University Press) 1960.

Arrow, Kenneth J. and Hoffenber, M. :
A Time Series Analysis of Inter-Industry Demands
(Amsterdam: North Holland) 1959.

Arya, K.C. :
Decentralised Planning in India,
Manuscript (Moradabad: Deptt. of Economics, Hindu College) 1988.

Ashraf, A. :
"Report of the Rural-Urban Relationship Committee, 1966 : A Critical Review",
Indian Journal of Public Administration, Vol. 14, No. 3, July 1968.

Asian & Pacific Development Centre :
"Project Review Meetings on Decentralisation for Rural Development",
Papers & Proceedings of Seminar, held between 29th Sept.

1986 & 3rd October 1986 at Kuala Lampur and Trengganu, Malaysia.

Association of Voluntary Agencies for Rural Development :
Development of a Tribal Region; Banpur Block , District Puri, Orissa,
(New-Delhi : Sagar Publications) 1977.

Association of Voluntary Agencies for Rural Development:
Meiti Villages Imphal (East Block) Manipur: Rural Development Plan
(New-Delhi : AVARD) 1975.

Association of Voluntary Agencies for Rural Development:
Socio-Economic Development of a Dacoit Affected Area in Chambal Valley, Joura Block, Morena District, M.P. (India)
(New - Delhi : AVARD) 1976.

Athwal, S.S. :
"Development of a Tribal District",
Socialist India, 21st September 1974.

Aurangabad and Jalna Regional Planning Board :
Regional Plan For Aurangabad And Jalna Region,
Aurangabad 1976.

AVARD :
Democratic Decentralization in Rajasthan- Report of a Study Team
(New- Delhi : Association of Voluntary Agencies for Rural Development) 1961.

Azad, R.N. :
"Integrated Rural Development",
Paper presented at the Seminar on Industries Participation in Rural Development (Lucknow : Govt. of Uttar Pradesh) 1978 mimeographed.

Aziz, Abdul (ed.) :
Studies in Block Planning,
(New-Delhi : Concept Publishers) 1983.

Aziz, Abdul :
Integrated Rural Development Programme in Karnataka: An Evaluation
(Bangalore: Institute for Social and Economic Change) 1986, (unpublished).

Aziz, Abdul :
"Approaches to Integrated Rural Development, Some Reflections",
in Naidu, K.M. :
Area Planning For Regional Development,
(New-Delhi : Inter-India Publications) 1984.

Aziz, Abdul :
"District Plan Process : The Karnataka Case",
in Aziz, Abdul and Racine, Jeane,:
About Decentralization : Two Studies in Multi-Level Planning in South India
(Pondicherry: French Institute of Pondicherry) May 1989.

Aziz, Abdul and Bisaliah, S.:
Some Issues in Employment Planning at the Block Level,
in Aziz, A :
Studies in Block Planning
(New-Delhi : Concept Publishers) 1983.

Aziz, Abdul and Rayappa, P.H.:
Employment Potential of Plan Schemes in Karnataka
(Bangalore: Institute for Social and Economic Change) 1978, unpublished.

Azzam, H.T. :
Human Resources Planning : Methods and Problems
(Beirut, LPME) International Labour Organisation, Working Paper No. 10, 1981.

B

Babu, P. Krishna:
Regional Planning in India,
(Allahabad : Chugh Publications) 1987.

Bacharach, M.:
Bi-proportional Matrices and Input-Output Change,
Cambridge University, Department of Applied Economics, Monograph No. 16. (Cambridge: Cambridge University Press) 1970. This contains discussions on the validity of Input-Output approach to planning.

Bacharach, M.:
Input-Output Analysis: An Appraisal
(Princeton: Princeton University Press) 1955. Discusses the validity of Input-Output approach to Planning.

Backmann, Martin J. :
"The Analysis of Spatial Diffusion Processes",
Papers and Proceedings of the Regional Science Association Vol. 25, 1970.

Bagchee, Sandeep and Bagchee, Aruna:
"Dantwala Committee and After: A Reply",
Economic and Political Weekly, Vol. 15, Nos. 45-46, November 1980.

Bagchee, Sandeep and Bagchee, Aruna:
"Whither Goes Block Level Planning, Dantwala Report",
Kurukshetra Vol. 28, No. 20, August 1980.

Bagchi, K.G. and Pathak, C.R. (eds.):
Regional Development And Planning: Strategies & Case Studies,
(Calcutta : University of Calcutta, Department of Geography) 1976.

Bagcni, K.G. and Pathak, C.R. (eds.) :
"Regional Development and Planning",
Proceedings of the 8th Regional Science Seminar, December 20th to 21st, 1974, Kharagpur, Indian Institute of Technology.

Balakrishna, S. :
"Calculation of Population Threshold in Regional Planning Exercises: An Alternative Method",
Behavioural Sciences and Community Development, September 1976.

Balasubramanian, M. :
"Balanced Regional Economic Development",
Indian Journal of Economics, 1970.

Baldev, Singh:
Regional Planning : Exploration in Agriculture and Industry,
(New-Delhi: Oxford & IBH) 1981.

Ball, R.J. :
"Economic Model Building for Control",
Advancement of Science, Vol. 23, 1967.

Bandopadhaya, D. :
"An Evaluation of Policies and Programmes for the Alleviation of Rural Poverty in India",
in Islam, Rizwanal (ed.): Strategies for Alleviating Poverty in Rural Asia (Geneva : ILO, ARTREP) 1985.

Bandopadhaya, Kalyani:
Industrialisation through Industrial Estates : A Pattern of Economic Decentralisation
(Calcutta : Bookland) 1969.

Banerjee, Debdas and Ghosh, Anjan :
"Indian Planning and Regional Disparity in Growth",

in Bagchi Amiya (ed.): Economy Society and Polity, (Oxford University Press) 1988.

Banerjee, Shyamadas and Fischer, Benjamin H.:
"Hierarchial Location Analysis for Area Planning in Rural India",
Papers of the Regional Science Association, Vol. 33, 1974.

Banerjee, Shyamadas and Fischer, Benjamin, H.; et. al.:
"Micro Regional Planning for Rural India: Experiences of the Pilot Research Project in Growth Centres",
Paper presented to the Annual Meeting of the American Institute of Planners, Atlanta, U.S.A. 1973.

Banerjee, Shyamdas and Fischer, Benjamin H. :
"Spatial Analysis for Integrated Area Planning in India",
Urban and Rural Planning Thought, January 1974.

Banerjee, Sujit :
The Spatial Dimension of Urbanization in Relation to Development Planning in India
(New-Delhi : Associated Publishing House) 1980.

Banfield, E.C.:
"Ends and Means in Planning",
International Social Science Journal, Vol. 11, No. 3, 1959, pp. 361-368.

Bapat, N.G. :
Economic Development of Ahmadnagar District 1881-1860
(Bombay: Progressive Corporation) 1973.

Bardhan, P.:
"On 'Welfarism' vs. 'Radicalism' in Planning",
Economic & Political Weekly, Vol. IX, No. 9, March 1974.

Bardhan, P.K., :
Land, Labour and Rural Poverty
(New-Delhi: Oxford University Press) 1984.

Bardhan, P.K.:
"Inequality of Farm Incomes - A Study of Four Districts",
Economic and Political Weekly, Annual Number, 1974.

Barker, T.S. and Lecomber, J.R.C. :
Economic Planning for 1972: An Appraisal of the Task Ahead
(London : PEP Broadsheet 515) 1969.

Barnabas, A.P. :
Social Change in a North Indian Village
(New-Delhi : The Indian Institute of Public Administration) 1968.

Barnabas, A.P. :
"Sociological Implications of Multi-Level Planning",
The Indian Journal of Public Administration, Vol. XIX, No. 3, 1973.

Baruth, K.H. :
Physical Planning of Israel : The Legal and Technical Basis
(London : Shindler & Golombo) 1949.

Basu, Asok :
Importance of Decentralised Planning in India and Its Problems,
(Midnapore: Vidyasagar University; Deptt. of Commerce) Manuscript, 1988.

Basu, Kaushik:
"Food For Work Programmes: Beyond Roads that Gets Washed Away",
Economic And Political Weekly, 3rd to 10th January 1981.

Basu, S.K. :
"Determinants of the Regional Distribution of Bank Credit", Indian Journal of Regional Science, Vol. V, No. 2, 1973.

Basu, Sukumar:
Decentralised Planning in India,
(Hooghly: S.B. College, Mogra) Manuscript, 1988.

Batten, T.R. :
Communities And Their Development
(London: Oxford University Press) 1957.

Bauchet, P. :
Economic Planning : The French Experience
(London: Heinemann) 1964.

Bawa, D.S. :
Rural Project Planning: Methodology and Case Studies
(New Delhi: Calcutta Press) 1976.

Bawa, R.L. et. al. :
"Market Towns & Spatial Development : A Case Study of North Bihar",
in NCAER : Market Towns and Spatial Development, (New Delhi : NCAER) 1972.

Baxi, C.V. :
"Backward Area Development: Expanding Institutional Set-up",
Economic Times, 12th June, 1974.

Beckerman W. (et. al.) :
The British Economy in 1975
(Cambridge : Cambridge University Press) 1965.

Beckerman Wilfred :
Methodological Links Between Economic and Social Planning,
Paper presented at Seminar on Social Planning : Puerto Rico, Balliol College, Oxford, July 18-22, 1966.

Beckmann, Martin :
"Some Reflections on Losch's Theory of Location",
Papers and Proceedings of the Regional Science Association, Vol.1, 1955.

Beckmann, Martin and Marschak, Thomas :
"An Activity Analysis Approach to Location Theory",
Kyklos, Vol. p, 1955.

Beed, Thomas and Stimson, Robert (eds.):
Survey Interviewing : Theory and Techniques,
(Sydney: Allen & Unwin) 1985.

Bell, C.L.G. and Duloy J.H.:
"Formulating A Strategy",
in Chenery, H. et. el.: Redistibution with Growth (London : Oxford University Press) 1974. This establishes that in South Asia, the comparative advantage in the long term appears to lie outside agriculture and long term development strategy must concentrate on labour intensive industrialisation.

Belshaw, D.G.R. :
"An Evaluation of Foreign Planning Assistance to Tanzania's Decentralized Regional Planning Programme 1972-1981",
Applied Geography, Vol. 2, 1982.

Belshaw, D.G.R. :
"Linkages Between Policy Analysis, National Planning And Decentralized Planning for Rural Development",
in Proceedings of the Expert Consultation, Kathmandu, 28th Nov. to 2nd December 1988, (Rome : Food & Agriculture Organization of the United Nations) 1989.

Belshaw, D.G.R. :
"Regional Planning in Tanzania : the Choice of Methodology for Irringa Region",
in Livingstone, I. (ed.): Issues in Development Studies : Essays in Honour of Athole Mackintosh (Farnborough : Dover Press) 1979.

Belshaw, D.G.R. :
"Regional Development Programmes and Their Impact on Subsistence Agriculture",
in Report of the Workshop on Planning, Policies and Programmes for Increased Food

and Agricultural Production in Traditional Subsistence Agriculture in Africa (Rome: Food & Agriculture Organization) 1985.

Belshaw, D.G.R. and Chambers, R. :
"A Management Systems Approach to Rural Development",
Discussion Paper No. 161, (Nairobi: Institute of Development Studies) 1973.

Belshaw, D.G.R. and Douglass, C.M. :
"Rural Regional Planning in Less Developed Countries : Irrelevant Theory versus Uninformed Practice ?"
Development Studies Discussion Paper No. 90. (Norwich: University of East Anglia) 1981.

Belshaw, D.G.R.:
An Application of the "Rehovot Approach" to Integrated Rural Development in Venezuela : A Methodological Appraisal,
Development Studies Discussion Paper No. 111, (Norwich : University of East Anglia) 1982.

Bendavid-Val, Avrom :
Regional Economic Analysis for Practitioners
(New-York : Praeger) 1974.

Bendavid-Val, Avrom :
Local Economic Development Planning: From Goals to Projects,
Planning Advisory Service Report Number 353, (Chicago: American Planning Association) 1980.

Benninger, C. and Benninger, A. :
Simplified Methodology for Formulating Integrated Rural Development Plans
(Poona: Centre for Development Studies and Activities) 1981 Mimeographed.

Bergman, Edward:
Citizen Guide to Economic Development in Jobless Communities
(Chapel Hill: Centre for Urban and Regional Studies, North Carolina) 1981.

Berry B.J.L. :
"Hierarchical Diffusion: The Basis of Development Filtering and Spread in a System of Growh Centres",
in Hansen, Niles M:
Growth Centres in Regional Economic Development
(New-York: Free Press) 1972.

Berry, B.J.L. :
Geography of Market Centres and Retail Distribution
(Englewood Cliffs, N.J. : Prentice Hall) 1967.

Berry, B.J.L. :
"An Inductive Approach to Regionalisation of Economic Development",
in Ginsburg, N. (ed.) :
Essays on Geography and Economic Development
(Chicago: University of Chicago Press) 1960.

Berry, B.J.L. :
"Basic Patterns of Economic Development", Part VIII,
in Ginsberg, N.(ed.) :
Atlas of Economic Development
(Chicago : University of Chicago Press) 1961.

Berry, B.J.L. :
"Policy Implications for an Urban Location Model for the Kanpur Region",
in Desai, P.B.; Grossack, J.M. and Sharma, K.N. (eds.) :
Regional Perspectives of Industrial and Urban Growth:The Case of Kanpur
(Bombay)1969.

Berry, B.J.L. :
"Recent Development in Central Place Theory",
Papers & Proceedings of the

Regional Science Association, Vol. 4, 1958, pp. 107-20.

Berry, B.J.L. and Garrison, W.L.,
"The functional Bases of Central Place Hierarchy",
Economic Geography, Vol. 34, 1958 pp. 145-154. This is a study of the early fifties of central places in Washington State that classified central place function into variates and attributes : the former are those that are present in varying quantities at different levels of central places and the latter as those either present or absent.

Berry, B.J.L. and Garrison, W.L. :
"Recent Development of Central Place Theory",
in Lesby, W.L.; et. al. (eds.):
Urban Economics Theory, Development and Planning
(New-York : Free Press), 1970.

Berry, B.J.L. and Garrison, W.L. :
"A Note on Central Place Theory and the Range of a Goods",
Economic Geography, Vol. 34, 1958.

Berry, B.J.L. and Garrison, S.L.:
Recent Development of Central Theory,
Papers & Proceedings of the Regional Science Association, Vol. 4, 1958.

Berry, B.J.L. and Horton, F.E.:
Geographic Perspectives on Urban System With Integrated Readings,
(Englewood Cliffs, New-Jersey: Prentice Hall) 1969.

Berry, B.J.L. and Marble, D.F. (ed.):
Spatial Analysis
(Englewood Cliffs, New-Jersey: Prentice Hall Inc.) 1968.

Berry, B.J.L.:
Spatial Analysis : A Reader in Statistical Geography,
(New-Jersey: Prentice Hall, Englewood Cliffs) 1967.

Berry, B.J.L.:
"Hierarchial Diffusion : The Basis of Developmental Filtering and Spread in a System of Growth Centres",
in English, P.W. and Mayfields, R.C. (eds.):
Man, Space and Environment,
(Oxford: Oxford University Press) 1972.

Berry, Brian J.L., et al.:
Essays on Commodity Flows and the Spatial Structure of Indian Economy
(Chicago: Department of Geography, Research Paper No. 111, University of Chicago) 1966.

Berry, David and Steiker, Gene:
The Concept of Justice in Regional Planning : Some Policy Implications
(Peace Dale, Virginia: Regional Science Research Institute) Discussion Paper No. 67, November 1973.

Berry, J.N.L. and Prakasa Rao, V.L.S. :
Urban Rural Inequality in the Regional Structure of Andhra Pradesh : A Challenge to Regional Planning and Development
(Weisbaden: F-Steiner Verlag) 1968.

Bethleheim, Charles:
Studies in the Theory of Planning
(New-Delhi: Asia Publishing House) 1961.

Beyers, W.B. :
"On The Stability of Regional Inter-Industry Models : The Washington Data for 1963 and 1967",
Journal of Regional Science, 1973.

Bhadouria, B.P.S. :
Disparities and Development Policies
(New-Delhi : Anmol Publications) 1986.

Bhadouria, B.P.S. :
"August Losch's Model of Spatial General Equilibrium and Its Applicability to Development Regions",
Indian Economic Journal, Vol. XIX, No. 2, 1971.

Bhadouria, B.P.S. and Bose, A.N.:
"Decentralisation for Fasters Rural Development",
Yojana, July 1-15, 1988.

Bhadouria, B.P.S.:
Decentralized Planning for Development of India,
(Delhi: Commonwealth Publishers) 1988.

Bhagatwar, P.A. :
Community Development Programme - A Psycho -Social Study (Nagpur: Anand Prakasan) 1972.

Bhagwati, J. and Chakravaty, S.:
Contributions to Indian Economic Analysis,
(Bombay: Lalvani Publishing House) 1971.

Bhagwati, Jagdish and Padma Desai,
India : Planning for Industrialisation,
(London: Oxford University Press) 1970.

Bhalerao, C.N.:
"Changing Patterns of Development Administration in the District",
The Indian Journal of Public Administration, Vol. XII, No. 1, January-March 1966. A good paper depicting the problems of the District Magistrate/Collector in co-ordinating planning effort.

Bhalla, G.S. and Tyagi, D.S. :
Patterns in Indian Agricultural Development : A District Level Study,
(New-Delhi : Institute for Studies in Industrial Development) 1989.

Bhalla, G.S.:
"Sectoral Income Multipliers in the Punjab and India",
Ninth Indian Econometric Conference, Patna, 1969 published in Anvesak, December 1971.

Bhambhri, C.P. :
"Official-Non-Official Relationship in Panchayati Raj",
Indian Journal of Political Science, Vol. XXVIII No. 3. July-September 1967. This paper describes how the Panchayati Raj institutions were rarely consulted in Plan formulation and how in their own plans, suggestions by the Departmental Heads were dutifully incorporated.

Bharadwaj, S.P.; Pandey, R.K. and Dixit, U.N. :
"Decentralised Planning for Balanced Cropping Patterns,
(New-Delhi: Indian Agricultural Statistics Research Institute) manuscript, 1988.

Bharathan, K. :
"Backward Area, Industrialisation",
Bulletin, Madras Development Seminar, Series XI, October 10th, 1981.

Bhardwaj, V.P. and Parmar, B.D. :
"Planning for Regional Development: A Case Study of Saurashtra Economy",
Paper presented at the National Seminar on Planning for Regional Development, Saurashtra University, 1982.

Bhargava Gopal:
"District Level Planning",
Capital, 28th April, 1980.

Bhargava, Gopal :
"Need for Regional Planning",
Khadi Gramodyog, August 1973, pp. 512-517.

Bhargava, Gopal:
"Towards District Level Planning",
Young India, 12th July 1973.

Bhargava, Gopal:
"Approach Towards District Level Planning",
Khadi Gramodyog, 11th August 1978.

Bhat, L.S. :
Central Place Hierarchy for a Developing Agricultural Region Karnal Area (Haryana) : A Case Study
(New-Delhi: Indian Statistical Society) 1973.

Bhat, L.S. and Das, B.N.:
Regional Physical Complexes for Agricultural Land use Planning,
Discussion paper No. 23 (New-Delhi: Indian Statistical Institute, Regional Survey Unit) 1967.

Bhat, L.S. and Prakasa Rao, V.L.S.:
" A Regional Framework for Resource Development",
Bombay Geographical Magazine, Vol. 10, No.1, 1964

Bhat, L.S. and Sharma, A.N. :
"Functional- Spatial Organization of Human Settlements for Integrated Area Study",
Paper read at the 13th Indian Econometric Conference, Ahmedabad, 1974.

Bhat, L.S. et. al.:
Micro-Level Planning : A Case Study of Karnal Area, Haryana India,
(New-Delhi : K.B. Publications) 1976.

Bhat, L.S.:
Strategy for Integrated Area Development: Case Study of North Kanara District (Karnataka)
(New-Delhi: Concept Publishing Co.) 1988.

Bhat, L.S.:
"Aspects of Regional Planning in India",
in
Liverpool Essays in Geography,
(London : Longmans) 1964. This essay suggests seven macro-economic regions based on distribution of resources and possibilities of developing regional production complexes.

Bhat, L.S.:
"Regional Concept and Planning Regions with Special Reference to India",
in Mishra, R.P., et. al. (eds.):
Regional Planning: Concepts, Techniques, Policies and Case Studies,
(Mysore, Prasaranga : University of Mysore Press) Mysore 1969. Here the author suggests grouping togather of States in regions instead of inter regional multi sectoral plan within the national Plan.

Bhat, L.S.:
"Regional Development- Some Dimensions of the Concept with Special Reference to Planning in India",
Indian Journal of Regional Science, Vol.V, No. I, 1973.

Bhat, L.S.:
"Regional Planning in India - A suggested Model",
in NCAER
Market Towns & Spatial Development
(New-Delhi : National Council of Applied Economic Research) 1972.

Bhat, L.S.; Kundu A.; Das, B.N.; Sharma, A.N.; Bhat D.R.; Sastry C.S. and Mahapatro, R.C. :
Micro-Level Planning - A Case Study of Karnal Area
(New - Delhi : K.B. Publications) 1976.

Bhat, L.S.; Pal M.N.; Komar I.V. and Papov K.M.:
"Problems of Regionalisation for the Development of National Economy",
Sankhaya, Series B, Vol. 25, 1963.

This paper brings out an important point that each region should have their own economic specialisation, for regionalisation to be meaningful in the context of planned development. The advantage of each region should be tapped to the maximum possible extent.

Bhat: L.S.:
Regional Planning in India,
(Calcutta: Statistical Publishing Society) 1972.

Bhati, J.P. and Guleria, A.S. :
Watershed Planning for Decentralized and Sustainable Development in Hilly Areas,
(Simla: Deptt. of Economics, Himachal Pradesh University) manuscript, 1988.

Bhatia, B.M.:
"Perspective Plan: Developing the Rural Sector",
Statesman, 28th February 1976.

Bhatia, B.M.:
"Planning for Janata: Square Deal for All",
Statesman, 10th February 1978.

Bhatia, S.S. :
"Spatial Variation, Changes and Trends in Agricultural Efficiency in Uttar Pradesh 1953-63",
Indian Journal of Agricultural Economics, Vol. 22, 1967.

Bhatia, V.G. et. al. :
"Economic Interdependence and Regional Development",
Arthavijnana, Vol. 9, No. 3-4. 1967.

Bhatnagar, S.C.; et. al. :
"Decision Support systems for District Administration", in Rural Regional Development Network Newsletter,
No. 6, (Bangkok: Asian Institute of Technology) April 1987.

Bhattacharjee, A.K. :
"Regional Frame for Rural Urban Planning: Some Basic Considerations",
in Misra R.P. et. al. (eds.):
Urban Systems and Rural Development
(Prasarang, Mysore : University of Mysore) 1972.

Bhattacharjee, Ajit:
"Planning in Blinkers",
Indian Express, 3rd September 1977.

Bhattacharjee, Dhires :
India's Five Year Plans
(Calcutta : Progressive Publishers) 1978.

Bhattacharjee, Mohit :
"Urban Development in The Perspective of Multi-Level Planning",
The Indian Journal of Public Administration, Vol. XIX, No. e, 1973.

Bhattacharya, Asit:
"Economic Regions in the Context of Development : Some Basic Considerations",
Vol. XV, March 1973.Artha Vijnana.

Bhattacharyya, J :
Administration Organization for Development
(Brussels : International Institute of Administrative Sciences) 1973.

Bhattacharyya, N. :
"Nature of Decentralised Planning in India",
Mainstream, March 4, 1989.

Bhattacherjee, Dhires :
"Evaluation of the Strategies of Regional Planning",
in Bagchi, K.G. and Pathak, C.R.:
Regional Development and Planning
(Calcutta & Kharagpur: Deptt. of Geography, Calcutta University & Regional Science Association of India) 1976.

Bhattacherjee, J.P. :
"Interaction of Urbanization and Rural Development in India",

Ekistics, Vol. 17, No. 98, Janurary 1964.

Bhattacherjee, Mohit :
"The Poorest of the Poor - A Story of a Backward Area", The Indian Journal of Public Administration, Vol XXII, No. 4, 1977.

Bhaumick, Alok K. :
"Micro-Level Planning - Theory, Practice and Lessons (With Special Reference to State-Level Planning)",
Indian Journal of Regiona Science, Vol. X, No. 2, 1978.

Bhoothalingam, S.:
"Planning: Need for Fresh Thinking",
Indian Express, 30th May 1977.

Bhuvaneshwari, M.:
"Industrial Development of Backward Areas with Special Reference to the Role of State Industries Promotion Corporation of Tamilnadu in North Arcot",
Unpublished Ph.D. dissertation, University of Madras, Madras, 1987.

Bhuvaneswari, M. :
Need for Decentralised Planning in Backward Area Development,
(Madras: University of Madras, Ethiraj College, Deptt. of Economics) manuscript, 1988.

Bilgrami, S.A.R.:
Micro-Local Planning Framework for Agricultural Sector
(Delhi: Zamia Millia, Deptt. of Economics) Manuscript 1988.

Bisaliah, S. and Srinivasamurthy, J.:
Methodology of Micro-Level Employment Planning
(Bangalore: University of Agricultural Science) 1983.

Bisaliah, S.; et. al. :
A Full Employment Plan for Bhalki Block, Bidar District, Karnataka
(Bangalore : Planning Department, Govt. of Karnataka) 1978, Mimeographed.

Bisaliah, S.; et. al.:
A Full Employment Plan For Basavakalyana Block, Bidar District
(Bangalore: Planning Department, Government of Karnataka), 1978 Mimeographed.

Bisaliah, S.; et. al.:
A Full Employment Plan for Muddabihal Block, Bijapur District
(Bangalore : Planning Department, Government of Karnataka) 1978, Mimeographed.

Bisaliah, S.; et. al.:
A Full Employment Plan For Badami Block Bijapur District
(Bangalore: Planning Department, Government of Karnataka) 1978, Mimeographed.

Biswas, S.K.:
"Spatial and Demographic Behaviour Among the Million Cities of India and Other Leading Countries of the World",
Indian Journal of Regional Science, Vol. IX, No. 2, 1977.

Black, J.:
"The Theory of Indicative Planning",
Oxford Economic Papers, Vol. 20, 1968.

Black, John, et. al. :
Rural Planning of One County: Worcester County
(Cambridge, Mass: Harvard University Press) 1959.

Blaike, P.M. :
Spatial Planning For Diffusion of Family Planning in India
(London: Edward Arnold) 1975.

Blair, H.W. :
"Approaches to Integrated Social Development Planning and

Implementation at The Local Level",
Regional Development Dialogue Vol. 7, No. 1, 1986.

Blair, John :
Industrial Polarization And The Location of New Manufacturing Firms: An Empirical Application
(Peace Dale, Virginia: Regional Science Research Institute) Discussion Paper No. 89, June 1976.

Bluestone, Barry and Harrison, Bennett, :
Capital and Communities: The Causes and Consequences of Private Disinvestment
(Washington D.C. : Progressive Alliance) 1980.

Boaden, N.; Goldsmith M., Hampton W, and Stringer P.:
Public Participation in Local Services,
(London : Longman Group Ltd.) 1982. This small book assesses the relationship between policy, service provision, public participation and development.

Boaden, N.; Goldsmith M.; Hampton, W. and Stringer, P. :
Planning and Participation in Practice : a study of Public Participation in Structure Planning,
(Oxford : Pergamon) 1980.

Bohra, G.S. and Mehta, S.S.:
"An Input-Output Table for Rajasthan's Industrial Economy 1964",
Anvesak, December 1971.

Boisier, Sergio:
Planning a System of Regions, Methods, And Techniques of Inter-regional Planning
(Santiago: United Nations) 1981.

Bombay Metropolitan Regional Planning Board :
Regional Plan for Bombay Metropolitan Region 1970-90,
(Bombay: Bombay Metropolitan Regional Planning Board) 1974.

Bordia, Otima :
"District Administration - Problems of Co-Ordination",
(Jaipur: H.C. Mathur State Institute of Public Administration) Mimeographed, 1970.

Borts, G.H. :
"Review of Richardson's Regional Growth Theory",
Journal of Economic Literature, Vol. XII, 1974.

Bos, H.C. :
The Spatial Dispersal of Economic Activity
(Rotterdam: Rotterdam University Press) 1965.

Bosch, H. :
"Central Functions as a Basis for Systematic Grouping of Localities",
International Geographical Union, 17th Abstract of Papers, National Geographic Society, Washington, 1952.

Bose, A.N. :
"Economics and Politics of Decentralized Planning",
Indian Journal of Regional Science Vol. XXI, No. 1, 1989.

Bose, A.N. :
"Regional Development - A Precondition for Metropolitan Development",
Indian Journal of Regional Science, Vol. 5, No.2., 1973.

Bose, A.N.:
"Regional Planning in the Era of Transition from Povery to Plenty",
Indian Journal of Regional Science, Vol. VI, No. 2, 1974.

Bose, Ashish,:
"Urbanization in the Face of Rapid Population Growth and Surplus Labour: The Case Study of India",
Papers read in the Asian

Population Conference, New-Delhi, December 1963.

Bose, D.K.:
"Dynamic Programming for Decentralized Planning",
Indian Economic Journal, Vol. 3, 1965.

Bose, S.R. :
"Locating the Depressed Areas of Bihar",
Indian Journal of Agricultural Economics, Vol. 2, 1956.

Boudeville J.R.,:
Problems of Regional Economic Planning
(Edinburgh: Edinburgh University Press) 1966, reprinted 1974. It is considered by many as still the best book on the subject.

Boudeville, J.R. :
"A Survey of Recent Techniques for Regional Economic Analysis",
in Isard, W and Cumberland, J.H. (eds.):
Regional Economic Planning : Techniques of Analysis
(Paris: OECD) 1960.

Boventer, E. von :
"Spatial Organizational Theory as a Basis for Regional Planning",
Journal of the American Institute of Planners, Vol 30, 1964.

Bracey, H.E. :
English Central Villages : Identification, Distribution and Functions,
Paper presented at the Lund Symposium on Problems of Urban Geography, 19th International Geographical Congress, 1960.

Bracey, H.E. :
"A Rural Component of Centrality Applied to Six Southern Countries of the United Kingdom",
Economic Geography, Vol. 32, 1956.

Bradford, C. ; Finney, L.; Hallet, S. and Knight, J. :
Structural Disinvestment : A Problem in Search of a Policy,
(Evanston, Illinois: Northwestern University Centre for Urban Affairs) 1981.

Braescher, Curtis; Kuchn, J.A. and Croll, John :
The Community Economic Base How to Compute, Evaluate and Use, Guide DM 3005.
(Columbia: University of Missouri Extension) 1977.

Brahme, S.:
"Approach to Rural Area Development",
Indian Journal of Regional Science, Vol. 4, No. 1, 1972.

Brahme, S.; et. al. :
Regional Planning
(Poona: Gokhale Institute of Economics & Politics) 1975.

Brahme, Sulabha; Pare, Kumud; and Pore, S.H.:
"Regional Planning : A Case Study of Marathawada Region"
Artha Vijnana, Vol. XVII, Numbers 1 and 2, March-June 1975.

Brara, J.S. :
The Political Economy of Rural Development: Strategies for Poverty Alleviation
(New-Delhi: Allied Publishers) 1983.

Breheny, M.J. and Hooper, A.J.:
Rationality in Planning : Critical Essays on the Role of Rationality in Urban and Regional Planning
(London : Pion Ltd.) 1985.

Brenner, Y.S. :
Theories of Economic Development and Growth,
(London: George Allen & Unwin) 1984.

Brien, Robert :
"Some Issues on Social Skills And

Attitude Training for Decentralized Planning",
in Proceedings of the Expert Consultation, Kathmandu, Nepal, 28th Nov. to 2nd Dec. 1988, (Rome: Food & Agriculture Organisation of the U.N.) 1989.

Brillantes, Alex B. :
"The Regional Development Council as a Mechanism for Co-ordination and Effective Performance",
Phillipines Journal of Public Administration, Vol. XXIV, No. 1, 1980.

Broadbent, T.A. :
An Introduction to Factor Analysis and Its Application to Regional Science,
(London : The Centre For Environmental Studies) Paper No. 13.

Bromley, R.J. :
"Markets in the Developing Countries: A Review",
Geography, Vol. 56, 1971.

Bromley, R.J. :
"The Spatial Pattern and Temporal Synchronization of Periodic Markets",
Swansea Geographer, Vol. 12, 1973, pp. 15-25.

Bronger, D. :
"The Dilemma of Developing Country Research"
Inter-Economics, Vol. 9 & 10, 1977.

Broniewski, S. and Jastrzetoski, B. :
"Optimisation Method" in Optimising Planning Unit: Threshold Analysis
(Edinburgh : University of Edinburgh) 1970.

Brown, A.J. :
"Surveys of Applied Economics: Regional Economics with Special Reference to United Kingdom",
Economic Journal, December 1969.

Brown, A.J. and Burrows, E.M.:
Regional Economic Problems,
(London : George Allen & Unwin) 1977.

Brown, A.J. et. al. :
"Regional Multipliers",
National Institute Economic Review, No. 40, May, 1967.

Brown, H.J. :
"Shift and Share Projections of Regional Economic Growth, an Empirical Test",
Journal of Regional Science, Vol. 9, No. 1, April 1969, p. 1-18.

Brown, L.A. :
Diffusion Processes and Location: A Conceptual Framework and Bibliography
(Philadelphia: Regional Science Institute) 1965.

Brown, L.A., and Harton F.E.:
"Functional Distance and Operational Approach",
Geographical Analysis, Vol. 2. 1970.

Brown, Lawrence :
Diffusion Processes and Location Theory
(Peace Dale: Regional Science Research Institute, U.S.A.) 1968.

Brown, Lawrence :
The Diffusion of Innovation : A Market Chain Approach, paper No. 3,
(Wanston: North Western University, Deptt. of Geography) 1963.

Brown, M. :
On The Theory and Measurement of Technological Change
(Cambridge: Cambridge University Press) 1966. Contains a general discussion of production function.

Brush, J.E. :
"The Hierarchy of Central Places in South Western Wisconsin",
Geographical Review, Vol. 43, No. 3, 1953.

Buck, T.W. :
"Shift and Share Analysis - A Guide to Regional Policy",
Regional Studies, Vol. 4, No. 4, 1970.

Budhraja, J.C. :
"Organizational Framework for District Planning and Involvement of People in Development Process",
Indian Journal of Regional Science Vol. XIX, No. 2, 1987.

Bulsara, J.F. :
Problems of Regional Economic Planning,
(Edinburgh : Edinburgh University Press) 1966.

Butler, Lawrence and Howell, R.E. :
Coping With Growth: Community Needs Assessment Techniques
(Corvallis: Oregon State University, Western Rural Development Centre) 1980.

Byfuglenen, J. and Nordgard, A.:
"Types or Regions?"
Norsk Geography, Tidsskr, Vol. 28, 1974.

Byres, T.J.:
" Agrarian Transition and the Agrarian Question",
in Harriss, J. (ed.):
Rural Development: Theories of Peasant Economy and Agrarian Change,
(London: Hutchison) 1982.

C

Calcutta Metropolitan Organization :
Notes on Plan Allocation, Financing Principles, Unit and Operating Costs of Some Community Facilities.
(Calcutta : Calcutta Metropolitan Planning Organisation) 1965

Calsamiglia, X. :
"Decentralized Resource Allocation and Increasing Returns", Journal of Economic Theory, 1977, pp. 263-283.

Cambridge University, Department of Applied Economics :
A Programme for Growth, Vol. 1 : A computable Model of Economic Growth 1962,
(London : Chapman and Hall) 1962.

Cambridge University, Department of Applied Economics:
A Programme for Growth, Vol 2: A Social Accounting Matrix for 1960,
(London : Chapman and Hall) 1962.

Cambridge University, Department of Applied Economics:
A Programme for Growth, Vol. 3 : Input-Output Relationships 1954-1956,
(London : Chapman and Hall) 1963.

Cambridge University, Department of Applied Economics:
A Programme for Growth Vol. 4, Capital Output and Employment 1948-1960,
(London : Chapman & Hall) 1964.

Cambridge University, Department of Applied Economics:
A Programme for Growth Vol. 5 : The Model in its Environment: A Progress Report
(London: Chapman and Hall) 1964.

Cambridge University, Department of Applied Economics:
A Programme for Growth; Vol 6: Exploring 1970 : Some Numerical

Results,
(London : Chapman and Hall) 1965.

Cambridge University, Department of Applied Economics:
A Programme for Growth, Vol 7: The Owners of Quoted Ordinary Shares : A Survey for 1963
(London : Chapman and Hall) 1966.

Cambridge University, Department of Applied Economics:
A Programme for Growth, Vol. 8: The Demand for Fuel : A Sub-model for the British Fuel-Economy
(London : Chapman and Hall) 1968.

Cambridge University, Department of Applied Economics:
A Programme for Growth, Vol. 10: The Determinants of British Imports 1949-1966
(London : Chapman and Hall) 1970.

Cameron, B. :
"The Production Function of Leontief Models",
Review of Economic Studies, Vol. 20, 1952-53.

Cameron, G.C. :
Regional Economic Development : The Federal Role
(Baltimore : Johns Hopkins University Press) 1971.

Cameron, Gordon C.:
"Growth Areas, Growth Centres, and Regional Conversion", Scottish Journal of Political Economy, Vol. 18, 1970.

Cao, Pinna V. :
"Problems of Establishing and Using Regional Input-Output Accounting",
in Isard, W. and Cumberland, J.H. (ed.):
Regional Economic Planning - Techniques of Analysis
(Paris : OECD) 1961.

Carlisle,L. :
"New Strategies for Local Economic Development",
Carolina Planning, Vol. 2, No. 4, 1978.

Carrothers, G.A.P. :
"An Historical Review of the Gravity and Potential Concepts of Human Interaction",
Journal of the American Institute of Planners, Vol. 22, 1956.

Carter, Robert :
"The Spatial Basis for Economic Development and Adjustment Policies", in Regions in Transition,
(Canberra: Government of Australia, Department of Local Government and Administrative Services) 1984.

Casetti, E. :
"Why Diffusion Processes Conform to Logistic Trends?",
Geographical Analysis, Vol. 1, 1969, pp. 101-105.

Central Regional and Urban Planning Organization:
Guide to Preliminary Planning Survey for small And Medium Sized Towns
(New Delhi: C.R.U.P.O.) 1962

Chakrabarti, Milindo :
Information Data Base as Infrastructure of Decentralised Planning : A Case Study of Three North Bengal Districts
(Darjeeling : Deptt. of Economics, St. Joseph's College) manuscript, 1988.

Chakraborty, S. :
The Planning Progress in India: An Appraisal and Framework,
paper Circulated in Ahmedabad Institute in Training Programme for Planning Officers 1987. Chakravaty demonstrates that there could be no regional planning without there being inner logic in State Plans.

Chakraborty, S. and Bhagwati, J.N.:
Indian Economic Analysis : A Survey
(Bombay : Lalvani Publishing House) 1971.

Chakraborty, S.:
The Logic of Investment Planning
(Amsterdam: North Holland Publishing Co.) 1968. This deals beautifully with the two Sector Model of Mahalanobis and four Sector Model of Feldman.

Chakravaty, S. :
A Note on the Structure of Multi-Level Planning for India,
(New-Delhi: Planning Commission) 1977 Mimeographed.

Chakravaty, S. :
"Planning Techniques in India", in Survey of Research in Economics,
(Bombay: Allied Publishers) 1977 Vol. I.

Chambers, Robert :
Rural Development : Putting the Last First,
(London: Longman) 1983.

Chandra, G.S. :
"Regionalisation in Management of Forests in India":
Indian Journal of Regional Science, Vol. 2, No. 2, 1969.

Chandrasekhar, C.S. and Sundaram, K.V.,:
Planning Regions of India
(New-Delhi : Town and Country Planning Organisation) 1968 Mimeographed.

Chandrasekhar, C.S. and Sundaram, K.V.:
"Population Growth and Urban and Regional Planning in India",
Journal of the Institute of Economic Geography, India, Vol. I, 1970.

Chauduri, M.R. :
Indian Industries Development and Location
(Calcutta : Oxford & IBH Book Co.) 1970.

Chatterjee, S. :
"Multi-Level Planning : Some Problems and Issues",
Indian Journal of Regional Science, Vol. X, No.1, 1978.

Chatterjee, A.B. :
"Nature of Commodity Flow of a Market in the Fringe Area of Calcutta",
Geographical Review of India, Vol. XXXI, No. 3, 1969.

Chatterjee, A. :
"Trends in Rural Urban Relations in Bengal : A Historical Appraisal",
Geographical Review of India, Vol. 30, Sept. 1968.

Chatterjee, Biswajit :
"Decentralized Planning in India - Conceptual Issues and Policy Options",
Conference Volume Indian Economic Association, Calcutta, December 1988.

Chatterjee, M. :
"A Scheme of Decentralized Decision-Making in India",
Indian Journal of Public Administration, Vol. XVI, No.4, Oct-Dec. 1970.

Chatterjee, M. :
"Regional Economic Planning: Importance for India",
Indian Journal of Economics, 1970.

Chatterjee, M. :
"Regional Planning Approach to Calcutta Metropolitan Area",
Indian Journal of Regional Science, Vol 2, No. 2, 1969.

Chatterjee, M. and Isard, W.:
"Potentialities of Regional Methods and Techniques in Attacking Indian Regional Science Problems",
Indian Journal of Regional Science, Vol 1, No. 1, 1968.

Chatterjee, S. :
"Organisation of Rural Poor - The Main Tool for Micro-Level Planning in Rural Areas",
Indian Journal of Regional Science, Vol. IX, No. 2, 1977.

Chatterjee, S.P. :
"Region, Regionalism and Economic Regionalisation",
The Geographer, Vol. XIV, 1967.

Chatterjee, Susmiti :
An Analysis of Conceptual Theoretical and Realistic Basis of Decentralised Economic Planning,
Manuscript, 1988.

Chattopadhyay, Boudhayan and Raza, Moonis :
"Regional Development : Analytical Framework and Indicators",
Indian Journal of Regional Science, Vol VII, No. 1, 1975.

Chaudhari, T.P.S. (ed.) :
Selected Readings in Community Development
(Hyderabad : National Institute of Community Development, since renamed National Institute of Rural Development) 1967.

Chaudhary, K.K. :
Decentralised Planning in India,
(Gaya: Deptt. of Economics, Sanjay Gandhi Mahila College) Manuscript, 1988.

Chaudhuri, Mrinal Dutta:
"The problems of Multilevel Planning and Decision Making in India",
in Kuklinski A. (eds.):
Social Issues in Regional Policy and Regional Planning,
(The Hague: Mouton & Co.) 1977.

Chaudhury, A.M. :
"Local Level Planning & People's Participation",
Bangladesh Journal of Public Administration, Vol. 2, No. 2, July 1988.

Cheema, G.S. and Rondinelli, D.A. :
Implementing Decentralized Programme in Asia : Local Capacity for Rural Development
(Nagoya, Japan; UNCRD) 1983.

Cheema, G.S. and Rondinelli, D.A. (eds.) :
Decentralisation and Development,
(Beverly Hills : Sage) 1983.

Chenery H.; Ahluwalia, M.S.; Bell, C.L.G.; Dubey, J.H.; and Jolly, R.:
Redistribution with Growth
(London: Oxford University Press) 1974.

Chenery, H.B. :
Studies in Development Planning,
(Cambridge, Mass : Harvard University Press) 1971.

Chenery, Hollis B. and Bruno, M. :
"Development Alternatives in an Open Economy"
Economic Journal, 1962.

Chenery, Hollis B. and Clark, P.G. :
Inter Industry Economics
(New York : Wiley) 1959.

Chenery, Hollis B.; Clark, P.G. and Christ, C.:
"A Review of Input-Output Analysis",
in Studies in Income and Wealth
(New-York: National Bureau of Economic Research) Vol. 18. This is an authoritative discussion on the validity of input-output approach.

Chhabra, K.M.L. :
"District Planning in India",
Indian Journal of Public Administration, Vol. XXV, No. 2, 1979.

Chinitz, B. :
"Appropriate Goals for Regional Economic Policy",
Urban Studies, Vol. III, 1966.

Chisholm, Michael :
Rural Settlement And Land Use
(London : Hutchinson

University Library) 1968, Second Revised Edition.

Chiswick, B.R. :
Income Inequality : Regional Analysis with a Human Capital Framework,
(New York : National Bureau of Economic Research) 1974.

Chopra, P.N. :
Development Planning
(Jullundur : Vishal Publications) 1974.

Chopra, R.N. :
"Administrative Machinery for Agricultural Production at District Level",
Indian Journal of Public Administration, Vol XIII, No. 3, 1967.

Chopra, R.N.:
"Administrative Organization for Regional Development: The Experience of Punjab",
The Indian Journal of Public Administration, Vol. XI, Oct-Dec. 1965.

Chopra, R.N.:
"Removal of Poverty : Some Suggestions and Administrative Implications",
The Indian Journal of Public Administration, Vol. XVIII, April-June 1972.

Chorley, R.J. and Hagget, P. :
Socio-Economic Models in Geography
(London : Methuen) 1967.

Choudhari, M. Dutta :
"Regional Planning in India" - Seminar on Regionalisation of National Policies
(The Hague: Institute of Social Studies) 1970.

Choudhury, M.D. :
Regional Income Accounting in an Under-Developed Economy: A Case Study of India
(Calcutta: Firma KLM) 1966.

Choudhury, Rabindra Kumar:
Micro-Level Planning in India - Why has the Objective Remained Unrealised,
(Gauhati: Deptt. of Economics, Gauhati University) Manuscript, 1988.

Christaller, W.:
The Central Places in Southern Germany,
translated from original German by Baskin, C.W. (Englewood Cliffs, New Jersey : Prentice Hall) 1966.

Clark, C. :
The Conditions of Economic Progress,
(London: MacMillan & Co) 1935.

Clark, J.A. and Hoeven, R. Vander :
"Industrialisation and Employment in Developed and developing Countries"
in
Methods for Development Planning : Scenarios, Model's and Micro-Studies,
(Paris : UNESCO) 1981.

Clark, P.G. :
Planning Import Substitution,
(Amsterdam : North Holland) 1970.

Clark, P.G. and Evans, F.G. :
"Distance to Nearest Neighbour as a Measure of Spatial Relationship in Population",
Ecology, Vol. 35, 1954.

Cliff, A.D. and Haggett, P. :
"On the Efficiency of Alternative Aggregations in Region Building Problems",
Environmental Planning, Vol. 2, 1970.

Cnudde, Charles F. :
"Towards a Communication Theory of Democratic Political Development : A Causal Model",
The American Political Science Review, Vol. LXI, No.1, March 1967.

Cochrane, W.W. :
Agricultural Development and Planning : Economic Concepts, Administrative Procedure and Political Process
(New-York) 1974.

Cohen, John and Uphoff, N.T. :
Rural Development Participation : Concepts and Measures of Project Design, Implementation and Evaluation,
(Ithaca, New-York : Cornell University) 1977.

Cohen, S.I. :
Development in the Analysis and Planning of Labour and Manpower,
(Geneva: I.L.O.) Working Paper No. 12, 1986.

Cohen, S.S. :
Modern Capitalist Planning - The French Model,
(London : Weidenfeld and Nicolson) 1969.

Cohen, S.S. and Zysman, J. L.:
Manufacturing Matters
(New-York : Basic Books) 1987.

Cole, J.P. and King, C.A.M. :
Quantitative Geography - Techniques & Theories in Geography
(London : John Wiley & Sons) 1968.

Conroy, M.F. :
"Rejection of Growth Centre Stretegy in Latin American Regional Development Planning",
Land Economics, Vol. XLIX, No. 4, 1973.

Converse, P.D. :
"Laws of Retail Gravitation",
Journal of Marketing, Vol 14, No.3, 1949.

Conyers, D. :
Decentralised Planning in Papua New Guinea
(Geneva: I.L.O.) Working Paper No. 107, 1981.

Conyers, Dianna :
"Decentralisation : The Latest Fashion in Development Administration?"
Public Administration and Development, Vol. 3, 1983.

Conyers, Dianna :
"Decentralization and Development : A Review of Literature",
Public Administration And Development, Vol 4, No.2, 1984.

Conyers, Dianna and Raymond, Apthrope :
"Decentralisation, Recentralisation and Popular Participation : Towards a Framework of Analysis",
Development & Peace, Vol. 3, 1982.

Corporation of Enterprise Development :
Investing in Poor Communities
(Washington, D.C. : Corporation of Enterprise Development) 1982.

Correa, R.L. :
"Rethinking in Central Place Theory",
Market Studies, Vol. 1, Nos. 1 & 2, 1983.

Cowling, T.M. and Steely, G.C.:
Sub-Regional Planning Studies
(Oxford: Pergaman Press) 1973.

Cremer, J. :
"A Comment on 'Decentralized Planning and Increasing Return",
Journal of Economic Theory, 1978, pp. 217-221.

Cullingworth, J.B.,
Town and Country Planning in Britain
(London: Allen and Unwin) 1972.

Cumberland, J.H. (ed.) :
Regional Economic Planning - Techniques of Analysis
(Paris : OECD) 1960.

Cumberland, J.H. :
"Regional and Environmental Planning in Social Perspective", in Kuklinski, A. (ed.): **Social Issues in Regional Policy and Regional Planning** (The Hague: Mouton & Co.) 1977.

Czamanski, S. :
Regional Science Techniques in Practice (Lexington, Mass.: D.C. Heath & Co.) 1972.

D

Dahiya Bhagwan :
Planning Theories and Techniques in India: A Critique (New-Delhi : Concept Publishing Co.) 1989.

Dahiya, S. Bhagwan :
Development Planning Models Vols. I & II, (New-Delhi : Inter-India Publications) 1982.

Dahiya, S.B. :
"A Comparative Dynamic Optimising Planning Model". Kurukshetra University Research Journal, Vol. 12, 1978.

Daniels, B. and Tilly, C. :
"Community Economic Development : Seven Guiding Principles", Resources, Vol. 11, 1985 (Washington D.C. : Congress for Community Economic Development).

Dantwala, M.L. :
"Rationale and Limitation of Decentralised Planning", in Dantwala M.L., et. al. (eds.): **Asian Seminar on Rural Development** (New-Delhi : Oxford & IBH) 1986.

Dantwala, M.L.:
"Consistency Between Macro and Micro Planning", in Dantwala, M.L. et. al.: (eds.): **Asian Seminar on Rural Development,** (New Delhi : Oxford & IBH) 1986.

Dantwala, M.L.:
"Approaches to Growth and Employment", Economic and Political Weekly, 16th December, 1972.

Dantwala, M.L.:
"Block Level Planning Revisited", Economic and Political Weekly, 26th July 1980.

Dantwala, M.L.:
"Two-way Planning: Logic and Limitations : A Critical Review of the Asian Experience", Paper prepared for F.A.O., Regional Office for Asia and the Pacific, Bangkok, 1981.

Darwent, D.F. :
"Growth Poles and Growth Centres in Regional Planning - A Review", Environment and Planning, Vol. 1, 1969.

Das Gupta, B. :
"Socio-Economic Classification of Districts - A Statistical Approach", Economic and Political Weekly, Aug. 14, 1971.

Das Gupta, S. :
History of Rural Development in Modern India, Vol. I (New-Delhi: Impex India) 1967.

Das, Amritendra:
"Decentralisation of Developmental Planning and

Implementation",
Indian Journal of Public Administration, Vol. XXIV, No. 3, 1978. A Case is made out for having District as both a planning and implementational unit.

Das, B.N. and Sarkar, A.K.,:
"Rural Area Development, Karnal Area: A Case Study",
Indian Journal of Regional Science, Vol. IV No. 2, 1972.

Das, Bibekananda and Buchi, K. Nana:
Evaluation of District Planning in India,
(Berhampur: University Deptt. of Economics, Berhampur University, Orissa) manuscript, 1988.

Das, K.B. :
Principle of Decentralisation in the Strategy of Economic Development of India,
(Bhubaneshwar: Utkal University) manuscript, 1988.

Das, L.N. :
Concept and Approaches of Decentralised Planning
(Nawada : K.L.S. College, Magadh University) mansucript, 1988.

Das, Narain and Sardesai, D.B.:
"Location of Industries in India - Transport Cost Minimization",
Arthavijnana, vol. 9, No. 3-4, 1967.

Das, P.K. :
"Basic Issues, Macro-Policies and Components of a Programme of Development",
Industry and Development, New-York, No. 4, 1979.

Das, R.B. and Singh, D.P. :
Formulation and Execution of Block Plans - A Case Study
(Lucknow : The Institute of Public Administration, Lucknow University) 1968.

Das, R.B. and Singh, D.P.:
Formulation and Execution of Block Plans: A Case Study of Barabanki District Two Blocks
(Lucknow: Institute of Public Administration, University of Lucknow) 1967.

Das, R.R.L. :
Decentralised Planning in India,
(Bhagalpur: T.N.B. College, Deptt. of Economics) manuscript, 1988.

Datta, A.K. (ed.):
India-Resources, Potentialisties and Planning
(New - Delhi : Oxford & IBH) 1975, Revised Indian Edition.

Datta, Bhabatosh:
The Contents of Economic Growth and Other Essays,
(Calcutta : Research India Publications) 1977.

Datta, K.L. :
Impact of Planning on the Cost of Services
Paper read at the XVI Annual Town and Country Planning Seminar, held at Calcutta, in 1967, organised by Institute of Town Planners, India, New-Delhi.

Datta, Vijay Ranjan :
"Planning from Below: A New Role of Panchayati Raj Institutions",
Khadi Gramodyog, August, 1968, pp. 797-800.

Day, R.H. :
"A Theoretical Note on the Spatial Diffusion of Something New",
Geographical Analysis, Vol. 2, 1970.

De Guzman, Raul P. :
"Co-ordination in Government Development Delivery Systems: Problems and Prospects"
in Cuyno, R.V. et. al. (eds.) :
Management of Rural Development in the 80's

(College Laguna: MARD, U.P. Los Bonos) 1982.

Degaonkar, C.K. :
District Planning for Development : A Case of Gulbarga District in Karnataka,
Ph. D. Dissertation, University of Gulbarga, (Jaipur : Aavishkar Publishers) under print.

Demaine, H. and Malong, R.E. (eds.) :
Decentralization: Area Development Practice in Asia,
(Bongkok: Asian Institute of Technology) 1987.

Deman, Suresh :
"Political Economy of Regional Development - A Review of Theories",
Indian Journal of Regional Science, Vol. XVI, No. 2, 1984.

Deman, Suresh :
"Political Economy of Regional Development : A Case Study of Orissa",
Indian Journal of Regional Science, Vol. XI, No. 2, 1979.

Deman, Suresh :
"Region-Regionalisation And Regional Planning: Review of Techniques",
Anvesak, Vol. XIV, No. 2, December,1984.

Denton, G.R.; Forsyth, M. and MacLenan, M. :
Economic Planning and Policies in Britain France and Germany,
(London: Allen & Unwin) 1968.

Deogaonkar, S.G.:
Problems of Development of Tribal Areas
(Delhi: Leeladevi Publishers) 1980.

Department of Architecture & Planning :
Training Programme on District Level Planning - Aspects And Methodology
(Kharagpur: Indian Institute of Technology) 1970.

Desai, A.K.R. :
Rural India in Transition,
(Bombay : Popular Book Depot) 1961.

Desai, B.M. et. al.:
Rural Development for Rural Poor: Dharampur Project
(Ahmedabad : Institute of Management) 1976.

Desai, D.K. and Prakash, Hari :
"Planning and Implementation of Financing the Area Development Scheme",
Economic & Political Weekly, Special Number, 25th March 1972, pp. A-13 to A-22.

Desai, M.B. and Mehta, R.S. :
Community Development and Change : Case Study of a Block in Gujarat
(Hyderabad: National Institute of Community Development, since renamed National Institute of Rural Development) 1967.

Desai, P.B.: (ed.)
Regional Perspective of Industrial and Urban Growth: The Case of Kanpur,
(Bombay: Macmillan) 1969. This is a collection of papers read at the International Seminar held at Indian Institute of Technology, Kanpur dealing with spatial dimensions of the development problems of Kanpur.

Desai, S.S.N. and Bhalerao,C.N.:
Economic Planning And Policy,
(Bombay: Himalaya Publishing House) 1987.

Deshmukh, C.D. :
"On Rural Growth Centres and Area Development", in
Community Development and Panchayati Raj Digest, Vol. 2, 1970, pp. 174-179.

Deva, Raj :
"Multilevel Planning and Local Government Structure",

The Indian Journal of Public Administration, Vol. XIX, No. 3. July-Sept. 1973,

Dey, B.K. :
Village Planning & Development in a Block Frame:
A Case Study of Nepura Village, unpublished Ph.D. Thesis of Berhampur University, Berhampur, Ganjam 1987.

Dhakar, B.L. :
"An Approach to Planning Regions of Rajasthan",
in Papers and Proceedings of Seminar on Regional Development in Rajasthan, (Jaipur : University of Rajasthan) 20th March 1974.

Dhakar, B.L. :
"Concept of Regional Development",
Economic Times, 1st September 1975, p.5.

Dhakar, B.L.:
"Regional Aspects of State Planning",
Modern Review, April 1973, p. 295-301.

Dhar, P.N. :
"Strategy to Industrialise Rural and Backward Areas",
Kurukshetra, 1st December 1973.

Dhar, P.N. and Lydall, H.F.:
Role of Small Enterprises in Indian Economic Development
(Bombay : Asia Publishing Co.) 1961. This is a classic treatment of the subject and is still an authoritative work.

Dhar, R. :
"Inter-Regional, Inter-Sectoral Relation of Industries in India",
Artha Vijnana, Vol. 9, No. 3-4, 1967.

Dhar, R. and Kadekodi, G.K.
A Consistency Model of Regional Survey Unit,
(New-Delhi: Indian Statistical Institute)1980.

Dhar, R.:
"The Nature of Spatial Clusters of the Indian Economy", Anvesak, Vol. III, No. 1-2, June-December 1973.

Dhar, Ranjit; Rao, M.R. and Srinivasan, V.:
"A Full Employment Model of A Regional Economy of India - with an Empirical Analysis of Bangalore District",
Indian Journal of Regional Science, Vol. XI, No. 1, 1979.

Dhar, Ranjit; Robert, Venning and Brian, J.L. Berry:
"Inter-Regional Inter-Sectoral Relations of the Indian Economy",
in Brian J.L. Berry, (ed.):
Essays on Commodity Flows and the Spatial Structure of the Indian Economy,
(Chicago : Department of Geography Research Paper No. 111, University of Chicago) 1966.

Dharamraj, S. :
Decentralised Planning in India,
(Madras : Institute of Correspondence Education, University of Madras) manuscript, 1988.

Dharia, Mohan :
"Planning for Development of Backward Areas and Weaker Sections of Society",
Indian Journal of Public Administration, Vol. XIX, No. 3, 1973.

Dhesi, A.S. and Bhullar, N.S.:
"Aspects of District Planning in India",
Social Sciences Research Journal 3rd November 1977.

Dholakia, R.H. :
"Block Level Planning And Employment Generation for Jambughoda Taluka of Panchmahal District,
(Ahmedabad: Sardar Patel

Institute of Economic and Social Research) 1979, mimeographed.

Di France, Joseph :
"A Collection of Principles and Guides : Difference Between Extension Education and Community Development
(Ithaca : Cornell University, New-York) Comparative Education Publication No. 4, and 6.

Dillon, J.L. and Anderson, J.R.:
"On Estimating Allocating Efficiency in Cross Sectional Analysis of Production",
Australian Journal of Agricultural Economics, Vol. 53, Feb. 1971.

Divakar, Rao, T.:
"Some Aspects of State Level Planning in India",
Yojana, Vol. 26, No. 16, September 1982.

Dixit, R.S. :
"Role and Rationale of Market centres in Integrated Rural Development",
Symposium Proceedings, Indian Council of Geographers, 1980.

Dobb, M. :
An Essay in Economic Growth and Planning
(London: Routledge and Kegan Paul) 1960.

Dobhal, G.L. :
Development of Hill Areas - A Case Study of Pauri Garhwal District
(New Delhi: Concept Publishing Co.) 1987.

Dogett, R.P. :
"The Development Sector Approach to Regional Planning",
Journal of the American Institute of Planners, Vol. XXXV, No. 3, May 1969.

Dohety, Joseph :
"Urban Places and Third World Development",
African Urban Notes, Series B., No. 2, 1975.

Dorfman, R. :
The Price System
(Englewood Cliffs: Prentice-Hall) 1964. Maximization and programming are discussed in this book.

Dresch, S and Goldberg, R.D.
"India : An Inter-industry, National Regional Policy Evaluation model",
Annals of Social and Economic Management, Vol, 2, 1975.

Drewnowaski, J. :
Social and Economic Factors in Development
(Geneva: UNRISD) Report No. 3, February 1968.

Du Soutoy, P. :
Community Development in Ghana
(London: Oxford University Press) 1958.

Du Soutoy, P. :
The Organization of Community Development Programme
(London : Oxford Univerisity Press) 1962.

Dubashi, P.R. :
The Grammer of Planning
(New-Delhi : Indian Institute of Public Administration on behalf of Deptt. of Personnel & Administrative Reforms, Government of India) 1984 reprint. Chapters III, IV & V specially.

Dubashi, P.R. :
"Co-ordination and Communication in Government",
Indian Journal of Public Administration, Vol. 12, No. 3, July-September 1966.

Dubashi, P.R. :
"Decentralization, Planning and Public Administration",

Indian journal of Public Administration, Vol. 12, No. 1, 1966.

Dubashi, P.R. :
"Gaps in the Indian Planning Process of Planning: Importance of Regional Planning",
The Indian journal of Public Administration, Vol. XIX, No. 3, 1973.

Dubasi, P.R. :
"Adminstration of Backward Areas",
The Indian Journal of Public Administration, Vol. XXII, No. 4, 1977.

Dube, Rajive :
Some Aspects of Block Level Planning in Education,
(Rawa: School of Studies in Business Economics, A.P.S. Viswavidyalaya) manuscript, 1988.

Dube, S.C. :
"Bureaucracy and Economic Development",
Indian Journal of Public Administration, Vol. 12, No. 3, July-September 1966.

Dube, S.C.:
Tribal Heritage of India
(New Delhi : Vikas Publishing House Pvt. Ltd.) 1977.

Dube, Sumati :
"Organizational Strains in Community Development Blocks in India",
Indian Journal of Social Work, Vol. 29, No. 2, July 1968.

Dubey, K.N. and Singh, R.P.:
"Centralised and Decentralised Planning: A Dialogue", in Dubey, K.N.: Planning and Development in India,
(New Delhi: Ashish Publishing House) 1990.

Dubey, K.N.:
"District Planning Models" in Dubey K.N. (ed.): Planning and Development in India,
(New Delhi: Ashish Publishing House) 1990.

Dubey, K.N.:
"The Role of Decentralised Planning in Removing Inter-District Imbalances".
Paper read at National Seminar on Decentralised Planning,
organised by State Planning Institute, Government of Uttar Pradesh, Lucknow, 13th & 14th February, 1988.

Dubey, S.N. and Murdia, Ratna :
Administration of Policy and Programmes for Backward Classes in India
(Bombay : Somaiya Publications) 1976.

Duncan, O.T. :
"Service Industries and The Urban Hierarchy",
Papers and Proceedings of the Regional Science Association, Vol. 4, 1958, pp. 105-120.

Dunham, D.M. and Hilhorst, J.G.M. :
Issues in Regional Planning
(The Hague : Institute of Social Studies, Mouton & Co.) 1971.

Dunn, Edgar S. Jr. :
"Spatial Organisation Theory as a Basis for Regional Planning",
Journal of the American Institute of Planners, Vol. 30, 1964.

Dusseldorp van, D.B.W.M. :
Planning of Service Centres in Rural Areas of Developing Countries
(Wageningen: International Institute for Land Reclamation and Improvement) 1971.

Dutta Choudhury, M. :
A Methodological Note on Spatial Planning in India
(New Delhi : Plannig Commission) 1973 Mimeographed.

Dutta, Choudhury, M :
"Regional Planning in India",
in Dunham, D.M. and Hilhorst, J.G.M. :
Issues in Regional Planning
(The Hague: Institute of Social Studies, Mouton & Co.) 1971.

Dutta, Debabrata :
Popular Participation in Planning Process - The West-Bengal Experience
(Calcutta : Ashutosh College, Deptt. of Economics) manuscript, 1988.

Dwett, K.K. and Wadhawan, Satish :
Economics of Development Planning,
(New-Delhi : S. Chand & Co. Ltd.) 1989.

Dziewonski, K. :
"The Theory of Economic Regions",
Geographic Survey, Vol. 1, No. 39, 1967, Warsaw.

Dziewonski, Kazimeirz :
"Theoretical Problems in the Development of Economic Regions",
Papers & Proceedings of the Regional Science Association, Vol. 8, 1962.

Dziewonski, Kazimierz :
"Theoretical Problems in the Development of Economic Regions",
Papers and Proceedings of the Regional Science Association Vol. 1, 1955.

E

Easterlin, Richard E. :
"Long Term Regional Income Changes : Some Suggested Factors",
Papers and Proceedings of the Regional Science Association, No. 4, 1958.

Eckaus, R.S. :
"Planning in India",
in Millikan, M.F. (ed.):
National Economic Planning in NBER
(Calcutta : Scientific Book Agency, Indian Printing) 1971.

Eckaus, R.S. and Parikh, K.S.:
Planning for Growth: Multi-Sectoral, Inter-Temporal Models Applied to India
(Cambridge, Mass: M.I.T. Press) 1968.

Elhance, Arun :
"Location of Social Facilities: An Analytical Approach",
Indian Journal of Regional Science, Vol. XV, No.1, 1983.

Elvin, Varrier (ed.):
A New Deal For Tribal India,
(New Delhi: Ministry of Home Affairs, Govt. of India) 1963.

Ensminger, Douglas :
A Guide to Community Development
(Calcutta: Ministry of Community Development, Government of India Press) 1962.

Ensminger, Douglas :
An Evolving Strategy for India's Agricultural Development (Delhi: Ford Foundation) 1968.

ESCAP :
Guidelines for Rural Centre Planning
(New York : United Nations) 1984.

ESCAP :
Local Level Planning for Integrated Rural Development Report of an Expert Group

Meeting 6th to 10th November 1978,
(Bangkok : ESCAP) 1978.

ESCAP :
The Practice of Local-Level Planning
(Bangkok : ESCAP) 1980.

ESCAP :
"Guidelines for Local Level Planning in Rural Areas", in Report of National Workshop held in Six Asian Countries
(Bangkok: ESCAP) 1981.

Esteben-Marquillas, J.M. :
"Shift and Share Analysis Revisited",
Regional and Urban Economics, Vol. 2, No. 3, October, 1972, pp. 249-255.

European Free Trade Association :
National Settlement Strategies: A Framework For Regional Development
(Geneva : E.F.T.A. Secretariate) 1974.

Expert Committee on Assessment and Evaluation:
Intensive Agricultural District Programme,
(Delhi: Ford Foundation) 1966.

F

Faludi, A. :
Planning Theory
(Glasgow: Pergamon Press) 1973.

Fernando, L. Loyd :
"Development Planning in Sri Lanka - Study of Innovative Methods and Approaches Used",
in UNESCO :
Innovative Approaches to Development Planning
(Paris : UNESCO) 1988.

Fischer, Benjamin H. and Andrade, C.P. :
"Pilot Research Project in Growth Centres",
Paper presented at the II International Seminar on Change in Agriculture, (Overseas Development Institute and University of Reading, U.K.) 1974.

Fischer, Benjamin H. and Rushton G. :
"Rural Growth Centres - Experiences in Pilot Research Project",
Paper read at the Annual Meeting of the Association for Asian Studies, San Fransisco, U.S.A., 1975.

Fischer, Benjamin H.:
"Growth Centre Planning in India",
in Misra R.P. and Sundaram, K.V. (eds.):
Rural Area Development Perspective and Approaches
(Delhi: Sterling Publishers) 1979.

Fisher, J.C. :
City and Regional Planning in Poland
(Ithaca ; New-York : Cornell University Press) 1966.

Fisher, J.L. :
"Regional Planning :Determining the Public Interest",
in Hufschmidt, M.M.:
Regional Planning - Challenge & Prospect
(New York : Frederick A. Praeger) 1969.

Fisher, Joseph L. :
"Concepts in Regional Economic Development Programmes",
Papers and Proceedings of the Regional Science Association, Vol. 1, 1955.

Floyd, C.F. and Sirmans, C.F.
"Shift and Share Projections Revisited",
Journal of Regional Science, Vol. 13, No. 1, April 1973.

Folke, S. :
Central Place System and Spatial Interaction in Nilgiris and Coorg,
Paper read at XXI, International Geographical Congress, 1968.

Food & Agricultural Organization :
Regional Decentralization for Agricultural Development Planning in the Near East And North Africa,
Economic and Social Development Paper No. 73, (Rome : Food and Agriculture Organisation of the United Nations) 1988.

Food & Agriculture Organization:
Planning Training Manual Sub-District Level
(Kathmandu : Food & Agriculture Organisation and Agricultural Projects Services Centre) 1986.

Food and Agricultural Organisation; and Assistance for National Inservice Training for Agricultural and Rural Development:
Agriplan Training System: Trainers Manual,
(Rome :FAO & UNDP) 1981.

Food And Agricultural Organisation:
An Introduction to Planning Forestry Development
(Rome:FAO of the U.N.) 1974.

Food and Agriculture Organisation :
Toward Improved Multi-Level Planning for Agriculture and Rural Development in Asia and the Pacific
(Rome : Food and Agriculture Organization of the U.N.) 1985 being FAO Economic and Social Development Paper No. 52.

Food and Agriculture Organisation:
Small Farmers Development Manual
(Bangkok: Food and Agriculture Organisation, Regional Office for Asia and the Far East) 1978.

Food and Agriculture Organisation :
Planning Training Manual: Crop Production
(Kathmandu: FAO & Agricultural Projects Services Centre) 1986 (2nd edition).

Food and Agriculture Organisation:
Training Material for Decentralized Planning District Officers' Level,
(Kathmandu : FAO & Agricultural Projects Services Centre) 1988.

Food and Agriculture Organisation:
Project Planning Handbook Vol. I
(Rome : FAO & UNDP) 1981.

Food and Agriculture Organisation:
Project Planning Handbook Vol. II
(Rome : FAO & UNDP) 1981.

Food and Agriculture Organization :
Proceedings of Expert Consultation on Multi-Level Planning and Two-Way Process in Agriculture and Rural Development Planning
(Bangkok: Food and Agriculture Organization of the United Nations, Regional Office for Asia & the Far East) 1983.

Ford Foundation :
Guidelines for Block Level Planning
(New-Delhi: Ford Foundation, Central Research Cell, Growth Centres Project) 1974.

Forbes, Jean:
Studies in Social Science and Planning
(Edinburgh: Scottish Academy Press) 1974.

Ford Foundation :
Draft Plan for Integrated Area Development, Turkulia Block, Champaran District
(New-Delhi : Ford Foundation, Bihar Central Research Cell Growth Centres Project) 1973.

Ford Foundation :
Pilot Projects for Integrated Area Development
(New-Delhi : Govt of India) 1973, mimeographed.

Ford Foundation :
Pilot Research Projects in Growth Centres -Draft Design Statement
(New-Delhi : Central Research Cell, Ford Foundation) 1970 mimeographed.

Ford Foundation :
Village Re-development Project: A Case Study
(New-Delhi : Food Foundation) 1959.

Fouraker, L. :
"A Note on Regional Multipliers",
Papers and Proceedings of the Regional Science Association, Vol. 1, 1955.

Fox, K.A.; Sen Gupta J.K.; and Thorbecke, E. (eds.):
The Theory of Quantitative Economic Policy
(Amsterdam: North Holland) 1962.

Fox, Karl A. :
"Study of Interactions Between Agriculture and the Non-Farm Economy, Local Regional and National",
Journal of Farm Economics, Vol 44, 1964.

Franda, Marcus:
Voluntary Association and Local Development
(New-Delhi : Young Asia Publishers) 1984.

Friedman, J. :
"Regional Planning as a Field of Study",
in Friedman, John and Alonso, W. (ed.) :
Regional Development and Planning - A Reader,
(Cambridge, Mass : M.I.T. Press) 1964.

Friedman, J. :
"The Concept of a Planning Region"
Land Economics, February 1956.

Friedman, J. and Weaver, C.:
Territory and Functions, The Evolution of Regional Planning
(Berkeley: University of California Press) 1979.

Friedman, John :
"A Generalised Theory of Polarised Development"
in Hansen, N.M. (ed.) :
Growth Centres in Regional Economic Development
(New-York : The Free Press) 1972.

Friedman, John and Alonso, W. (eds.):
Regional Development and Planning: A Reader
(Cambridge, Massachusetts: M.I.T. Press) 1964 (fourth reprinting 1969). A pioneering work in defining various definitions about regional and multi-level planning.

Friedman, John and Douglass, M. :
"Agropolitan Development - Towards a New Strategy for Regional Planning in Asia",
in Growth Pole Strategy and Regional Development Planning in Asia (Nagoya, Japan: United Nations Centre for Regional Development) 1985. A Study of the application of growth centres in the planning process in various countries.

Friedman, John R. :
"Regional Planning : A Problem in Spatial Integration",
Papers and Proceedings of Regional Science Association, Vol. 5, 1959. pp. 167-179.

Friedman, John:
Regional Development Policy - A Case Study of Venezuela (Cambridge, Mass: M.I.T. Press) 1969.
Friedman points out that in developing countries, spatial dimensions come up as issues in development policy during transitional phases in the evolution of the national economy.

Friedman, John:
"Regional Planning As a Field of Study",
Journal of the American Institute of Planners, Vol. 29, 1963.

Friedmann, J. :
"Regional Planning and Nation Building : An Agenda for International Research",
Economic Development and Cultural Change, Vol. 16, No. 1, 1967.

Frisch, R. :
Planning for India : Selected Explorations in Methodology,
(Delhi: Asia Publishing House) 1960.

Funnel, O.C. :
"The Role of Small Service Centres in Regional and Rural Development with Special Reference to East Africa",
in Gilbert, A. (ed.) :
Development Planning and Spatial Structure,
(London: Edward Arnold) 1976.

G

Gadgil, D.R. :
Planning and Economic Policy in India,
(Poona: Gokhale Institute of Economics and Politics, distributed by Orient Longmans) 1972.

Gadgil, D.R. :
Supplementary Note to the Notes on the Present Position of Wardha Plan
(Poona : Gokhale Institute of Economics & Politics) 1965. (Mimeographed).

Gadgil, D.R. :
Wardha Plan - A Comment
(Poona : Gokhale Institute of Economics & Politcs) 1965 (Mimeographed).

Gadgil, D.R.:
District Development Planning
(Poona : Gokhale Institute of Politics and Economics) 1967. An able treatment of the subject . It emphasies the need to bridge the gap of knowledge and information at District Level and relevance of technical and economic information.

Gadgil,D.R.:
"Approach to the Development of Backward Areas",
Speech delivered at the meeting of National Development Council Committee of Chief Ministers on 26th September 1969, Maharashtra Co-operative Quarterly, Oct. 1969,pp.103-105.

Gaekwad, V.R. :
"Management of Rural Development Programmes - Organizational Deficiencies and Strategies for Improvement",
The Indian Journal of Public Administration, Vol. XXI, No. 4, Oct-Dec. 1975.

Gaekwad, V.R. :
"Rural Development Strategies: Evaluation of Some Early Experiments in India",

in Dantwala, M.L. and others (eds.):
Asian Seminar on Rural Development,
(New Delhi : Oxford & IBH) 1986.

Gammon, Colin A.:
On The Loschian Spatial Demand Curve
(Peace Dale:Regional Science Research Institute) Discussion Paper No.32, April 1969.

Ganapathy, R.S. :
"Methodologies for Development Planning: A Critical Review with Special Reference to Social & Cultural Factors",
UNESCO : Socio-Economic Studies Vol. 12. (Paris : UNESCO) 1986.

Gandhi, A.C. :
Decentralised Planning in India, Problems & Prospects,
(Surat: S.V. College of Engineering) manuscript, 1988.

Ganeriwal, A.L.:
"Some Questions of Plan Formulation and Implementation at the District Level",
Public Administration, Kanpur, June 1974.

Gangrade, K.D. :
"Development and People - A Participatory Approach",
The Indian Journal of Social Work, Vol. XLV, No. 2, July 1984.

Ganguli, B.N. and Devendra, B. Gupta:
Levels of Living in India - An Inter State Profile
(New-Delhi : S. Chand & Co. Ltd.) 1976.

Gant, G. :
Regional and Local Organization for Development Administration
(Madison : University of Wisconsin Press) 1979.

Garcia, Mannuel P. Jr. :
"Managing Social and Economic Development through Community Organisations",
Occassional Paper Series on Community Management, Vol. 1, No.3, February 1986.

Gardner, L.M.:
Community Economic Development Strategies: Creating Successful Business, Building the Base, (Vol. I)
(Berkeley, California: National Economic Development and Law Centre) 1983.

Garnsey, M.E. :
"The Dimensions of Regional Science",
Papers & Proceedings of the Regional Science Association, Vol. II, 1956.

Gates, L.; Dermatt, A.M., and Perroux, F. :
"Notes on Concepts of Growth Poles",
in McKee, D.L. et. al. (ed.):
Regional Economics-Theory and Practice (London : The Free Press and Collier MacMillan) 1970.

Gaur, A.K. and Sharma, R. :
Gandhiji on the Orbit of Decentralization,
(Muzzaffarpur: Bihar University, M.P.S. Science College, Deptt. of Economics) manuscript, 1988.

Gaur, M.K. :
"Local Level Planning and Rural Development",
Indian Journal of Public Administration, Vol. XXVI, No. 4, 1980.

Gauthier, Howard, L. :
"Economic Growth and Growth Poles: A Search for Geographic Theory",
in Helleiner, F.M. and Stohr, Watter B. (eds.):
Paper s and Proceedings of the Commission on Regional Aspects of Development, International Geographical Union,

Methodology and Case Study, Vol. II,
(Toronto: Allister Typesetting & Graphics for CRAD) 1974.

Geiger, P.P. and Davidovich, F.R. :
"Urban Growth as a Factor of Regional Balance-Imbalance",
in Thomon, Richard S. :
Papers and Proceedings of the Commission on Regional Aspects of Development, International Geographical Union, Methodology and Case Studies, Vol. I,
(Toronto : Allister Typesetting & Graphics for CRAD) 1974.

George,K.K.:
"Development of Backward Regions: Strategy Distorted",
Economic Times , October 1st, 1976 and October 2nd, 1976, pages 5.

Ghadwick, George :
A Systems View of Planning
(Oxford: Pergamon Press) 1971.

Ghatak, Subrata :
Development Economics,
(New York: Longman Group Ltd.) 1978.

Ghildyal, V.C. :
"The Ecology of Community Development in India",
Community Development and Panchayati Raj Digest, No. 2, 1970.

Ghorpade, M.Y. :
"Centre, States and Panchayats : The Planning Process",
Economic Weekly July 1964. The author describes the involvement of the Panchayati Raj Institutions in the planning process during the second and Third Five Year Plan formulation.

Ghosh, Alok, and Ghosh, Sujit Kumar:
Planning Techniques and Indian Plans,
(Allahabad : A.H. Wheeler & Co.) 1983.

Ghosh, A. :
"Economic Classification of Agricultural Regions",
Sankhya, Vol. 10, 1960.

Ghosh, A. :
Inter-Regional Input-Output Analysis and Linear Programming,
(Cambridge University Press)

Ghosh, A. :
Efficiency in Location and Inter-Regional Flows
(Amersterdam: North Holland Publishing Co.). This raises the point that diminishing return to scale may make development of an area beyond a point rather regressive.

Ghosh, A. :
"Input-Output Analysis with Substantially Independent Groups of Industries",
Econometrica, Vol. 28, 1960.

Ghosh, A. :
"Inter-Regional Models & Problems of Substitution",
Indian Economic Journal, Vol. 14, No.2, 1967.

Ghosh, A. and Chakraborty, D. (eds.):
Contributions To National And Regional Planning Problems,
(Calcutta : K.P. Bagchi & Co.) 1983.

Ghosh, A. and Dhar, R. :
"Implications of Regional Balance in Planned Growth",
Indian Economic Journal, Vol. 8, 1960.

Ghosh, Alak :
New Horizons in Planning : Studies in the Techniques of Planning with Special Reference to India's Five Year Plans, 3rd edition
(Calcutta : World Press) 1982.

Ghosh, Arun :
West-Bengal Landscape,

(Calcutta & New Delhi: K.P. Bagchi & Co.) 1989.

Ghosh, Arun, :
"Education and Environment",
Economic and Political Weekly, October 10, 1987.

Ghosh, Arun:
"Decentralized Planning: West-Bengal Experience",
Economic and Political Weekly, (Review of Agriculture), March 26th, 1988.

Gnosh, Sujit Kumar :
"Perspective of Balanced Growth and Indian Planning",
Economic Affairs, July, 1978.

Ghosh, Sujit Kumar :
"Social Action, The Vital Need for Indian Planning",
in Roy, H. (ed.):
Collected Essays on Economic Problems of India
(Calcutta : World Press) 1978.

Ghuman, B.S. :
"A Planning Model for Punjab in Consistency Framework", The Indian Economic Review, Vol. XXIV, January-June 1989, No. 1.

Gibson, L.J. and Warden, Marshall A. :
"Estimating the Economic Base Multiplier: A Test of Alternative Procedures",
Economic Georgraphy, Vol. 57, 1981.

Gibson, Lay J. and Simpson, Robert J. (eds.):
Regional Structural Change : Experience and Prospects in Two Mature Economics,
(Peace Dale : Regional Science Research Institute, USA) 1989.

Gidadhubly, R.G. and Bhat, L.S.:
"Economic Regions and Regional Flows - A Case Study in the Flow Patterns and Trends in Selected Commodities in India",
in
Economic and Socio-cultural Dimensions of Regionalisation
(Census of India, 1971, Centenary Monograph No. 7).

Gilbert, A. (ed.) :
Development Planning and Spatial Structure
(London : John Wiley & Sons) 1976.

Gilbert, A.G. :
"Growth Poles - The Instant Solution to Regional Problems",
in Thomon, R.S. (ed.):
Papers and Proceedings of the Commission on Regional Aspects of Development, International Geographical Union, Methodology and Case Study, Vol. I,
(Toronto: Allister Typesetting & Graphics for CRAD) 1974.

Gilbert, A.G. and Gugler, J. :
Cities, Poverty and Development : Urbanization in The third World
(Oxford: Oxford University Press) 1982.

Gilbert,A.:
"A Note on the Incidence of Development Vicinity of a Growth Centre",
Regional Study, Volume 9, No. 4, 1975,

Gilbt, Alan, G. and Goodman, D.E.:
"Regional Income Disparities and Economic Development : A Critique",
in Gilbert, Alan G. (ed.):
Development Planning and Spatial Structure
(London : John Wiley) 1976.

Gille, F.B. :
Basic Thinking in Regional Planning
(The Hague : Mouton & Co.) 1967.

Gillie, F.B.:
Thinking in Regional Planning
(The Hague : Mouton & Co.) 1967.

Ginsburg, N. (ed.) :
Essays on Geography and

Economic Development
(Chicago: University of Chicago Press) 1960.

Giullemero, Mariano J. :
"Local Level Planning for Rural Development",
Paper presented at the National Workshop on Local Level Planning, December 9th and 10th, 1980, at U.P. College of Public Administration, Manila.

Glasson, J.:
An Introduction to Regional Planning
(London: Hutchinson) 1978.

Glasson, John.:
An Introduction to Regional Planning : Concepts, Theory and Practice
(London : Hutchinson & Co. Ltd. Second Impression) 1957.

Glikson, A. :
Regional Planning and Development
(Six lectures delivered at the Institute of Social Studies, at the Hague, 1953, Leiden 1955).

Gokhale Institute of Economics & Politics :
Wardha District Development Plan -Important Features
(Poona : Gokhale Institute of Economics & Politics) 1963.

Goldstein, Benjamin and Davis, Ross (eds.):
Neighbourhoods, in the Urban Economy : Dynamics of Decline and Revitalization
(Cambridge, Mass.: Lexington Books) 1977.

Goldstein, Harvey A. and Bergman, Edward M.:
"Institutional Arrangements for State and Local Industrial Policy",
Journal of the American Planning Association, Vol.52, Summer 1986.

Goldstein,H.A.:
Planning for Community Economic Development: Some Structural Considerations,
Paper for the Conference on Planning Theory and Practice (New York:Cornell University) 1979.

Gopal, M.H.:
"Region as Development Concept",
The Indian Economic Journal, Vol. XIX, No. 1., July-Sept., 1971.

Gopinath, C.; Asan, G.C.M. and Mukund Das, V.:
Pilot Intensive Rural Employment Project in Trithala Block of Kerala : An Evaluation
(Ahmedabad: Centre for Management of Agriculture) 1976 (Unpublished).

Gorenman, S. :
"Regionalisation as an Operational Procedure - Some Comments on di Tella's Report",
in Kuklinski, A. and Pretella, R.: Growth Poles and Regionalisation Policies (Hague: Mouton & Co.) 1972.

Gorzebak, G. :
Regional Dynamics of Socio-Economic Change : Experiences and Prospects in Europe and Latin America
(Warsaw : University of Warsaw) 1987.

Goswami, Prabhas Chandra :
A Study in Rural Change in Assam : Dispur
(Jorhat : Agro-Economic Research Centre for North East India) 1967.

Govil, Minnie :
Indian Social and Economic Development,
(New-Delhi: Sage Publications India Pvt. Ltd.) 1988.

Govindarajan, P. :
Decentralised Planning in India,
(Vellore: M.G. Arts College, Deptt of Economics) manuscript, 1988.

Govindarajan, P. :
"Decentralised Planning in India", Conference Volume, Indian Economic Association, 71st Conference, Calcutta, December 1988.

Gowde, K.S. Rane :
"Regional Planning for Integrated Rural Urban Development in Mysore State", in Misra R.P. et. al. (eds.): **Urban Systems and Rural Development** (Prasarang : University of Mysore) 1972.

Goyal, Vibhooti :
"Settlement Planning: Case Study Strategy Options of a Backward District", Economic Times, March 1st, 1977.

Goyal, Vibhooti:
"Area Development Strategy : Diffusion of Growth Forces", The Economic Times, 9th December 1975.

Greary, R.C., (ed.):
Europe's Future in Figures (Amersterdam: North Holland) 1962.

Green, H.L. :
"Hinterland Boundaries of New-York City and Boston in Southern New-England", Economic Geography, Vol. 31, 1955.

Grieve, R. and Robertson, D.J.:
The City and The Region (Edinburgh : Edinburgh University Press) 1964.

Groteworld, Andreas :
"Von Thunen in Retrospect", Economic Geography, Vol. 35, 1959.

Grover, Deepak :
"Planning Minimum Needs of Rural Population", in Aziz, Abdul (ed.): **Studies in Block Planning,** (New-Delhi: Concept Publishing Co.) 1983.

Growth Centre Research Cell:
Integrated Area Development Plan for Pondicherry (Pondicherry: Govt. of Pondicherry) 1974.

Gruchman, B. :
"Training of Regional Development Planners: An International Viewpoint", in Mathur, O.P. (ed.): **Training for Regional Development Planning : Perspectives for the Third Development Decade** (Singapore: Maruzen Asia, UNCRD) Vol. 9, 1981.

Guha, Sabita. :
"District Level Planning: A Pragmatic Approach", Yojana, 16th November 1978.

Guha, Sunil, :
Rural Manpower and Capital Formation in India, (New Delhi : Academic Books Ltd.) 1969

Gulati, I.S. :
"Decentralised Planning: Loopholes that Remain", Economic & Political Weekly, August 6, 1986.

Guplin, C.J.:
"The Social Anatomy of an Agricultural Community", Research Bulletin , No.34, University of Wisconsin Agricultural Experiment Station, Madison,U.S.A.

Gupta Ranjit :
Prelude to Block-Level Planning in Gujarat, Report of November 1978 Workshop (Ahmedabad: I.I.M. Ahmedabad) 1978.

Gupta, Anil :
Decentralised Planning in India

(Muzzaffarnagar : S.D. College, Deptt, of Economics) manuscript, 1988.

Gupta, R.L.:
"13-Point to Develop Backward Areas,
Financial Express,September 3rd,1974,p.4.

Gupta, Ram Gopal:
"Planning From Below",
Rural India, Vol. 51, No. 10-11, October-November, 1988.

Gupta, Ranjit:
" Sustained Development Through People: Insight from an Experience",
Vikalpa, Journal of the I.I.M. Ahmedabad, Janurary-March 1988.

Gupta, Ranjit:
"Institutional Support",
Appendix V of the
Report of the Working Group on Block Level Planning
(New Delhi: Planning Commission, Government of India) 1978.

Gupta, S.P. :
Planning Strategies and Techniques in India: Sub-Regional Symposium on the Critical Analysis of Development
(New Delhi: UNESCO Papers) 1987.

Gupta, S.P. and Singh, J.P. (eds.) :
Regional Dimensions of India's Economic Development,
(New-Delhi : Planning Commission, Govt. of India) 1983.

Gupta, Surendra Kumar :
District Planning - An Appraisal,
(Muzzaffarpur: Bihar University, Deptt. of Economics), manuscript 1988.

Gupta,L.C.:
"Decentralised Implementation: Some Administrative Problems", The Indian Journal of Public Administration, Vol.XI, No.2, 1965.

Gupta,R.L.:
"Rational Plan to Develop Backward Areas",
Economic Times, May 11th, 1974,p.5.

Gyaneband, B.R. :
"Strategy for Rural Development",
Khadi Gramodyog, Vol. 15, No. 1, 1958.

H

Hackett, J. and Hackett, A.M.:
Economic Planning in France
(London: Allen & Unwin) 1963.

Hagerstrand, T.:
Innovation Diffusion in Spatial Process,
Translated by Pred Allen (Chicago: University of Chicago Press) 1967. He suggests that communication fields operate at local, regional and national levels to form a mean communication field hierarchy.

Hagerstrand, T.:
Propagation of Innovative Waves,
Lund Studies in Geography, Series B, Human Geography, 1952.

Hagerstrand, T.:
"On Monte Carlo Simulation of Diffusion",
in Garrison, W.L.:
Quantitative Geography,
(Evanston: Department of Geography, North-Western University) 1967.

Hagget, P.:
Locational Analysis in Human Geography,

(London: Edward Arnold Publishers Ltd.) 5th Edition, 1969.

Haggett, P. and Gunawardena, K.A.:
"Datermination of Population Thresholds for Settlement Function by Reed-Muench Method",
Professional Geographer, Vol. 16, No.4, 1964.

Hagood, M.J. :
"Statistical Method for the Purpose of Delineation of Regions Applied to Data on Agriculture and Population",
Social Force, Vol. 21, 1943.

Hajnal, A. and Kiss, I. :
"Systems Approach to Planning Integrated Development",
in UNESCO : Innovative Approaches To Development Planning, (Paris: UNESCO) 1988.

Haldipur, Krishna:
"Wither Decentralization",
The Indian Journal of Public Administration, Vol. XXIV, No. 3, 1978.

Haldipur, R.N. :
Local Government, Rural Development and Micro-Level Planning
(New Delhi: Cabinet Secretariate, Department of Personnel & Administrative Reform, Ministry of Home, Government of India) 1974.

Haldipur, R.N. :
"Bureaucracy's Response to New-Challenges",
Indian Journal of Public Administration, Vol. XXII, No. 1, 1976.

Haldipur, R.N. :
"On Remodelling Panchayati Raj",
Indian Journal of Public Administration, Vol. 17, 1971.

Haldipur, R.N. :
"Whither Community Development",
Community Development And Panchayati Raj Digest, Vol. 2, 1970 New-Delhi. @TITLE = Haldipur, R.N. and Ghildyal, V.C. :
"Relevance of Community Development",
Kurukshetra, Vol. 20, 1971.

Haldipur, R.N.:
"Some Dimensions of Planning",
The Indian Journal of Public Administration, Vol. XIX, No. 3, 1973.

Hale, C.W. :
"The Mechanism of the Spread Effect in Regional Development",
Land Economics, November 1967.

Hall, Peter.:
The Theory and Practice of Regional Planning.
(London : Pemberton Publishing Co. Ltd.) 1970.

Hall, P.:
Urban and Regional Planning,
(Harmondsworth: Penguin) 1975.

Hansen, B. :
Long and Short Term Planning in Under-Developed Countries
(Amsterdam : North Holland) 1967.

Hansen, N. :
"Development from Above: the Centre-Down Development Paradigm",
in Stohr, W. and Taylor, D.R.F. (eds.):
Development from Above or Below? The Dialectics of Regional Planning in Developing Countries
(New York: John Wiley) 1981.

Hansen, N.M. (ed.) :
Public Policy and Regional Economic Development,
(New-York: Ballinger Publishing Co.) 1974.

Hansen, N.M. :
Public Policy And Regional Economic Development
(Cambridge: Cambridge University Press)

Hansen, N.M. :
"Development Pole Theory in a Regional Context",
Kyklos, Vol. 20, 1967.

Hansen, N.M. :
"How Regional Policy Can Benefit From Economic Theory", Growth and Change, January 1970.

Hansen, N.M. :
"Regional Planning in a Mixed Economy",
The Southern Economic Journal, 1965.

Hansen, Niles M. (ed.).
Growth Centres in Regional Economic Development
(New York: The Free Press) 1974.

Hansen, Niles M. (ed.):
Growth Centres in Regional Economic Development
(New York: Free Press) 1972.

Hanson, A.H. :
"Power Shifts and Regional Balances"
in Streeten, Paul and Lipton, Michael (eds.):
The Crisis of Indian Planning: Economic Policy in the 1960s
(London: Oxford University Press) 1968.

Hanson, A.H.:
The Process of Planning: A Study of India's Five year Plans
(London: Oxford University Press) 1966.

Haragopal, G.; Prasad, V.S. and Manohar, K. Murli :
Grass Roots Planning for Development
(Warangal: Kakatiya School of Public Administration) 1985.

Harman, Harry H.:
Modern Factor Analysis
(Chicago : The University of Chicago Press) 1967.

Harmston, F.K. :
The Community as an Economic System
(Ames: Iowa State University Press) 1983.

Harper, E.B. and Durham, Arthur:
Community Organization in Action
(New-York: Associated Press) 1959.

Harris, John (ed.):
Block Level Planning in Gujarat
(Baroda: M.S. University) 1980.

Harriss, J. (ed.):
Rural Development: Theories of Peasant Economy and Agragian Change,
(London: Hutchinson University Library) 1982.

Hart, P.K.; Mills, G. and Whitaker, J.K. (eds.):
Econometric Analysis for National Economic Planning
(London: Butterworth) 1964.

Hartshorne, R. :
Perspective on the Nature of Geography
(Chicago: Rand McNally) 1959.

Hartshorne, R.:
The Nature of Geography
(Lancaster PA : Association of American Geographers) 1946.

Hartshorne, R.:
"The Concept of Geography as a Science of Space from Kant and Humboldt to Hettner",
Annals of the Association of American Geographers, Vol. 48, No. 2, 1958.

Harvey, S. Perloff et. al. :
Regions Resources And Economic Growth
(Baltimore : Johns Hopkins University Press) 1960.

Hasan, H. :
Regional Planning

Harmonization
(Karachi : Pakistan Institute of Development Economics) 1965.

Hashim, S.R. :
"Inter-Regional Linkages and Economic Regionalisation",
Indian Journal of Regional Science, Vol. II, No. 1, 1970.

Hashim, S.R.:
"Locational Flows and the Problem of Regional Development: Some Views along with an Historical Review of the Indian Situation",
Balanced Regional Development, Proceedings of the Indian Economic Association (Bombay: Popular Prakashan) 1969.

Hasain, Nadeem:
Tribal India Today
(New Delhi: Harnam Publishers) 1983.

Haswell, M.R. :
Economics of Development in Village India
(Bombay: Allied Publishers) 1967.

Hatch, Spencer :
Towards Freedom From Want: From India to Mexico
(London: Oxford University Press) 1959.

Hauser, Philips M., and Matras Judah:
"Areal Unit for Urban Analysis",
in Hauser, P.M. (ed.): Handbook for Social Research in Urban Areas (Belgium: UNESCO) 1965.

Hazari, R.K.:
Industrial Planning and Licensing Policy, Report to the Planning Commission,
(New Delhi: Govt. of India) 1967.

Heesterman, A.R.G.:
Forecasting Models for National Economic Planning
(Dortrecht : Reidel Publishing Co.) 1970.

Hegde, Ramkrishna:
Planning and States' Right
(Bangalore: Government of Karnataka) August 1988.

Henderink, J. and Titus, M.J. :
"Paradigms of Regional Development and the Role of Small Centres"
Development and Change, Vol. 19, 1988.

Herfindahl, O.C. :
Natural Resource Information for Economic Development
(Baltimore: The Johns Hopkins University Press) 1969.

Hermansen, T. :
Growth Poles and Growth Centres in National and Regional Development - A Synthetical Approach, Part - I,
(Geneva: UNRISD) 1969.

Hermansen, T.:
Development Poles and Development Centres in National and Regional Development - Elements of a Theoretical Framework for a Synthetical Approach
(Geneva: UNRISD) 1969.

Hermansen, T.:
Inter-regional Allocation of Investments for Social and Economic Development: An Elementary Model Approach to Analysis, Report No. 70.4
(Geneva: UNSIRD) 1970. It is suggested here, based on a model approach, that appropriate choices on spatial investments is possible only on the basis of analysis of development goals, and the time horizon is of critical importance.

Hermansen, T.:
"Development Poles and Related Theories",
in Hansen, N.M. (ed.) Growth Centres in Regional Economic Development, (New York : The Free Press) 1974.

Hermansen, Tormod:
Spatial Organization and Economic Development, Scope and Task of Spatial Planning
(Mysore: Institute of Development Studies, Mysore University) Development Studies Number 1, 1971.

Hermansen, Tormod:
"Development Poles and Development Centres in National and Regional Development",
in Kuklinski, A. (ed.) Growth Poles and Growth Centres in Regional Planning (The Hague: UNRISD Mouton & Co.)1972.

Hermansen, T. :
"Regional Disaggregation of National Plans within the Context of National Sectoral and Regional Planning",
in Kuklinski, A. : (ed.): Regional Disaggregation of National Policies and Plans (The Hague: Mouton & Co.) 1975.

Hicks, U.K. :
Development from Below: Local Government and Financing in Developing Countries in Commonwealth,
(Oxford: The Clarendon Press) 1961.

Higgins, B. :
"Integrated Approach to Rural Uplift",
Journal of Industry and Trade, India, Vol. 18, No. 5, May 1968.

Higgins, B.:
Regional Integration and National Development,
(Cairo) 1963.

Higgins, Benjamin:
"Development Poles: Do They Exist?"
Economic Bulletin for Asia and the Pacific, Vol. XXIX, No. 2, December 1978.

Hilhorst, J.G.M. :
Regional Planning : A Systems Approach
(Rotterdam : Rotterdam University Press) 1971.

Hilhorst, J.G.M. :
Rural Development: Theories of Peasant Economy and Agrarian Change
(London: Hutchinson University Library) 1982.

Hilhorst, J.G.M. :
"Territory Vs. Function : A New Paradigm ?",
in I.S.S. Occasional Papers, No. 89, (The Hague: Institute of Social Studies) August 1981.

Hilhorst, J.G.M.:
Regional Development Theory: An Attempt to Synthesize
(The Hague: The Institute of Social Studies) 1967.

Hill, Morris :
Planning for Multiple Objectives
(Peace Dale : Regional Science Research Institute, U.S.A.) 1973.

Hiremath, S.C.; Bisaliah, S.; and Hiremath K.C.:
A Full Employment Plan for Basavakalyan Taluk, Bidar District,
(Bangalore: University of Agricultural Sciences) 1978 (unpublished).

Hirschman, A.O. :
"A Generalised Linkage Approach to Development with Special Reference to Staples",
in Essays in Economic Development and Cultural Change in Honour of Best F. Hoselitt (Chicago: University of Chicago Press) 1976.

Hirschman, A.O.:
"Inter-regional and International Transmission of Economic Growth",
in Mckee, D.L., et. al. (eds.): **Regional Economics: Theory and Practice,**
(New York: Free Press) 1970.

Hirschman, A.O.:
The Strategy of Economic Development:
(New Haven: Yale University Press) 1969. A classic treatment of the continuing debate on balanced versus unbalanced growth strategy.

Hirway, Indira :
Block Level Planning in Gujarat :Policy Limitations and Suggestions for An Alternative Approach,
(Ahmedabad : Sardar Patel Institute of Economic & Social Research) 1980 Mimeographed.

Hirway, Indira :
"A Critical Evaluation of the First Phase of Block Level Planning Experiment in Gujarat",
Journal of the Sardar Patel Institute of Economic and Social Research, Vol. 11, Nos. 1 & 2, June-December, 1980.

Hoffsomer H. and Dubey, D.C.:
A Sociological Study of Panchayati Raj
(Mussoorie: Central Institute of Study and Research in Community Development) 1961.

Holland, Stuart :
The Regional Problems,
(London: MacMillan Press) 1976.

Holland, Stuart:
Capital Vs the Region
(New York: St. Martin's Press) 1976.

Holzinger, K.J. and Harmon, H.:
Factor Analysis : A Synthesis of Factorial Methods
(Chicago: Univeristy of Chicago Press) 1961.

Hooja, Bhupendra:
" Functional Approach to Panchayat Development - A Post Asoka Mehta Committee Perspective",
Administrative Change, Vol. 6, No. 1 & 2, July 1978- June 1979.

Hooja, Rakesh :
"District and Regional Planning in India - Some Reflections",
in Arora, Ramesh K. :
Administrative Change in India,
(Jaipur: Aalekh Publishers) 1974.

Hooja, Rakesh and Hooja, Bhupendra:
"Land-Water Management and Productivity",
The Indian Journal of Public Administration, Vol. XXIII, No. 3, July-Sept. 1982.

Hooja, Rakesh and Seth, Ajit
"District Planning Guidelines and the Uttar Pradesh Model",
Unpublished paper, Mussoorie 1975.

Hooja, Rakesh:
District Planning : Concept, Setting and State Level Applications,
(Jaipur: Aalekh Publishers) 1986. This book among other things, examines the rationale of Planning at decentralised level and the suitability of the District as an appropriate planning unit.

Hooja, Rakesh:
"Micro-Level Credit Planning and the Rural Delivery-cum-Recovery System",
Administrative Change, July 1978-March 1979. A Comprehensive credit planning scheme is suggested in this paper, and the linkage between District Plan and District Credit Planning is emphasized.

Hooja, Rakesh:
" State Level Planning : The Rajasthan Case",
The Indian Journal of Public Administration, Vol. XXII, NO. 3, July-Sept 1976.

Hooja, Rakesh:
"District as a Planning Unit-Style and Locus",
Indian Journal of Public Administration, No. 3, Vol. XIX, July-Sept. 1973.

Hooja, Rakesh:
"District Planning: Some Assumptions and Implications",
in Arora, Ramesh et. al. (ed.):
The Indian Administrative System,
(Delhi: Associated Publishers) 1978.

Hooja, Rakesh:
"People's Participation in Comprehensive Watershed Development Programmes",
in Singh, Hoshiar (ed.):
Rural Development in India
(Jaipur : Printwell) 1984.

Hooja, Rakesh:
"Planning Commission at the State Level in India - Some Reflections on Problems and Prospects",
Journal of the National Academy of Administration, Vol. XVII, NO. 3, 1972. A strong case is made out about a stronger and more important State Planning Bodies.

Hooja, Rakesh:
"Project Formulation and Planning - Special Problems of Rural Projects and Some Examples of Rajasthan Responses",
Prashasnika, Vol. XII, No 1&2; Jan-June 1983.

Hooja, Rakesh:
"Various Units of Regional Planning - A Case for Improved District Planning",
Prashasnika, Vol. 2, No. 1, Jan-March 1973. Here the author focusses attention on conflict arising out of Town Planning and District Planning.

Hoover, E.M. :
An Introduction to Regional Economics
(New-York : A. Knopf) 1971.

Hoover, E.M. and Czamanski, S.:
"Techniques for Estimating Local and Regional Multiplier Effects of Change in the Level of Government Programmes",
in Butter, G.J. and Mandeville, P.D. (ed.):
Regional Economics,
(St. Lucia: Queensland University Press) 1981.

Hoover, E.W. :
An Introduction to Regional Economics
(New-York: Alfred A. Knopf) 1974.

Hoover, Edgar M. :
The Location of Economic Activity
(New York : McGraw Hill Book Company) 1963.

Hopkins, M.J.D. and Hoeven, R. vander :
Basic Needs in Development Planning,
(Aldershot, Hampshire: Gower) 1983.

Hopkins, M.J.D.; Rogers, G.B., and Wery, R.:
A Structural Overview of Bachue - Phillipines
(Geneva :ILO) 1976 mimeographed.

Horst, Siebert :
Regional Economic Growth : Theory and Policy
(Scranton) 1969.

Hoselitz, Best F. :
"Generative and Parasite Cities",
Economic Development & Cultural Change, Vol. VIII, No. 3, 1955.

Houston, D.B. :
"The Shift and Share Analysis of Regional Growth, A Critique",
Southern Economic Journal, Vol: 32, No. 2, April 1967.

Hoyle, B.S. (ed.):
Spatial Aspects of Development
(London: John Wiley & Sons) 1974.

Hudson, J.C. :
"Diffusion in Central Place System",
Geographical Analysis, Vol. 1, 1969.

Huestedde, Ron; Shaffer, R. and Pulver, G. :
Community Economic Analysis : A How To Manual,
(Ames, Iowa: North Central Regional Centre for Rural Development) 1984.

Hufschmidt, Maynard M.:
Regional Planning: Challenge and Prospects
(New York : Frederick A. Preager) 1969.

Hughes, J.T. and Kozlowski, J.:
"Threshold Analysis - An Economic Tool for Town and Regional Planning",
Urban Studies, Vol. 5, 1968.

Hughes, Rufus B. :
"Inter-regional Income Differences: Self Perpetuation",
Southern Economic Journal, Vol. 28, 1961.

Hunter, Guy and Jiggins, Janice :
Local Diagnosis Farmer Groupings & Co-ordination of Services
(London : Overseas Development Institute, Agricultural Administration Unit) paper IV, 1976.

Hymer, S. and Resnick, S. :
"A Model of an Agrarian Economy with Non-Agricultural Activities", The American Economic Review, Vol. LIX, No. 4, September 1969.IDS Bulletin Vol. 8, No. 1, 1976 Special Issue on "The Limits of Planning",
Reviewed by Hooja, Rakesh in Development Policy and Administration Review, Vol. 3, No. 1, Jan-June 1977. This paper sobers fearless pursuit of decentralized planning.

I

Iglesias, Gabriel U. :
"Implementation and the Planning of Development: Notes on Trends and Issues, Focussing on the Concept of Administrative Capacity",
in Iglesias, Gebriel U. (ed.):
Implementation, The Problem of Achieving Results - A Case of Asian Experiences
(Manila :EROPA) 1976.

Iglesias, Gabriel U. :
"Political And Administrative Issues in Regional Planning and Development",
Phillipine Journal of Public Administration, Vol. XXI, No. 3 & 4, July-Oct. 1977. N.R. :
"District Planning in Maharashtra",
Indian Journal of Public Administration, No. 3, 1973. This is a good account of District Planning exercise based on Zilla Parishad Model.

Inamdar, N.R. :
Report of the Survey of the Administration of the Community Development Block Haveli
(Poona : University of Poona) 1962.

Inamdar, N.R. and Kshire, V.K.:
"Process, Machinery and Problems of District Planning in Maharashtra",
in Singh, Hoshiar (ed.): Rural Development in India Evaluative Studies in Policies and Programmes (Jaipur: Print well) 1985.

Inamdar, N.R. and Kshire, V.K.:
District Planning in India
(New Delhi: Oxford & IBH) 1987.

Inayatullah :
"Development of Monitoring and Evaluation System for Rural Development in Asia",
in Mathur, Kuldip and Inayatullah (eds.):
Monitoring and Evaluation of Rural Development : Some Asian Experience,
(Kuala Lumpur: APDAC) 1980.

Indian Economic Association:
Balanced Regional Development:
Conference Papers,
(Bombay: Popular Prakashan) 1970.

Indian Institute of Management :
Rural Development for Rural Power,
CMA monograph No. 63, 1976.
Indian International Centre, Council for Social Development:

Action for Rural Change:
Readings in Indian Community Development
(New Delhi : Munshiram Manoharlal) 1970.

Institute of Area Planning:
Integrated Area Plan for Talela Block.
(Ahmedabad: Gujrat Institute of Area Planning) 1974.

Institute of Regional Development Planning :
Wardha District Plan
(Wardha : IRDP) 1965 (Mimeographed).

Institute of Social Studies Advisory Service :
The Theory and Practice of Regional Rural Development and Planning: A Review of the Literature
(The Hague: Food & Agriculture Organization, of the United Nations) 1968.

International Geographical Congress:
Proceedings of Symposium on Regional Planning of the XXI International Geographical Congress
(Calcutta : National Committee for Geography) 1968.

International Labour Office :
Employer's & Worker's Participation in Planning, Chapters 4 & 5
(Geneva : International Labour Office) 1984.

International Labour Office:
Employment Resource Mobilisation and Basic Needs Through Local Level Planning
(Bangkok : ARTEP) 1979.

International Labour Office :
Employment Expansion Through Local Resource Mobilisation: Papers and Proceedings of a Workshop, Comilla, Bangladesh 1-3 July 1981
(Bangkok : ARTEP) 1981.

International Labour Office:
Proceedings of the First Meeting of the Asian Employment Planners,
Bangkok, Thailand, 26th to 29th November, 1985 (New Delhi :ARTEP)1986.

International Labour Organisation:
The Asian HRD Planning Network,
Proceedings of a technical workshop convened in Bangkok, 16-18 December 1986 to establish an Asian Network of Resource Development Planning Institutes (New-Delhi).

International Labour Organization:
Manpower Assessment and Planning Projects
(Geneva: ILO) 1978.

International Labour Organization:
Information System for Monitoring Development Indicators at District Levels:

A Demonstration Exercise for Nuwara Eilya
(Bangkok: ARTEP) 1982

International Labour Organization :
Employment and Manpower Planning : A Mannual for Training in Basic Techniques
(Bangkok: ARTEP) 1984.

International Perspective Planning Team:
Development of Small Scale Industries in India
(New-Delhi: The Ford Foundation) 1963.

Isard, Walter and Reiner, Thomas :
"Regional and National Economic Planning and Analytical Techniques for Implementation",
in Isard, Walter and Cumberland, J.H. (eds.):
Regional Economic Planning: Techniques of Analysis
(Paris: OECD) 1961.

Isard, W. and Cumberland, J.H. (eds.):
Regional Economic Planning: Techniques of Analysis
(Paris : OECD) 1961.

Isard, W. and Cumberland, J.H.:
"A Synthesis of Operational Methods in Regional Analysis",
in Isard, W. and Cumberland, J.H.:
Regional Economic Planning: Techniques of Analysis
(Paris: O.E.C.D) 1961.

Isard, Walter & Smith T.E.:
"On the Resolution of Conflicts Among Regions of a System",
Papers & Proceedings of the Regional Science Association, Vol. XIX, 1967.

Isard, Walter :
"Game Theory, Location Theory and Industrial Agglomeration",
in Papers and Proceedings of the Regional Science Association, Vol. XVIII, 1966.

Isard, Walter :
Location and Space Economy: A General Theory Relating to Industrial Location, Market Areas, Land Use Trade and Urban Structure
(New York: John Wiley & Sons) 1950.
Location Space Economy,
(Cambridge, Mass: M.I.T. Press) 1956.

Isard, Walter and Chatterjee, M.:
"Potentialities of Regional Methods and Techniques in Attacking Indian Regional Science Problems",
Indian Journal of Regional Science, Vol. 1, 1969.

Isard, Walter and Frental, G. :
"Regional and National Product Projections and Their Inter-relations",
in National Bureau of Economic Research:Studies in Income and Wealth:
Long Range Economic Projection,
Vol. 16, (Princeton: Princeton University Press) 1954.

Isard, Walter and Smith T.E.:
"Coalition Location Games",
Papers & Proceedings of the Regional Science Association, Vol. XX, 1968.

Isard, Walter:
Introduction to Regional Science
(New York: Prentice Hall) 1975.

Isard, Walter:
Method of Regional Analysis,
(Cambridge : M.I.T. Press) 1960.
This contains a good treatment of the concept of industrial complex analysis.

Islam, N. and Renault, G.M.:
Changing Notions of Development, Development Administration and Administrative Development: Prologues. Paradoxes and Perspectives
(Ottawa : Institute for International Co-operation, University of Ottawa) 1979.

Islam, R. (ed.):
Strategies for Alleviating Poverty in Rural Asia
(Bangkok: Bangladesh Institute of Development Studies. Dhaka, ARTEP) 1985.

Isserman, Andrew:
"A Bracketing Approach for Estimating Regional Economic Impact Multipliers and a Procedure for Assessing Their Accuracy",
Environment and Planning, Vol, 49. 1977.

Isserman, Andrew:
"The Location Quotient Approach to Estimating Regional Economic Impacts",
Journal of the American Institute of Planners, Vol. 57, 1977.

Iswaran, K.:
Shibapur : A South Indian Village,
(London: Routledge K. Paul) 1968.

J

Jacobson, L. and Prakash, Ved:
"Urbanization and Regional Planning In India",
Urban Affairs Quarterly, Vol. II, No. 3, March 1967. The paper emphasises urban regions for planning.

Jain L.C. :
"Panchayati Raj and Decentralisation",
Kurukshetra, February 1989.

Jain, L.C. ,
"Central Planning and Karnataka's Decentralised Planning",
Mainstream, 25th April 1987, Vol 25 No. 32. This is an excellent summary of the Planning formulation process in Karnataka.

Jain, L.C. et. al. :
Grass Without Roots Rural Development Under Government Auspices,
(New Delhi: Sage Publications) 1985.

Jain, L.C.,
"Decentralised Planning: Karnataka Innovation",
Economic Times, 11th May 1987. A fine article on decntralised plan administration of Karnataka.

Jain, L.C.:
"Central Planning in Karnataka's Decentralised Planning",
Paper read at Seminar on New Thrust in Democratic Decentralisation, Lucknow, U.P. Regional Branch of the Indian Institute of Public Administration, 1987.

Jain, L.C.:
"Decentralised Planning in U.P.: District Committees Help the Poor",
Times of India, August 8, 1978.

Jain, R.B.,:
" Planning in the Third World - An Overview of Experiences in India",
Indian Journal of Public Administration, No. 3, Vol. 30., July-Sept. 1984.

Jain, S.P. :
"Panchayati Raj and Agricultural Development: Some Issues",
The Indian Journal of Public Administration. Vol. XXIII, No. 4, 1977.

Jain, Sugan Chand :
Community Development and

Panchayati Raj in India
(Bombay: Allied Publishers Pvt. Ltd.) 1968.

James, P.E. and Jones, C.F. (eds.):
American Geography Inventory and Prospect
(Syracuse : Syracuse University Press) 1954.

Jathar, S.N. :
"Tribal Sub-Plan of Maharashtra State",
Co-Operative Perspective, October - December 1975, pp. 2833.

Jauhari, B.M. :
Cottage and Small Scale Industries in India - The Genesis of Decentralised Planning
(Ghaziabad: Deptt. of Economics, MMH College) Manuscript, 1988.

Jayaraman, T.K. and Savdasia, V.B. :
"Development of Backward Areas in Gujarat State",
The Indian Journal of Public Administration, Vol. XXIII, No. 4, 1977.

Jensen, R.C. and West, R.G. :
"A Graduated Approach to the Construction of Input-Output Tables",
paper presented to the Input-Output Workshop of the IX Conference of the Regional Science Association, Australia and New-Zealand Section, University of Melbourne, December 3rd to December 5th, 1984.

Jensen, R.C.; Mandeville, T. and Karunarten, N.:
Regional Economic Planning
(London: Croom Helm) 1979.

Jha, D. and Roy, Prasoon Kumar :
Agricultural Processing Activity - A Solution to Regional Disparity,
(Muzzaffarpur: Department of Economics, Bihar University) manuscript 1988.

Jha, Sailendra :
Planning from Below For The Transformation of India's Rural Economy,
(Darbhanga: Deptt. of Economics, L.N. Mishra University) manuscript, September 1989.

Jha, Shailendra :
Planning from Below for the Transformation of Indian Rural Economy,
(Darbhanga : L.N. Mithila University, Department of Economics) manuscript 1988.

Jha, U.M.:
Nature and Scope of Decentralised Planning,
(Bhagalpur University) manuscript, 1988.

Johnson, E.A.J.:
Organization of Space in the Developing Countries
(Cambridge, Mass : Harvard University Press) 1970. An authoritative theoretical work on spatial planning.

Johnson. E.A.J.:
Market Towns and Spatial Development in India
(New Delhi: National Council for Applied Economic Research) 1965. This is one of the many earlier case studies about the requirements of growth points, assuming that each growth point will serve 1.5 lakh population. The ideas are still relevant.

Johnston, B.J. and Kilby, P. :
"'Unimodal' and 'Bimodal' Strategies of Agrarian Change",
in Harriss, J.: Rural Development: Theories of Peasant Economy and Agrarian Change (London: Hutchinson) 1982.

Johnston, Bruce F. and Clark, W.C. :
Redesigning Rural Development
(Baltimore: Johns Hopkins University Press) 1982.

Jones, B.G. and Clark, P.G. :
"Psychological Factors in Regional Economic Development",
in Chatterjee, M.:
Space, Location Plus Regional Development
(London : Pion) 1976.

Jones, G.W. :
"Links Between Urbanization and Sectoral Shifts in Employment in Java",
Bulletin of Indonesian Economic Studies, Vol. 20, No. 3, pp. 120-157, 1984.

Jose, A.M. :
"A Note on Integration and Development",
Economic Affairs, Vol. 29, Dec. 1984.

Jose, A.M. :
"Decentralised Planning in India, A Review in the Background of Seventh Five Year Plan",
Southern Economist, Vol. 24, No. 20, February, 1986.

Jose, A.M. :
"People's Participation in Rural Development",
Southern Economist, Vol. 26, No. 16, December 1987.

Joshi, B.M. :
"Monitoring of District Plans in Uttar Pradesh",
Paper presented at the National Seminar on Monitoring and Cost Management of Projects held at Yojana Bhawan, 23rd to 25th March 1988

Joshi, Samir :
"Financial Institutions' Role in Industrialisation of Backward Regions",
Indian Management, (Journal of the All India Management Association) Special Issue on Corporate Finance, Vol. 26, No. 1, January 1987.

Joshi, B.M. :
"Decentralised Planning and Inter-District Disparities in Uttar Pradesh",
Paper presented at the National Seminar on Decentralised Planning, February 13th & 14tn 1988 (Lucknow: State Planning Institute, Planning Deptt., Govt. of Uttar Pradesh) 1988.

Joshi, B.M. :
"Evolution and Practice of Decentralised Planning in India",
in the Indian Journal of Public Administraiton, Vol. XXXV, No. 1, Jan-March 1989.

Joshi, B.M. and Verma, H.S. :
"Decentralised Planning in Uttar Pradesh: An Examination of the Experience of Its First Stage",
Indian Journal of Regional Science, Vol. XIX, No. 1, 1987.

Joshi, N.D. :
"Integrated Area Development with Reference to District Planning",
Indian Journal of Agricultural Economics, October-December, 1973.

Joshi, N.D.,
"Review of the Policy for the Development of Backward Regions in India",
Arth Vikas, Vol IX. 1977.

Joshi, S.S.A and Rao, Bhaskar:
"Regional Development Experience in U.P. Hills - A Note",
Indian Journal of Regional Science, vol. XX No. 1, 1988.

Joshi, Samir :
"Role of Central Public Enterprises in the Development of Industrially Backward Regions - An Inter State Analysis",
Paper read at the National Seminar, held in August 1987 at the Department of Economics, University of Hyderabad, Hyderabad.

Joshi, Samir:
"Economic Planning: To be

Centralised or Decentralised to Correct Regional Imbalances",
(Bharuch, Zadeshwar: Narmada College of Science, Technology & Commerce, Deptt. of Economics) manuscript 1989.

Joshi, V.H. :
"Concept of Regional Analysis: Its Application to the Study of the Development of Backward Areas",
Arth-Vikas, Jan-July 1973, No. 1, pp. 64-68.

Joshi, V.H.:
"Strategy for the Development of Backward Areas (With Special Reference to Gujarat)"
Paper delivered at the A.N. Sinha Institute of Social Studies, Patna, January 1979 at the National Seminar on the Design of Development of Backward Areas, 1979.

Joshi, V.H.:
Economic Development and Social Change in South Gujarat
(Ahmedabad: S.P. Institute of Economic & Social Research) 1983.

K

Kabra, K.N. :
"Planning of Plan Implementation in India",
Indian Journal of Public Administration. Vol. XXX, No. 3, 1983.

Kabra, Kamal Narayan :
"Some Remarks on Regional Planning",
Journal of Development Planning, No. 3, 1973 (published by centre for Development Planning, Projections and Policies Secretariate, New York).

Kabra, Kamal Narayan :
Planning Process in a District,
(New Delhi: Indian Institute of Public Administration) 1977.

Kabra, Kamal Nayan:
"Notes Towards a Theory of Indicators of Development",
The Indian Journal of Public Administration, Vol. XXIII, No. 4, 1977.

Kannan, K.P. :
Of Rural Proletarian Struggles : Mobilisation and Organization of Rural Workers in South-West India
(Oxford: Oxford University Press) 1988. It would be of use to refer to review of this book in the Sunday Herald, 31st July, 1988, by N. Jayaram.

Kant, Surya :
"District Plans in India: Punjab Experience",
The Indian Journal of Public Administration, Vol XXXIV, No. 2, April-June 1988.

Kant, Surya and Dubey, K.N. :
"Spatial Structure of Administrative Unity and the Development Process, A Case Study of Uttar Pradesh",
The National Geographical Journal of India, Vol. 30, Part I, 1984.

Kapde, M.V. :
Decentralised Planning in India
(Indore: D.A. Vishwavidyalaya, Department of Economics) manuscript, 1988.

Kapoor, M.M. :
Constraints to Decentralised Planning in India
(Indore: G.S. Institute of Technology and Science,

Department of Humanities) manuscript, 1988.

Kar, N.R. :
Urban Hierarchy and Central Functions around Calcutta and their Significance,
proceedings of the International Geographical Union Symposium in Urban Geography, Lund, 1962.

Karnataka Government :
Papers Relating to the Two-Days Workshop on District Planning, 28th and 29th January 1976
(Bangalore: Planning Department) 1976.

Kashyap, S.P. :
"Growth Variants of a Regional Economy : Implications for Reduced Inequalities",
Institute Seminar on Regional Economic Planning, held in March 1973, reproduced in Anvesak, June-December 1973.

Kashyap, S.P. :
Regional Planning in a Consistency Framework - A Study of Gujarat,
(Ahmedabad: Sardar Patel Institute of Economic and Social Research) 1979, distributed by Allied Publishers, New-Delhi.

Kashyap, S.P. and Alagh, Y.K.:
A Consistency Framework for the Perspective Plan for Gujarat 1974-84,
(Ahmedabad: Govt. of Gujarat).

Kasturi, K :
"Development of Backward Regions: Need for a Selective Approach",
The Indian Journal of Public Administration, Vol. XXIII, No. 4, 1977.

Kayastha, S.L. and Singh, Rambabu:
"Regional Development Through Social Planning - A Micro-Level Case Study From India",
Indian Journal of Regional Science, Vol. XIII, No. 1, 1981.

Kellerman, Aharon:
Agricultural Location Theory: A Review and Bibliography of Theory and Application,
(Peace Dale, Virginia: Regional Science Research Institute) Discussion Paper No. 1-9, December 1983.

Kelly, R. :
Community Participation in Directing Economic Development,
(Cambridge, Mass: Centre for Continuing Economic Development) 1976.

Kenessey, Z. :
The Process of Economic Planning,
(New York: Columbia University Press) 1978.

Kesik, M. and Komorowski, S.M. (eds.):
A Systems Approach to Regional Studies
(University of Waterloo, Faculty of Environmental Studies) 1985.

Kessler, Edward, S :
Guides for Community Planning
(Chicago: American Society of Planning Officials) 1954.

Khakhar, K.K. :
Decentralised Planning Under the Process of Polarisation Reversal,
(Rajkot: Saurastra University) manuscript 1988.

Khan, M. Baseer Ahmed:
Regional Planning and Economic Development,
(Jaipur: Pointer Publishers) 1988. This is a collection of papers of a Seminar held in Poona. The papers are on theoretical issues of Regional Planning, District Planning and applied Regional Planning Problems.

Khan, M.M. :
"Development: Meaning,

Strategies and Goals",
Development Policy and Administrative Review, Vol. IV, No. 1, 1978.

Khan, M.M. :
"Process of Decentralisation in Bangladesh",
Community Development Journal, Vol. XXI, No. 2, April 1986.

Khan, W. and Ramesh K.S.:
Plan for Integrated Area Development, Plan for West District, Manipur
(Hyderabad: National Institute of Community Development) 1977.

Khan, W. and Tripathi, R.N. :
Plan for Integrated Rural Development in Pauri Garhwal,
(Hyderabad: National Institute of Community Development) 1977.

Khatu, K.K. :
"Rural Planning System",
The National Geographical Journal of India, Vol. XXI, Parts 3 and 4, 1975.

Khera, S.S. :
District Administration in India
(Bombay : Asia Publishing House) 1964.

Khurana, I.R. :
"Regional Planning: A Basic Model for Administrative Set Up",
Enterprise, December 1970.

Khusro, A.M. :
Economic Development With No Population Transfers
(Bombay : Asia Publishing House) 1962.

Kiker, B.F. and Vasconcellos, A.S.:
"The Performance of the French Economy Under Planning 1949-1964",
Economics of Planning, Vol. 8, 1968.

Kimani, S.M. and Taylor, D.R.F.:
"Growth Centres and Rural Development in Kenya"
(Thika : Kenya) 1973.

King, Clarence :
Working with People in Small Communities : Case Records of Community Development in Different Countries,
(New York: Harper Row) 1958

Kintaner, Augustin, Jr. :
"Seminar On Administration of Economic Administration",
(P.A. 331) June 201, 1955, U.P. College of Public Administration, Manila.

Kistaiah, M. :
Sub-Regionalism in India,
(Hyderabad: Book Links Corporation) 1977.

Klaasen, L.H. :
Area Economic and Social Redevelopment : Guidelines for Programme,
(Paris : OECD) 1965.

Klaasen, L.H.:
Growth Poles in Economic Theory and Policy,
Paper prepard for the Expert Group on Growth Poles and Growth Centres, Toulouse, May 1969, mimeographed. It gives an interesting argument that even consumption of very important amenities is influenced by distance from where the amenities are to be brought or availed of.

Klassen, L.H. :
Social Amenities in Area Economic Development : An analysis of Methods Defining Needs
(Paris: OECD) 1968.

Knetsch, Jack L. and William, J. Hart:
"Watershed as an Entity in Development Planning"
Journal of Farm Economics, Vol. 43, 1961.

Kolawale, A.:
" The Role of Grassroots

Participation in National Development : Lessons from Kwara State of Nigeria",
Community Development Journal, Vol. 17, No. 2, 1982.

Kolb, J.H. :
"Service Relations of Town and Country",
Research Bulletin, University of Wisconsin Agricultural Experiment Station Madison, U.S.A., No. 58, 1923.

Kolb, J.H. and Marshall, D.G. :
"Neighbourhood Community Relationships in Rural Society",
Research Bulletin, University of Wisconsin Agricultural Experiment Station, Madison, U.S.A., No. 154, 1944.

Kolosovosky, N.N.:
"Some Theoretical Problems of Economic Regionalisation",
Geografia, Vol. 2, 1961.

Komar, I.V. and Popov, K.M. :
"Problems in the Economic Regionalisation of India",
Soviet Geography: Review and Thought, Vol. 3, No. 5, 1962.

Konar, Dhirendra Nath:
A Study of the Inter-District Variation in the Growth Rates of Production of Rice in West -Bengal and the District-Level Planning in India
(Kalyani, West-Bengal: Kalyani University, Deptt. of Economics) manuscript 1988.

Kornai, J. :
"Multi-Level Programming - A First Report on the The Model on the Experimental Computations",
European Economic Review, 1969.

Kornai, J. :
Mathematical Planning in Structural Decisions
(Amsterdam : North Holland Publishing Co.) 1967.

Kornai, J. and Liptak, T. :
"Two-Level Planning",
Econometrica, Vol. 33, 1965.

Kosta, M. :
"Dynamics of Structural Changes as Background of Growth Poles Theory",
in Mishra, R.P. et. al. (eds.):
Regional Planning and National Development
(New Delhi: Vikas) 1976.

Kothari, Ashok and Bharati, Rajiv:
"Narmada Valley Project: Development or Destruction",
Economic & Political Weekly, June 2-9, 1984.

Kothari, Rajni:
" Challenge of the Hustings",
Economic and Political Weekly, Special Number, Vol. 6, No. 30-32, July 1971. An article, slightly removed from techniques of planning but rightly emphasizes the need to remove complacency about the policy making process, affecting our bureaucracy and politicians.

Kothari, S. and Ray, R. :
Relation Between Politicians and Administrators at the District Level
(New Delhi: Indian Institute of Public Administration & Centre for Applied Politics) 1971.

Koul, O.N. :
"Kashmir Plan: Focus on Neglected Areas",
Economic Times, January 6th, 1973, p.7.

Kozlowski J. and Hughes, J.T. :
"Urban Threshold Theory and Analysis",
Journal of the Town Planning Institute, Vol. LIII, 1967.

Kozlowski J. and Hughes, J.T. :
"Threshold Analysis: An Economic Tool for Town and Regional Planning",
Urban Studies, Vol. V, 1968.

Krishanmachari, V.T. :
Planning in India - Theory and Practice,
(New Delhi: Orient Longmans) 1977.

Krishna, Mridula:
Project Planning in India,
(Delhi : Indian Institute of Public Administration) 1980. This provides a national perspective on project approach being applied to national planning.

Krishna, Raj :
"Rural Unemployment : A Survey of Concepts",
in Shah, V.H. and Vakil, C.N. : (eds.): Agricultural Development of India: Policy and Problems (New Delhi: Orient Longmans) 1979.

Krishna, Raj:
Report of Indian Mission to Kenya,
(New Delhi: Govt. of India) 1972 unpublished. An excellent work spelling out the newer approaches of economists to District Planning.

Krishnamachari, T.T. :
Community Development In India,
(New-Delhi: Govt. of India, Ministry of Information & Broadcasting) 1958

Krishnaswami, O.R. :
"Area Development Approach and District Planning",
Kurukshetra, 1st June 1974, pp. 4-5.

Kuch, Y.Y. :
Local Level Planning in China
(Geneva: I.L.O.) Working Paper No. 44, 1982.

Kuklinski A.:
"Progress and Change in the Industrialisation of Poland",
Geographica Polonica, Vol. 3. It shows that even in centrally planned economies, development of regional economy is not attainable by mere location of a few industrial units in backward areas.

Kuklinski, A (ed.):
Regional Policies in Nigeria, India and Brazil
(The Hague : Mouton & Co.) 1978.

Kuklinski, A. (ed.):
Social Issues in Regional Policy and Regional Planning
(The Hague : Mouton & Co.) 1977.

Kuklinski, A.:
"Regional Policies - Experience and Prospects",
International Social Science Journal, No. 112, May 1987.

Kuklinski, A.R. (ed.):
Growth Poles And Growth Centres in Regional Planning,
(Geneva: U.N. Research Institute for Social Development) 1972.

Kuklinski, A.R. :
"Some Basic Issues in Regional Planning",
in Misra, R.P.; Urs, D.V. and Nataraj, V.K. (eds.):
Regional Planning and National Development,
(New Delhi: Vikas) 1978.

Kuklinski, A.R. :
"Training for Regional Development: Agenda for Future Research",
in Mathur, O.P.:
Training for Regional Development Planning: Perspectives for the Third World Decade
(Singapore: Maruzen Asia, UNCRD, Vol. 9) 1981.

Kuklisnski, Antoni:
Contribution to Regional Planning and Development
(Mysore: Development Studies No. 3, Institute of Development Studies, University of Mysore) 1971.

Kulkarni, N.K.:
"District Planning",
Public Administration, Kanpur, June 1974.

Kullar, M.S. and Degaonkar, C.K. :
District Planning - Scope and Implementation,
(Gulbarga: Gulbarga University, Deptt. of Economics) manuscript 1988.

Kulp, E.M. :
Rural Development Planning: Systems Analysis and Working Method,
(New york: Prgeaer) 1970.

Kumar, Rajendra and Ali, Mansoor:
"Decentralised Planning in India - A Mere Slogan or Solution",
(Roorkee: University of Roorkee, Deptt. of Humanities & Social Sciences) manuscript, 1988.

Kumar, Surendra:
Decentralised Planning : Some Issues
(Lari Darheta, Jahanabad: S.B.A.N. College, Department of Economics) manuscript, 1988.

Kumarappa Institute :
Block Development Plan of Bandikui Panchayat Samiti Bapunagar,
Jaipur, 1982.

Kumaresan, G. and Ramaswamy, C. :
"Sectoral Interdependency and Regional Planning - The Case for Central Tamilnadu",
Journal of Rural Development, Vol. 8, No. 1, 1989.

Kundu A. and Sidhu H.S. :
"Complete and Incomplete Schemes of Regionalisation",
Indian Journal of Geography, Special Issue, University of Jodhpur, 1980.

Kundu, A. :
"Construction of Indices for Regionalisation: An Enquiry Into the Methods of Analysis",
Geographical Review of India, Vol. 37, No. 1, March 1975.

Kundu, Amitabh :
"Nodal Regions - Some Conceptual Issues in Measurement and Regionalisation",
Indian Journal of Regional Science, Vol. XIX, No. 1, 1982.

Kundu, Amitabh :
"Problems and Possibilities of Decentralized Planning in Multi-Regional Economy",
Indian Journal of Regional Science, Vol. IV, No. 2, 1972.

Kundu, Amitabh :
Decentralised Planning in Education: A Framework Synthesising Formal and Informal Approaches
(New Delhi :NIEPA) 1981, Mimeographed. This is an able treatment of assimilation of formal and informal approaches to planning in education sector.

Kundu, Amitabh :
Measurement of Urban Processes: A study in Regionalisation
(Bombay: Popular Prakashan) 1980.

Kundu, Amitabh and Raza, Moonis:
Indian Economy - The Regional Dimension,
(New Delhi: Jawaharlal Nehru University) 1981.

Kunwar, U.:
Decentralised Planning in India,
(Darbhanga: C.M. College, Department of Economics) manuscript 1988.

Kurien, C.T. :
"Decentralisation Perspective in the Seventh Plan",
in Adiseshiah, M.S. (ed.):
Seventh Plan Perspectives
(New Delhi: Lancer International) 1985 pp. 283-303.

Kurien, K.T.:
"Decentralised Planning: The

Indian Experience in Development",
in Brahmananda P.R. (eds.) (Bombay: Himalaya Publishing House) 1987.

Kurien, Paul :
"Commercialisation of Common Property Resources",
Economic and Political Weekly, 16th January 1988. This exhibits how gross neglect of local population caused widespread agitation against forest policy of Karnataka.

Kushwaha, D.S. and Mathur, R.N. :
"District Planning: An Overview and Prospects", in Conference Volume,
Indian Economic Association, Calcutta, December 1988, Part III, pp. 136 to 144.

Kutty, M.A. :
"The Challenge of Regional Planning", Geographical Review of India,
Vol. XXIX, No. 2, June 1967.

Kuyvenhoven, Arie :
"New Industrial Planning Techniques : Macro, Sectoral and Project Linkages",
in Industry and Development, No. 5, UNIDO, 1980.

Kuznets, Simon:
"Quantitative Aspects of the Economic Growth of Nations: VIII - Distribution of Income Size",
Economic Development and Cultural Change, Vol XI, No. 2, January 1963. These empirical guesses are suggestive of a systematic relationship between national development levels and regional inequality or geographic dispersion.

L

Lahiri, T.B.:
Balanced Regional Development, Concepts, Strategies and Case Studies
(Calcutta: Oxford & IBH) 1972.

Laird, William and Rinehard, James R. :
"Regional Development in Developing Nations"
in Developing Economies, Vol. 7, 1969.

Lakdawala, D.T.; Alagh, Y.K. and Sharma, Atul:
Regional Variations in Industrial Development,
(Ahmedabad: Sardar Patel Institute of Economic and Social Research) Monograph series No. 2, 1974.

Lakshmanan, M.S. :
"Decentralised Planning in India", in Conference Volume,
Indian Economic Association, Calcutta, Dec. 1988.

Lal Bahadur Shastri National Academy of Administration:
Journal of the Lal Bahadur Shastri National Academy of Administration, Vol. XX No. 1, Spring 1975. One of the earlier attempts to discuss District Planning was topical enough.

Lal Bahadur Shastri National Academy of Administration:
Report of the Sub-Group on Growth Centre Theory -
Its Applicability in India, Second Seminar on District Planning, held at the National Academy, Mussoorie, June 24th to 26th 1974. This group favours district as a planning unit.

Lal, Deepak:
"Agricultural Growth, Real Wages and the Rural Poor in India", Economic and Political Weekly, 26th June 1976.

Lal, M.B. :
"Regional/District Planning: Concept and Experience India", in Ahuja, Kanta (ed.): **District Planning in Rajasthan** (Jaipur: H.C.Mathur State Institute of Public Administration) 1977. This is a summary of the position of District Level Planning Boards/Committees/Councils in 15 States.

Lal, M.B. :
"The Structure and Process of Micro Level Planning", in Micro-Level Planning - Case studies Paper Contributed to Workshop, August 24th to 30th, 1981 (Mysore: Institute of Development Studies) 1981, Mimeographed.

Lal, M.P. :
"Micro-Level Planning in India - The Need For Strengthening the States' Capabilities for Plan Formulation at District and Block Levels", in Singh, Hoshiar (ed.): **Rural Developments in India-Evaluative Studies in Policies and Programmes** (Jaipur: Printwell) 1985. Lal here bemoans the paucity of commitment to the process of planning at the District Level.

Lal, R. :
Community Development-Principles Practices and Problems, (Calcutta : Bookland Pvt. Ltd.) 1963.

Lal, Tarsem :
District Development Planning, A Case Study of Two Districts, (New Delhi: Concept Publishing Co.) 1985.

Lalwani, K.C.:
"Regional Planning - Its Concepts, Methods and Techniques", Indian Journal of Regional Science, Vol. 1, 1968.

Landis, John :
"Electronic Spreadsheets in Planning", Journal of the American Planning Association (Planners' Note Book Section) Vol. 5, No. 2, Spring 1985.

Lasuen, J.R.:
"Multi-Regional Economic Development - An open System Approach", in Information System for Regional Development : A Seminar, Lund Studies in Geography, Series B, No. 31, Human Geography, 1971.

Lasuen, J.R.:
" On Growth Poles", Urban Studies, Vol. 6, No. 2, June 1969.

Lausen, J.R. :
"A Generalisation of the Growth Pole Notion", in Thomson, Richard S. (ed.): **Papers and proceedings of the Commission on Regional Aspects of Development, International Geographical Union, Methodology & Case Study** (Toronto: Allister Typesetting & Graphics) 1974.

Lausen, J.R. :
"On Growth Poles", in Hansen, N.M. (ed.): **Growth Centres in Regional Economic Development,** (New York: The Free Press) 1972.

Lavania, G.S. :
"Approach to Integrated Area Development", Indian Journal of Agricultural Economics, October-December 1973, pp. 22-26.

Lean, W :
"An Economist,s Note on the Validity of Urban Threshold Theory",
Journal of Town Planning Institute, Vol. LV. July -August, 1969.

Lean, W. :
"On the Validity of Urban Threshold Theory : A Rejoinder",
Journal of Town Planning Institute, Vol. LVI, March 1970.

Learmont, A.M. and Learmont A.T.A. :
"Regional Concept and National Development"
Economic Weekly, January, 1958.

Learmonth, A.T.A. :
"A Regional Survey of Mysore State for Planning Purposes", Bombay Geographical Magazine, Vol. 6 & 7, No. 1, Sept. 1959.

Leckachman, Robert:
"Who Plans What For Whom and Why",
Encounter, Vol. 23, No. 5, 1964. An excellent treatment of the logic of decentralised planning.

Lefeber, L. :
"Planning in a Surplus Labour Economy",
American Economic Review, Vol. 88, June 1968.

Lefeber, L. :
Regional Allocation of Resources in India
(New Delhi : Perspective Planning Division, Planning Commission), also in Friedman, J. and Alonso, W. (ed.):
Regional Developmental Planning: A Reader
(Cambridge, Mass: M.I.T. Press) 1964.

Lefeber, L. and Dutta Choudhuri, M.:
Regional Development : Experiences and Prospects South and South East Asia, Report No. 70. 21,
(Geneva : UNRISD) 1970. Here a case is established that expensive attempts at diverting industries to rural areas need not be made. There are criticisms of this approach. See Misra R.P. (et. al.) 1974, Chapter V. They also point out that as the specificity of decentralised or regional planning increases the difficulties of vertical and horizontal consistency, are excrabated.

Lefeber, L.:
"Regional Allocation of Resources in India",
in Misra R.P., et. al. (eds.):
Regional Planning: Concepts, Techniques, Policies and Case Studies
(Mysore: University of Mysore) 1969.

Lefeber. L. :
Allocation in Space: Production Transport and Industrial Location
(Amsterdam: North Holland) 1958.

Leff, Nathniel H :
"Economic Development and Regional Inequality: Origins of the Porazitian Case Study",
Quarterly Journal of Economics, Vol. 86, 1972.

Lehman, F. and Ascoli, W. (eds.) :
In Economic Planning Compatible with Democracy, Political and Economic Democracy
(New York: W.W. Norton & Co) 1937. An old treatise raising the fundamental issue of antagonism, which is still largely validated by current experience.

Leibenstein, Harvey:
Economic Backwardness and Economic Growth: Studies in Theory of Economic Development
(New-York: John Wiley) 1957.

Leonard, David K. and Marshall, Dale Rogers (eds.):
Institutions for Rural Development: Decentralization and Organizational Linkages,
(Berkeley: University of California Press) 1982.

Leontief, W.W. :
The Structure of the American Economy 1919-1929
(New York: Oxford University Press) 1941.

Leven, C.:
Research and Education for Regional and Area Development, (Ames, Iowa : Iowa State University Press, Iowa State University Centre for Agriculture and Economic Development) 1962.

Leven, C.L. :
"Establishing Goals for Regional Economic Development", Journal of the American Institute of Planners, Vol. XXX, 1964.

Leven, Charles:
"Establishing Goals for Regional Economic Development",
in R.P. Mishra (ed.):
Regional Planning: Concept, Techniques, Policies and Case Studies
(Mysore : University of Mysore) 1969.

Levis, E. and Howells, R.E. :
Coping With Growth: Community Needs Assessment Techniques
(Corvallis: Oregon State University, Western Rural Development Centre) 1981.

Lewis, W.A.:
Development Planning: The Essentials of Policy
(London: Allen & Unwin) 1966.
This is a seminal work in the area of planning by a celebrated scholar.

Limcaoco, J. Andres A. :
"Integrated Area Development Approach to Regional Development",
Philippines Planning Journal, Vol. XV, No. 2, April 1984.

Lingaiah, K.; Krishna, S. Radha; and Bavinder, P. :
Importance of Decentralised Planning in India: Some Suggestions,
(Secunderabad: New Government College, Department of Economics) manuscript 1988.

Lipton, M. and Streeten, Paul :
"Introduction : Two Types of Planning",
in Streeten, Paul and Lipton, M:
The Crisis of Indian Planning: Economic Policies in the 1960s
(London : Oxford University Press) 1968.

Lisk, F. (ed.):
Popular Participation in Planning for Basic Needs: Concepts, Methods and Practices,
(Aldershot, Hampshire: Gower) 1985.

Little, I.M.D. and Mirrless, J.A. :
Project Appraisal and Planning for Developing Countries
(New York : Basic Book Publishers) 1975.

Lo, Fu-Chan and Salih, K. :
Growth Pole Strategies and Regional Development Policy, Asian Experience and Alternative Approaches,
(Oxford: Pergamon Press) 1978.

Lo, Fu-Chen (ed.):
Rural-Urban Relations and Regional Development U.N.C.R.D. Regional Development Studies Series 5,
(Nagoya : Maruzen Asia) 1981.

Lo, Fu-Chen and Salih, K. :
"Growth Poles, Agropolitan Development and Polarization Reversal : The Debate and Search for Alternatives",

in Stohr, W.B. and Taylor, D.R.F. (eds.):
Development from Above or Below ? The Dialectics of Regional Planning in Developing Countries
(Chichester: Wiley) 1981.

Lokamanya, D.S.; Bisaliah, S. and Hirenath, K.C. :
A Full Employment Plan for Badami Taluk, Bijapur District,
(Bangalore: University of Agricultural Sciences) 1978 (unpublished).

Losch, A.:
Die raumliche ordung der wirtschaft sweite neu durchgearbeitete Auflage, Juna 1944, translated by Stopler, W.F. as The Economics of Location,
(New-Haven : Yale University Press) 1954. A brilliant analysis on a theoretical plane of the issues relating to location of economic activities. A rare contribution to economics.

Luning, Henk A. :
The Need for Regionalized Agricultural Development Planning
(Laguna: SEARCA) 1981.

Luther, N.:
"Developing Backward Regions: Operation 'Leap Forward'", Economic Times, March, 31st, 1972, p. 6.

M

Mackay,D.I.:
"Industrial Structure and Regional Growth: A Methodological Problem",
Scottish Journal of Political Economy, Vol.XV, June 1968.

Madan, B. :
"Economics of the Indian Village and Its Implications in Social Structure", Social Change & Economic Development
(Paris: UNESCO) 1963.

Maddick, H. :
Public Administration Research on Panchayati Raj
(New Delhi: Ford Foundation) 1962.

Maddick, H.:
Democracy Decentralization and Development
(Bombay: Asia Publishing House) 1963.

Mahajan, O.P. :
"Convergence in Regional Economic Development in India",
Kurukshetra; 1972.

Mahapatro, P.C. :
"Spatial Dimension of Tribal Development: Regional Approach",
Indian Journal of Regional Science, Vol. XIII, No. 2, 1981.

Maharaja Sayaji Rao University:
Block Development Plan for Jabergam
(Baroda: M.S.University) May 1979.

Maharaja Sayaji Rao University:
Block Development Plan for Chhotanagpur Taluka
(Baroda: M.S.University, September,1980.

Maharashtra Government:
A Brief Note Regarding Formulation of District Plans
(Bombay: Government of Maharashtra, Planning Department) 1973, May 25th.

Mahood, T. and Ghosh, A. :
Handbook of Community

Economic Development, Sponsored by the U.S. Department of Commerce, Economic Development Administration, Washington D.C.
(Los Angeles: Community Research Group of the East Los Angeles Community Union) 1979.

Maikap, A.K.:
"Role of Market Centres in Indian Economic Development with special Reference to West-Bengal
in NCAER:
Market Towns and Spatial Development
(New Delhi: NCAER)1972.

Makhija, B.N.:
"District Planning and the Adivasi Question",
Public Administration, Kanpur, 1974, June.

Malassis, C.:
"The Relationship Between Farm Analysis and Regional Economic Studies",
in Isard, W. and Cumberland, J.H. (eds.):
Regional Economic Planning - Techniques of Analysis
(Paris: OECD) 1961.

Malhotra, D.K. :
"Planning Techniques in India, Problems of Area Development - Need for Scientific Area Surveys",
in Major Industries of India, Annual Number 1964-65.

Malhotra, R.C. and Vadakan, V.V. :
Alternative Strategies for Development with Focus on Local Level Planning and Development
(Bangkok: UNAPDI) 1979.

Malinvard, E.and Bucharach, M.O.L.:
Activity Analysis in the Theory of Growth and Planning (New York: St. Martin's Press)1967

Malinvard,E:
"Decentralised Procedure for Planning"
in Malinvard,E. and Bacharach, M.O.L.:
Activity Analysis in the Theory of Growth and Planning
(New York:St.Martin's Press)1967

Malinvaud,E.:
"A Planning Approach to the Public Good Problem,"
Swedish Journal of Economics, Vol.11, 1971.

Malisz, Boleslaw:
"Implications of Threshold Theory for Urban and Regional Planning",
Journal of Town Planning Institute, Vol. LV, 1969. This is a pioneering work on the subject.

Malizia, E. :
"Contingency Planning: A New Approach to Local Economic Development Planning",
Manuscript, 1981.

Malizia, E. :
A Guide to Planning Economic Development in Small Communities and Rural Areas
(Charlotte, North Carolina: Division of Community Assistance, North Carolina, Department of Natural Resources and Community Development) 1981.

Malizia, E.:
"Planning Economic Development in Smaller Communities",
Paper prepared for the National Planning Conference, Rural and Small Town Planning Division, Boston, 28th April 1981.

Mallet, J.A. :
Planning for Agricultural Development,
(New York: St. Martin's Press) 1984.

Mandal, B. (ed.):
Patterns of Regional Geography: An International Perspective, Vol.

I, II & III
(New Delhi: Concept Publishing Co.) 1985.

Mandal, S.K.:
Regional Disparities and Imbalances in India's Economic Development
(New Delhi: Deep and Deep Publishers)1987.

Mandal, S.K.:
"People's Involvement in District Planning: Organisation Framework",
Indian Journal of Regional Science, Vol. XIX, No. 1, 1987.

Mandal,S.K.:
Regional Disparities and Imbalances in India's Planned Economic Development
(New Delhi: Deep & Deep Publications)1987.

Mann, Harbans Singh:
Analysis of Some Community Developments in India
(Delhi: Atma Ram & Sons) 1967.

Mann, R.S. :
"Functional Interpretation of Rural Settlements in Hansi Tehsil (Haryana)",
Indian Journal of Regional Science, Vol VI, No. 1, 1974.

Manne, A.S. :
"DINAMICO, A Dynamic Multi-Sector, Multi-Skill Model",
in Goreax, L.M. and Manne, A.S. (eds.):
Multi-Level Planning: Case Studies in Mexico
(Amsterdam : North Holland Publishing Co.) 1973.

Manne, A.S. :
"Multi Sector Models for Development Planning A Survey", Journal of Development Economics, Vol. I, June 1974.

Manne, A.S. :
"Sufficient Conditions for Optimality in an Infinite Horizon Development Plan",
Econometrica, January, 1970.

Manne, A.S. and Markowitz, H.M.:
Studies in Process Analysis
(New York: Wiley)1963

Manne, A.S. and Weisskopf, T.E. :
"A Dynamic Multi-Sectoral Model for India, 1967-75",
in Caxter, A.P. and Brody, A. (eds.):
Contributions To Input-Output Analysis
(Amsterdam: North Holland Publishing Co.) 1969, Vol. II.

Mansfield, E. :
"Intra-Firm Rates of Diffusion of Innovations",
Review of Economics & Statistics, Vol. 45, 1963, pp. 348-359.

Maranzana, F.E. :
"On The Location of Supply Points to Minimize Transport Costs",
Operational Research Quarterly, Vol 15, 1964, pp. 261-270.

Marschack, J. and Marschack, T. :
"Centralization and Decentralization in Economic Organization",
Econometrica, July 1959.

Marschak, T. :
"An Activity Analysis Approach to Location Theory",
Kyklos, 1955, pp. 125-145.

Martin, A. and Williams, E. :
"Agricultural Planning Focus on Regional Constraints",
Economic and Political Weekly, Vol. VI, Special Number, 1971.

Martin, Fernand:
"Regional Factor in the Diffusion of Innovations",
University of Montreal Papers, Paper, No. 7601, 1976, Mimeographed.

Masaldan, P.N. :
Planning and the People: A Study

of Public Participation in Uttar Pradesh
(Bombay: Asia Publishing House) 1964.

Masser, I. :
Analytical Models for Urban and Regional Planning
(Newton Abbot: David & Charles) 1972.

Massey, Doreen:
Problems of Location : Game Theory and Gaming Simulation, Paper No. 15.
(London: The Centre for Environmental Studies).

Massey, Doreen:
Problems of Location: Lenear Programming, Paper No. 14
(London: Centre for Environmental Studies).

Mathew, George:
Panchayati Raj in Karnataka
(New Delhi: Concept Publishing Co.) 1985.

Mathur P.C.:
"Multi-Level Planning in Rajasthan",
Voluntary Action, Vol 11, No. 4, July-August 1966.

Mathur, Ashok :
"Regional Growth and Income Disparities in India",
(New-Delhi: Centre for Regional Development, Jawaharlal Nehru University) Mimeographed. Undated.

Mathur, D.P.:
"Planning for the Districts - Some Problems in Developing an Analytical System",
Journal of the LBS National Academy of Administration, Vol. 20, No. 1, 1975. Here the stress is laid on ideology and political reasons, and on social and individual costs, for making District the basic planning unit.

Mathur, K.:
"Promise and Prospect of Local Level Planning in India", Indian Journal of Public Administration, Vol. XXVI, No. 3, 1980.

Mathur, Kuldeep:
Bureaucratic Response to Development (A Study of Block Development Officers in Rajasthan and Uttar Pradesh),
(New Delhi: National Publishing House) 1972.

Mathur, Kuldip and Gupta, A.K.:
"Action Research for Micro Level Planning - A Self Appraisal",
International Review of Administrative Sciences, No. 1, 1984. This is a competent summary position of the performance of specifially created District Planning Cells in various parts of the country, particularly with regard to Data Collection.

Mathur, Kuldip and Inaytulla (eds.):
Monitoring and Evaluation of Rural Development: Some Asian Experiences
(Kuala Lumpur: APDAC) 1980.

Mathur, M.V. :
Multilevel Educational Planning and Administration in India
(Paris: International Institute of Education)1980 Mimeographed.

Mathur, M.V. and Narain, Iqbal (eds.):
Panchayati Raj Planning and Democracy,
(Bombay: Asia Publishing House) 1969.

Mathur, O.P. :
"National Policy for Backward Area Development: A Structural Analysis"
The Indian Journal of Public Administration, Vol. VI, No. 1, 1974.

Mathur, O.P. and Misra, R.P.:
Planning for the Backward Areas: Some Contributions, Development Studies No. 9
(Mysore: Institute of Development Studies) 1974.

Mathur, O.P.:
Backward Areas in Poor Countries - Problems and Perspectives of Development with Special Reference to India,
Development Studies No. 9, Institute for Development Studies (Mysore: University of Mysore) 1973.

Mathur, O.P.:
"Planning Districts: Some Problems in Developing an Analytical System",
Urban and Rural Planning Thought, Vol. 16, No. 4, 1973.

Mathur, O.P.:
"Planning for Districts: Some Problems in Developing a Conceptual Framework",
Prajnan, Vol. 2, No. 3, 1973.

Mathur, P.C. :
"The Development of Backward Areas, A Crucial Policy Issue", The Indian Journal of Public Administration, Vol.XXIII, No. 4, 1977.

Mathur, P.C.:
"Development Reorientation of Panchayati Raj in India",
in Singh, Hoshiar (ed.):
Rural Development in India
(Jaipur: Printwell) 1983. This has a good summary of the Report of the Committee of Panchayati Raj Institutions (Asoka Mehta Committee Report) 1979.

Mathur, P.M. :
"New Strategy for Backward Areas",
Yojana, 1st July 1972, pp. 483-485.

Mathur, P.N. and Hashim, S.R. :
"A Model for Location of Industries and Inter-Regional Commodity Flows",
Indian Journal of Regional Science, Vol. 1, No. 1 1968.

Mathur, Subodh :
"Decentralisation of Development Planning : The Economic Area Approach",
Development Policy and Administration Review, July-December, 1975.

Mathur, V.K. :
"Concept of Area Development as Applicable to Tribal India",
Social Welfare, September, 1968, pp. 8-9.

Mathur,Gautam:
Planning for Steady Growth
(New Dellhi: Oxford University Press)1965.

Mathur. O.P., et. al.:
Cost of Urban Infrastructure for Industry as Related to City Size in Developing Countries: Indian case Study,
(Hyderabad : Small Industries Extension Training Institute) 1968. A Case Study of Planning of infrastructure.

Matuszerski, T.I.; Pitts, P.R. and Swayer, J.A.:
"Linear Programming Estimates of Changes in Input Co-efficient",
Canadian Journal of Economics and Political Sccience, Vol.30, 1964.

Mavlankar, P.D. and Ghaiara, B.M.:
"Regional Development : Where and How ?"
in Sen, L.K., (ed):
Readings in Micro-Level Planning and Rural Growth Centre,
(Hyderabad: National Institute of Community Development) 1972.

Mayer, Albert et. al. :
The Story of Rural Development in Etawah
(Los Angles: University of California Press) 1958.

Mayer, J.P.:
"Regional Employment and Development, The Evolution of Theory and Practice",

International Labour Review, No. 1, Jan-Feb. 1984.

Mayers, J.R.:
"Regional Economics: A Survey" in American Economic Association and Royal Economic Society (ed.):
Survey of Economic Theory, Vol.II.
(New York: St. Martins Press) 1965.

Mayfield, R.C. :
"A Central Place Hierarchy in Northern India",
in Garnsom and Marble (eds.) Quantitative Geography, Part I, Illinois, 1967.

Mayfield, R.C. :
"Range of Central Goods in the Indian Punjab",
Annals of the Association of American Geographers, Vol. 53, 1963.

Mayor, H.M. and Kohn, C.F.:
Readings in Urban Geography
(Chicago: University of Chicago Press) 1965, in particular Sections 4, 5, 7 and 8.

McFarquhar, A.M.M. and Evans, M.C.(eds):
Europe's Future Agriculture
(Amsterdam: North Holland)1970.

Mckee, D.L.; Dean, R.D.; and Leahy, W.H. (eds.):
Regional Economics: Theory and Practice
(New York: The Free Press) 1970.

Mclouglin, J.B. :
Urban and Regional Planning: A Systems Approach
(London: Faber & Faber) 1969.

McLoughlin, Irian J.:
Urban and Regional Planning: A Systems Approach,
(London: Faber & Faber) 1969. A good theoretical discussion adopting a systems approach.

McMohan, C.W.:
Techniques of Economic Forecasting
(Paris: OECD)1965. This is a good treatment of short-term forecasting.

McNeely, John G. :
Influence of Specific Agriculture Resource Adjustments on the Growth and Development of the Rural Sector in the District of Burdwan, India,
(New Delhi: Ford Foundation) 1958

Meacock, Michael:
"Pace Setter District in Planning for Action",
Economic Affairs, Vol. 25, No. 9-10, 1980.

Mead, Margaret (ed.) :
Cultural Pattern & Technological Change
(Paris: UNESCO) 1955.

Meade, J.E.:
The Theory of Indicative Planning
(Manchester:University of Manchester Press)1970.

Mehta, B.C. and Menaria, Rajendra:
"Decentralised Planning and Environmental Improvement",
Conference Volume, Indian Economic Association, Calcutta, December 1988, Part III pp. 71-79.

Mehta, Dinesh:
"Micro-Level Planning in a Multi-Level Planning Framework: Towards an Approach",
Indian Journal of Regional Science, Vol. X, No. 2, 1978.

Mehta, Meera :
"Service Centres for Area Planning Towards An Integrative Approach",
Indian Journal of Regional Science, Vol. XIV, No. 2, 1982.

Mehta, N.; Rahman, A. and Wingerja, P.:
Towards A Theory of Rural

Development,
(The Hague:United Nations Asian Development Institute)1975

Mehta, Sanat:
"Planning in Gujarat",
The Economic Times, October 30th and 31st, 1985.

Mellor, J.W. :
The New Economics of Growth - A Strategy for India and Developing World
(Ithaca : Cornell University Press) 1976.

Mellor, John W. :
Developing Rural India: Plan and Pracice
(Ithaca : Cornell University Press) 1968.

Mcloughlin, J. Brian :
Urban and Regional Planning - A Systems Approach
(London: Faber & Faber) 1970

Mennes, L.B.M.; Tinbergen, J. and Waardenberg, J.G. :
Elements of Space in Development Planning,
(Amsterdam: North Holland) 1969.

Mennon, K.S.V.:
"Backward Areas Development",
The Economic Times, 27th May,1979

Menon, K.S.V.:
Development of Backward Areas through Incentives: An Indian Experience
(New Delhi: Vidya Vahini) 1979.

Mera, Koichi :
"Trade off between Aggregate Efficiency and Inter-regional Equity, A Static Analysis",
Quarterly Journal of Economics, Vol. 81, 1967, pp. 658-674.

Merriam, C.E. :
Pacific Northwest Regional Planning - A Review,
(Washington : State Printing Plant) 1963, Bullentin No. 6, Division of Power Resources, Olympia, Washington. It is an interesting early book that reminds us of the limits of decentralisation in planning so as to decentralise everything is anarchy.

Metropolitan Applied Research Centre:
A Relevant War Against Poverty
(New-York : Metropoliton Research Council) 1968.

Metwally, M.M. and Jensen, Rodney C.:
" A Note on the Measurement of Regional Income Disparities",
Economic Development and Cultural Change, Vol. 22, 1973.

Meyers, J.R.:
"Regional Economics : A Survey",
in L. Needleman (ed.):
Regional Analysis,
(Penguins, Modern Economics Readings) 1968.

Michalos, A.C. :
"Integrated Development Planning Using Socio-Economic and Quality of Life Indicators",
in UNESCO:
Innovative Approaches to Development Planning
(Paris: UNESCO) 1988.

Midgley, J. et. al. (eds.):
Community Participation, Social Development and The State, (New-York: Metheun) 1986.

Miernyk, W.H. :
"A Note on Recent Regional Growth Theories",
Journal of Regional Science, Vol. 19, No. 3, 1976.

Miernyk,W.H.:
The Elements of Input-Output Analysis
(New York:Random House)1965.

Miernyk,W.H.:
"Long-range Forecasting with a Regional Input-Output Model",

Western Economic Journal, Vol.6, 1968.

Miller, J.C. :
"Regional Development : Review of the State of the Art",
(Washington D.C.: Agency for International Development, State Department, Government of United States) 1979.

Mills, E.S. and Lav, M.R. :
"A Model of Market Areas with Free Entry",
Journal of Political Economy Vol. 72, 1964.

Minns, Richard and Thoornley, Jennifer:
"Do Local Authorities Have a Role in Economic Planning?" Planner, Vol. 63, No. 3, May 1977.

Minocha, A.C. :
Decentralised Planning in India - The Madhya Pradesh Experience
(Bhopal: Bhopal University, Department of Economics) manuscript 1988.

Minocha, A.C. :
Growth Performance of an Underdeveloped Economy
(Bhopal: P.S. Publications) 1988.

Minocha, A.C. :
"Decentralised Planning in India and the Role of Administration",
Indian Journal of Regional Science, Vol. XIX, No. 1, 1987.

Minocha, A.C. :
"Regional Planning in India", in Mahajan, V.S. (ed.): Studies in Indian Planning
(New-Delhi: Deep & Deep Publications) 1988.

Minocha, A.C.:
A Conceptual Framework For Multi-Level Planning and Spatial Analysis,
Unpublished manuscript. No date.

Minocha, A.C.:
"Some Aspects of Income Distribution in India",
Indian Economic Journal, Vol.25, No.2, October-December 1977.

Minocha, A.C.:
"Planning for Social Services in Backward Region",
Indian Journal of Regional Science, Vol.VI. No.2, 1974

Mishra, R.P. and Ramesh, A:
Fundamentals of Cartography
(revised edition, New-Delhi: Concept Publishing Co.) 1989.

Mishra, R.P. :
"Growth Poles and Growth Centres in the Context of Indian Urban and Regional Development Problems",
in Kuklinski, A. (ed.): Growth Poles and Growth Centres (The Hague: Mouton & Co.) 1972.

Mishra, R.P. and Sundaram, K.V. (ed.):
Rural Area Development - Perspectives and Approaches,
(New-Delhi: Sterling Publishers) 1979. This has listed the ingredients of the policies and programmes which guided rural development in India during the relevant peiod.

Mishra, S.K. :
"Simultaneous Equations Models in Regional Analysis",
Indian Journal of Regional Science, Vol. XII, No. 2, 1980.

Misra, R.P. :
Development Issues of Our Time
(New Delhi: Concept Publishing Co.) 1985.

Misra, R.P. and Prantilla, E B.:
"Basic Needs and Development Planning",
in Nagamine, H. (ed.):
Human Needs and Regional Development,
(Singapore: UNCRD, Regional Development Series, Maruzen Asia) 1981.

Misra, R.P. and Sundaram, K.V. :
"Growth Foci as Instruments of Modernisation in India",
in Kuklinski, A. (ed.):
Regional Policies in Nigeria, India and Brazil
(The Hague: Mouton & Co. 1978.

Misra, B.:
"Growth Pole and Growth Centre Strategy in Metropolitan Regional Development",
Indian Journal of Regional Science,Vol.III, No.1, 1971

Misra, G.K. :
"Computer in Regional Planning",
Indian Journal of Regional Science, Vol. X, No. 1, 1978.

Misra, G.K.:
Regional Planning
(Mysore: University of Mysore) 1969

Misra, G.K.:
"The Centrally Oriented Connectivity of Roads in Miryalguda Taluka, A Case Study",
Behavioural Sciences and Community Development, special number on Rural Growth Centres,Vol.6,1972.

Misra, Girish K. :
"Spatial Organization of Service Centres in Rural India",
The Indian Journal of Public Administration, Vol. XXIII, No. 4, 1977.

Misra, Girish K. and Kundu, Amitabh:
Regional Planning at the Micro-Level: A Study of Rural Electrification in Bastar and Chandrapur
(New Delhi: Indian Institute of Public Administration) 1980.

Misra, K.; Mahanti, T.K. and Pathak, C.R.:
"Micro-Level Planning for Agricultural Development: A Case Study of East Champaran District Bihar",
Indian Journal of Regional Science, Vol. X, No. 1, 1978.

Misra, K.K. :
"Service Centre Strategy in the Development Planning of Hamirpur District, U.P.",
Indian Journal of Regional Science, Vol. XIX, No. 1, 1987.

Misra, K.K.:
System of Service Centres in Hamirpur District U.P. India,
unpublished Doctoral Dissertation, Bundelkhand University, Jhansi, 1981.

Misra, R.P. (ed):
Regional Planing: Concepts Techniques, Policies and Case Studies
(Mysore: University of Mysore)1969.

Misra, R.P. (ed.):
Local Level Planning and Development
(New-Delhi : Sterling Publishing Co.) 1983.

Misra, R.P. (ed.):
District Planning - Essays in Honour of Dr. K.V.Sundaram,
(New Delhi: Concept Publishers) 1990.

Misra, R.P. (ed.):
Regional Development, Essays in the Honour of Prof. M. Honjo,
(Singapore: Maruzen Asia) 1981.

Misra, R.P. :
Research Methodology: A Handbook
(New Delhi: Concept Publishing Co.) 1989.

Misra, R.P. :
"Growth Pole Strategy for Rural Development in India",
Journal of the Institute of Economic Geography, 1970, pp. 33-38.

Misra, R.P. :
"Social Dimensions of Regional

Development",
in Kuklinski, A.(eds.):
Regional Dynamics of Socio-Economic Change
(Tampere: Finn Publishers) 1979.

Misra, R.P. :
"Target Groups and Regional Development",
Regional Development Dialogue, Vol. 1, No. 1, 1980.

Misra, R.P. :
"The Challenge of Culture Neutral Development Planning",
in Misra, R.P. and Honjo, M. (eds.):
Changing Perception of Development Problem
(Singapore: UNCRD and Maruzen Asia, Regional Development Series Vol. I) 1981.

Misra, R.P. :
"Regional Development Planning: Search for Bearings",
in Misra, R.P. (ed.):
Regional Development: Essays in Honour of Masanhiko Honjo
(Singapore: Maruzen Asia) 1982.

Misra, R.P. and Honjo, M. (eds.):
Changing Perception of Development Problem
(Singapore: UNCRD and Maruzen Asia, Regional Development Series Vol. 1) 1981.

Misra, R.P. and Misra, H.N. :
"Ruralization of Indian Cities: A Study of the Process of Penetration of Rural Functions in Urban Areas of Slow Growing Economies", Urban Studies, Vol. III, No. 3, 1983.

Misra, R.P. and Natraj, V.K. :
"India: Blending Central Roots Planning",
in Stohr, W.B. and Taylor D.R.F. (ed.):
Development from Above or Below?
(New York : John Wiley & Sons Ltd.) 1981

Misra, R.P. and Prantilla, E.B.:
"Emerging Trends in Regional Development Planning: The South - East Asian Experience",
in Chatterjee, Lata and Nijkamp, Peter (eds.):
Urban and Regional Policy Analysis in Developing Countries
(London: Gower Publishing Co.) 1982.

Misra, R.P. and Shivalingaih, M.:
"Growth Pole Strategy for Development in India",
Journal of the Institute of Geography, Vol. 1, 1970.

Misra, R.P. and Sundaram, K.V.:
Multi-Level Planning and Integrated Rural Development in India,
(New-Delhi: Heritage Publishers)1980

Misra, R.P.:
Diffusion of Agricultural Innovation,
(Mysore: University of Mysore) 1968.

Misra, R.P.:
District Planning, Development Studies No. 6.
(Mysore: Institute of Development Studies, Univesity of Mysore) 1973. A status report on progress and methodology for District Planning.

Misra, R.P.:
Growth Poles and Growth Centres in Urban and Regional Planning in India, And Training Programme for Regional Development in Developing Countries, An Experiment in India,
(Mysore: Institute of Development Studies, Mysore University) Development Studies Number 2, 1971.

Misra, R.P.:
Methodology of District Planning, Development Studies No. 6,

(Mysore: Institute of Development Studies) 1972.

Misra, R.P.:
"Diffusion of Information in the Context of Development Planning",
in
Information System for Regional Development,
Lund Studies in Geography, series B, No. 37, 1971. This is a seminal paper dealing with diffusion process development on account of non-adopters delaying the diffusion process.

Misra, R.P.:
"Framework of a modified Growth Pole Strategy for Urban and Regional Planning in India",
in Misra R.P., Mahadev, P.D., and Jayashankar, D.C.:
Urban Systems and Rural Development
(Mysore: Institute of Development Studies, Mysore University) 1972 Part I.

Misra, R.P.:
"Growth Pole Policy for Regional Development in India",
in Lahiri T.B. (ed.):
Balanced Regional Development, Concepts, Strategy and Case Study
(Calcutta: Oxford & IBH Publishing Co.) 1970.

Misra, R.P.:
"On the Concept of Region", in Mishra R.P., et. al. (eds.) Regional Planning: Concepts, Techniques, Policies and Case Studies. (Mysore : University of Mysore) 1969. This paper demonstrated various taxomonic ranks by groups areas according to the purpose and scale of development.

Misra, R.P.:
"Regional Issues, Investment Criteria and Strategies for Development", in Misra, R.P. (ed.) with assistance of Masood, M.S. and Mahadev, P.D.,Census of India 1961.
(Mysore: Unversity of Mysore) 1969.

Misra, R.P.:
Regional Planning: Concepts, Techniques, Policies and Case Studies
(New Delhi: Concept Publishing Co.) 1990.

Misra, R.P.:
Micro-Level Rural Planning, Principles, Methods and Case Studies
(New Delhi: Concept Publishing Co.) 1990.

Misra, R.P.; Urs D.V., and Natraj V.K. (eds.):
Regional Planning and National Development,
(New-Delhi : Vikas Publishing House Pvt. Ltd.) 1978. This book is the by product of the First Asian Symposium on Regional Planning and National Development, held in Mysore, July 1974. It has collection of papers on regional perspectives in national development, growth poles and growth centres in regional development and on several related subjects by experts in their field.

Misra, R.P.;Sundaram, K.V.; and Prakasa Rao, V.L.S. :
Regional Development Planning in India A New Strategy
(Delhi: Vikas Publishing House Pvt. Ltd.) 1974.

Misra, S.K. :
"Simultaneous Equation Models in Regional Analysis",
Indian Journal of Regional Science, Vol. XIII, No. 2, 1980.

Misra,J. and Sinha, C.:
Planning and Development in India
(New Delhi: Sterling Publishers)1985.

Mitra, Ashok:
Levels of Regional Development in India, Regional Planning: Concepts, Techniques Policies and Case Studies,
(New Delhi: Government of India) 1965.

Mitra, Ashok:
"Levels of Regional Development in India",
in Sdasyuk, G. and Sen Gupta, P.:
Economic Regionalization in India: Problems and Approaches
(Census of India 1961, Monograph series Vol.I, No,8) 1961.

Mitra, Ashok :
Micro-Planning for Space,
First Lecture Delivered at the Academy of Sciences in the Institute of Geography, Moscow, June 1973.

Mitra, Ashok:
Multi-Level Planning,
Second Lecture delivered at the Academy of Sciences in the Institute of Geography at Moscow, June 1973.

Mitra,Ashok:
"A Function Classification of Indian Town",
in Bose, A.O (ed):
Pattern of Population Change in India 1951-61
(Bombay: Allied Publishers)1967.

Mobugunje, Akin :
"Growth Poles and Growth Centres in Regional Development in Nigeria",
in Kuklinski, A. (ed.):
Regional Policies in Nigeria, India and Brazil,
(The Hague: Mouton Co.) 1978.

Mohamad, Afzal :
"Compugraphics Application for District Planning",
in Sanwal, Mukul (ed.):
Computer Application in District Administration,
(Nainital: Administrative Training Institute) 1986.

Mohandass, M:
"Decentralised Planning at Panchayat Level",
Paper read at Workshop on Decentralised Planning held at the John Mathai Centre, Calicut University, Trichur, on January 10th, 1989.

Montgomery, J.D.:
"The Populist Front in Rural Development",
Public Administration Review, Jan-February 1979.

Montias,J.M.:
Central Planning in Poland,
(New Haven: Yale University Press)1962.

Moore, F.T. and Peterson J.W.:
"Regional Analysis: An Inter-Industry Model of Utah",
Review of Economics & Statistics, Vol.37,1955. The inclusion of the household sector within the input-output sector structure is discussed here in this paper.

Morgan, Theodore :
"The Long-Run Terms of Trade Between Agriculture and Manufacturing", Economic Development and Cultural Change, Vol. 8, 1959.

Morril, R.L. :
The Spatial Organisation of Society,
(Belmont, C.A.: Duxburg Press) 1970.

Morril, R.L. :
"The Shape of Diffusion in Space and Time",
Economic Geography, Vol. 46, 1970.

Morril, R.L.:
"Waves of Spatial Diffusion",
Journal of Regional Science, Vol. 8, 1968.

Morrill, R.L.:
The Spatial Organization of Society
(Belmont: Duxburge Press) 1974 2nd edition.

Morrill, R.L. :
"The Development of Spatial Distribution of Towns",
Annals of the Association of American Geographers, Vol. 53, 1963.

Morrill, R.L.:
"Growth-Centre Hinterland Relations",
in Helleiner, F.M. and Stohr, W.B.F.: (eds.):
Papers and proceedings of the Commission on Regional Aspects of Development, International Geographical Union, Spatial Aspects of the Development Process Vol. II
(Toronto: Allister Typesetting and Graphics for CRAD) 1974.

Moseley, M.J. :
Growth Centres in Spatial Planning
(Oxford: Pergamon Press) 1974.

Moseley, M.J. :
"Growth Centres - A Shiboleth",
Area, Vol. 5, No. 2, 1973.

Moseley, Malcolm J.:
Growth Centres in Spatial Planning
(Oxford: Oxford University Press) 1974.

Mosher, Arthur Theodore:
Varieties of Extension Education and Community Development, Comparative Extension Education Publication No. 2.
(Ithaca, New - York: State College of Agriculture) 1958.

Mukherje,R.C.:
"Case Study of Growth Function and Regional Relationship in Small Towns",
Geographical Review of India, Vol.30,No.3, September 1968.

Mukherjee, Amitava:
"Decentralised Planning - A Rejoinder",
Economic Times, New-Delhi, 13th December, 1989

Mukherjee, Amitava:
"Decentralised Planning - Economic Issues",
Economic Times, New-Delhi, 14th December 1989.

Mukherjee, Amitava:
"Growth Centres: Need for Change in Approach",
Economic Times, January 8th, 1990.

Mukherjee, Dhurjati and Shah, O.P.:
"Indian Planning: Need for Developing Rural Economy",
Khadi Gramodyog, Vol. 22, No. 5, February 1976.

Mukherjee, Nirmal:
"Decentralisation Below The State Level",
Economic & Political Weekly, March 4, 1989.

Mukherjee, Radha Kamal :
Social Ecology
(New-York: Century & Co.) 1935.

Mukherjee, Radha Kamal:
Regional Sociology
(New-York: Century & Co.) 1926.

Mukhopadhyay, A.K.:
"The Structure of Land Relations in Tribal Communities in India",
in Perspectives on Tribal Development and Administration (Hyderabad: National Institute of Community Development)1975.

Mukhopadhyay, Sampat and Sarkar, Utpal :
"Micro-Level Planning in Backward Areas",
Financial Express, August 5th, 1976, p. 4.

Mundle, Sudipto:
Surplus Flows And Growth

Imbalances
(New Delhi: Allied Publishers Pvt.Ltd.) 1981.

Mundle, Sudipto:
"Developing Backward Areas: Some Questions Concerning Strategy",
The Indian Journal of Public Administration, Vol. XXIII, No. 4, 1972.

Murk, Peter J.; & Wells, John H.:
"A Practical Guide to Programme Planning",
in Training & Development Journal, Vol. 42, No. 10, Oct. 1988.

Murray, James:
"Population - Employment Ratios as Supplement to Location Quotient and Threshold Estimates",
Community Economics, Vol. 21, June 1978.

Murty, K.L. Narasimha and Sarma, P.V. :
"Identification of Service Centres in Tanuku Taluk - An Approach Towards Micro Regional Level Planning",
Indian Journal of Regional Science, Vol. XVII, No. 2, 1985.

Muthuswamy, S. :
Decentralised Planning for Human Development
(Namakkal: A.A. Governments Arts college, Department of Economics) manuscript 1988.

Muttiah, M.:
Decentralised Planning in India,
(Madras: Presidency College, Department of Economics) manuscript 1988.

Myint H.:
The Economics of the Developing Countries
(New-Delhi:B.I. Publishers, First Indian Edition) 1974.

Myrdal, Gunnar :
Economic Theory and Under-Developed Regions
(London: Metheun & Co.) 1963.

Myrdal, Gunnar:
An International Economy: Problems and Prospects
(New-York : Harper low) 1956.

Myrdal, Gunnar:
Asian Drama : An Inquiry Into the Poverty of Nations, Vols. I, II, & III,
(New-York: Pantheon) 1968. A monumental work on development issues of developmental economies of Asia.

Myrdal, Gunnar:
Economic Theory and Underdeveloped Regions,
(London: Duckworth) 1957.

N

N.C.A.E.R. :
District Planning Moradabad,
(New Delhi : National Council for Applied Economic Research) 1968.

Nagaiya, D. :
The Identification of Growth Centres - A Study of Vardha Region Hyderabad,
SIET Studies, Winter 1972.

Nageswara, Rao V.:
"Integrated Area Development with Reference to District Planning",
Indian Journal of Agricultural Economics, Vol. 28, No. 4, 1973.

Naidu, K. Munirathna (ed.) :
Area Planning for Regional Development

(New Delhi: Inter-India Publishers) 1984.

Naidu, K. Munirathna :
"Planning in India - The Need for An Alternative Approach-Attempt at District Planning"
Economic Studies, 1981.

Naidu, K. Munirathna :
"Regional Development and a New-Strategy - Problems & Perspectives",
Economic Studies, Nos. 1,2,3,& 4, 1981.

Naidu, N.Y.:
"Tribals -Pains of Industrialisation",
Economic and Political Weekly, 5th June 1976.

Naik, J.P. :
Educational Planning in the District
(New-Delhi : Asian Institute of Educational Planning & Administration) 1969.

Nair, K.R.G.:
Regional Experience in a Developing Economy
(New-Delhi : Wiley Eastern Ltd.) 1981.

Nair, K.R.G.:
"Inter-State Income Disparities in India",
Indian Journal of Regional Science, Vol. 3, No. 2, 1974.

Nair, M.N.V.; Srinivasan, V. and Kumar, S.P.:
"Need for New Policy Perspectives on Regional Developments"
in Backward Area Development: Strategies and Policies (New Delhi : Management Development Institute) 1977.

Nandekar, V.G. :
Zila Parishads as Local Governments and Development Bodies,
Ph.D. dissertation, University of Poona, 1972, (unpublished).

Nandekar, V.G.:
Local Government: Its Role in Development Administration
(Delhi: Concept Publishing Co.) 1979.

Nanjundappa D.M.:
Area Planning and Rural Development
(Delhi : Associated Publishers) 1981. This is a book from a practical planner and distinguished academician. A good blend of theory and practice.

Nanjundappa, D.M. :
"Decentralized Planning - Problems of Administration and Co-ordination",
A paper read at the National Seminar on Decentralised Planning and Implementation held at the Institute for Social and Economic Change, Bangalore, November 29th to 1st December, 1984.

Nanjundappa, D.M.:
"Karnataka Block Planning: Methodology and Project Criteria",
Economic Times, 2nd January, 1982.

Narain, Iqbal :
"Democratic Decentralisation: The Idea, Image and The Reality",
Indian Journal of Public Administration, Vol 9, No. 1, 1963.

Narain, Iqbal :
"Democratic Decentralisation and Rural Leaderships in India : The Rajasthan Experiment",
Asian Survey, Vol. IV, No. 8, 1964.

Narain, Iqbal :
"Development Administration Under Panchayati Raj - The Rajasthan Experience",
The Indian Journal of Public Administration, Vol. XIV, No. 1, January-March 1968.

Narayan, B.K., and Rao, D. Vasudeva :
"Regional Planning: Growth Centre Technique",
Indian Journal of Regional Science, Vol. VI, No. 1, 1974.

Narayan, B.K.; and Vasudev, Rao D.:
"Regional Planning: Growth Centre Technique",
Indian Journal of Regional Science, Vol. VI, No. 1, 1974.

Narayana, B.K. :
"Backward Area Development: A Conceptual Framework",
in Brahmananda P.R. and Panchmukhi, V.R. (eds.):
Indian Economic Development and Policy,
(New Delhi: Vikas) 1989.

Narsimhan, N.V.A.:
"Principles of Integration of Local and National Plans", Behavioural Sciences and Community Development, Vol. 1, No. 1, 1967.

Nasbeth, L and Ray, G.F. :
The Diffusion of New-Industrial Processes
(Aberdeen: Cambridge University Press) 1974.

Nasir, Ali S.:
"Plan Implementation Through District Administration",
Indian Journal of Politics, Vol. 6, No. 2, 1972.

Nataraj, V.K. :
Decentralised Planning in India,
(Mysore: Institute of Development Studies) Studies No. 10, 1974.

Natarajan, K.V. :
"Some Aspects of Local Planning in Andhra Pradesh",
Asian Economic Review, May 1965, pp. 329-346.

Natarajan, Nalini :
"Role of Valuntary Organizations in the Development of Backward Areas: Nagaland",
The Indian Journal of Public Administration Vol. XXIII, No. 4, 1977.

Nath V.:
"Regions for Planning",
The Indian Journal of Public Administration, Vol. 22, No. 1, 1966. @TITLE = Nath, V. :
"Planning for Panchayati Raj Institutions",
in Mathur, M.V. and Narain, I.:
Panchayati Raj, Planning & Democracy
(Bombay: Asia Publishing House) 1969.

Nath, V. :
"Progress of Rural Development Programmes : Regional Differences",
Economic Weekly, February 1963, Annual Number, pp. 175-177.

Nath, V. :
"Regional Planning in the National Plan",
Artha Vijnana, Vo. 9, No. 1, 1967.

Nath, V.:
"Area Development : Planning at District and Block Level",
Indian Journal of Public Administration, Vol. XXI, No. 2, 1965. A six fold classification of central places of different regions is suggested.

Nath, V.:
"Regional Development in Indian Planning",
Economic and Political Weekly, Annual Number 1970.

National Capital Region Planning Board :
Draft Regional Plan 2001 National Capital Region,
(New Delhi : Ministry of Urban Development, Government of India) July 1987.

National Council for Applied Economic Research:
Market Towns and Spatial Development,
(New Delhi: NCAER) 1971.

National Council for Applied Economic Research :
Survey of Backward Districts of Andhra Pradesh
(New Delhi: NCAER) 1970.

National Council for Applied Economic Research:
Survey of Backward Districts of Orissa
(New Delhi : NCAER) 1969.

National Council for Applied Economic Research:
Survey of Hilly and Backward Areas of Punjab
(New Delhi : NCAER) 1966.

National Council for Applied Economic Research:
Techno-Economic Survey of Andaman And Nicobar Islands,
(New Delhi: NCAER) 1966.

National Council for Applied Economic Research:
Techno - Economic Survey of Manipur : Economic Report
(Imphal: Manipur Administration) 1961.

National Council for Applied Economic Research:
Techno - Economic Survey of NEFA
(New Delhi : NCAER) 1967.

National Council for Applied Economic Research:
Techno - Economic Survey of Orissa
(New Delhi : NCAER) 1962.

National Council for Applied Economic Research:
Techno Economic Survey of Tripura
(New- Delhi :NCAER) 1961.

National Council of Applied Economic Research:
Socio-Economic Conditions of Primitive Tribes in Madhya Pradesh,
(New Delhi : NCAER) 1963.

Nayar, Vaneet :
"Methodology of Area Planning: The Karnal Case Study",
Management in Government, October-December, 1969.

Needleman, L.:
Regional Analysis
(Penguin Modern Economics Readings) 1968.

Negi, S.S. :
Tribal Welfare, Development And Administration
(Dehradun : International Book Distributors) 1986.

Newcomb, V.Z.:
"Creating An Industrial Development Pole in Southern Italy",
Journal of the Town Planning Institute, Vol. 55, No. 4, April 1969.

Newcombe, Vernon Z. :
"Some Observations on Planning for Regional Development",
Indian Journal of Regional Science, Vol. X, No. 2, 1978.

Ng Lu Siong:
An Income Distribution and Employment Consistency Model of the Philippines
(Ames : Iowa State University, Department of Economics) 1975.

Nicholas, Ralph W. :
"Structure of Politics in the Villages of Southern Asia",
in Singer, Hans; Milton and Chon, B.S. (eds.):
Structure and Change in Indian Society
(Chicago: Aldine Publishing Co.) 1968.

Nichols, Vida :
Growth Poles : An Investigation of Their Potential as Tool for Regional Economic Development,
(Peace Dale : Regional Science Research Institute) Discussion Paper No. 30, May 1969.

Nilakantan, S.:
"District Planning Concept Revived",
Rising Sun, 20th July 1973.

Nizamuddin, K., et. al. :
"Parameters Influenceing Planning of District Level Towns in Bangladesh. A Case Study of Jhenaidah Town",
Bangladesh Journal of Public Administration, Vol. 2, No. 2, July 1988.

Noble, A.G. and Dutt, Ashok K., (eds.):
Indian Urbanization and Planning : Vehicles of Modernization,
(New-Delhi : Tata McGraw Hill Publishing Co. Ltd.) 1977.

North, D.C. :
"Location Theory and Regional Economic Growth",
Journal of Political Economy, Vol. LXII, 1955, p 243-258.

North, Douglass C. :
"Exports and Regional Economic Growth, A Reply",
Journal of Political Economy, Vol. LXIV, 1956.

North, Douglass C. :
"The Spatial and Inter-regional Framework of the United States Economy : An Historical Perspective",
Papers and Proceedings of the Regional Science Association, Vol. 2, 1956.

Nourse, Hugh O. :
Regional Economics : A Study in the Economic Structure, Stability and Growth of Regions
(New York : McGraw Hill) 1968.

Noyelle, T. :
"The Rise of the Advanced Services",
Journal of the American Planning Association, Vol. 49, No. 3, Summer, 1983.

O

O.E.C.D. :
Regional Development and Accelerated Growth
(Paris :OECD) 1965.

O.E.C.D. :
Multi- Disciplinary Aspects of Regional Development
(Paris : Organisation of European Community Development) 1969.

O.E.C.D.:
The Regional Factor in Economic Development Policies in Fifteen Industrialised O.E.C.D. Countries
(Paris : OECD) 1970. Attention to problems at regional level helps in counteracting centripetal forces inherent in economic development that widens the disparities between regions.

Olsson, Rune :
"Commodity Flows and Regional Inter-Dependence",
Papers and Proceedings of the Regional Science Association, Vol. 19, 1964.

Oza, Nila :
Decentralised Planning: A Study of Bhavnagar District,
(Bhavnagar: Bhavnagar University, Deptt. of Economics) mansuscript, 1988.

P

Padmanabhan, K.:
"Issues Before District Planning",
in V.S. Mahajan (ed.):
Studies in Indian Planning
(Chandigarh: Centre for Indian Economic Development Studies) 1986.

Padmanabhan, K. :
Industrial Development in Kanyakumari District - A Decentralised Approach ,
(Tirupathur : Sacred Heart College Society) 1982, mimeographed.

Paelinck, J.H.P.:
Programming for Europe's Collective Needs
(Amsterdam : North Holland) 1970.

Pal M.N.:
"Regional Information, Regional Statistics and Regional Planning in India",
in Kukliuski, A. (ed).:
Regional Information and Regional Planning, UNRISD, Regional Planning
Vol.6, (The Hague: Mouton & Co.) 1974.

Pal, M.N. :
An Introduction to Regional Planning:
(Calcutta : Indian Statistical Institute, Regional Survey Unit) 1963.

Pal, M.N. :
Methods and Techniques for Regional Planning
(New Delhi: Indian Statistical Institute) 1964.

Pal, M.N. :
"Discriminatory Power of the V.L.S. over the OLS Regression Techniques and Some Uses in Regional Analysis",
Indian Journal of Regional Science, Vol. XVIII, No. 1, 1986.

Pal, M.N. :
"Operations Research Techniques in Indian National and Regional Planning",
Opsearch, Council for Scientific and Industrial Research, New-Delhi, Vol. 2, Nos. 1 and 2, 1965.

Pal, M.N. :
"Regional Disparities in the Level of Development in India", Indian Journal of Regional Science, Vol. VII, No.1, 1975.

Pal, M.N. :
"Regional Disparities in the Level of Development in India (Addenda) of Previous Article of Vol. VII, No. 1",
Indian Journal of Regional Science, Vol. VII, No. 2, 1975.

Pal, M.N. and C.Subramaniam:
"An Optimal Evaluation of Spatial Linkage in South India," Indian Journal of Regional Science, Vol. IX, No.1, 1977.

Pal, M.N. and Learmouth, A.C.A. :
An Appraisal of Regionalisation of Economic Development of India
(Canberra: Australia and New-Zealand Association for Advancement of Science) 1964.

Pal, M.N. and Subramanian, C:
" Indian Planning :Need for Greater Emphasis on Regional development",
AICC Economic Review, 1966.

Pal, M.N.:
Regional Analysis for National Development : Techniques and Case Studies,
unpublished doctoral dissertation (Delhi: University of Delhi)1968.

Pal, M.N.:
"Quantitative Delimitation of Regions",
Bombay Geographical Magazine, 1961,pp. 8-9.

Pal, M.N.:
"Regional Information, Regional Statistics and Regional Planning in India",
in Kulinski, A. (ed.):
Regional Information and Regional Planning,
(The Hague : Mouton & Co.)

1974, UNRISD/Regional Planning, Vol. 6.

Pal, M.N.:
"Quantitative Techniques for Regional Planning",
Indian Journal of Regional Science, Vol.III, No.1, 1971.

Pal, M.N.:
"A Method of Regional Analysis of Economic Development with Special Reference to South Region",
Journal of Regional Science, Vol.5, 1963, pp. 41-58. A Pioneering study.

Pal, M.N.:
"Regional Studies and Research for Consistent and Optimal Plan Formulation,: The Need for Right Kind of Orientation,"
Indian Journal of Regional Sciences, Vol.V., No.1, 1973.

Pal, M.N.;Prakasa Rao, V.L.S. and Tiwari A.:
"Techniquie of Ranking Central Places and Determining Linkages",
Papers of the 21st International Geographical Congress, Mysore,1968.

Palanidurai, K.V. :
Decentralised Planning in India - Precept and Practice - Experience of Karnataka & Tamilnadu;
(New-Delhi: Indian Institute of Economic Growth) 1988.

Pande, V.P. :
Village Community Projects in India: Origin, Development and Problems
(Bombay: Asia Publishing House) 1967.

Pandey, M.P. :
"Regional Planning in Bihar",
Eastern Economist, August 7th, 1974.

Pankert, F.; Skolka, J. and Maton, J.:
Redistribution of Income, Patterns of Consumption and Employment: A Case Study of the Phillipines
(Geneva: ILO) 1974, mimeographed.

Pant, Bishnu Dev :
"Estimation of Regional Production Function of Manufacturing Industries in Nepal",
Indian Journal of Regional Science, Vol XVII, No. 1, 1985.

Paranjape, H.K. :
"Planning from Below: Why and How",
Economic Weekly, December 19th, 1964.

Parida, B.C. :
Operational Constraints and Their Solutions of Decentralised Planning in India
(Cuttack: University of Cuttack, Deptt of Economics) manuscript, 1988.

Parikh, Udai and Sudarshan, R. :
Human Resources Development for Panchayati Raj, A Report Sumbitted to the Karnataka Government,
(New-Delhi : Ford Foundation) 1988.

Park, Richard L.:
"Administrative Co-ordination and Economic Development in the Districts of India"
in Bralbanti, Ralph J.D. and Spengler, Joseph J.:
Administration And Economic Development in India,
(Durham, North Carolina : Duke University Press) 1963.

Patankar, P. :
Planning for Mico-Regions and the Plan for Infrastructure in Wardha
(Wardha: Wardha Institute) 1968.

Patel, G.D. :
"District Area Development",
Indian Journal of Public

Administration, Vol XII, No. 3, 1966.

Patel, M. L. :
Dilemma of Balanced Regional Development in India
(Bhopal : Progress Publishers) 1975.

Patel, M.L. :
"Role of Rural Industrialisation in Community Development", Rural India, Vol. 31, No. 9, Nov. 1968.

Patel, V.G.:
An Analysis of Plan Implementation in India
(Ahmedabad: Balgovind Prakashan) 1969. This book is indicative of the fact that National Plans approved by National Development Council mirrored an impression that spatial breakdown of sectoral plan was not considered necessary and hence planning at District level remained the weakest link. The observations in the book are still largely relevant.

Pathak, C.R. :
"Development : Search for a Conceptual Frame",
Indian Journal of Regional science, Vol. IV, No. 2, 1972.

Pathak, C.R. :
"Integrated Area Developmetn",
Geographical Review of India, Vol. XXXV, No. 3, Sept. 1973.

Pathak, C.R. and Kundu,A. :
"Regionalisation and Regional Planning: An Axiomatic Approach",
Indian Journal of Regional Science, Vol. V, No. 2, 1973.

Pathak, C.R.:
" A Note on Problems of Micro-Level Planning for Integrated Area Development",
Indian Journal of Regional Science, Vol.III, No. 2, 1971.

Pathak, C.R.:
"District Development Planning in India",
Indian Journal of Regional Science, Vol. VII, No. 2, 1975.

Pathak, C.R.; Aziz, A. and Chattopadhyay, R.N.:
"Identification of Planning Areas in the Three State Regions-Bihar, Orissa and West-Bengal-with Reference to their Levels of Development and Planning Problems",
Indian Journal of Regional Science, Vol. 2, 1970.

Pathak, Mahesh T.:
"Development of Backward Areas: Problems and Prospects", Artha Vikas, Vol.X, January-July 1973.

Patil, G.P. :
"District Area Development",
Indian Journal of Public Administration, Vol. XII, No. 3, July-Sept 1966.

Patnaik, N.:
Tribes and Their Development: A Study of Two Blocks in Orissa,
(Hyderabad:NICD) 1978.

Patnaik, Nityananda and Bose, Saradindu:
An Integrated Tribal Development Plan for Keonjhar District
(Hyderabad: NICD) 1976.

Patnaik, S.C. :
Economics of Regional Development and Planning in Third World Countries
(New Delhi: Associated Publishing House)1981.

Patnaik, S.C. :
"Regional Problem and The Strategy of Sub-National Planning in Developing Countries",
Planning and Regional Development in India,
(Jallandhar: Gaurav Publishing House) 1985.

Patnaik, S.C. and Chattopadhyay, R.N. :
"Spatial Variations in Levels of Development in Orissa",
Indian Journal of Regional Science, Vol. 7, No. 1, 1975.

Paul, Samuel:
"Micro-Planning: The Neglected Interface",
Economic and Political Weekly, February 27th, 1971.

Paul, Satya:
" Unemployment and Under-employment in Rural India",
Economic & Political Weekly, Vol. XXIII, No. 29, July 16, 1988.

Pederson, O.P.:
"Innovative Diffusion in Urban System",
in Information System for Regional Development - A Seminar, Lund Studies in Geography, series B, No. 37, 1971. This is a seminar paper on diffusion process.

Pelz, Donald C.:
"Co-ordination and Communication in Agricultural Development",
Indian Journal of Public Administration, Vol. 12, No. 1, 1966.

Penouil, M:
"Growth Poles in Underdeveloped Regions and Countries",
Kuklinski, A. and Petralla, R. (ed.):
Growth Poles and Regional Policies
(The Hague: Mouton & Co.) 1972.

PEP:
Regional Development in the European Economic Community
(London: George Allen & Unwin) 1962. This work relates the experiencs of Southern Italy with regard to the critical minimum effort required for stimulating development.

Perloff, H.:
"Natural Resource Endowments and Regional Economic Growth",
in Friedman, J. and Alonso, W. (eds.):
Regional Development and Planning
(Cambridge, Mass: M.I.T. Press) 1964.

Perloff, H.S. :
"Education for Regional Planning in Less Developed Countries" in
Dunham, D.M. and Hilhoust, H.G.M. ;
Issues in Regional Planning
(The Hague: Institute of Social Studies and Mouton & Co.) 1971.

Perloff, H.S.; Dunn, E.S.; Lampard, E.E., and Muth, R.F.:
Regions, Resources and Growth
(Baltimore: Johns Hopkins University Press) 1960.

Perloff, Harvey S.:
Education for Planning City, State and Region
(Baltimore: The Johns Hopkins University Press) 1957.

Perloff, Harvey S.:
"Regional Planning in Less Developed Countries,"
in Maynard, M. Hryschmidt (ed.):
Regional Planning: Challenge and Prospect
(New York:Frederick A. Praeger) 1969.

Perroux, F.:
"Note Sur la Notion de la Pole de Croissance",
Economic Applique, Vol. 8, 1955, translated from original French, in Livingstone, I. (ed.):
Economic Policy for Development (Penguin) 1971.

Perroux, F.:
"Economic Space, Theory and Application",

Quarterly Journal of Economics, February,1955.

Perroux, Francois :
"The Dominance Effect and Economic Theory",
Social Research, Vol. 17, 1950.

Philbrick, A.K. :
"Principles of Areal Functional Organization in Regional Human Geography",
Economic Geography, Vol. 33, 1957.

Philbrick, A.K.:
"Areal Functional Organization in Regional Functional Geography", Economic Geography, Vol.33, 1957,pp. 380-402.

Pilot Research Project Cell :
Integrated Area Plan for Phirangipuran Block
(Hyderabad: Govt. of Andhra Pradesh) 1974.

Pilot Research Project in Growth Centre Cell :
Integrated Area Plan through Growth Centres for Schore Block (Bhopal: Government of Madhya Pradesh) 1974.

Pioro, Zygmut :
"A Sociological Concept of Polarised Development",
in Kuklinski, A. (ed.):
Growth Poles And Growth Centres
(The Hague: Mouton & Co.) 1972.

Plaff, Martin:
"Inter-Regional Transfers Through Environmental Policy",
in Misra, R.P.; Urs D.V. and Natraj V.K. (eds):
Regional Planning and National Development
(New-Delhi: Vikas Publishing House Pvt. Ltd.) 1978.

Podal, Richard L.:
Problems and Prospects of Administrative Decentralisation in Nepal
(Nepal : USAID) 1969.

Pokshiskevsky, V.V.:
"Population Geography: Problems of Planning Development of Economic Regions of Developing Countries,"
in
Economic and Socio-Cultural Dimensions of Regionalization,
Census of India, 1971, Centenary Monograph No.7(New Delhi: Government of India) 1971.

Pontifica academica scientarum :
The Econometric Approach to Development
(Amsterdam: North Holland) 1965.

Popov, I.V. and Komar, I.V. :
Certain Problems of Scientific Study of Economic Regionalisation of India for Purposes of Planning
(Calcutta : Indian Statistical Institute) 1962.

Popovic, B.:
Some Techniques for Regionalised Long Term Planning of the Size and Structure of Employment, Work Employment Programme Workshop on Quantitative Techniques for Employment Planning and their implication for Labour Market Analysis and Data Base, International Labour Organisation,
Geneva Working Paper No.10. (Geneva: International Labour Organisation) 1986.

Porter, David O. and Olson, Eugene O. :
"Some Critical Issues in Government Centralization and Decentralisation",
Public Administration Review, Vol. 36, No. 1, Jan-Feb 1976.

Poruit, K.:
Central Planning: Evaluation of

Variants,
(London: Pergamon) 1967.

Prabhakar, K.V. and Degaonkar, C.K. :
"District Planning : An Approach to Regional Development",
in Khan , M. Basheer Ahmed:
Regional Planning And Economic Development,
(Jaipur: Poiner Publishers) 1988.

Pradhan, B.B. :
"Integrated Rural Development Projects in Nepal: A Review"
ICIMOD, Occasional Paper No. 2, Kathmandu, 1985.

Prakash, Gian :
"District Administration and Urban Local Bodies",
Indian Journal of Public Administration, Vol. 12, No. 3, 1966.

Prakash, Om :
"Planning for Socio Economic Development and Environment Management in West District of Sikkim",
Journal of Rural Development, January 1987, Vol. 6, No. 1.

Prakash, Ved:
New Towns in India,
Monograph No.8 under the Programme in Comparative studies in Southern Asia, (Durham: Duke University) 1969.

Prantilla, B. (ed.):
The Process of Local Level Development Planning
(Nagoya, Japan: UNCRD) Mimeographed, 1981.

Prasad, Kamta :
Planning for Poverty Alleviation
(New-Delhi: Agricole Publishing Academy) 1985.

Prasad, Kamta :
Report on a Study of the Planning Process for Rural Development at the Block and District-Level,
(New-Delhi; Indian Institute of Public Administration) 1985.

Prasad, Kamta (ed.):
Planning and Its Implementation: Selected Articles
(Delhi: Indian Institute of Pubic Administration, Silver Jubilee Volume) 1984.

Prasad, Kamta :
Planning At the Grassroots,
(New Delhi: Sterling Publishers Pvt. Ltd.) 1988.

Prasad, Kamta :
"Area Planning Approach to Rural Development and the Problem of Consistency Between National And Local Planning",
in Johnson, G. and Maunder, A. (eds.):
Rural Change
(Farnborough: Gower & Co.) 1981.

Prasad, Kamta :
"Industry and Balanced Regional Development in India",
Indian Journal of Economics, 1970.

Prasad, B.:
District Planning in Bihar,
unpublished Ph.D. dissertation, Magadh University, Bodh Gaya, 1988.

Prasad, H. :
"Integrated Area Development and Its Appraisal in Dehradun",
Indian Journal of Regional Science, Vol. IV, No. 2, 1972.

Prasad, K.N.:
"Growth Centres in Theory and Practice",
Indian Journal of Economics, Vol. 1, No.1, December 1973.

Prasad, K.N.:
"Input-Output Table for Bihar",
Seminar on Quantitative Economics (Ahmedabad: Sardar

Patel Institute of Economic Research) 1971.

Prasad, Nageshwar :
Decentralisation in Yugoslavia and India
(Varanasi: Navachetna Prakashan) 1972.

Prasad, Narendra :
Relevance of Decentralised Planning in India
(Nawadah, Bihar : S.N. Sinha College, Warisaliganj : Deptt. of Economics) manuscript, 1988.

Prasad, Pradhan Harishankar :
"Sectoral Models of Growth : A Critique",
The Indian Economic Review, April 1966.

Prasad, R.C. :
Development And Democracy: The Grass-Roots Experience in India
(New Delhi: Rachna Prakashan) 1972.

Prasad, Ramayan :
Decentralised Planning in Bihar - A Case Study
(Bakhtiyarpur, Patna: R.L.S.Y. College, Deptt. of Economics) manuscript, 1988.

Prasad, Tribhuvan:
"Concepts, Significance and Limitations of District Planning",
Journal of the Lal Bahadur Shastri National Academy of Administration, Vol. 20, 1975. Prasad has suggested representation of the plan in terms of four categories, viz., District Schemes, schemes planned at State Levels but located at District, Inter-District Schemes, and Central Projects/Schemes, located at the District.

Prasad,P.H.:
Economic Benefits in the Kosi Command Area
(Patna:A.N.Sinha Institute of Social Studies) 1972 Mimeographed.

Preston, Andrade:
" A Graphical Approach to Settlement Planning for Integrated Area Development",
Urban and Rural Planning Thought, July 1974.

Prime Minister's Economic Advisory Panel Report:
on "Decentralisation of Development Planning and Implementation Systems in States",
(New Delhi: Government of India) 1983.

Purohit, M.C. :
"Identification of Backward Areas and Its Policy Imperatives: A Case Study of Rajasthan",
The Indian Journal of Public Administration, Vol. XXIII, No. 4, 1977.

Putnam, Steven H.:
An Empirical Model of Regional Growth,
(Peace Dale : Regional Science Research Institute) 1975.

Pyatt, F.G. and Roe, A.R.:
Social Accounting Methods for Development Policy and Planning : A Case Study of Sri Lanka
(London: Cambridge University Press)1979.

Pyatt, F.G.; Bharier, J.; Lindley, R.M.; Mabro, R.; and Sabolo, Y.:
Methodology for Macro-Economic Projections
(Geneva: ILO)1973 Mimeographed.

Pyatt, Graham and Thorbecke, Erik:
Planning Techniques For A better Future,
(New Delhi: Oxford & IBH Publishing Co.) 1984.

R

Raghavaiah, V. :
"District Planning and Administrative Case of Unified and Integrated Approach",
Indian Journal of Public Administration, Vol. XXIII, No. 4, 1967. This is a very good analysis of the utility of District as the Unit of Planning in the context of decentralization.

Raghaviah, Y. :
"Theory and Practice of Local Planning in India",
Journal of the National Academy of Administration, December 1968.

Raghvan, V.P. .
Planning in India: Lessons of Experience
(Kanhangad, Kerala:,Nehru Arts and Science College, Deptt. of Economics) manuscript, 1988.

Rahman, Atiur :
"Where Do the Poor Stand in the Process of Nation Building",
Paper read at a seminar on Nation Building in Bangladesh, Institute of International and Strategic Studies, Dhaka, Oct 13-14, 1985.

Rahman, Atiur Md. :(ed.):
Grass-Roots Participation and Self Reliance
(New Delhi: Oxford & IBH Publishing Co.) 1984.

Rahman, M.A.:
"Regional Allocation of Investment",
Quarterly Journal of Economics, Vol. LXXVII, 1963.

Rai, H.:
Co-ordination of Development Programmes at the District Level with Special Reference to Role of District Officer in Bihar",
The Indian Journal of Public Administration, Vol. XII, No. 1, Jan-March 1966.

Rai, Haridwar :
"Co-ordination of Development Programme at the District Level with Special Reference to the Role of the District Officer in Changing Administration",
Indian Journal of Public Administration, Vol. 12, No. 1, 1966.

Rai, S.C. :
Bhattrat Block, Gorakhpur District, U.P.: A Study in Service Centre Planning and Rural Development
(Varanasi: Banaras Hindu University) 1979.

Raj, Dev:
"Multi-Level Planning and Local Government Structure",
Indian Journal of Public Administration Special Number on Multi Level Planning Vol. XIX, No. 3, July-Sept. 1973,

Raj, K.N. :
"Planning from Below With Reference to District Development and State Planning - A Preliminary Note",
Economic and Political Weekly, (Annual Number 1971) Vol. VI, No. 30-32, September, 1971.

Raj, K.N.:
"Decentralization in Perspective",
Mainstream, Dec. 22, 1984.

Raj, K.N.:
"Growth and Stagnation in Indian Industrial Development",
Mainstream, 21st February 1976.

Raj, K.N.:
"Some Questions Concerning Growth, Transformation and Planning of Agriculture in

Developing Countries",
in Robinson,E.A.G. and Kidron, M. (eds.):
Economic Development of South Asia,
(London:Macmillan) 1970.

Raj, K.N.:
"Some Thoughts on Decentralization of Development Planning and Implementation",
Keynote paper presented to the Seminar on Decentralised Planning and Implementation, at the Institute for Social and Economic Change, Bangalore, 1984.

Rajaram, M.G. :
"Backward Areas: A Strategy for Development",
Economic Times, December 31st, 1972.

Ramachandran, N. :
Village Clusters and Rural Development
(New Delhi: Concept Publishing Co.) 1980.

Ramesh, K.S.:
"Application of Certain Mathematical Techniques in Locating Growth Impulses and Services Centres",
Behavioural Sciences and Community Development, Special Number on Rural Growth Centres, Vol. 6, March 1972.

Rangarajan, C.; Sah, R.K. and Reddy, K.S. :
"Impact of Hike in Prices of Coal and Petroleum Products in other Sectors of the Economy - An Application of Input-Output Techniques", Arth Vijnana, Vol. 23, No. 2, 1981.

Rao Prakash, V.L.S. :
Readings in Planning and Development,
(Madras: Madras University, Department of Geography) 1976.

Rao, C.H. Hanumantha and Rangaswamy, P.:
"Efficiency of Investments in IRDP : A study of Uttar Pradesh",
Economic and Political Weekly, June 25, 1988.

Rao, C.R., (ed.):
Essays in Econometrics and Planning
(London: Pergamon) 1965.

Rao, D. Vasudeva :
"Identification of Potential Growth Centres - An Alternative Method",
Indian Journal of Regional Science, Vol. IX, No. 1, 1977.

Rao, D. Vasudeva :
"Population Threshold for Location of Industrial Agglomeration : A study in Andhra Pradesh",
Indian Journal of Regional Science, Vol VII, No. 2, 1975.

Rao, Hanumantha, C.H.:
"Factor Endowments, Technology and Farm Employment",
Economic and Political Weekly, 26th September 1976.

Rao, Hemlata:
" Identification of Backward Regions and the Trends in Regional Disparities in India",
Artha Vijnana, Vol 19, No. 2, June 1977.

Rao, K. Nageswara and Rao, G. Bhaskar:
District-Level Planning and Drought Mitigation in Anantapur District
(Anantapur, Andhra Pradesh: Sri Krishnadevaraya University) manuscript, 1988.

Rao, K.R.M.:
"Growth From the Grass Roots",
Democratic World, Vol. 16, No. 28, 10th July, 1977.

Rao, K.V. Narayan:
"Education and Employment

Policy Towards Scheduled Tribes in India",
in NICD,
Perspectives on Tribal Development and Administration,
(Hyderabad: National Institute of Community Development) 1975.

Rao, K.V. Narayana; Shastri, K.R.; and Vithal C.P. :
"Decentralisation of Planning Process",
Journal of Rural Development No. 3, Vol. 6, 1987.

Rao, M.L. Kantha et. al. :
Decentralised Planning - A Case Study of Rayalseema in Andhra Pradesh,
(Anantapur, Andhra Pradesh: SriKrishnadevaraya University, Department of Economics) manuscript, 1988.

Rao, P. Prabhakar and Sundaram, K.V.:
Regional Imbalances in India: Some Policy Issues and Problems,
(New Delhi: Town and Country Planning Organisation) 1971, Mimeographed. Subsequently published in the Indian Journal of Regional Science, Vol. V, No. 1, 1973.

Rao, S.K. :
"A Note On Measuring Economic Distances Between Regions",
Economic & Political Weekly, Vol. VIII, No. 17, April 1973.

Rao, V. Nageswara:
"Integrated Area Development with Reference to the District Planning",
Indian Journal of Agricultural Planning, October-December 1973.

Rao, V.K.R.V. :
Issues and Problems of Development of Tumkur
(Bangalore: Institute for Social and Economic Change) 1978.

Rao, V.K.R.V. :
"District Planning Concept Getting to the Grassroots",
Times of India, May 23rd, 1973. Rao talks about planning at Districts at two levels: "District Level" dealing with matters like areawise sectoral allocation, distribution of employment oriented schemes and solving of organizational problems; "Area Level" dealing with matters like conservation of natural resources, production targets etc..

Rao, V.K.R.V. :
"Some Neglected Factors in Integrated Rural Development",
Address delivered on the occasion of the XVI Convocation of the Indian Agricultural Research Institute, New-Delhi, 1977.

Rao, V.K.R.V.:
Planing Unit Area for Integrated Rural Development-An Exercise,
(New-Delhi: Ashish Publishing House)1980.

Rao, V.K.R.V.:
"An Integrated Approach to Rural Development",
Yojana, 15th to 28th February 1977.

Rao, V.K.R.V.:
"District Planning Concept: Getting to the Grass Roots", Co-operative News Digest, Vol. 25, No. 1, 1974.

Rao, V.L.S. Prakasa and Bhat L.S.:
"A Regional Framework for Resource Development In India",
Bombay Geographical Magazine, Vol. 10, 1962. This is in fact the Regional Survey Unit's (of Planning Commission) tentative regional framework for resource develpment of India. The study identified 11 major regions and 51 sub-regions, with

qualitative description of their regional characteristics and regional norms of development. Prakasa Rao and Bhat had developed a fund of ideas for further research.

Rao, V.L.S. Prakasa:
Development Strategy for An Agricultural Region - A Case Study of Muzaffarnagar District U.P.
(Mysore: Institute of Development Studies)

Rao, V.L.S. Prakasa:
Regional Planning
(Bombay: Asia Publication House and Calcutta : Statistical Publication Society) 1963.

Rao, V.L.S. Prakasa; Mazumdar, H.K.; Thimmaiah, G. and Seshaiah, S. (eds.):
Working Paper on District Planning Officers' Programme ISEC staff Paper No. 7.
(Bangalore: Institute of social & Economic Change) 1973. A paper which favours District as the appropriate unit for decentralized Planning.

Rao, V.L.S. Prakasa :
Bhongiri - A Case Study of Market Towns, Census of India Monograph, No. 12,
(New-Delhi: Registrar General) 1961.

Rao, V.L.S.Prakasa and Bhat, L.S.:
Regional Planning in the Mysore State-The need for Readjustment of District Boundaries,
(New Delhi: Indian Statsitical Institute)1960.

Rao, V.M. :
Rural Development and The Village Perspectives for
(New-Delhi: Sterling Publishers) 1980.

Rao, V.M. :
"Decentralised Planning : Priority Economic Issues",
Economic & Political Weakly, 24th June 1989.

Rao, V.M. :
"Spatial Aspects of Integrated Rural Development",
in Thimmaiah, G. (ed.):
Studies in Rural Development
(Allahabad: Chugh Publications)

Rao, V.M. and Erappa, S. :
"IRDP and Rural Diversification : A Case Study in Karnataka",
Economic and Political Weekly, December 27th, 1987 (Review of Agriculture).

Rao, V.M.:
Interventions for the Poor, Critical Dimensions, Potentialities and Limitations,
(Bangalore: Institute for Social and Economic Change) 1988, mimeographed.

Rao, V.M.:
"Changing Village Structure: Impact of Rural Development Programme",
Economic and Political Weekly (Review of Agriculture) 28th March 1987.

Rao, V.M.:
"Sustained Development Through People: The Need For Political Activisation",
July-September 1988, Vikalpa, Journal of the I.I.M. Ahmedabad.

Rastogi, R.K. :
Decentralised Planning in India
(Moradabad: Hindu College, Deptt. of Economics) manuscript, 1988.

Rath, Binayak:
Decentralised Planning in India: Is it the Appropriate Means to Achieve on Planned Goal of Equity and Social Justice
(Kanpur: Indian Institute of Technology, Deptt. of Humanities and Social Sciences) Manuscript, 1988.

Rathod, S.G.; Basaliah, S. and Hirenath K.C.:
A Full Employment Plan For Muddebihal Taluk Bijapur District
(Bangalore: University of Bangalore) 1978.

Ray, Amal:
"Organizational Aspects of Rural Development: Taluk-Level Administration in an Indian State,
(Calcutta: World Press) 1976.

Ray, Amal:
"Agrarian Structure and Issues in Organising Small Farmer Development",
The Indian Journal of Public Administration, Vol. XXIII, No. 4, 1977.

Rayappa, P.H. and Grover, D. :
"Employent Planning for Scheduled Castes and Scheduled Tribes"
Economic and Political Weekly, Vol. XIV, No. 24, 1979.

Raza, Moonis (ed.):
Renewable Resources for Regional Development: The Indian and the Soviet Experience
(New Delhi: Concept Publishing Co.) 1988.

Raza, Moonis:
Regional Development
(New Delhi: Heritage Publishers) 1988.

Recine, J.:
Urban Strategies in Rural Development: The State, The Space and The Dynamics of Change in a Tamil District,
(Madras: Institute of Development Studies) Working Paper No. 62, December 1985.

Reddy, E. Sudhakar and Nimbur, B.N.:
"Decentralized Planning for India: Some Paradigmic Issues",
Journal of Rural Development, Vol. 8, No. 1, 1989.

Reddy, V.S.; Rao, R.J. and Sarma, A.V.K.:
"Packing of Areas in Regional Studies",
Behavioural Sciences and Community Development, Vol. 6, 1972.

Reddy, Y. Venugopal :
"A Note on Regionlisation and Regional Development With special Reference to Multi-level Plan Process in India",
Indian Journal of Regional Science, Vol. VI, No. 1, 1974.

Reddy, Y. Venugopal:
Multi-Level Planning in India
(Vikas Publishing House : New-Delhi) 1979. This gives a good idea about plan formulation at various levels.

Reddy, Y. Venugopal:
Multi-Level Planning In India: Emerging Issues,
Lecture delivered at the National Institute of Planning and Economic Policy, Karl Marx University of Economics, Budapest, June 1st & 2nd, 1988.

Reddy, Y. Venugopal:
State Market and Planning in the Ninties,
Paper delivered at Centre for Economic And Social Studies, Hyderabad (date not known) but received as Manuscript on 25/11/89.

Reddy, Y.Venugopal and Kosalram, K. (eds):
Multi-level Planning in India: Processes and Perceptions
(Hyderabad: Centre for Economic and Social Studies, and Booklinks Corporation)1988.
SEE ALSO UNDER VENUGOPAL

Reilly, W.J.:
The Law of Retail Gravitation
(New York)1931.

Reilly, W.J.:
"Method for the Study of Retail Relationships," Bulletin No. 2944.
University of Texas Buletin, No.2944 (1929).

Renukarya, C.K. :
"Decentralised Planning in Gandhian Perspective", in Conference Volume,
71st Conference Indian Economic Association, Calcutta, December 1988.

Richardson, H.W. :
"Empirical Aspects of Regional Growth in the United States", Annals of Regional Science 1974, pp. 8-23.

Richardson H.W.:
Elements of Regional Economics
(Harmondsworth Penguin Modern Economic Texts) 1973.

Richardson, H.W. (ed):
Regional Economics: A Reader,
(London & Basingstoke: Macmillan & Co., St. Martin's Press)1970.

Richardson, H.W. :
"The Relevance and Applicability of Regional Economics to Developing Countries",
Regional Development Dialogue, Vol. 1, No. 1, 1980, (U.N. Centre for Regional Development, Nagoya, Japan)

Richardson, H.W.:
A Teaching Manual for Community Economic Development
(Davis: University of California, Department of Agricultural Economics) 1986.

Richardson, H.W.:
Regional Economics
(London: Weidenfeld & Nicholson) 1969.

Richardson, H.W.:
Regional Growth Theory,
(London: The Macmillan Press Pvt. Ltd.) 1973.

Richardson, H.W.:
Regional and Urban Economics
(London: Penguin)1979.

Rief, Benjamin:
Models in Urban and Regional Planning
(London: Leonard Hill) 1973.

Robinson, J.N. :
Planning and Forecasting Techniques: An Introduction to Macro-economic Applications
(London: Weidenfeld and Nicolson) 1972.

Rociznewski, M. :
"Problems of Regional Development in Third World Countries: Analysis Criteria of Peripheral Areas",
Report of the Committee on Spatial Economy and Regional Development, Warsaw, 1972.

Rociznewski, M. :
"Socio-Economic Aspects of Space Organization and Regional Development in the Third World Countries",
Culture & Society, No. 1, 1974, Warsaw.

Rodell, Michael J.:
"Growth Centres - Two Recent Contributions : Review Article",
Economic Development & Cultural Change, Vol. 25, 1975.

Rodgers, A.:
" Migration and Industrial Development: The Southern Italian Experience",
Economic Geography, Vol. 46, No. 2, April 1970.

Rodwin, L. et. al. (eds.):
Planning Regional Development
(Cambridge, Mass. : M.I.T. Press) 1969. A competent treatment of the problems and apportunities of decentralised Planning, based on the experiences of Ciudad Guayana.

Rondinelli, D.A. :
Secondary Cities in Developing

Countries : Policies for Diffusing Urbanisation,
(Sage: London and Beverly Hills) 1983.

Rondinelli, D.A. :
"Government Decentralisation in Comparative Perspective : Theory and Practice in Developing Countries",
International Review of Administrative Sciences, Vol. XLVII, No. 2, 1981.

Rondinelli, D.A. :
"Implementing Decentralised Programmes in Asia : A Comparative Analysis",
Public Administration and Development, Vol. 3, 1983, pp. 181-208.

Rondinelli, D.A. and Evans, H.:
"Integrated Regional Development Planning: Linking Urban Centres and Rural Areas in Bolivia",
World Development, Vol. 11, No. 1, 1983.

Rondinelli, D.A. and Ruddle, K. :
Urbanization and Rural Development: A Spatial Policy for Equitable Growth
(New-York: Praeger) 1978.

Rondinelli, D.A.:
"Decentralisation and Development -Policy Implementations in Developing Countries",
World Bank Staff Papers, No. 581, 1983.

Rondinelli, D.A.:
"National Investment Planning and Equity Policy in Developing Countries: The Challenge of Decentralised Administration",
Policy Sciences, Vol. 10, No. 1, 1978.

Rondinelli, D.A.; Nellis, J.R.; Cheema, G.S.:
"Decentralisation in Developing Countries : A Review of Recent Experience",
World Bank Staff Working Papers No. 581, (Washington: World Bank) 1984.

Rondinelli, Dennis A. :
Spatial Analysis for Regional Development : A Case Study in the Bicol River Basin of the Philippines, Resource systems Theory and Methodological Series, No. 2.
(Tokyo : United Nations University) 1980.

Rosciszewski, M.:
"Problems of Spatial Structure in the third World Countries"
paper read at the Polish Russian Geographical seminar on Developing Countries, November 1973 at Warsaw (Mimeographed).

Rosenstein-Rodan, Paul (ed.):
Capital Formation and Economic Development,
(London: Allen & Unwin) 1964.

Ross, Murray G. :
Community Organization: Theory and Principles
(New York: Harper & Row) 1955.

Rossi, Doria M.:
"Analysis of Agricultural Structure for Regional Planning", in Isard, W. and Cumberland, J.H. (ed.): Regional Economic Planning-Techniques of Analysis
(Paris: OECD) 1961.

Roupp, Phillip (ed.):
Approaches to Community Development, papers of a symposium Introductory to Problems and Methods of Village Welfare in Underdeveloped Areas
(Bandung: W. Van House Ltd.) 1953.

Routray, J.K. and Patnaik, M. :
"Transformation of Rural Habitat: Concept and Approaches",
Kurukshetra, Vol. 30, No. 8, 1982

Routray, J.K.L:
"Approaches to Backward District Planning: Case Study of Boudh-Khandhmal District in Orissa",
Indian Journal of Regional Science, Vol.XVI, No.1, 1984.

Roy Barman, B.K.:
"Social Process in the Wake of Economic Change of a Backward Region - A Case Study",
Paper presented to the Seminar on Planning for Social change, organised by Council for Social Development, New-Delhi, 1969.

Roy Barman, B.K.:
"Towards an Integrated Regional Frame",
in
Economic and Socio-Cultural Dimension of Regionalisation,
(Census of India, 1971, Centenary Monograph No. 7, Government of India) 1971.

Roy, B.K. :
"Potentiality of Evirons of Growth Centres in India", in Lahiri T.B. : Balanced Regional Development: Concepts, Strategies and Case Studies,
(Calcutta: Oxford & IBH) 1972.

Roy, Durgadas:
Some Thoughts on Decentralisation of Development Planning and Its Implementation,
(Calcutta: Rabindra Bharati University, Deptt. of Economics) manuscript, 1988.

Roy, G.G.:
"A Multiple Criteria Appoach to Regional Planning",
Environmental Planning, Vol 6, 1974.

Roy, Pradipto and Patil B.R.:
Manual For Block Level Planning,
(Delhi: Macmillan) 1977.

Roy, Pradipto et. al. :
Patterns of Agricultural Diffusion in Rural India
(Hyderabad : National Institute of Community Development) 1968.

Roy, Pradipto:
"Micro-Regional Planning for Management of Agriculture",
Social Change, Journal of the Council for Social Development, March-June 1973.

Roy, Prasun Kumar:
"Agricultural Processing Activity - A Solution to Regional Disparity in India", Manuscript
(Muzzaffarpur: Deptt. of Economics, Bihar University) 1989.

Roy, Prodipto and Andrade Preston:
Pilot Projects for Integrated Area Development,
(Delhi : Council for Social Development and Ford Foundation) 1969.

Roy, Turner (ed.):
India's Urban Future
(Berkeley: University of California Press) 1962.

Rudra, Asok :
"L'echee de la Planification decentralisee en Inde", in Novelles de l' Econdevelopment
(Paris: Maison des Sciences de l'Homme) No. 35, 1985.

Rudra, Asok:
Indian Plan Models
(New Delhi: Allied Publishers Pvt. Ltd.)1975.

Rudra, Asok :
"Decentralized Long Term Planning : A Frame",
Indian Economic Review, April 1966.

Rudra, Asok:
"A Model Maker's Model",
Economic and Political Weekly,February 1972.

Rudramoorthy, B. :
Extension in Planned Social Change

(New Delhi: Allied Publishers) 1964.

Rural Development Agency:
A Prototype Plan for Raiganj Upazila
(Bogra: RDA)1985.

Ruston, Gerard; Goodchild, M.F. and Ostresh, L.M. (eds.):
Computer Programmes for Location Allocation Problem,
(Ames: Department of Geography, University of Iowa) 1973.

Ruttan, V.W.:
"Integrated Rural Development Programs : A Skeptical Perspective", International Development Review, No.4, 1975.

Ryan, W.J.L.:
Price Theory
(London: Macmillan) 1958. This contains a classic treatment of Production functions but somewhat specialised.

S

Sachs, Ignacy:
Development and Planning,
(Cambridge: Cambridge University Press) 1987. Translated to English from French Original by Peter Fawcett. This is a good discussion that brings out the importance of local level participation in development.

Sardar Patel Institute of Economic and Social Research :
Gujarat Economy in 2001 A.D.: A Study in Perspective, 1981., distributed by Allied Publishers, New-Delhi.

Sadasyuk, Galina V.:
"Urbanisation and the Spatial Structure of Indian Economy", in Economic and Socio-Cultural Dimensions of Regionalisation,
(Census of India 1971, Centenary Monograph) 1971.

Sadhu, Urmila:
"Identification of Backward Regions - A Brief Critical Review",
Margin, New Delhi, Vol. 9, No. 2, 1977.

Sain, K. and Bagchi, B. :
"New Strategy of Comprehensive Area Development Programmes in West-Bengal: An Analytical Study",
Indian Journal of Agricultural Economics, October-December, No. 4, 1973.

Saini, Nayan S. :
"Rural-Urban Communities in the Coastal Region of India, Problems and a Concept of Development",
Journal of the Institute of Town Planners, New-Delhi, March 1970.

Saini, Nayan S.:
"District Planning For Service Centres, A Technique",
Voluntary Action, Vol. 16, No. 1, January-February 1974.

Sakashita, Noboru:
Production Function, Demand Function and Location Theory:
(Peace Dale, Virginia: Regional Science Research Institute) Discussion Paper No. 15, June 1967.

Samonte, Abelardo G.:
"Decentralisation and Development : Some Basic Issues",
Philippine Journal of Public Administration, Vol. XI, No. 2, 1967.

Sankaranarayana, M.:
"Role of the District Officer in Changing Administration",
Indian Journal of Public Adminsitration, Vol. 12, No. 4, 1966.

Sankaranarayanan, M.:
"Role of the District Officer in Changing Administration",
The Indian Journal of Public Administration, Vol. XII, No. 4, Oct-Dec. 1966.

Santhanam, M.L.; Sastry, C. Yoganand; and Vijayakumar, S.:
"People's Participation - Some Psychological Dimensions",
Journal of Rural Development, Vol. III No. 4, July 1984.

Sanwal, M.:
Computer Applications in District Administration
(Nainital: Administrative Training Institute) 1986.

Sanwal, Mukul:
"The Implementation of Decentralization : A Case Study of District Planning in Agra District; Uttar Pradesh, India",
Public Administration And Development, Vol. 7, 1987.

Sanwal, R.D.:
Social Stratification in Rural Kumaon
(Delhi: Oxford University Press) 1976.

Sapru, R.K.:
Management and Planning of Rural Development,
(New Delhi: Ashish Publishing House) 1989.

Sarkar, A.K.:
"Role of Market Centres and Regulated Marketing in the Development Process",
in NCAER:Market Towns and Spatial Development (New-Delhi: NCAER) 1972.

Sarkar, Subhash Chandra:
"Ideological-Political Parameter of District Planning",
Modern Review, February, 1974.

Sarma, P.V. and Mohan Kumar, K.V.:
"Planning for Integrated Area Development - A Case Study of Konaseema Region of Andhra Pradesh",
in Pandey, D.C. and Tiwari, P.C.:
Dimensions of Development Planning,
(New Delhi: Criterion Publications) 1989.

Sarma, P.V. and Mohan Kumar, K.V.:
"Planning for Integrated Area Development - A Case Study of Huzvid Block, Krishna District, Andhra Pradesh",
in Area Planning by Naidu, K. Munidoraswami, 1984.

Sarma, P.V. and Ramana, K.V.:
"Disparities in Development - A Block Level Study of Telangana Region",
Indian Journal of Regional Science, Vol. XI, No. 1, 1979.

Sarma, P.V. and Sarveswara Rao, B.:
"Regionalisation for Growth and Balance in the Agricultural Sector",
Indian Journal of Regional Science, Vol. XII, No. 1, 1980.

Sarma, R.P.:
Planning Model for a Tribal District
(Berhampur: Berhampur University, Department of Economics) manuscript, 1988.

Sarupia, Shantilal:
"Approach to Regional Development in India",
in Peter Meyer-Dohm (ed.):
Economic and Social Aspects of Indian Development
(Tubingen-Basel : Horst Endmann Verlag, and Bombay : Shakuntala Publishing House) 1975.

Sarveswara Rao, B.:
A Case Study of Rural Poverty in

a Developed District
(Waltair: Agro-Economic Research Centre, Andhra University) 1976.

Sastry, M.V.R.:
"Integration of National and Regional Economic Models in the United States",
The Indian Economic Journal, Vol. 16, No. 1, 1965.

Sathe, M.D. :
Regional Planning An Areal Exercise,
(Poona: S.G. Saraswat Publishers) 1973.

Satya Sundaram, I.:
"District Planning for Social Justice",
Mainstream, Vol. 18, No. 7, October 1979.

Sau, Ranjit :
"Multi-Level Planning",
Economic and Political Weekly, Vol. VI, 1971.

Sau, Ranjit:
"The New Economics",
Economic And Political Weekly, Special Number, 1972.

Saxena, A.P. :
Some Common Problems in Project Formulation
(New-Delhi: Indian Institute of Public Administration) 1970, mimeographed.

Saxena, A.P. :
"Backward Area Development Issues in Administrative Planning",
The Indian Journal of Public Administration, Vol. XXIII, No. 3, July-Sept. 1977.

Saxena, D.K. :
"Planning from Below in Rajasthan",
Political Science Review, Vol. 1, No. 2, 1962.

Saxena, P.S. :
Strategy for Decentralised Planning in India
(Moradabad: Hindu College, Department of Economics) manuscript 1988.

Schmenner, R. :
"How Corporations Select Communities for New Manufacturing Plants",
in Siegfried, J. (ed.):
Firm Size, Market Structure and Social Performance,
(Washington D.C. : Govt. Printing Office) 1980.

Schneider, Jerry B. and Symons, John G.:
Regional Health Facility System Planning: An Access Opportunity Approach,
(Peace Dale, Virginia: Regional Science Research Institute) Discussion Paper No. 48, July 1971.

Schwartzberg, I.E.:
Occupational Structure and Level of Economic Development in India: A Regional Analysis , Census of India 1961, Monograph No. 4.
(New Delhi: Government of India) 1969.

Scott, Allen J. :
A Statistical Analysis of the Functional and Spatial Structure of the London Region
(Peace Dale, Virginia: Regional Science Research Institute) Discussion Paper No. 21, January 1968.

Scott, Peter:
"The Hierarchy of Central Places in Tasmania",
The Australian Geographer, Vol. 9. 1964. .

Sebastian, M. :
"Regional Planning in Tamilnadu",
in Naidu, Munirathna K. (ed.):
Area Planning for Regional Development

(New Delhi: Inter-India Publishers) 1984.

Secomski, K. :
Goods in Regional Policies and Objectives in Regional Planning: Contributions to the Discussion Based on Polish Experience, Committee for Space, Economy and Regional Planning
(Warsaw: Polish Academy of Sciences) 1969.

Seetharam, G.N.:
"Multi-Level Planning: Issues in Decentralization",
in Bhadouria B.P.S. (ed.):
Decentralised Planning for Development in India,
(Delhi: Commonwealth Publishers) 1988.

Sen Gupta, J.K., and Fox, K.:
Economic Analysis and Operations Research: Optimisation Techniques in Quantitative Economic Models
(Amsterdam: North Holland) 1969.

Sen Gupta, N.:
Destitude and Development: A Study of the Bawri Community in Bokaro Steel Region
(Patna: A.N. Sinha Institute of Social Studies) 1976..

Sen Gupta, P. and Sdasyuk, Galina V.:
Economic Regionalisation of India: Problems and Approaches,
(New Delhi: Census of India) Monograph series No. 8, Vol I, 1968. This book gives a division into regions of the economy on the basis of resources potentials and the existing stock of human, infrastructural and capital resources. An interesting work.

Sen Gupta, P.:
"Framework of Economic Regions",
in
Economic Regionalization of India; Problems and Approaches,
(Census of India 1961), Monograph Series Vol. I, No. 8.

Sen Gupta, P.:
"The Methodology of Delineating Economic Planning Regions of Different Orders",
Paper presented to Summer School in Applied Geography, Banaras Hindu University, November 1965.

Sen Gupta, P.:
"Planning Regions for Resource Development in India",
Paper presented to the XX International Geographical Congress, New Delhi, 1964.

Sen Gupta, P.:
"The Principles and Techniques of Regional Planning",
The Geographer, Vol. XIV, 1967.

Sen, A.K. :
Choice of Techniques, 3rd Edition,
(Oxford: Basil Blackwell) 1968.

Sen, A.K. :
"Control Areas And Accounting Prices : An Approach to Economic Evolution",
Economic Journal, Vol. 82, March 1972, Supplement.

Sen, Amartya :
"Strategies of Economic Development: Feasibility Constraints and Planning",
in Robinson, E.A.G. and Kindron, Michael (eds.):
Economic Development in South Asia
(London: MacMillan) 1970.

Sen, Lalit K.:
"Role of Area Development in Multi-Level Planning",
Indian Journal of Public Administration, No. 3, Vol. 19, 1973. Sen makes the important point that there is a definite pattern in the dispersal of concentration of activities in space.

Sen, Lalit K.:
" An Exercise in Micro-Level Planning for a Rural Taluka - The Miryalguda Experience",
Urban and Rural Planning Thought, April 1972.

Sen, Lalit; Wanmali, Sudhir; Bose, Saradindu; Mishra, Girish and Ramesh, K.S. (eds.):
Planning Rural Growth Centres for Integrated Area Development
(Hyderabad: National Institute of Community Development) 1971. A pioneering work on the application of Growth Centre concept in Indian planning process.

Sen, A.C. et. al. (eds.) :
Comprehensive Area Development : Proceedings and Papers of a Workshop on District Mirzapur, February 19th to Feb. 22,
(New Delhi: Association for Voluntary Agencies for Rural Development) 1976.

Sen, Lalit K. (ed.):
Readings in Micro Level Planning and Rural Growth Centres
(Hyderabad: National Institute of Community Development) 1972.

Sen, Lalit K. :
Integrated Area Development Concepts and Methods,
(New-Delhi: Department of Personnel, Cabinet Secretariate Govt. of India) 1972.

Sen, Lalit K. :
"A New Strategy for Community Development Planning for Integrated Area Development and Rural Growth Centres",
in Community Development & Panchayati Raj Digest, C.D. Week Special Number, Vol. 2, No. 2, October 1970.

Sen, Lalit K. :
"Rural Growth Centres And Unemployment",
Kurukshetra, 1972.

Sen, Lalit K. :
"The Growth Centre and Its Application to Development Planning,
ASCI Journal of Management, Hyderabad, 1971.

Sen, Lalit K. and Misra, G.K, :
Regional Planning for Rural Electrification: A Study of Suraypet Taluk Nalgonda District, Andhra Pradesh
(Hyderabad: National Institute of Community Development) 1974.

Sen, Lalit K. and Thaha, A.L.:
Regional Planning for a Hill Area - Case Study of a Tehsil in Pauri Garhwal District
(Hyderabad: National Institute of Community Development, Now NIRD) 1974.

Sen, Lalit K. et. al.:
Growth Centres in Raichur: An Integrated Area Development for a District in Karnataka
(Hyderabad: National Institute for Community Development) 1974.

Sen, Lalit K. et. al.:
People's Image of Community Development and Panchayati Raj
(Hyderabad: National Institute of Community Development) 1967.

Sen, Lalit K. and Roy, Pradipto :
Awareness of Community Development in Village India,
(Hyderabad: National Insitutute of Community Development) 1967.

Sen, Lalit K.:
"Growth Centres and Rural Unemployment",
Community Development and Panchyati Raj Digest, C.D. Week Special Number, No. 3, No. 2, 1971.

Sen, Lalit K. :
"The Role of Rural Electrification Corporation in the Development of Backward Areas",
The Indian Journal of Public Administratio, Vol XXIII, No. 4, 1977.

Sen, Raj Kumar and Roy, K.C. :
"Decentralised Planning and Primary Health Care in LDCs, with Reference to India", in
Conterence Volume, Indian Economic Association, Calcutta, December 1988, Part III, pp. 63-70.

Sengupta, P. (Miss) Dr.:
"Territorial Association of National Resources with Natural Regions",
in Sen Gupta, P. and Sadasyuk, G.:
Economic Regionalization of India : Problems and Approaches,
(Census of India 1961: Monograph Series) Vol. I, No. 8.

Seshadri, K :
"Co-ordination of Development Programmes at the Block-Level", Indian Journal of Public Administration, Vol. 12, No. 1, 1966.

Sethi, Harsh :
"A Methodological Note on Area Development Programming : Some Reflections on Western Rajasthan",
Development Policy and Administrative Review, January-June 1975, pp. 65-71.

Setty, E. D. :
"People's Participation in Rural Development : A Critical Analysis",
The Indian Journal of Social Work, Vol. XLVI, No. 1, April 1985.

Shah, Anil C. and Patel, V.G.:
"An Integrated Strategy for Backward Districts, Industrial Development",
Artha Vikas, Vol IX.

Shah, M. :
Rural Development: Planning and Reforms,
(New Delhi: Abhinav Publications) 1977.

Shah, S.M. :
"Growth Centres for Economic Development",
Eastern Economist, New-Delhi September 1972, pp. 604-606.

Shah, S.M. :
"Growth Centres for Rural Development and Modernization in India",
in Kuklinski, A. (ed.): Readings in Regional Planning(Geneva: UNRISD).

Shah, S.M. :
"Growth Centres as a Strategy of Rural Development: Indian Experience",
Economic Development & Cultural Change, Vol. 22, 1974.

Shah, V. :
Planning for Talala Block - A Study in Micro-Level Planning
(Ahmedabad: Gujarat Institute of Area Planning) 1974.

Sharma, A.N.:
Spatial Approach for District Planning - A Case Study of Karnal District,
(New-Delhi: Concept Publishing House) 1980.

Sharma, B.D. :
"Administration for Tribal Development",
The Indian Journal of Public Administration Vol. XXIII, No. 4, 1977.

Sharma, B.D. :
"Planning from Below with Special Reference to Tribal Areas",
Community Development and Panchayati Raj Digest, July 1976, p. 12-19.

Sharma, K.L.:
"Spatial Disparities in Rajasthan: A Comparative Study of Levels of Developments Between Two Points of Time",
Indian Journal of Regional Science, Vol. 10, No. 1, 1975.

Sharma, L.R. :
"Development Problems of a Hill Region: With Special Reference to Himachal Pradesh",
AICC Economic Review, September, 15th, 1966, pp. 33-35.

Sharma, P.N. :
"Backward Region: A Case Study - Identification and Location of Growth Centres for Development",
Economic Times, September 6th, 1973, p.5.

Sharma, P.N. and Katiyar, P.C. :
"Identifying Under-Developed Districts in Uttar Pradesh", Indian Journal of Regional Science, Vol. 6, No. 1, 1971.

Sharma, P.N. and Shastri, C.:
Social Planning- Concepts and Techniques,
(Lucknow: Print House) 1984.

Sharma, P.N.:
"Operationalising the Concept of Decentralised District Planning",
in Dubey, K.N.:
Planning and Development in India
(New Delhi: Ashish Publishing House) 1990.

Sharma, P.S. :
Agricultural Regionalisation of India,
(New Delhi: Heights Publishers) 1973.

Sharma, P.V. :
"Regionalisation for Agricultural Development in Andhra Pradesh",
Indian Journal of Regional Science, Vol. VI, No: 2, 1974.

Sharma, Parameswar :
"The Role of the Community Development Block in Multi-Level Planning: Some Lessons from the Restructuring of the Panchayat System in Assam",
Indian Journal of Regional Science, Vol. XI, No. 1, 1979.

Sharma, R.C. :
Regional Planning for Social Development: Concepts, Approaches and Application
(New Delhi: Criterion Publications) 1989.

Sharma, Ramesh C.:
" A Conceptual Chronological and Attributive Treatment to the Approach to Integrated Area Development",
Indian Journal of Regional Science, Vol. XII, No. 2, 1980.

Sharma, S.C. :
Landuse Survey in Terai Tract of Eastern U.P.
(New-Delhi: Concept Publishing Co.) in press.

Sharma, S.K. :
"Democratic Decentralisation and Development of Backward Areas",
The Indian Journal of Public Administration, Vol. XXIII, No. 4, 1977.

Sharma, S.K. and Malhotra, S.L. :
Integrated Rural Development: Approach, Strategy and Perspective
(New-Delhi: Abhinav Publications) 1977.

Sharma, S.K. and Roy, Pradipto:
Awareness of Community Development in Village India
(Hyderabad: National Institute of Community Development) 1966.

Sharwan, Kumar :
"Strategy for Backward Area Development",
Economic Times, April 17th, 1974.

Shastri, Siddharth :
District Planning - The Rajasthan

Experience (Banasthali Vidyapith: Department of Economics), manuscript 1988.

Shetty, S.L.:
"Structural Regression in the Indian Economy since the Mid-Sixties", Economic and Political Weekly, Annual Number, February 1978.

Shilaber, Caroline :
References on City and Regional Planning (Cambridge, Mass : M.I.T. Press) TechnologyMonographs, Library Series No. 2 1959.

Shimokobe, A.:
"Concept and Methodology of Regional Development", Developing Economics, Vol. 8, 1970. pp. 496-510.

Shiva, Vandana and Bandopadhyay, J.:
"Environmental Conflicts and Public Interest Science", Economic and Political Weekly, January 11th , 1986. Shows how lack of local participation led to agitation in Doon Valley against quarrying of Stone.

Shiwalkar, R.S. :
The Twin Problems of Rural Development and Agricultural Production (Allahabad: Kitab Mahal) 1968.

Shrestha, Surendra Bahadur :
"Development through Decentralisation", in Srestha, T.N.: (ed.): District Administration in Nepal (Lalitpur, Nepal: Nepal Administrative Staff College) 1985.

Shridharan, L. :
Block Level Planning in Uttar Pradesh (Pune : Centre for Development Studies and Activities) 1982.

Shridharan, L. :
"Decentralisation and District Planning: Some Issues", Economic Times, 9th August 1986.

Shridharan, L. :
"District Planning - A Review", Indian Journal of Regional Science, Vol. XIX, No. 1, 1987.

Shrivastava, V.K. :
"Central Place Theory in an Indian Context", Indian Journal of Regional Science, Vol. XII, No. 2, 1980.

Shukla, Tara:
"Integrated Area Development with Special Reference to District Planning", Indian Journal of Agricultural Economics January-March, No. 1, 1974, pp. 16-18.

Siebert, H.:
Regional Economic Growth: Theory and Policy, (Scranton: International Textbook Co.) 1969.

Singh, Abhimanyu:
Planning for Developing A Backward Economy, (New Delhi: Vikas Publishing House Pvt. Ltd.) 1989.

Singh B.N. :
Decentralised Planning in India: Ambitions Vs. Realities (Muzzaffarpur: Bihar University, Deptt. of Economics) manuscript 1988.

Singh S.P.:
Development Needs Decentralised Planning, (Gonda, U.P. : L.B.S. (PG) College, Department of Economics) manuscript, 1988.

Singh, A.J. and George , M.V.:
"Regional Economic Development in India", Indian Journal of Economics, 1970. This raises the question of a conflict between regional and national goals.

Singh, A.K. :
"Decentralized Planning in U.P. - A Critical Appraisal", Indian Journal of Regional Science, Vol. XIX, No. 1, 1987.

Singh, A.K.:
"Decentralized Planning Under Five Year Plans: Emerging Perspectives",
Journal of Rural Development, Vol 8, No. 3, 1989.

Singh, Abha Lakshmi and Tyagi, Sadhna :
"Identification of Planning Areas in Aligarh District with Respect to Their Levels of Development",
Indian Journal of Regional Science, Vol. XXI, No. 2, 1989.

Singh, Ajit Kumar:
Allocation of Plan Funds to Districts Under Decentralised Planning,
(Lucknow: Giri Institute of Development Studies) manuscript 1988.

Singh, Ajit Kumar:
"A Policy Framework for Metropolitan Regional Development", Indian Journal of Regional Science, Vol. 11, No. 2, 1969.

Singh, Ajit Kumar:
"Integrated Area Development: Concept and Issues",
Indian Journal of Agricultural Economics, October-December 1973, pp. 27-31.

Singh, Ajit Kumar:
"Regional Economic Growth and Planning",
Eastern Anthropologist, October-December 1973, pp. 329-337.

Singh, Ajit Kumar:
"States as Planning Regions",
Indian Journal of Regional Science, Vol. IV, No. 1, 1972.

Singh, Amar:
"Area Development Administration",
in Pandiankar, P. (ed.):
Development Administration in India
(Delhi: MacMillan) 1974. This paper stresses block as the key unit of decentralized planning.

Singh, B.:
A Planned Economy: India's Model
(Budapest: Hungarian Academy of Sciences) 1967.

Singh, Baldev :
Integrated Local Level Planning Some Empirical Explorations: A Study of Surendranagar District
(Ahmedabad: S.P. Institute of Economic & Social Research) 1983.

Singh, Baldev :
Regional Planning - Explorations in Agriculture and Industry
(New Delhi: Oxford & IBH) 1987.

Singh, Bhagwan Prasad :
Decentralised Planning in India: Rationale and Requirements,
(Patna: B.N. College, Deptt. of Economics) manuscript 1988.

Singh, Bikram Singh:
Decentralised Planning in India
(Gaya, Bihar: Gaya College, Deptt. of Economics) manuscript 1988.

Singh, D. Bright Singh:
"District Planning and VI Plan",
Yojana, Vol. 21, No. 15, September 1977.

Singh, D.N. and Rai, S.C. :
"Spatial Organizations of Service Centres: A Strategy for Rural Development : A Study of Kopaganj Block, Azamgarh District, U.P.",
Indian Journal of Regional Science, Vol. XX, No. 1, 1988.

Singh, D.P. :
Introduction to District Plan 1951-52,
(Lucknow: Superintendent

Printing & Stationary, Govt. of U.P.) 1951.

Singh, G. Raj:
"Pattern of Decentralisation in Nepal",
Vasudha, Vol. XI, Ashad, 2025, p. 51.

Singh, H.P.:
"Development Pole Theory: Review and Appraisal - A Case Study of Bundelkhand",
National Geographer, Vol. XIII, No. 2, December 1978.

Singh, J.:
Central Places and Spatial Organization in a Backward Economy: Gorakhpur Region - A Study in Integrated Regional Development
(Gorakhpur: Uttar Bharat Bhoogol Parishad) 1979.

Singh, J.:
"Nodal Accessibility and Central Place Hierarchy - A Case Study of Gorakhpur Region",
National Geographer, Vol. XI, No. 2, 1976.

Singh, Jagpal:
"How Best to Plan for Rural Uplift",
Yojana, March 1-15, 1986.

Singh, K.K. and Ashraf, Ali:
"Bureaucracy and Economic Development in the District", Indian Council for Social Science Research, Research Abstracts Quarterly, October 1971, pp. 7-24.

Singh, Kartar:
"Approach to Integrated Area Development",
Indian Journal of Agricultural Economics, October-December 1973.

Singh, Kashinath:
"Functions and Functional Classification of Towns in Uttar Pradesh",
The National Geographical Journal of India, Vol. V, Part IV, 1959.

Singh, L.S. :
"Decentralised Planning in India",
Conference Volume, Indian Economic Association, Calcutta: Part III, December 1988.

Singh, M. and Sharma , R.N. :
Rural Development: Select Bibliography.
(New Delhi: Uppal Publishing House) 1978.

Singh, M.L. :
Sectoral Terms of Trade and Economic Growth in India,
(New Delhi: Sterling Publishers) 1976.

Singh, Madhusudan :
Decentralised Planning in India,
(Goya, Bihar: Goya College, Deptt. of Economics) manuscript 1988.

Singh, O.P.:
"Hierarchy of Towns as Service Centres in Varanasi Region",
Uttar Bharat Bhoogol Patrika, Vol. XIV, No. 1, June 1978.

Singh, O.P.:
"Central Places, Identification and Types",
Uttar Bharat Bhoogol Patrika, Vol. X, Nos. 3 & 4, Sept-Dec. 1974.

Singh, O.P.:
"Functions and Functional Classification of Central Places in U.P.",
National Geographical Journal of India Vol. XIV, No.2 & 3, June-Sept., 1968.

Singh, P.B. and Mazumdar, Kumkum:
"An Approach Towards Modelling Spatial Planning - In An Indian Perspective",
Indian Journal of Regional Science, Vol. X, No. 1, 1978.

Singh, R.L.; Singh, Rana P.B.; Mazumdar, K. and Singh, C.B.:
"Spatial Planning An Approach

towards Theory and its Applications in Indian Perspectives",
National Geographical Society of India Research Bulletin, Vol. 28, 1977.

Singh, R.L.; Singh, Rana P.B. and Singh, C.B.:
"Bundelkhand Region, A Study in Population Resources Regionalisations and Development Models",
National Geographical Journal of India, Vol. 22. 1971.

Singh, R.N. and Kumar, A.:
"Classical Theories of Spatial Organization: Scope and Limitations", National Geographer, Vol. XVIII, No. 2, December 1982.

Singh, R.N. and Pathak, R.K.:
"The Delimitation of Growth Centre Regions in Faizabad District (India)"
Indian Journal of Regional Science, Vol. XVI, No. 2, 1984.

Singh, R.R.:
Studies in Regional Planning and Rural Development
(Patna: Associated Book Agency) 1982.

Singh, R.S. and Singh, Chandra Prakash :
Rationale for Decentralised Planning in India: An Assessment
(Raj Mahal, Bihar: B.L.N. Bohra College, Bhagalpur University, Department of Economics) manuscript 1988.

Singh, Radha Raman :
"Multi-Level Planning for Achieving Integrated Area Development",
Khadi Gramodyog, January 1971, pp. 208-216.

Singh, Radha Raman:
Decentralised Planning in India: Retrospect and Prospect
(Muzzaftarpur: Bihar University, Department of Economics) manuscript 1988.

Singh, Rana P.B. and Mazumdar, K.:
"An Approach Towards Modelling Spatial Planning in an Indian Perspective",
Indian Journal of Regional Science, Vol. X, No. 1, 1978.

Singh, S.C. :
"Regional Development in Pauri Garhwal District of Uttar Pradesh",
Indian Journal of Regional Science, Vol. XX, No. 1, 1988.

Singh, S.C. :
"Service Centres in Pauri Garhwal District",
National Geographic Journal of India, Vol. 32, Part 41, 1985.

Singh, S.C. :
"Some Observations on the Development Project (IRDP) in Garhwal Himalaya",
The Economic Journal of Nepal, Vol. 10, No. 4, 1987.

Singh, S.M. :
"The Stability Theory of Rural Central Place Development", National Geographical Journal of India, Vol. XI, No. 1, March 1965.

Singh, T.:
"Resource Development and Regional Planning",
Geographical Review of India, Vol. XXVIII, No. 1, March 1966.

Singh, Tarlok :
"Planning for Economic Development in India",
in Planning for Economic Development, Vol. 2, Studies in National Planning Experience, Document No. A/5533/Rev.1/ Add. 1 (New-York : United Nations)

Singh, Tarlok :
"Development and Disparities: Analysis and Approach",

Yojana, March 29th, 1964 pp. 10-13.

Singh, Tarlok :
"Meaning of Integration in Rural Development and Instruments for Achieving It",
in Gangrade, K.D. :
Integrated Approach to Rural Develpment and Social Justice
(Delhi: NSS Unit, University of Delhi) 1977.

Singh, V.S. :
"Development Strategy for Backward Regions in U.P.",
Kurukshetra, March 16th 1974.

Singh, V.S. :
"Integrated Area Development Approach in Formulating District Plans",
Journal of Rural Development, Vol. 7, No. 5., 1988.

Singh, V.S. :
"Spatial Planning and Techniques of Identification of Growth Centres",
Indian Journal of Regional Science, Vol. XVIII, No. 2, 1986.

Singh, V.S.:
"Decentralised Planning Needs Reorientation",
Yojana, July 1-15, 1987.

Singh, Vishwa Nath :
Decentralisation of Planning in India: Problems and Prospects
(Bodh Gaya: Magadh University, Department of Economics), manuscript 1988.

Sinha, Ajit Kumar:
Incongruous Indian Planning System,
(Muzzaffarpur: Bihar University, Deptt. of Economics) manuscript 1988.

Sinha, B.N. :
Urban Studies : An Aid to Research
(Dharwar: Karnataka University) 1968.

Sinha, C.D. :
Decentralised Economic Planning in India Retrospect and Prospect
(Jamalpur, Bihar: J.R.S. College, Deptt. of Economics) manuscript, 1988.

Sinha, J.K.P. :
Decentralised Planning in India
(Patna: Kautilya Institute of Economic Administration, Kadam Kuan) manuscript, 1988.

Sinha, K.K. and Sinha, Uma :
"A Welfarist Approach to Indian Planning",
Indian Economic Association
Conference Volume,
1986. This paper emphasises the relevance of participation, in a society of unequals, in organised effort to increase control over resources and regulating local institutions.

Sinha, K.K. and Sinha, Uma :
"Sub-Regional Planning in India: Blocks Versus Districts",
Conference Volume,
Indian Economic Association, Calcutta, December 1988, Part III, pp. 127 to 135.

Sinha, R.K. :
Evolution of Fiscal Federalism in India
(New-Delhi: South Asian Publisher) 1981.

Sinha, R.K. :
"Novel Way of Dispersing Industries in Backward Areas",
Khadi Gramodyog, March 1974.

Sinha, R.K.:
Planning in India A Critique
(New Delhi: South Asian Publishers) 1987.

Sinha, S.P.:
"Planned Change in Tribal Areas",
The Indian Journal of Public Administration, Vol. XIX, No. 3, 1973.

Sinha, Savita :
Regional Structure, Process and Patterns of Development: A Case Study of Chotanagpur
(New Delhi: Concept Publishing Co.) 1988.

Sinha, V.C. :
Gandhian Approach to Balanced Regional Development,
(Rewa : A.P.S. University, Department of Economics) manuscript, 1988.

Sinha, Vishwanath Prasad :
Chotanagpur Plateau: A Study in Settlement Geography
(New Delhi: K.B. Publications) 1976.

Sivaraman, T.V. :
"Anatomy of Mysore Backward Districts",
Economic Times, 27th November 1972, p. 13.

Small Industries Extension Training Institute:
A Study of the Pochampad Ayaent - An Orderly Development of Additional Processing Storage, Marketing and Other Infrastructure Facilities,
(Hyderabad: SIET) 1972.

Smith, Derek Payton:
"Focus for Development in Regional Policy",
Indian Finance, April 22nd , 1972.

Smith, Herbert H. :
Citizen's Guide to Planning
(New-Jersey: Chandler-Davis) 1961.

Smith, Tony E. :
A Choice Theory of Spatial Interaction
(Peace Dale, Virginia: Regional Science Research Institute) Discussion Paper No. 74, June 1974.

Smith, Tony E. :
Spatial Discounting And The Gravity Hypothesis
(Peace Dale, Virginia: Regional Science Research Institute) Discussion Paper No. 82, November 1975.

Smith, V.:
"Experiments with a Decentralized Mechanism for Public Good Decisions",
American Economic Review, Vol. 70, September 1980.

Smithies, A. :
"Optimum Location in Spatial Competition",
Journal of Political Economy, Vol. 49, June 1941.

Sahoo, Basudeb:
Socio-Economic Schism Indian Policy and Decentralised Planning
(Cuttack: Ravenshaw College, Deptt. of Economics) manuscript, 1988.

Somani, G.D.:
"Industrialisation of Backward Areas: National and Regional Growth",
Economic Times, August 31st , 1965, p.5.

Somasekhara, N.:
State's Planning in India Techniques, Procedures and Management - An Across the States Account, Vol. I,
(Bombay: Himalaya Publishing House) 1984, reprinted in 1985.

Somasekhara, N. :
State's Planning in India : Techniques, Procedures and Management State Profiles, Vol. II,
(Bombay: Himalaya Publishing House) 1985 Reprint.

Somasekhara, N. :
"Identification of Less Developed Regions: A Case Study of Mysore,
Indian Journal of Regional Science Vol. 2, No.2, 1969.

Spate, O.H.K.:
Memorandum on Geographical

Studies in Relation to Planning in India,
Planning Commission, November 1956 Mimeograph. This early pioneering study provides the rationale of decentralized planning as securng maximum return by organisation of planning the relationship between the natural resources and the people exploiting them with least friction.

Spate, O.H.K., and Learmonth, A.T.A.:
India and Pakistan - A General and Regional Geography
(London: Methuen & Co. Ltd.) 1954. Here the scheme of macro-economic regions has been analysed.

Special Schemes Organisation:
Draft Guidelines for Preparation of Rural Growth Centre Projects,
circulated at the Second Special Schemes Organisation Meeting, Govt. of Rajasthan, held on 21st to 25th October, 1980.

Special Schemes Organisation:
Rural Growth Centre-Pacheswar Project Report (mimeographed),
(Jaipur: Special Schemes organisation, Govt. of Rajasthan) 1980.

Special Schemes Organisation:
Guidelines for Formulation of Block Development Plans
(Jaipur: Special Schemes Organisation, Govt. of Rajasthan) 1980 (mimeographed).

Special Schemes Organisation:
Guidelines for Formulation of Block Level Credit Projects Under Integrated Rural Development Programme,
(Jaipur: Special Schemes Organisation, Govt. of Rajasthan) 1980 mimeographed. This is one of the Government guidelines on credit planning, an important but rather neglected angle of decentralised planning.

Spiegelman, Robert C. et. al.
Application of Activity Analysis of Regional Development Planning,
(Washington D.C.: U.S. Department of Agricultural Technical bulletin) 1939.

Sreekantaradya, B.S.:
"Reflectoins on District Planning with Special Reference to Karnataka",
Journal of the Mysore University, March 1976. The constraints to successful District Planning in the shape of paucity of competent planning machinery, lack of knowledge of financial local resources, lack of local level data etc., are discussed with special reference to Karnataka.

Sreekantoradhya, B.S. :
"The New Phase in Decentralised Planning in Karnataka",
in
Conference Volume,
Indian Economic Association, Calcutta, December 1988, Part III pp. 80-88.

Sridharan, L.:
"District Planning Process - A Case Study of Karnataka", The Indian Journal of Public Administration, October-December 1987. This seeks to highlight the importance of genuine political commitment in favour of decentralised and district planning.

Srinivasan, A.V.:
Lead Industry Strategy for Developing Backward Areas,
(Delhi: Faculty of Management Studies, Delhi University) 1978.

Srinivasan, N.S. :
"Some Aspects of Capacity and

Safety in Road Planning", paper read at the XVI Annual Town & Country Planning Seminar held in Calcutta, organized by Institute of Town Planners, New-Delhi, in 1967.

Srivastava, V.K. :
"Central Place Theory in an Indian Context",
Indian Journal of Regional Science, Vol. XII, No. 2, 1980.

Srivastava, K.R. :
"Spatial Distribution of Rural Markets in Meerut District", Uttar Bharat Bhoogol Patrika, Vol. XII, No. 1, June 1976.

Srivastava, S.C. :
Some Paradigms of Decentralised Planning
(Bilaspur: C.M.D. College, Department of Economics) manuscript, 1988.

Srivastava, V.K. :
"Hierarchy of Market Centres - A Methodological Approach", Uttar Bharat Bhugol Patrika, Vol. 14, No. 2, 1978.

Srivastava, V.K. and Rai, J.P. :
"Hierarchy of Market Centres: A Methodological Approach",
Uttar Bharat Bhoogol Patrika, Vol. XIV, No. 2, December 1979..

Stabler, J.C.:
"Exports and Evolution : The Process of Regional Change",
in David L. Mckee, Robert D. Dean, and William H. Leahy (eds.):
Regional Economics: Theory and Practice
(New York : The Free Press) 1970.

Stafford, H.A.:
"The Functional Bases of Small Towns",
Economic Geography, Vol. 39, April 1963.

Stamp, L.D.:
"The Determination of Planning Region",
National Geographer, Vol. 5, Allahabad 1952. Stamp emphaises that on account of a dynamic environment, "Planning regions" are adequately dynamised, and related to time perspective.

Stein, J.H. :
"Temporal Aspects of Tertiary Production Elements in Korea",
in Pittz, E.R. (ed.):
Urban Systems and Economic Development
(Oregon) 1962.

Stevens, B.H.:
"Regional Multipliers in Great Britain",
Oxford Economic Papers, Vol. XXI, 1969.

Stevens, Benjamin :
Location Theory and Programming Models: The Von Thunen Case
(Peace Dale, Virginia: Regional Science Research Institute) Paper No. 19, November, 1967.

Stevens, Benjamin H. and Moore, Graig:
A Critical Review of the Literature on Shift Share As A Forecasting Technique
(Peace Dale, Virginia: Regional Science Research Institute) Discussion Paper No. 109, December 1978.

Stevens, Benjamin H. :
A Note on the Usefulness, Even in the Computer Age, of the Round-By-Round Method of Performing Input-Output Impact Calculations
(Peace Dale, Virginia: Regional Science Research Institute) Discussion Paper No. 132, October 1988.

Stevens, Benjamin H.; Bower, James R. and Ehrlich, David J. :
Effects of Neighbourhood Economic Development on the

Economic Health of the Central Business District
(Peace Dale, Virginia :Regional Science Research Institute) Discussion Paper No. 127, October 1981.

Stevens, Benjamin H.; Douglas, Robert C. and Neighbor, Carolyn B.:Stevens, Benjamin H.; Douglas, Robert C. and Neighbor, Carolyn B.
Trends in Industrial Location And Their Impact on Regional Economic Development
(Peace Dale, Virginia: Regional Science Research Institute) Discussion Paper No. 31, May 1969.

Stewart, C.T. :
"The Size and Spacing of Cities",
The Geographical Review, 1958, p. 222-245.

Stewart, Q.J. :
"Empirical Mathematical Rules Concerning the Distribution and Equillibrium of Population",
The Geographical Review, Vol. 37, 1979.

Stewart, Q.J. :
"The Development of Social Physics",
American Journal of Physics, Vol. 18, 1950.

Stewart, Q.J.:
"Demographic Gravitation: Evidence and Application",
Sociometry, Vol. 11, 1948.

Stillwell, F.J.B.:
"Further Thoughts on the Shift and Share Approach",
Regional Studies, Vol. IV, No. 4, 1970.

Stilwell, F.J.B.:
"Regional Growth and Structural Adaptation",
Urban Studies, Vol. VI, 1960.

Stoer, W.:
"Toward 'another' Regional Development ? - In Search of Strategy of Truly 'integrated' Regional Development",
in Mishra R.P. and Honjo, M. (eds.):
Changing Perceptions of Development Problems,
United Nations Centre for Regional Development, Regional Development Series Vol. 1 (Singapore: Maruzen Asia) 1971.

Stohr, W.B. :
"Development from Below: The Bottom-Up and Periphery Inward Development Paradigm",
in Stohr, W.B. and Taylor: D.R.F. (eds.):
Development form Above or Below? The Dialectics of Regional Planning in Developing Countries
(Chichester: Wiley) 1981.

Stohr, W.B. and Todtling:
"Spatial Equality - Some Antitheses to Current Regional Development Doctrine",
in Folmer, H. and Oosterhaven, J. (eds.):
Spatial Inequalities and Regional Development
(Leiden: Nijhoff) 1979.

Stone, J.N.R. and Craft-Murray, G.:
Social Accounting and Economic Models
(London: Bowes & Bowes) 1959.

Stone, J.R. :
"Social Accounts at the Regional Level: A Survey",
in Isard, W. and Cumberland, J.H.:
Regional Economic Planning
(Paris: OECD) 1961. This is easily the best treatment of regional accounts.

Stone, J.R.N.:
Mathematical Models for the Economy And other Essays,
(London: Chapman & Hall) 1970.

Stone, Richard:
A Programme for Growth, 12 Vols.

(London: Champman and Hall) 1962. This is the outcome of research of a team working under Sir Richard Stone at the University of Cambridge, Department of Applied Economic Research. See under C earlier.

Streeten, Paul:
"From Growth to Basic Needs",
Finance and Development, Vol. 16, No. 3, Sept. 1979.

Subramaniam, C.:
"Strategy for Integrated Rural Development",
in Community Development and Panchayati Raj Digest, Vol. X, No. 2, 1976.

Subramanian, G. and Pal, M.N.:
"An Optimal Evaluation of Spatial Linkages in South India", Indian Journal of Regional Science, Vol. IX, No. 1, 1977.

Subramanian, N.R.:
"Development of Backward Regions",
Swarajya, 15th April, 1972, pp. 5-6.

Subramanian, V.:
"Decentralised Planning for Full Employment",
The Indian Journal of Public Administration, Vol. XXIII, No. 4, 1977.

Subramanian, V.:
"Planning and the Citizen",
The Indian Journal of Public Administration, Vol. XXII, No. 3, Special Number, July-September, 1976.

Subrahmanyam, S.:
Levels of Poverty and Unemployment and Perspective of Development: A Case Study of East Godavari District Andhra Pradesh.
unpublished Ph.D. dissertation, Andhra University, Waltair.

Subrahmanyam, S.:
Poverty, Unemployment And Perspective of Development,
(Allahabad: Chugh Publications) 1987.

Subramanyam, S.:
"Macro-Programming Model for Regional Industrialisation: An Application to East Godavari District",
Indian Journal of Regional Science, Vol XIX, No. 1, 1982.

Sudarshan, P.:
"Identification of Backward District, in Andhra Pradesh - An Application of Factor Analysis",
Indian Journal of Regional Science, Vol. XVIII, No. 2, 1985.

Sundaram K.V. and Mishra R.P.:
"Local and Intermediate Level Development in India - A Case Study",
in papers contributed to UNIDS National Correspondence Seminar on Mico-Level Planning (Mysore: Institute for Development Studies) 1981.

Sundaram, K.V. (ed.):
Geography And Planning - Essays in Honour of V.L.S. Prakasa Rao
(New Delhi: Concept Publications) 1985.

Sundaram, K.V.:
Geography of Under-development - The Spatial Dynamics of Underdevelopment,
(New Delhi: Concept Publishing Co.) 1983.

Sundaram, K.V.:
Urban & Regional Planning in India
(New Delhi : Vikas) 1977.

Sundaram, K.V.:
"Pre-requisites for Decentralized Planning in View of Ensuring Appropriate Utilization of Trained Manpower",
In Proceedings of the Expert Consultation held in

Kathmandu, 28th November-2nd December 1988, (Rome: Food & Agriculture Orgnization of the U.N.) 1989.

Sundaram, K.V. :
"Towards a National Urban Policy in India",
Fulbright Newsletter, March 1973. Describes the process of how spatial planning started receiving attention from Fourth Five Year Period.

Sundaram, K.V. and Palanidurai, K.V.:
"Development of Hill Areas in India - Some Lessons for Strategy Formulation and Planning",
Indian Journal of Regional Science, Vol. XX, No. 1, 1988.

Sundaram, K.V. and Rao, V.L.S. Prakasa:
"Regional Planning in India",
Paper read at the XXI Inter-national Geographical Congress, Symposium on Regional Planning (Calcutta: National Committee of Geography) 1968.

Sundaram, K.V.:
Urban and Regional Planning in India
(New Delhi: Vikas Publishing House Pvt. Ltd.) 1977.

Sundaram, K.V.:
"A Study of Bastar District, With Special Reference to Spatial Organisation and Problems of Development",
in Mishra, R.P., et.al. (eds.):
Growth Poles and Centres in Regional Planning and Development in India, Report No. 70. c. 58.
(Geneva: UNRISD) 1970. Stresses the importance of transition policy in promoting development in tribal areas which have a long way to go before reaching levels of development obtaining in other parts of the country.

Sundaram, K.V.:
"Agricultural Programme for Backward Areas",
The Indian Journal of Public Administration, Vol. XXIII, No. 3, 1977.

Sundaram, K.V.:
"District Planning: The Case of Maharashtra",
Indian Journal of Public Administration, Vol. 25, No. 1, January to March 1979.

Sundaram, K.V.:
"Measurement And Analysis of Development at the Regional And Local Levels: Some Issues and Problems",
Proceedings of Seminar at Nainital April 22-24, 1982, entitled Regional Dimensions of India's Economic Development,
(Lucknow: State Planning Commission, Planning Deptt., Govt. of Uttar Pradesh) 1983.

Sundaram, K.V.; Misra, R.P. and Tiwari, P.S.:
Micro Level Planning and Development Process",
(Mysore: University of Mysore, Institute of Development Studies) Vol. II, 1976.

Sundaram, S.K.G. :
"Voluntary Agencies in Decentralized Planning (A Case Study in Tribal Development in Maharastra)", in
Conference Volume,
Indian Economic Association, December 1988, Part III, pp. 100-126.

Suresh, K.A. and Joseph, Molly:
"Peoples' Participation and Decentralised Planning: A Case for Village Level Organisation",
Conference Volume
of the Annual Conference of the Indian Economic Association
(Bombay: University of Bombay) 1986.

Suri, P.C. :
"Panchayat and District Development Administration",
Indian Journal of Public Administration Vol. 3, No. 1, 1957.

Swaminathan, E. :
"A Quantitative Approach to the Study of the Spatial Distribution and Functional Hierarchy of Shopping Centres in Coimbatore City",
The National Geographical Journal of India, Vol. XXV, Parts 3 & 4, September-December 1979.

Swaroop, A.:
"District Planning for Integrated Development
(New Delhi: Planning Commission) 1972, Mimeographed.

Swaroop, Anand:
" District Planning for Integrated Development",
Journal of the LBS National Academy of Administration, No. 1, Vol. XX, 1975.

Swaroop, Anand:
" A Methodology for Estimating District Domestic Product: A Case Study of U.P.",
in
Regional Dimensions of India's Economic Development,
proceedings of the seminar held at Nainital, April 22-24, 1982 (Lucknow: State Planning Commission, Planning Deptt., Govt. of U.P.) 1983.

T

Tambi, J.M.L.:
"Strategy for Development of Backward Areas",
Financial Express, 23rd August, 1974.

Tamilnadu State Planning Commission:
District Planning Guidelines to District Collectors and Proforma for Data Collection
(Madras : Govt. of Tamilnadu) 1972.

Tamilnadu State Planning Commission:
Towards Better Urban Development: Report of the Task Force on Urban Development Including Urban Housing and Regional Planning and Tourism 1972-84
(Madras: Govt. of Tamilnadu) 1972.

Tandon, B.C. :
Economic Planning
(Allahabad: Chaitanya Publishing House) 1963.

Taylor, Carl C. :
A Critical Analysis of India's Community Development Programme
(New Delhi: Govt. of India, Community Project Administration) 1956. @TITLE = Taylor, D.R.F. and Obudho, R.A. (eds.):
The Spatial Structure of Development: A Case Study of Kenya
(Boulder : West view Press) 1979.

Taylor, L. :
Decentralised Planning : A Case Study of Zambia,
(I.L.O.: Geneva) Working Paper No. 43, 1982.

Taylor, Lance et. al. :
Models of Growth and Distribution for Brazil
(New York: Oxford University Press) 1980.

Taylor, R.H. and Hobart, P.M. (eds.):
Context and Meaning of Development in Southeast Asia
(Ithaca : Connell University Press) 1986.

Tella, T.S.D. :
"The Concept of Polarised Development in Regional Planning - A Sociological Interpretation",
in Kuklinski, A. and Petrellar, R. (eds.):
Growth Poles and Regional Policies
(The Hague: Mouton & Co.) 1972.

Tewari, R.T. :
"Applications of Cluster Analysis for Identification of Planning Regions in Uttar Pradesh",
Indian Journal of Regional Science, Vol. XIII, No. 2, 1981.

Thaha, Mumtaz and Shanthundu, D. :
"Cluster Plan for Production And Employment: Sindhnur Cluster, Raichur District : An Evaluative Study",
Journal of Rural Development, Vol. 1, No. 4, 1982 July.

Thakker, Jyoti D.:
"A Note on the level and Structure of Gujarat's Inter-regional Trade",
Anvesak, June 1971.

Thapliyal, B.K., :
"Spatial Planning for IAP Project in Gazipur and Ballia Districts in U.P.",
Behavioural Sciences and Rural Development, Vol. 2, No. 2, 1979.

Thapliyal, B.K.:
"Integrated Rural Development Planning in India: Planning Methodologies in Practice and An Alternative Framework",
Journal of Rural Development, Vol.2, No. 4, July 1983.

Thimmaiah, G.:
"Block Level Planning: A Critique",
in Aziz, Abdul (ed.):
Studies in Block Level Planning
(New Delhi: Concept Publishers) 1983. This is an attempt at showing that district is a big unit for achieving social and economic unity.

Thimmaiah, G. :
India's Development Experience
(New Delhi: Ashish Publishing House) 1985.

Thimmaiah, G. :
"District Level Planning",
Economic Times, November 1983.

Thimmaiah, G.:
"Block Level Planning",
Economic Times, 26th & 27th March 1982.

Thimmaiah, G.:
"Case Study No. 3: India"
in Maetz, M. and Quieti M.S., (eds.):
Training for Decentralised Planning : Lessons from Experience,
(Rome: Food & Agriculture Organization of the U.N.) 1987. This paper shows that only two states, Maharastra and Gujarat, have reached a stage of having a settled methodology for District Planning.

Thimmaiah, G.:
"District Level Planning: Need for Clear Cut Guidelines",
Times of India, 1st November 1983.

Thimmaiah. G. :
"District as a Unit of Sub-Regional Planning in India",
in Mishra, R.P.; Urs, D.V. and Nataraj, V.K. (eds.):
Regional Planning and National Development,
(New Delhi: Vikas Publishing House) 1978.

Thimmaiah, G. :
"District Level Planning: Lessons from Experience",
in Naidu, K. Munirathna (ed.):

Area Planning for Regional Development
(New Delhi: Inter-India Publishers) 1984.

Thirlwall, A.P.:
"Regional Phillips Curve", Oxford University,
Bulletin of Economics & Statistics 1970.

Thomas Jr., N.L. (ed.):
Man's Role in Planning Rural Growth in Changing the Face of the Earth
(Chicago: University of Chicago Press) 1956.

Thomas, E.N. :
"Towards an Expanded Central Place Model",
Geographical Review, Vol. 51, 1961.

Thomas, M.D. :
"The Regional Problems, Structural Change and Growth Pole Theory"
in Kuklinski, A. (ed.):
Growth Poles and Growth Centres
(The Hague; Mouton & Co) 1972.

Thomas, Morgan D. :
"Growth Pole Theory: An Examination of Some of Its Basic Concepts",
in Hansen, Niles M. (ed.):
Growth Centres in Regional Economic Development
(New York: Free Press) 1972.

Thomas, P.A. and Padmanabhan:
Development Perspectives of North Arcot District of Tamilnadu
(Tirupattur : Sacred Heart College) 1985.

Thompson, I.B. :
"Some Problems of Regional Planning in Predominantly Rural Environment",
Scottish Geographical Magazine, Vol. 85, 1966.

Thorbecke, E. and Sen Gupta, J.K.:
A Consistency Framework for Employment Output and Income Distribution Projections Applied to Columbia
(Washington D.C.: World Bank Development Research Centre) 1972, mimeographed. This is a model for Columbia which attempts to evaluate the recommedations contained in the report of the ILO Comprehensive Employment Strategy Mission Towards Full Employment: A Programme for Columbia (Geneva: ILO) 1970.

Tiebout, C.M. :
"A Pure Theory of Local Expenditure",
Journal of Political Economy, Vol. 64, October 1956.

Tiebout, C.M. :
"Exports and Regional Economic Growth",
Journal of Political Economy, Vol. 64, April 1956.

Tiebout, C.M.:
The Community Economic Base Study,
Supplementary Paper No. 16, Committee for Economic Development, New York 1962.

Tiebout, C.M.:
"Regional and Inter-Regional Input-Output Models: An Appraisal",
in L. Needleman (ed.):
Regional Analysis
(Penguin Modern Economics) 1968.

Tilak, J.B.G.:
"Block Level Planning in India",
Indian Journal of Public Administration, No. 3, July-Sept. 1984.

Tilak, J.B.G.:
Block Level Planning in Education,
(New Delhi: NIEPA) 1984 Mimeographed.

Tilak, J.B.G.:
"Approaches to Educational

Planning and their Applications in India",
Indian Economic Journal, January-March 1977. Here it is suggested that educational planning should have long term perspective and that the approach to planning in education should be different from that of other sectors of the economy.

Tilak, J.B.G.:
"Investment in Education in India",
Eastern Economist, Annual Number 1980. This is a reinforcement of Tilak J.B.G., (1977).

Tilanus, T.B. :
Input-output Experiments, The Netherlands 1948-1961
(Rotterdam: Rotterdam University Press) 1966.

Tinbergen, J. :
Economic Policy: Principles And Design
(Amsterdam : North Holland) 1966.

Tinbergen, J. :
"The Economic Framework for Regional Planning",
in The Econometric Approach to Development Planning, Pontificate Acadamiae Scientarum, scripta Via, No. 28 (Amsterdam) 1965.

Tinbergen, J.:
Essays in Regional And World Planning
(New Delhi: NCAER) 1966.

Tinbergen, Jan:
Development Planning,
(London: World University Library) 1967.

Tinberger, Jan :
"Links Between National Planning and Town and Country Planning", in Urbanization in Developing Countries, (The Hague: International Union of Local Authorities) 1968.

Tintner, Gerhard and Sen Gupta, J.K.:
Econometrics of Development and Planning,
(Amsterdam: North Holland) 1970.

Titus, M.J. :
"Socio-Spatial Consequences of the Integration of Serayu Valley Region into the Colonial System",
in O. van de Muiyzenberg, P. Steefland and W. Walters (eds.):
Focus on the Region in Asia
(Rotterdam: Erasmus University) 1982.

Tiwari, K.N. :
"Planning at the State And District Level",
Journal of the National Academy of Administration, Vol. 15, No. 3, 1970.

Todaro, Michael P. :
Development Planning: Models and Methods,
(Nairobi: Oxford University Press) 1971.

Town & Country Planning Organization:
Regional Development Plan for South East Resource Region, (New-Delhii: Ministry of Works & Housing, Government of India) 1973.

Town and Country Planning Department:
Regional Development Plan for Banda Hamirpur,
(Lucknow: Government of Uttar Pradesh) 1973.

Town and Country Planning Organisation:
Role of Growth Foci in Regional Development Strategy
(New Delhi: Town and Country Planning Organization Government of India) 1971

mimeographed. An attempt at showing that a suitably conceived hierarchy of centres, can be used to manipulate both, regional imbalances (growth poles) and inter-regional imbalances (growth centres).

Town Planning Organisation:
Draft Master Plan for Jaipur
(Jaipur: Town Planning Organisation) 1972.

Town Planning Organization:
Delimitation of Rural District for Planning,
(New Delhi: Town Planning Organization) 1956.

Tremoulet, A. and Walker, E.:
Predicting Corporate Failure and Plant Closings : Resources for Local Employment Planners
Manuscript, Department of City and Regional Planning, University of North Carolina, Chapel Hill, 1980.

Tribal Research and Development Institute:
A Study of The Tribal People and Tribal Areas of Madhya Pradesh
(Chhindwara: TRDI) 1968.

Tripathi, R.N. and Thapliyal, B.K.:
"Alternative Methodologies for Local Planning for Rural Poor",
Paper presented at National Seminar on Alternative Methodologies for Local Level Planning, sponsored by ESCAP and Ministry of Rural Development, April 14 to 16th, 1981. See also in UN (ESCAP) :Guidelines for Local Level Planning in Rural Areas (Bangkok: ESCAP) 1981.

Tripathi, V.B. and Chand, R.:
Micro-Level Locational Planning for Market Facilities: A Case Study of Bulandshahar District",
The Geographer, Vol. XXX, No. 2, July 1983.

Tripathy, R.N. :
Block Plan in a District Frame: A Developmental Plan for Modakasira Block, Anantpur District
(Hyderabad :NIRD) 1980.

Tripathy, R.N. et. al. :
Development Plan for a Block: Ibrahimpatnam Ranga Reddy District (AP)
(Hyderabad: NIRD) 1979.

Trivedi, I.M. :
Frame-Work of Decentralised Planning in Gujarat
(Bhavnagar: Bhavnagar University, Deptt. of Economics) manuscript, 1988.

Tungare, D.C.:
"Some Aspects of District Planning",
Kurukshetra, March, 1969.

U

U.N. Research Institute for Social Development:
Inter-regional Allocation of Investment for Social & Economic Development
(Geneva : United Nations Research Institute for Social Development of the U.N.) 1970 Report No. 70.4.

Uathavikul :
Decision Theory and Regional Economic Growth: A Model of Resource Utilisation in the Context of Regional Opportunity Loss
(Ithaca: Cornell University) unpublished Ph.D. dissertation 1966.

Ullman, E.L. :
"A Theory of Location of Cities",
American Journal of Sociology, Vol. XLVI, May 1941.

Ullman, Edward L. :
"Regional Development and the Geography of Concentration",
Papers and Proceedings of the Regional Science Association, Vol. 4, 1958.

Ullman, Edward L.:
American Commodity Flows
(Seattle: University of Washington Press) 1957.

UNCRD :
"Environmental Planning and Management Focus on Inland Waters", Regional Development Dialogue, Vol. 8, No. 3, (Nagoya: Japan United Nations Centre for Regional Development) Autumn 1987.

United Nations :
Decentralization for National and Local Government
(New York: United Nations) 1962, U.N. Sales No. 62 H.H.2.

United Nations Asia and Pacific Development Institute:
Local Level Planning and Rural Development - Alternative Strategies
(New Delhi: Concept Publishing Co.) 1980.

United Nations Centre for Regional Development :
Implementing Decentralisation Policies and Programmes, Report of the UNCRD Workshop
(Nagoya, Japan: United Nations Centre for Regional Development) 1981.

United Nations Economic Commission for Asia and the Far East:
Review of Long Term Economic Projections for Selected Countries in ECAFE Region: Report of the Fourth Group of Experts on Programming Techniques
(Bangkok: United Nations) 1964.

United Nations Economic Commission for Europe:
Economic Survey of Europe in 1962 Part 2: Economic Planning in Europe
(Geneva: United Nations) 1965.

United Nations Institute for Social Development:
Regional Development: Experience & Prospects, Vol. I, Part I, South & South East Asia,
(Geneva : UNRISD) 1970.

United Nations Research Institute for Social Development:
Measurement and Analysis of Progress at the Local Level, Vols. I and II,
(Geneva: UNRISD) 1978.

United Nations:
Community Development & National Development,
(New York: U.N.) The U.N. Sales No. 64. IV. 2.

United Nations:
Local Participation in Developing Economy
(New York : The United Nations)) 1967.

United Nations:
Policy Issues Concerning the Future Evolution of Community Development
(New York: The United Nations) April 1967.

United Nations:
Public Administration Aspects of Community Development
(New York : The United Nations) 1955. Report of the Workshop held in New York in 1955.

United Nations:
Regional Planning
(New York: Deptt. of Economics & Social Affairs, United Nations) 1959.

United Nations:
Report on Concepts and Principles of Community Development, Recommendations

on further practical measures to be taken by International organisations, EXN. 5/325 (New York: U.N.O.).

United Nations:
The Problems and Methods of Social Planning, Report of the Expert Group (Dubrownik : U.N.) Nov. 1963, the U.N., SOA/ESWP/1964/3.

United Nations:
"Concepts and Methods of Area Programming for Community Development", in Economic Bulletin for Latin America, Vol. XII, No. 1, 1967.

United States of America, Department of Commerce:
The Development of a Sub-National Economic Development Policy (Washington D.C.: U.S. Deptt. of Commerce) 1977.

Uphoff, N. and Easman, J:
Local Organisation and Rural Development-Analysis of Asian Experience (Connecticut :Cornell University Press) 1974.

Uphoff, N.T. and Easman, M.J.:
Local Organisation and Rural Development: Analysis of Asian Experience (Ithaca: Connell University Press) 1974.

Uphoff, Norman:
Approaches to Community Participation in Agriculture And Rural Development (Ithaca: Cornell University, Rural Development Committee, Review Paper) 1987.

V

V.M. Rao; and Kshirasagar, V.R. :
"Size Distribution of Towns and Economic Development - A Case study of Vidarbha, India", Indian Journal of Regional Science, Vol. 2, 1970. .

Valavanis, Stefan :
"Losch on Location", American Economic Review, Vol. XLV, 1955.

Van Dusseldorf, D.B.W.M.:
Planning Service Centres in Rural Areas of Developing Countries (Wageningen, The Netherlands: International Institute for Land Reclamation and Improvement) 1973.

Van Raay, H.G.T. :
"A Case for Regional Planning", in Development and Change, No. 3, 1970-71.

Van Raay, H.G.T.:
Regional Planning for Integrated Rural Development (The Hague: I.S.S.A.S) 1981.

Vancleef, E. :
"Hinterland and Umland", Geographical Review, Vol. 31, 1941.

Varadachary, T.R. :
"Planning and Project Formulation with Special Reference to Development of Backward Areas", State Bank of India Monthly Review, July 1974.

Varghuesc, M.M. :
"Development Planning in Rajasthan", in Papers contributed to Workshop on Micro Level Planning Case Studies, Vol. 2, (Mysore: UNIDS National Correspondence Seminar on Micro Level Planning, Institute

of Development Studies) 1981, (mimeographed).

Varshney, J.K. and Mathur O.N.:
Handbook of Rural Housing and Village Planning
(New Delhi: National Building Organization) 1968.

Vashi, D.G.:
" Development Planning Models",
The Economic Times, 21st December 1974.

Vasudevaraju, V.A.:
"Growth Centres Research and District Planning",
Indian Institute of Public Administration Bulletin (Pondicherry) September, 1972.

Vasudevraju, V.A. :
"Growth Centres Research and District Planning",
Indian Institute of Public Administration Bulletin, (Pondicherry) September 1972.

Veena, D.R. and Bhushri, N.K.:
"A Methodological Approach to District Income Estimation: A Study of Surendranagar",
Vishleshan, June 1979.

Veenstra, J.:
"Theory and Practice of Foreign Assistance to Regional Development Planning",
Public Administration and Development, Vol. 9, No. 5, November-December 1989.

Venkatarangaiya, M. and Pattabhiram, M. (eds.):
Local Government in India, Selected Readings,
(Bombay: Allied Publishers) 1969.

Venugopal, Reddy Y,:
"Limits to Block Level Planning",
Paper read at Seminar on Block Level Planning for Full Employment, August 17th & 18th, 1977, Planning Commission, New Delhi.

Venugopal, Reddy Y.:
" State Planning and Regional Development Objectives - Some Issues",
Indian Journal of Regional Science, Vol. 4, No. 1, 1972.

Vepa, Ram K. :
"Development of Backward Economy: Relevance of Gandhian Technology",
The Indian Journal of Public Administration, Vol. XXIII, No. 4, 1977.

Vepa, Ram K. :
"Multi-Level Planning for Industry",
The Indian Institute of Public Administration, Vol. XIX, No. 3, 1973.

Vepa, Ram K. :
"New Pattern of District Administration in Andhra Pradesh",
Indian Journal of Public Administration, Vol. 14, No. 1, 1968.

Verma, Amita and Sinha, Chandra:
Decentralised Planning in India: An Organisational Framework
(Muzzaffarpur: Bihar University, Deptt. of Economics) manuscript. 1988.

Verma, H.S., and Tripathi B.L.:
"Integrating Research, Training and Education",
in Gupta, Ranjit (ed.): Planning for Tribal Development (New Delhi: Ankur Publishing House) 1976.

Verma, M.M.:
Planning For The Poor,
(New Delhi : Gitanjali Publishing House) 1986.

Verma, R.V. :
"Decentralised Planning for Unified National Development", Indian Journal of Regional Science, Vol. XIX, No. 1, 1987.

Verma, R.V. :
"Spatial Reorganisation of Small Service Centres for Rural Development - A Case Study of Safipur Tehsil of Unnao District in Uttar Pradesh",
Indian Journal of Regional Science, Vol. XIV, No. 2, 1982.

Verma, Rajesh Kumar and Singh, Bhagwan:
Agricultural Analysis of Gandhian Concept of Decentralised Planning in Indian Context
(Etawah: Tilak P.G. College, Auraiya) manuscript 1988.

Victorisz, Thomas :
"Location Choices in Planning",
in Max Millikan (ed.):
National Economic Planning, Universities-National Bureau of Economic Research
(New York: Columbia University Press) 1967.

Vining, D.:
"Bad Model with Interesting Physics and Vice Versa : Some comments on the Casetti and Isard-Liossantos Papers",
in Papers of the Regional Science Association, Vol. 39, 1977.

Vir, Kamal:
Gandhian Concept of Decentralisation and Micro-Level Planning in India,
(Ghaziabad :M.M.H. College, Deptt. of Economics) manuscript 1988.

Vishveswaraya, M.:
District Development Scheme Economic Progress Forced Marches,
(Bangalore: Bangalore Press) 1942.

Vishwa Nath:
"Suitability of a District as Unit Formulation of Integrated Area Development Plans",
Indian Journal of Agricultural Economics Vol. 28, No. 4, October-December 1973.

Vithal, B.P.R.:
"District Planning in the Context of Multi-Level Planning",
Economic and Political Weekly, 3rd to 10th February, 1979.

Vivekananda, M. and Rao, V.K.R.V. (eds.):
Planning Unit Areas for Integrated Rural Development - An Exercise,
(New Delhi: Ashish Publishing House) 1980.

Von Boventer, E. :
"Regional Growth Theory",
Urban Studies, Vol. 12, 1975.

Von Thunen, H.J. (1826):
Isolated State,
translated from original German by Wartenbergh, C.M. (London: Oxford University Press) 1966.

Vyas, V.S.:
"Development Administration at Taluka Level",
Paper read at the Seminar on Rural Development, of United States Education Foundation in India, Srinagar , 1977, reprinted in Misra, R.P. and Sundaram, K.V. (ed.): Rural Area Development (New-Delhi: Sterling Publishers) 1979.

Vyas, V.S.; Bhatt, Anil; and Shah, S.M.:
Decentralised Planning in India
(New Delhi: Oxford & IBH) 1985.
Growth Centre approaches in 20 Taluka Plans 1978-79.

Vyas, V.S.; Moulik, T.K.; Desai, B.M. and Gupta, R.:
Rural Development for Rural Poor,
(Ahmedabad I.I.M.) 1976 Mimeographed.

W

Waardenberg, J.C. :
"Space in a Development Planning",
Papers and Proceedings of the Regional Science Association, Vol. 13, 1967.

Wade, Robert:
"The Management of Common Property Resources; Finding a Co-operative Solution",
World Bank Research Observer, Vol. 2, No. 2, July 1987. This demonstrates how efficient utilization of resources possible through local community involvement.

Wadhwa, C.D. (ed.):
Some Problems of India's Economic Policy,
(New Delhi: Tata McGraw Hill Publishing Co. Ltd.) 1973.

Wallace, L.T. and Ruttan, Vernon W. :
"The Role of Community as a Factor in Industrial Location",
Papers and Proceedings of the Regional Science Association, Vol. 7, 1961.

Walls, D. :
Central Appalachia : A Peripheral Region Within an Advanced Capitalist Country",
Journal of Sociology and Social Welfare, Vol. IV, No. 3, November, 1976.

Walters, A.A. :
"Production and Cost Functions: An Econometric Survey",
Econometrica, Vol. 31, 1963.

Wanmali, S.:
Regional Planning for Social Facilities: An Examination of the Central Place Concepts and Their Application- A Case Study of Eastern Maharashtra
(Hyderabad: National Institute of Community Development) 1970.

Wanmali,S. :
"Clustering of Services as a Function of Population Distance in Settlement System",
Journal of Behavioural Sciences and Community Development, Vol. VI, No. 1, (Hyderabad, NICD) 1972.

Wanmali, Sudhir :
"Zone of Influence of Central Villages in Miryalguda Taluka: A Theoretical Approach",
Behavioural Sciences and Community Development, Vol. 6, No. 1, 1972.

Wanmali, S. and Khan, Waheeduddin:
"Role of Location in Regional Planning with Particular Reference to the Provision of Social Facilities",
Behavioural Sciences and Community Development, Vol. IV, No. 2, Sept. 1970. Here a centre-periphery model of planning at the city level is set forth.

Wanmali, S.:
"Lessons of Work on Growth Centres for Micro- Level Planning",
Indian Journal of Public Administration, No. 3, Vol. 19, 1973. A relatively early work on the success of the application of Growth Centre approach in India's decentralized Planning attempts.

Wanmali, S.:
"Ranking of Settlements: A Suggestion",
Journal of Behavioural Sciences and Community Development, Vol. 5, No. 2, 1971.

Wanmali, Sudhir and Khan, Waheeduddin:
"Conceptual and Methodological Dimensions of Central Place Theory",
in Sen, L.K. (eds.):
Readings of Micro-Level Planning and Rural Growth Centres
(Hyderabad: National Institute for Community Development) 1972.

Wanmali, Sudhir:
A Note on Growth Centering Policy for Telengana Region: Perspective Plan for Telengana
(Hyderabad: Government of Andhra Pradesh, Deptt. of Planning & Co-operation) 1973.

Wanmali, Sudhir:
Report on the Provision of Social Facilities in Nagpur Metropolitan Regions
(Nagpur: Deptt. of Town Planning and Valuation, Govt. of Maharastra) 1969, mimeographed.

Wanmali, Sudhir:
Settlement Hierarchy in Telengana Region : Perspective Plan for Telengana, Technical Studies
(Hyderabad: Govt. of Andhra Pradesh, Deptt. of Planning & Co-operation) 1972.

Wanmali, Sudhir:
The Hierarchy of Towns in Vidharba, India and its Significance in Regional Planning
(London: Graduate School of Geography, London School of Economics) 1968, mimeographed.

Wanmali, Sudhir:
" Regional Imbalances and Rural Development: A Study of Spatial Distribution of Support Services in Singbhumi District",
Journal of Food Marketing Centre, Vol. 3, No. 1, 1974.

Wanmali, Sudhir:
"Growth Centres and Land Use Models: Some Observations", Community Development and Panchayati Raj Digest, Community Development Week Special Number, Vol. 2, No. 2, 1970. .

Warren, R.L. :
Studying Your Community,
(New York: Russell Sage Foundation) 1955.

Weaver, C. :
Regional Development and the Local Community: Planning, Politics and Social Context
(London: Wiley) 1984.

Weaver, C.:
"Development Theory and the Regional Question: A Critique of Spatial Planning and Its Detractors",
in Stohr W.B., and Taylor, D.R.F (eds.):
Development from Above or Below? The Dialectics of Regional Planning in Developing Countries
(Chichester: Wiley) 1981.

Weber, Alfred:
Theory of Location of Industries,
the French version of 1909 translated into English by Wartenberg C.M., (Chicago: The University of Chicago Press) 1979.

Weber, K.E. and Dhungal, Y.N.:
Manual on Rural Development Planning
(Bangkok: Division of Human Settlements Development, Asian Institute of Technology) 1988.

Weber, Max :
Theory of Social and Economic Organization,
(Glencoe: The Free Press) 1947.

Weiss, S.J. and Gooding, E.C. :
"Estimation of Differential Employment Multipliers in a

Small Regional Economy",
Land Economics, Vol. XLIV, 1968.

Weitz, R.:
Integrated Rural Development: The Rehovot Approach,
(Rehovot: Settlement Study Centre) 1979.

Weitzman, M. :
"Iterative Multi-Level Planning with Production Targets",
Econometrica, Vol. 38, 1970.

West, E.G. :
"Regional Planning- Fact and Fallacy",
Lloyds Bank Review, No. 80, April 1966.

Westgaard, Kristen:
People's Participation, Local Government and Rural Development: The Case of West Bengal, India
(Copenhagen: Centre for Development Research) 1986. See the review of this book by Arun Ghosh in Economic & Political Weekly, March 26th, 1988, in the section on Review of Agriculture.

Whittlesey, D.C. :
"The Regional Concept and the Regional Method",
in James, P.E. and Jones, C.F. (eds.):
American Geography: Inventory and Prospect
(Syracuse: Syracuse University Press) 1954.

Wigley, K.H.:
"The Development of the National Plan",
Journal of the Royal Statistical Society, Series A, 1966.

William, S. Rt. Hon. :
Local Employment Generation: The Need for Innovation, Information and Suitable Technology
(Paris: OECD)1986.

Williams, R.:
The Country and The City
(New York: Oxford University Press) 1973.

Williamson, J.G.:
" Regional Inequality and the Process of National Development: A Description of the Patterns",
Economic Development and Cultural Change, Vol. XIII, July 1965. This study reinforces Kuznets (1963) based on a thoroughgoing empirical investigations through connection approaches and time series analysis.

Williamson, J.G.:
"Regional Inequality and the Process of National Development : A Description of Patterns",
in Needleman, L.:
Regional Analysis,
(Penguin Modern Economics Readings) 1968.

Wilson, A.G.:
The Integration of Accounting and Location Theory Framework in Urban Modelling
(London: The Centre for Environmental Studies) Paper No. 11.

Wilson, M.L. :
Comments on Community Development Program in India: Report of a Survey,
(New Delhi : C.P.A., Govt. of India) 1956.

Wilson, T.:
"The Regional Multiplier-Critique",
Oxford Economic Papers, Vol. XX, 1968.

Woglom, W.H. and Stopler, W.F. :
The Economics of Location
(New Haven: Yale University Press) 1954.

Wolfson, Margaret, S. (ed.):
Regional Development and Accelerated Growth,

Papers and Proceedings of Seminar held in Herzlia, Israel, 1964, (Paris :OECD) 1965.

Wood, J. :
Town and Country Planning: A Bibliography
(New Delhi: The Oxford Book and Stationery Co.) 1958.

Wood, J.:
"Development of Urban and Regional Planning in India",
Land Economics, Vol. 34, 1958.

World Bank :
Rural Development: Bank Experience 1965-86,
(Washington D.C.) 1988.

World Bank:
Decentralisation in Developing Countries, World Bank Staff Working Paper No. 581,
(Washington, D.C.: World Bank).

World Bank:
Rural Development: Sector Policy Paper
(Washington D.C.: World Bank) 1975.

Wrobel, A. :
"Theories and Models of Regional Development : A Critical Examination"
in Thomon, Richard S.(ed.):
Papers and Proceedings of the Commission on Regional Aspects of Development, International Geographic Union, Methodology and Case Studies
(Toronto: Allister Typesetting & Graphics) 1974.

Y

Yan, C. :
Introduction to Input-Output Economics,
(New-York: Holt Rinehart Winston) 1969.

Yapa, I.S. :
"Computer-Assisted Regional Planning",
in Rural Regional Development Newsletter, No. 5, August, 1987, Asian Institute of Technology, Bangkok.

Z

Zaheer, M.:
"Regional Planning for Integrated Area Development",
Community Development and Panchayati Raj Digest, Oct., 1975, p. 43-46.

Ziolkowski, J.A. :
Sociological Problems of Regional Development, Proceedings of the First Scandanavian - Polish Regional Science Seminar
(Warsaw: Polish Scientific Publishers) 1967.

Ziolkowski J.A.:
"The Integrated Social Science Approach to Regional Planning",
in Kuklinski, A. (ed.):
Social Issues in Regional Policy and Regional Planning,
(The Hague: Mouton & Co) 1977.